# RECONSIDERING
# the BLUESTOCKINGS

Edited by

Nicole Pohl &

Betty A. Schellenberg

HUNTINGTON LIBRARY
SAN MARINO, CALIFORNIA

Cover illustration

James Barry, *The Distribution of Premiums in the Society of Arts,* fifth in the series *The Progress of Human Culture and Knowledge,* ca. 1777–84; oil on canvas (detail). R.S.A. London; UK/Bridgeman Art Library. Please also see pp. 75 and 79 of this volume.

Also published as volume 65, numbers 1 and 2, of the *Huntington Library Quarterly,* edited by Susan Green.

Library of Congress Cataloging-in-Publication Data

Reconsidering the Bluestockings / edited by Nicole Pohl & Betty A. Schellenberg.
    p. cm.
"Also published as volume 65, numbers 1 and 2 of the Huntington Library quarterly"—T.p. verso.
Includes bibliographical references and index.
  ISBN 0-87328-202-7 (alk. paper)
 1. English literature—18th century—History and criticism. 2. English literature—Women authors—History and criticism. 3. Feminism and literature—Great Britain—History—18th century. 4. Women and literature—Great Britain—History—18th century. 5. Great Britain—Intellectual life—18th century. 6. Women intellectuals—Great Britain—Biography. 7. Authors, English—18th century—Biography. 8. Women authors, English—Biography. I. Pohl, Nicole, 1961– II. Schellenberg, Betty A. III. Henry E. Huntington Library and Art Gallery. IV. Huntington Library quarterly.
  PR113.R43 2003
  820.9'9287'09033—dc21

                                                      2003003793

# Contents

**continued overleaf**

# Contributors

**Nicole Pohl** is a lecturer at University College Northampton. She has edited *Female Communities, 1600–1800: Literary Visions and Cultural Realities* (2000), with Rebecca D'Monte, and she is currently working on an edition of Sarah Scott's correspondence and researching women's utopianism.

**Betty A. Schellenberg,** an associate professor of English at Simon Fraser University, is the author of *The Conversational Circle: Rereading the English Novel, 1740–1775* (1996). She is coeditor of a book on sequels, and she is now completing a study on the professional careers of mid-eighteenth-century women writers.

❧ ❧

**Janice Blathwayt** is a recent graduate in women's studies at York University (Canada), where she completed a dissertation on Elizabeth Carter. Her previous publications are in the field of occupational therapy.

**Elizabeth Child** is an assistant professor of English at Trinity College, Washington, D.C. She completed her doctorate at the University of Maryland, College Park, where her dissertation was on gender and print culture in eighteenth-century English towns. An essay on women's writing and community in Bath was recently published in *Studies in Eighteenth-Century Culture*.

**Elizabeth Eger** is William Noble Research Fellow at the University of Liverpool. She is currently completing a study of the Bluestocking contribution to their national culture, titled "Living Muses: Women of Reason from Enlightenment to Romanticism. She is the editor of volume 1, on Elizabeth Montagu, of *Bluestocking Feminism* (1999; general editor Gary Kelly).

**Harriet Guest,** director of the Centre for Eighteenth-Century Studies at the University of York (U.K.), is the author of *Small Change: Women, Learning, Patriotism, 1750–1810* (2000).

**Deborah Heller**, a professor of English at Western New Mexico University, has published articles on the poets of Sensibility and on Bluestocking salon culture. She is currently working on an edition of the correspondence between Elizabeth Montagu and Elizabeth Vesey.

**Gary Kelly** is Canada Research Chair in Literature and Language in Society, University of Alberta. He is the author of *Women, Writing, and Revolution* (1993) and general editor of *Bluestocking Feminism* (1999) and of *Varieties of Female*

*Gothic* (2002). He has also edited Sarah Scott's *Millenium Hall,* Mary Wollstone-craft's two novels, and Felicia Hemans's selected poems and letters.

**Susan S. Lanser** is a professor of English and comparative literature and chair of the Women's Studies Program at Brandeis University. Her recent books include *Fictions of Authority: Women Writers and Narrative Voice* (1992) and two coedited volumes of eighteenth-century women's writings. The essay in this volume is part of a project on the cultural and political meanings of female intimacies in eighteenth-century Europe.

**Jane Magrath** is an assistant professor of English at the University of Prince Edward Island. Her current work concerns the representation of women's bodies in eighteenth-century texts, in particular exploring this subject in the Montagu correspondence.

**Emma Major** is a lecturer at the Centre for Eighteenth-Century Studies at the University of York (U.K.). She is completing a study based on her D.Phil. thesis, "Rethinking the Private: Religious Femininity and Patriotism, 1750–1789."

**Anna E. Miegon** is a doctoral candidate at Simon Fraser University. She recently completed her M.A. in the Department of British Literature and Culture at the University of Lodz, Poland, with a thesis on the fiction of Muriel Spark. Her current research interest is the construction of gender roles in the periodical press of the eighteenth century.

**Betty Rizzo,** a professor emerita at the Graduate Center of the City University of New York, is the author of *Companions without Vows: Relationships among Eighteenth-Century British Women* (1994). She has edited journals and letters of Fanny Burney, Sarah Scott's *The History of George Ellison* (1996), and the volume devoted to Elizabeth Griffith in *Eighteenth-Century Women Playwrights* (2001).

**Mary L. Robertson** is William A. Moffett Curator of Manuscripts at the Huntington Library.

**Susan Staves** is a professor emerita at Brandeis University. Her books include *Married Women's Separate Property in England, 1660–1833* (1990), *Early Modern Conceptions of Property in England, 1660–1833* (1995; coedited with John Brewer) and Elizabeth Griffith's *Delicate Distress* (1997; coedited with Cynthia Ricciardi). She is currently completing a literary history of women's writing in Britain.

# Introduction
## A Bluestocking Historiography

—————— Nicole Pohl and Betty A. Schellenberg

We have lived much with the Wisest, the best, & most celebrated Men of our Times, & with some of the best, most accomplish'd & most learned Women of any times. These things I consider, not merely as pleasures transient, but as permanent blessings, by such Guides & Companions we were set above the low temptations of Vice & folly, & while they were the instructors of our Minds they were the Guardians of our Virtue.

–Elizabeth Montagu to Elizabeth Vesey, 21 September 1781[1]

At Mrs Montagu's, the semi-circle that faced the fire retained during the whole evening its unbroken form, with a precision that made it seem described a Brobdignagian compass. The lady of the castle commonly placed herself at the upper end of the room, near the commencement of the curve, so as to be courteously visible to all her guests; having the person of rank, or consequence, properly, on one side, and the person the most eminent for talents, sagaciously, on the other; or as near to her chair, and her converse, as her favouring eye, and a complacent box of the head, could invite him to that distinction.

–Frances Burney, *Memoirs of Doctor Burney*, 1832[2]

These very different accounts of the Bluestocking circle point to the range of interpretations that have characterized both contemporary and subsequent understandings of this mid-eighteenth-century British phenomenon. Each retrospective to a degree, the first originates from within, written by one Bluestocking hostess to another; the second arises from the peripheral perspective of a middle-class

1. Elizabeth Montagu to Elizabeth Vesey, Montagu Collection 6566, 21 September 1781. All further citations from the Huntington's Montagu Collection will be given in the text, using the abbreviation "MO."
2. Frances Burney, *Memoirs of Doctor Burney, Arranged from his own Manuscripts, from Family Papers, and from Personal Collections*, 3 vols. (London, 1832), 2:270–71.

professional father and daughter needing to cultivate their places in the circle. Montagu's statement is a celebratory memorial of a particular intellectual community, formed in the 1750s around the prominent hostesses Elizabeth Montagu, Elizabeth Vesey, and Frances Boscawen and continuing well into the 1780s with a second generation of hostesses and societies in London and the provinces. Montagu, Vesey, Boscawen, and Elizabeth Carter were all close friends and eager correspondents who were united in the "blue stocking doctrine" of "rational conversation" (Montagu to Carter, MO 3151, 17 [August 1765]). These informal gatherings united men and women primarily of the gentry and upper classes, with the participation of a number of more middle-class professionals, in the pursuit of intellectual improvement, polite sociability, the refinement of the arts through patronage, and national stability through philanthropy. Underpinning Montagu's nostalgic hymn is a commitment to these ideals as the basis of civic virtue in a liberal society. The Bluestocking women can be seen to have played a central role in the cultural and social transformations of the second half of the century that entrenched this system of values in England.

As the moral and religious connotations of Montagu's language indicate, however, this elevation of the ideals of learning and virtue was part of a conservative, Anglican ideological project that distinguished the Bluestockings from both courtly and plebeian cultural ideologies and practices.[3] Thus Frances Burney's observation, from its alternative perspective, reveals how the supposedly informal intellectual meritocracy of the Bluestocking circle—symbolized by Bishop Benjamin Stillingfleet's coarse blue-worsted stockings, which seem to have been the source of the name—could rather be understood as an exclusive and hierarchically ordered hegemonic construct. The divergence between the two epigraphs reminds us of the extent to which the Bluestockings sought to fashion their own identity as moral and social models for the nation.[4]

Certainly, Montagu's rigid style of hosting her assemblies attracted criticism and led to unfavorable comparisons with Vesey's more informal hospitality, as Montagu herself reports to Carter:

> I hope you have met with an absurd paragraph in ye morning Herald, which says, that at Mrs Vs ye the other night, there happend such a dispute between ye blue stockings, that had it not been for the timely interference of ye unletterd part of ye company

3.  See the essays by Emma Major and Susan Staves in this volume.
4.  On the other hand, Betty A. Schellenberg has recently argued that Frances Burney, for her own purposes, elevated the relatively professional circle around Hester Thrale and Samuel Johnson at Thrale's Streatham house, of which she had recently become a part, over the amateur circle presided over by Elizabeth Montagu as patron (Schellenberg, "From Propensity to Profession: Frances Burney, *The Witlings*, and *Cecilia*," *Eighteenth-Century Fiction* 14 [2002]: 345–70).

> might have ended very fatally & then ... that there are now 2 par-
> ties of ye blue stockings. (MO 3565, 15 December 1783)[5]

However untrue, rumours of opposing factions among the Bluestockings make
it clear that these women's high public profile attracted expressions of anxiety
about learned and socially active women. For better or for worse, the Bluestockings as a specific cultural, social, and political phenomenon played a crucial
part in a widening and redefinition of women's social roles in the eighteenth century. Their own negotiations of female scholarship, literary genres, and participation in the public and political spheres mirrored intersecting and often
contradictory debates among their contemporaries about gender roles and the
demarcation of public and private. Furthermore, subsequent work on the Bluestockings, starting with late-eighteenth-century and nineteenth-century editions
of the members' correspondence and continuing through to current Bluestocking
historiography, reflects profound changes in the discipline of social and literary
history itself, changes that have determined if, and how, the Bluestockings have
been considered.

In her 1990 book *The Bluestocking Circle*, still the principal study of the
group, Sylvia Harcstark Myers has traced the label's complex semantic history.[6]
First used in the seventeenth century to describe the plain attire of the members
of the Little Parliament in 1653, it was taken up again in the mid–eighteenth century to characterize Stillingfleet, who eschewed full dress at evening assemblies.[7]
Frances Burney recalls:

> It owed its name to an apology made by Mr. Stillingfleet, in de-
> clining to accept an invitation to a literary meeting of Mrs. Vesey's,
> from not being, he said, in the habit of displaying a proper equip-
> ment for an evening assembly. "Pho, pho," cried she, with her well-
> known, yet always original simplicity, while she looked inquisitively,
> at him and his accoutrements; "don't mind dress! Come in your
> blue stockings!"[8]

5. Fifteen years earlier, Montagu similarly argues for the friendly collaboration of the Bluestocking hostesses,
   writing of Lady Hervey, "tho from being the only Women who have circles of beaux esprits, there might
   be supposed to be some envy, she takes pleasure in commending me beyond my deserts to every body.
   If she has a partie that she thinks may be particularly agreable for any reason whatever she never omits
   inviting me. . . . I am so disgusted with the silly way our Ladies have of getting into whispers like boarding
   school misses, that I reap but small delight in the parties I am ask'd to at most Houses, tho many of
   my acquaintance are so good as to compose ye circle for me with great indulgence to my love of Beaux
   esprits" (MO 5898, September 4 [1768]).
6. Sylvia Harcstark Myers, *The Bluestocking Circle: Women, Friendship, and the Life of the Mind in Eighteenth-
   Century England* (Oxford, 1990), 6–12.
7. See the *Oxford English Dictionary*.
8. Burney, *Memoirs of Doctor Burney*, 2:262–63.

The reference stuck, and it appears for the first time in Elizabeth Montagu's correspondence in 1756:

> [P]ray Madam be so good as to tell Stillingfleet I neither can nor will answer his questions till he returns to Clarges Street. Monsey swears he will make out some story of you & him, before you are much older. You shall not Keep Blew stockings at Sandleford for nothing. (Samuel Torriano to Elizabeth Montagu, MO 5153, 13 November 1756)

In the 1750s and 1760s, the term "Bluestocking" was used of the salon circles around Montagu, Boscawen, and Vesey in London, Bath, and Dublin. These assemblies differed from the traditional card-playing gatherings by nurturing intellectual pursuits, polite conversation, philanthropic projects, and publishing ventures among a mixed group of guests that included Elizabeth Carter, Lord Lyttelton, the earl of Bath, Horace Walpole, the earl of Orford, and Charles Burney.[9] Originally in the form of levées, the gatherings became informal receptions held in the late afternoons.[10] They were comparable to the French salons of Cathérine de Vivonne (Marquise de Rambouillet), Julie de Lespinasse, Suzanne Necker, and Marie-Thérèse Géoffrin in their principles of polite sociability, a limited social mobility based on merit, and equality between the sexes based on rational friendship and intellectual exchange. As with the Bluestocking salons, a new conception of civic virtue and political power based on "reciprocal exchange" and "natural sociability" defined the Parisian salons.[11] In both cases, the main force of this self-proclaimed civilizing process was located in the hostess, or *salonnière*.

9.     Charles Burney writes, "My publication [*The Present State of Music in Germany, the Netherlands, and United Provinces*, 1773] was honoured with the approbation of the blue-stocking families at Mrs. Vezey's and Mrs. Montagu's and Sir Joshua Reynolds's, where I was constantly invited and regarded as a member"; *The Early Journals and Letters of Fanny Burney*, ed. Lars E. Troide, 2 vols. (Montreal and Kingston, 1988), 1:266n. In her poem *The Bas Bleu; or, Conversation* (1786), Hannah More records Frances Boscawen, Elizabeth Montagu, Lord Lyttelton, William Pulteney, Horace Walpole, Elizabeth Carter, and Elizabeth Vesey as among the main members of the circle. Much more recently, Walter S. Scott lists Mary Delany, Elizabeth Carter, Elizabeth Montagu, Hester Chapone, Hester Lynch Thrale, Hannah More, Frances Burney, Elizabeth Vesey, Frances Boscawen, Ann Ord, Catherine Talbot, Frances Greville, Frances Anne Crewe, Charlotte Walsingham, and Mary Monckton as hostesses and members; Scott, *The Bluestocking Ladies* (London, 1947).

10.   Marie Anne Fiquet du Boccage recalls her experience of Mrs. Montagu's levée: "We breakfasted in this manner to-day at Lady Montagu's, in a closet lined with painted paper of Pekin, and furnished with the choicest moveables of China. A long table covered with the finest linen, presented to the view of thousand glittering cups, which contained coffee, chocolate, biscuits, cream, butter, toasts, and exquisite tea" (Fiquet du Boccage, *Letters Concerning England, Holland and Italy*, 2 vols. [London, 1770], 1:7).

11.   See Dena Goodman, *The Republic of Letters: A Cultural History of the French Enlightenment* (Ithaca, N.Y., 1994). While Elizabeth Montagu was interested in visiting French salons on her trip to France in 1775, Hannah More sought to distance herself and the Bluestockings from their French counterparts in her poem *The Bas Bleu*.

The late 1770s saw a change in usage of the term "Bluestocking"; increasingly it referred to the women of the groups only and, as Gary Kelly suggests, was used by those "who feared or felt excluded from Bluestocking Society," thus preparing the way for the later pejorative sense.[12] These decades also saw a second generation of Bluestockings, with hostesses such as Hester Thrale and Mary Delany, and Samuel Johnson, Frances Burney, Hannah More, and Hester Chapone among the guests. Elizabeth Montagu's own assemblies became more established after the death of her husband in 1775, when she remodeled and enlarged the salon in her new house in Portman Square. Provincial communities formed in Bath around Sarah Scott and Sarah Fielding, in Batheaston around Lady Miller, and in Lichfield around Anna Seward. The vast correspondence carried on between members of those original groups attests to the early establishment of a wider, virtual circle of friends who regularly communicated about politics and literature. The term "bluestockings" thus began to refer to learned women in general.[13]

At the same time, the reactionary political and intellectual climate of the 1790s, responding to the unfolding of the French Revolution, led, as Myers shows, to a pejorative understanding of a "bluestocking" as a dangerously intellectual woman—a trend that also produced a range of satires, of which Richard Polwhele's, *Unsex'd Females* (1798), Thomas Moore's *M.P.; or, The Bluestockings* (1811), and Lord Byron's *The Blues: A Literary Eclogue* (1821) are the most prominent examples.[14] In its most popular and often derogatory sense, the epithet "bluestocking" has retained its connotation of social privilege and conservatism, in addition to the denotation of intellectual or literary qualities in a woman. Increasingly for scholars of the original movement, however, the term "Bluestockings" encompasses a broad range of relations, originally mobilized by the actual Bluestocking salons, between men and women—but especially between women. As the essays in this volume indicate, the rationales and modes of expression of these networks were as varied as their members' activities and

12. Gary Kelly, "Bluestocking Feminism and Writing in Context," in Elizabeth Eger, ed., *Elizabeth Montagu*, vol. 1 of *Bluestocking Feminism: Writings of the Bluestocking Circle, 1738–1785*, gen. ed. Gary Kelly, 6 vols. (London, 1999), 1:ix–liv at x.

13. A note on capitalization is in order here. In this general sense of a learned or intellectual woman, the term is most correctly spelled with a lower-case "b," whereas the historically specific sense is indicated by capitalization. In this volume, use of the term is historically specific, though at times deliberately broadening the traditional boundaries of membership in the group (see in particular the essays by Gary Kelly and Susan Staves).

14. This was mirrored in France where, as Goodman has shown, the feminocentric salon culture was replaced in the 1780s and 1790s with an exclusively male culture of the "republic of letters" (*Republic of Letters,* 11). The anxieties conjured up by the "new woman" in late Victorian England resulted in very similar criticism and satirical iconography.

aspirations, including intellectual and religious exchange, political influence, literary publishing, commercial enterprises, philanthropic projects, social experiments, friendship, and same-sex love.[15]

❧ ❧

As Gary Kelly has shown in detail, it is clear that politically, the first generation of Bluestockings were committed to a "progressive-aristocratic" program that sought to amend traditional cultures of court libertinism and paternalism based on patronage and property, essentially transforming them in terms of gentry and middle-class values. This program's model of a civil society defined by egalitarian sociability, conversation, and the advancement of civic virtue relied on an essentialist and exclusive understanding of gender. In this view, the "feminization" of culture that critics have found characteristic of the period was welcomed as positive, since women played the role of a civilizing force in the progression of commercial capitalism and political "embourgoisement."[16] Separate, gendered spheres were seen to complement each other in the modernizing and commercializing of eighteenth-century society.

But with conservative social critics opposed to the increasing commercialization of culture and blaming "effeminacy" and luxury for social ills, the nature of the feminine became a proxy in ideological disputes between conservatives and liberals.[17] The Bluestockings both partook in and revised the terms of this dispute by creating a space—the salon—where women actively participated in the public sphere. Nevertheless, as Deborah Heller argues, the project of this egalitarian and intellectual circle grappled with gender contradictions: "on the

15.  Susan Frye and Karen Robertson suggest the term "alliance" for this range of interrelationships; Frye and Robertson, eds., *Maids and Mistresses, Cousins and Queens: Women's Alliances in Early Modern England* (Oxford, 1999).

16.  Gary Kelly, "Bluestocking Feminism," in Elizabeth Eger, Charlotte Grant, Cliona Ógallchoir, and Penny Warburton, eds., *Women, Writing, and the Public Sphere, 1700–1830* (Cambridge, 2001), 163–80 at 167, 169.

17.  Anxieties about femininity and learning are influentially expressed by Jean-Jacques Rousseau in his *Lettre à d'Alembert* (1758): "Chez nous, au contraire, la femme la plus estimée est celle qui fait le plus de bruit; de qui l'on parle le plus; qu'on voit le plus dans le monde; chez qui l'on dine le plus souvent; qui donne le plus impérieusement le ton; qui juge, tranche, décide, prononce, assigne aux talents, au mérite, aux vertus, leurs degrés et leurs places; et dont les humbles savants mendient le plus basement la faveur" (Rousseau, *Discours sur les sciences et les arts; Lettre à d'Alembert*, ed. Jean Varloot [Paris, 1987], 200). See also Goodman, *Republic of Letters*, for Rousseau's and his contemporaries' position on learned women. A century later, Jules Barbey D'Aurevilly's book *Les Bas-Bleus* (1878) is still echoing the condemnation of learned women in England: "Ce sont des hommes,—du moins de pretension,—et manqués! Ce sont des Bas-bleus, Bas-bleu est masculin. Les Bas-bleus ont, plus ou moins, donné la demission de leur sexe. Même leur vanité n'est plus celle de la femme.... Les Bas-bleu, c'est la femme littéraire. C'est la femme qui fait metier et merchandise de littérature. C'est la femme qui se croit cerveau d'homme et demande sa part dans la publicité et dans la gloire" (Barbey D'Aurevilly, *Les Bas-Bleus* [Paris, 1878], ix, xii).

one hand, the salon was grounded on the public sphere premise of universality and disembodied reason; on the other, the salonnières were nevertheless judged by standards of femininity that potentially constrained them."[18] The Bluestockings thus occupied a markedly contradictory position within the discourses of eighteenth-century femininity. While they furthered the advancement of women in education and in print publication, they at the same time enforced a feminine respectability that specifically concerned sexual conduct. For example, Catharine Macaulay's second marriage to the much younger and socially inferior William Graham in 1778 prompted defamatory attacks in Bluestocking letters; Sarah Scott even went so far to call upon "the pure Virgins & Virtuous Matrons who reside in this place [to] unite & drown her in the Avon" (Scott to Montagu, MO 5391, 27 November 1778). Hester Lynch Thrale's 1784 second marriage to Gabriel Piozzi, an Italian musician and the tutor of her daughter, was censured severely on the same grounds.

This conservatism regarding female conduct notwithstanding, nineteenth-century editors of Bluestocking letters apparently felt a need to locate the circle even more firmly within the domestic sphere, and they stressed the circle's involvement in the feminized realms of Christian philanthropy and education.[19] The representation of the Bluestockings in the late eighteenth and early nineteenth centuries thus exhibits the crucial tensions between the political radicalism of the 1790s, counter-Revolutionary politics, domestic ideology, and what Kelly calls the "remasculinisation of culture that characterized the Romantic movement."[20] Montagu Pennington's *Memoirs of the Life of Elizabeth Carter* (1808) praises his aunt Carter's determination to lead a single life as a scholar and her intellectual genius, but above all her piety and Christian humility: "But among her Studies there was one which she never neglected; one which was always dear to her from her earliest infancy to the latest period of her life, and in which she made a continual improvement."[21] The brief biography of Hester Chapone that prefaces the 1807 edition of her works again stresses Chapone's

---

18. Deborah Heller, "Bluestocking Salons and the Public Sphere," *Eighteenth-Century Life* 22 (1998): 59–82 at 72.

19. See, for example, the various prefaces and memoirs attached to Elizabeth Carter, *Letters from Mrs. Elizabeth Carter to Mrs. Montagu, between the years 1755 and 1770*, ed. Montagu Pennington, 3 vols. (London, 1817); *The Letters of Mrs. Elizabeth Montagu, with Some of the Letters of Her Correspondents*, 4 vols. (London, 1810–13); *Memoirs of the Life of Elizabeth Carter*, ed. Montagu Pennington, 2 vols. (London, 1808); Dr. Doran, *A Lady of the Last Century: Illustrated in her unpublished Letters* (London, 1873); and Hester Chapone, *The Works of Mrs Chapone: To which is prefixed an account of her Life and Character drawn up by her own family*, 4 vols. (London, 1807). This essential grounding of education in faith and piety is a common trope in the nineteenth century and also appears in didactic writings such as Jane Taylor's *Display: A Tale* (London, 1815).

20. Kelly, "Bluestocking Feminism," 177.

21. Pennington, *Memoirs of Carter*, 17.

eagerness to cultivate her mind through a close study of the Bible. Nor does this concern end with the Bluestockings' first editors; even Emily J. Climenson's 1906 edition of Montagu's correspondence accentuates her profound Christian faith, "a religion that prompted her ever to the kindest actions to all classes, that had nothing bitter or narrow in it, no dogmatism," and her quintessentially domestic and philanthropic qualities: "As a wife, a friend, a camarade in all things, grave or gay, she was unequalled; as a housewife she was notable, beloved by her servants, by the poor of her parish, and by her miners."[22]

However, there was another strand of literature, modeled on George Ballard's *Memoirs of Several Ladies of Great Britain who have been celebrated for their writings or skill in the learned languages, arts and science* (1752), which praised learned women without hiding their intellectual achievements under a eulogy on their Christian and domestic virtues.[23] Ballard's pioneering study of learned women went beyond the traditional range of female biographies in the form of family memoirs, martyrologies, and memoirs of philanthropic women and mystics to create a lineage of intellectual and literary women from the early modern period to the late seventeenth century.[24] Nevertheless, the attention paid to the Bluestockings in works following Ballard's lead often singled out the literary achievements of a few of them (such as Elizabeth Carter, Hester Thrale, or Hannah More) as individuals, or honored the Bluestocking circles as a worthy but bygone phenomenon. These studies thereby responded to a growing interest in intellectual and literary women of earlier times while marginalizing the significance of the Bluestockings as social and political innovators or reformers.[25]

In this context, Amelia Opie's *Detraction Displayed* (1828) is a very unusual polemical document that rescues the term "Bluestocking" from its derogatory association with "women on display." In the process, Opie uses the term to refer both to the historical group and to learned women in general, as a proto-feminist catchphrase:

22. Emily J. Climenson, *Elizabeth Montagu, The Queen of the Blue-Stockings: Her Correspondence from 1720 to 1761* (London, 1906), ix. Reginald Blunt, in a later, undated edition of the remaining correspondence, provides a brief introduction to the salons; *Mrs. Montagu, "Queen of Blues": Her Letters and Friendships from 1762 to 1800*, 2 vols. (London, n.d.), 2:1–11.

23. George Ballard, *Memoirs of Several Ladies of Great Britain who have been celebrated for their writings or skill in the learned languages, arts and sciences* (1752), ed. Ruth Perry (Detroit, 1985). The *Memoirs* were dedicated, incidentally, to Catherine Talbot and Mary Delany.

24. See Ruth Perry's introduction to Ballard's *Memoirs of Several Ladies* for an account of these biographical traditions.

25. Some important compilations of accounts of learned women are Horace Walpole, *A Catalogue of the Royal and Noble Authors of England, Scotland, and Ireland*, 5 vols. (London, 1806); Mark Noble, *A Biographical*

> I think it incumbent on all those women who are really blue-
> stockings, to dare to be themselves, and to shew by joining sea-
> sonably and modestly in intellectual converse, that all females of
> cultivated minds are not pedants or precieuses, and that they love
> information for its own sake, and not for the sake of display.... If
> ... they reply [to their detractor], "I am a blue-stocking, if to love
> knowledge better than ignorance entitles me to the name," the
> petty assaulter, be it man or woman, will soon lay down the weapon
> that is powerless to wound.[26]

Despite Opie's efforts, Thomas de Quincy's 1852 verdict on the Bluestockings as a "feeble minority" of mannish women, "not simply obsolete, but even unintelligible to our juniors," marked their disappearance from the literary canon and cultural history of the nineteenth century.[27]

While Climenson's 1906 edition, mentioned above, did little to draw attention to Elizabeth Montagu as anything other than a model of piety and domesticity, Chauncey Brewster Tinker's study *The Salon and English Letters* (1915) was in many ways a new departure. Tinker reintroduces French and English salon culture to his readers, makes a clear connection between the two cultures—something that has not been satisfactorily addressed in subsequent criticism—and prepares the ground for a more recent debate about public and private spheres. Indeed, he recognizes the permeability between the categories of literature and society, public and private, through polite conversation and sociability:

> The salon gave an opportunity for the development of ideas in a
> new medium—the liveliness of conversation. At such a time, when
> the formulation of opinion is stimulated by contact with other
> minds, when all barriers are down, all dread of critics forgotten, a
> man may give free rein to his doctrines and borrow all the bril-
> liancy that lives in exaggeration.[28]

*History of England*, 3 vols. (London, 1806); Jane Williams, *The Literary Women of England* (London, 1861); and Georgiana Hill, *Women in English Life from Mediæval to Modern Times*, 2 vols. (London, 1896).

26. Amelia Opie, *Detraction Displayed* (London, 1828), 264–66.

27. Thomas De Quincy, *Autobiography*, quoted in Sylvia H. Myers, "Learning, Virtue, and the Term 'Bluestocking,'" *Studies in Eighteenth-Century Culture* 15 (1985): 279–88 at 286.

28. Chauncey Brewster Tinker, *The Salon and English Letters: Chapters on the Interrelations of Literature and Society in the Age of Johnson* (New York, 1915); quotation at 39. See also Walter Scott, cited above, and Ethel Rolt Wheeler, *Famous Blue-Stockings* (London, 1910) for similar inquiries. Conspicuously, Myra Reynolds's *The Learned Lady in England, 1650–1760* (Boston, 1920) merely expands Ballard's list with entries on Elizabeth Carter, Sarah Fielding, Catherine Talbot, and Mary Delany. Elizabeth Montagu is also duly mentioned as the "Queen of the Blue-Stockings" but is praised for her knowledge of crafts, not her patronage, writing, or philanthropy (p. 263).

Tinker nevertheless confines his enthusiasm for the Bluestockings to their "high office as inspirer[s] and patron[s] of letters" and thus highlights the art of letter-writing more than the Bluestockings' own literary and critical oeuvre. In comparing the Bluestocking circles with the French salons, he comes to the conclusion that "the bluestockings never became, like their French models, true disseminators of new and daring philosophies and radical transitions. They were always on the side of law and order, and of a conservative tradition."[29] The premise of this comparison has been revised by subsequent feminist scholarship that acknowledges the debt of later, more radical feminist and egalitarian discourse to politically conservative women such as the Bluestockings.[30]

The project of rediscovery of women's writing was accelerated and politicized in the 1970s and 1980s in the context of second-wave feminism. Sandra M. Gilbert and Susan Gubar's seminal *The Madwoman in the Attic* addresses those issues that contributed to the writing of a canonical literary history that included or excluded specific writers—an approach that was later widened to an investigation of the politics of publishing and literary patronage.[31] Curiously, Ballard's meticulous but problematic encyclopedia proved again to be the foundation of some of these studies. Thus histories of eighteenth-century women's writing relying on the notion of a patriarchal social structure rigidly opposed to women's participation in any but the most narrowly conceived domestic sphere, and on dichotomous models of proper and improper women writers established by historians such as Ballard in the eighteenth century, found the Bluestockings both awkward and disappointing—awkward because they did not often choose fiction, a genre to which women were assumed to be relegated;[32] and disappointing because they did not articulate explicit critiques of contemporary gender roles

29. Tinker, *Salon and English Letters,* 99, 213. Tinker seems to welcome this conservatism, since, in a previous passage on early modern women, he criticizes the adoption of the *querelle des femmes* by late-seventeenth-century English writers such as Mary Astell and Judith Drake (p. 99).

30. See Harriet Guest's essay in this volume, and also her *Small Change: Women, Learning, Patriotism, 1750–1810* (Chicago, 2000). For a different political evaluation of the Bluestockings but a similar appraisal of their importance, see Anne K. Mellor, *Mothers of the Nation: Women's Political Writing in England, 1780–1830* (Bloomington, Ind., 2000).

31. Sandra M. Gilbert and Susan Gubar, *The Madwoman in the Attic: The Woman Writer and the Nineteenth-Century Literary Imagination* (New Haven, Conn., 1979); see also their *No Man's Land: The Place of the Woman Writer in the Twentieth Century* (New Haven, Conn., 1988). More importantly, however, Gilbert and Gubar identified strategies of resistance and negotiation that were used by nineteenth-century writers to overcome the exclusivity of the literary canon and publishing industry. A similar set of strategies of imitation, negotiation, and appropriation is suggested for early women poets such as Lady Mary Wroth and Aemilia Lanyer by Ann Rosalind Jones in *The Currency of Eros: Women's Love Lyric in Europe, 1540–1620* (Bloomington, Ind., 1990).

32. In fact, the Bluestockings' published writings ranged from poetry and fiction, through literary criticism, history, biography, translation, and essays, to educational treatises and didactic tracts.

and sexual practices in the manner of an Aphra Behn, a Mary Astell, or a Mary Wollstonecraft.[33] Marilyn L. Williamson and Moira Ferguson move away from this project of rediscovery and give credit to the Bluestockings' diversity and importance to eighteenth-century culture and society.[34] Both Williamson and Ferguson see the Bluestockings as a prominent example of female patronage that sought to make women writers and intellectuals visible. Williamson and Ferguson maintain that there is a very close relationship between the feminism of the *querelle des femmes*, seventeenth-century English feminism, and the rights that the Bluestockings claimed for themselves and other gentry and middle-class women—an issue that has been expanded more recently in Gary Kelly's work on Bluestocking feminism.[35]

With the publication in 1990 of Sylvia Myers's detailed research on the Bluestocking circle, the stage was set for the reconsideration of which this volume is one outcome. Inspired in part by a widening debate about the nature and relation of public and private, scholars have come to see the Blues as a collective, concerned, as we have outlined above, with articulating the relation between these spheres and also with defining a model of public life that incorporated the political, the intellectual, and the sociable. Implicit in this work is an engagement with Jürgen Habermas's *The Structural Transformation of the Public Sphere* (1962)—a work that has dominated eighteenth-century studies since its translation into English in 1989.[36] Habermas offers an account of the emergence of the bourgeois public sphere in the eighteenth century, relating its genesis to profound social and economic changes that transformed early modern Europe from absolutism and mercantilism to a modern civil society. Feminist studies of the eighteenth century have noted that Habermas's interpretation elides questions

33. See, for example, Jane Spencer, *The Rise of the Woman Novelist, from Aphra Behn to Jane Austen* (Oxford, 1986); and Janet Todd, *The Sign of Angellica: Women, Writing, and Fiction, 1660–1800* (New York, 1989). For a critique of such histories and their reliance on Ballard, see Margaret J. M. Ezell's *Writing Women's Literary History* (Baltimore, 1993), esp. chap. 4, "The Tedious Chase: Writing Women's Literary History in the Eighteenth and Nineteenth Centuries." A more recent review of the feminist project of recovery is presented by Isobel Grundy, "(Re)discovering Women's Texts," in Vivian Jones, ed., *Women and Literature in Britain, 1700–1800* (Cambridge, 2000), 179–96.

34. Marilyn L. Williamson, "Who's Afraid of Mrs. Barbauld? The Blue Stockings and Feminism," *International Journal of Women's Studies* 3 (January–February, 1980): 89–102; and Moira Ferguson, ed., *First Feminists: British Women Writers, 1578–1799* (Bloomington, Ind., 1985). See also Evelyn Gordon Bodek, "Salonnières and Bluestockings: Educated Obsolescence and Germinating Feminism," *Feminist Studies* 3 (Spring–Summer 1976): 185–99.

35. See esp. Gary Kelly's essay in *Women, Writing, and the Public Sphere,* ed. Eger et al.; and his general introduction to the six-volume *Bluestocking Feminism* anthology.

36. Jürgen Habermas, *The Structural Transformation of the Public Sphere: An Inquiry into a Category of Bourgeois Society* (1962), trans. Thomas Burger (Cambridge, Mass., 1989). See also Craig Calhoun, ed., *Habermas and the Public Sphere* (Cambridge, Mass., 1996).

of the gendered specificity of the public and the private.[37] Although Joan Landes influentially argued in 1988 that the dichotomy of spheres described by Habermas's model is fundamentally hegemonic, mutually exclusive, and gendered,[38] it is of particular interest to this volume that subsequent studies of French and English salons have shown that, historically, the public-private dichotomy was not as hegemonic as the model seems to suggest. Literary salons may have been located in the intimate domestic sphere, the salon, the parlor, or the *ruelle*, but were nothing less than an expansion of the authentic public sphere into institutions of "intellectual sociability."[39] Indeed, for Harriet Guest, ideological negotiations of the public and private in the eighteenth century are complex and ambivalent. She suggests that the discourse of the private and domestic allows women to intervene in public and political affairs if it is linked to a specifically conservative notion of propriety and patriotism. Guest argues further that domesticity can be a "site from which an oppositional political discourse can be articulated."[40] In contrast, Lisa Moore addresses the complicity of the "domestic" woman in the formation of gendered discourses of power. Using *Millenium Hall* as an example, Moore argues that while public/private ideologies might empower

37. For a general revision of Habermas, see Lawrence E. Klein, "Gender and the Public/Private Distinction in the Eighteenth Century: Some Questions about Evidence and Analytic Procedure," *Eighteenth-Century Studies* 29 (1995): 97–109.

38. Joan B. Landes, *Women and the Public Sphere in the Age of the French Revolution* (Ithaca, N.Y., 1988). For other feminist re-readings of Habermas, see Johanna Meehan, ed., *Feminists Read Habermas: Gendering the Subject of Discourse* (New York, 1995); Kathleen Wilson, "Citizenship, Empire, and Modernity in the English Provinces, c. 1720–1790," *Eighteenth-Century Studies* 29 (1995): 69–96; Margaret C. Jacob, "The Mental Landscape of the Public Sphere: A European Perspective," *Eighteenth-Century Studies* 28 (1994): 95–113; and Amanda Vickery, *The Gentleman's Daughter: Women's Lives in Georgian England* (New Haven, Conn., 1998).

39. For the specific context of salons, see Dena Goodman, *Republic of Letters*; Goodman, "Public Sphere and Private Life: Toward a Synthesis of Current Historiographical Approaches to the Old Regime," *History and Theory* 31 (1992): 1–20, quotation at 5; Heller, "Bluestocking Salons and the Public Sphere"; Erica Harth, "The Salon Woman goes Public . . . or Does She?" in Elizabeth C. Goldsmith and Dena Goodman, eds., *Going Public: Women and Publishing in Early Modern France* (Ithaca, N.Y., 1995), 179–93; Carla Hesse, *The Other Enlightenment: How French Women Became Modern* (Princeton, N.J., 2001); and Susan Stabile, "Salons and Power in the Era of Revolution: From Literary Coteries to Epistolary Enlightenment," in Larry E. Tise, ed., *Benjamin Franklin and Women* (University Park, Pa., 2000), 129–48. Goodman suggests that because Landes mistakenly amalgamates the Habermasian authentic public sphere with the state public sphere, she must necessarily arrive at an understanding of the public and private as fixed and hegemonic ("Public Sphere," 15). Jacob, in "Mental Landscape of the Public Sphere," goes even further in suggesting that a reading of public and private as a binary will inevitably retain its gendered bias and its focus on mainstream, urban culture, and is thus limited in its analysis of the "mental landscape" of the Enlightenment (pp. 98–99). Klein and Wilson (see nn. 34 and 35) make similar points.

40. Guest, *Small Change*, 18.

women within the domestic realm, they also legitimize bourgeois hierarchies and power relations:

> The women of Millenium Hall, then, enjoy their privilege only to the extent that they are willing to serve a hierarchized ideology in which they are inferior to the men who visit them from the "foreign" realms beyond the domestic sphere. Thus their efforts to extend their privilege cannot take the form of challenging that hierarchy; rather, they must attempt to extend the domestic sphere themselves.[41]

A further impetus to fresh analysis has been a widening debate about sexuality and gender as defined in the eighteenth century. In their manuscript and published writings, the Bluestockings left an extensive record of their theory and practice of female friendship. Recent critical and theoretical studies have revised Lillian Faderman's original dictum of a platonic but romantic friendship that brought the Bluestockings together.[42] Critics such as Moira Ferguson, George Haggerty, Susan Lanser, Celia Easton, and Lisa Moore address the intimate and more exclusive attachments that some of the Bluestockings formed and suggest a lesbian continuum expressed not only in these personal friendships but also in literary works such as Sarah Scott's *Millenium Hall* and Mary Wollstonecraft's *Mary*.[43] Ferguson also advocates a new way of reading these letters and fictions to

> probe beneath the surface of fiction's "harmless cover stories," expose political "subtexts," and identify the dual purposes of literary polemic that speaks softly, indistinctly, or disarmingly. Nor are the subsets of feminist polemic rigid, but open-ended, revealing what was previously hidden: two hundred years of complex and recorded protofeminist and feminist underground networks of resistance.[44]

41. Lisa L. Moore, *Dangerous Intimacies: Toward a Sapphic History of the British Novel* (Durham, N.C., 1997), 31.

42. Lillian Faderman, *Surpassing the Love of Men: Romantic Friendship and Love between Women from the Renaissance to the Present* (New York, 1981).

43. See Ferguson, *First Feminists;* George Haggerty, *Unnatural Affections: Women and Fiction in the Later Eighteenth Century* (Bloomington, Ind., 1998); Susan S. Lanser, "Befriending the Body: Female Intimacies as Class Acts," *Eighteenth-Century Studies* 32 (1998–99): 179–198; Celia Easton, "Were the Bluestockings Queer? Elizabeth Carter's Uranian Friendships" *Age of Johnson* 9 (1998): 257–94; and Moore, *Dangerous Intimacies.* Myers, however, strongly rejects the implication of any erotic relationship between the Bluestocking women (*Bluestocking Circle*, 18–19). For different evaluations of the Bluestockings' relationships with each other, see Janet Todd, *Women's Friendship in Literature* (New York, 1980); Betty Rizzo, *Companions without Vows: Relationships among Eighteenth-Century British Women* (Athens, Ga., 1994); Rebecca D'Monté and Nicole Pohl, eds., *Female Communities, 1600–1800: Literary Visions and Cultural Realities* (London, 2000).

44. Ferguson, *First Feminists*, 32.

Postcolonial theory has drawn increasing attention in eighteenth-century studies to issues of race—and specifically to the correlation between race, gender, and colonialism—and this has in turn influenced work on the Bluestockings. Laura Brown has shaped our understanding of femininity as the site where conspicuous consumption, domesticity, and colonialism are contested and negotiated.[45] Felicity Nussbaum has developed this argument further, showing that there is in fact a complex and complicit relationship between colonized and colonizer, between the domesticated European woman and the other, sexualized woman of the colonies: "The invention of the 'other' woman of empire enabled the consolidation of the cult of domesticity in England and, at the same time, the association of the sexualized woman at home with the exotic, or 'savage,' non-European woman." Sarah Scott's novel *Millenium Hall* (1762) is read as a rejection of this patriarchal discourse of the "Other" woman "in favour of a feminotopia" that paradoxically "substitutes benevolent confinement for colonization and enslavement at the time of the emergence of the Second Empire," thus retaining inequalities of class and race.[46] This novel, as well as its sequel *The History of Sir George Ellison* (1766), thereby maintains an inconsistent racial discourse that is both resistant to, and complicit in, contemporary mechanisms of racial discrimination.

❧ ❧

These recent attempts to reach beyond the divide of heavily edited nineteenth-century publications in order to reconstruct Bluestocking networks and the material conditions of their lives, their political interventions, and their publishing activities have led scholars to turn increasingly to collections of unpublished correspondence such as the Montagu Collection of the Huntington Library, as well as to original editions of their published works.[47] Several recent conferences or conference sessions on the Bluestockings, both in Britain and in North America, gave rise to a wish to gather together work that would represent some of these re-examinations. In reconsidering the Bluestockings, the ensemble of the following essays reveals an entity that functioned relationally to develop a collectively

45. Laura Brown, *Ends of Empire: Women and Ideology in Early Eighteenth-Century Literature* (Ithaca, N.Y., 1993).

46. Felicity A. Nussbaum, *Torrid Zones: Maternity, Sexuality, and Empire in Eighteenth-Century English Narratives* (Baltimore, 1995), 1, 161; see also Nussbaum, "Women and Race: 'a difference of complexion,'" in *Women and Literature in Britain, 1700–1800*, ed. Jones, 69–90; Markman Ellis, *The Politics of Sensibility: Race, Gender, and Commerce in the Sentimental Novel* (Cambridge, 1996); and Eve W. Stoddard, "A Serious Proposal for Slavery Reform: Sarah Scott's *Sir George Ellison*," *Eighteenth-Century Studies* 28 (1995): 379–96.

47. Gary Kelly's multivolume edition *Bluestocking Feminism* is a welcome corrective to the lack of modern editions of many of these texts.

articulated and recognizable, if informal, sense of identity. While individually authored texts have received considerable attention in recent years and are discussed at various points in this volume, the picture that comes into focus is one of the social and intellectual exchanges out of which individually authored texts emerged and that served to nurture the individual aspirations and achievements of their producers.

Harriet Guest's reconsideration of "bluestocking feminism-before-the-fact" sets this focus in detailing the Bluestocking women's particular historical place between the relatively isolated and politically inconspicuous women writers of the earlier eighteenth century and the more stridently politicized women, perceived as possessing a collective gender identity, of the 1790s. In this place—one characterized by a shift from the dominance of political and status-defined factions in the 1760s and early 1770s to increasingly rigid gender-defined and ideologically driven divisions between public and private—the educated circle presided over by Montagu in effect contributed to the transition that ultimately enabled the collective and political approach to gender that we call "feminism."

Partly because of the concern of feminist historiography of the Bluestockings to uncover and celebrate relations between women, the relations of members of this group with men have often been underemphasized or overlooked altogether. Susan Staves's essay on "Church of England Clergy and Women Writers" addresses this omission with respect to a specific group of men who "had a privileged monopoly on the prestigious forms of literary learning cultivated at the universities," and who therefore could provide "various kinds of educational and literary assistance" to women dependent on informal modes of education. Tracing a number of connections between clergymen and "high-minded, intellectually ambitious women" of the eighteenth century, including Elizabeth Carter and Hannah More as well as others viewed with suspicion by the Blues, such as Susannah Wesley, Lady Huntingdon, and Catharine Macaulay, Staves illuminates a range of dynamics, from those of mentoring and discipleship, to those of intellectual parity, to those of subordination and resistance.

Gary Kelly's examination of Clara Reeve as a "provincial Bluestocking" reveals a similarly complex and particularized set of relations for one writer who appears to have had no social contact with the London-based circles. In describing Reeve as a "Bluestocking with specifically provincial experience, viewpoint, and politics, . . . [which] gave her much in common with the metropolitan Bluestockings," Kelly not only tests the boundaries of the label but also details the extent to which one woman with roots in old Whig professional and commercial groups, and with links to publishing networks through a provincial firm based in Colchester, might have participated in the process of forming the modern liberal state in the nineteenth century. With *The Champion of Virtue* (1777; republished in London as *The Old English Baron* in 1778) and *The Progress of Romance* (1785), Reeve models "self-discipline, social loyalty, and civic virtue" and argues for the role of fiction-reading in forming these essential qualities of the modern sovereign subject. Reeve thereby joins her urban counterparts in having the "task of reforming the state in mind," and in believing that "literary and intellectual women—Bluestockings—could and should carry it out."

Elizabeth Eger examines another marriage of the literary and the political in her comparison of Elizabeth Montagu's and Elizabeth Griffith's 1769 and 1775 works of Shakespeare criticism. In nationalizing Shakespeare as the English bard and feminizing him as the source of morally improving analyses of human nature, Montagu and Griffith established the claim of women to cultural authority with respect to the vernacular canon, attracted the attention of a broad range of readers, and helped to set the terms of subsequent Shakespeare criticism. At the same time, Eger argues, Montagu and Griffith set the terms of their own disappearance from view as Shakespeare's position "became ever more prominent," in that their "reverential attitude to Shakespeare's work. . . . did not ultimately challenge masculine literary authority." Thus the paradoxical invisibility, yet influence, of the Bluestockings in the broader political and social landscape analyzed in Guest's essay is here manifested in these women's "largely . . . forgotten" yet "pioneering role as agents of change in the history of [Shakespeare's] reputation."

Elizabeth Child continues this focus on the best-known Bluestocking figure, Elizabeth Montagu, the "Queen of the Blues," in order to examine "a sphere of Montagu's life to which she herself devoted a great deal of attention but that has been all but ignored by subsequent accounts: Montagu as a Bluestocking businesswoman." Child observes that Montagu's writings about her management of the northern collieries and country estates that she eventually inherited from her husband show her as "pursu[ing] an alternative 'real-life' outlet for her Bluestocking ideals," and "suggest[ing] that benevolence, sensibility, altruism, and imagination can be the governing values not only for domestic economies or the cottage industries described in novels such as Sarah Fielding's *David Simple* and Sarah Scott's *Millenium Hall* but also for large-scale industrial enterprises." Montagu's "entrepreneurial persona" thus offers a strong contrast to the female economic vulnerability that is so dominant a motif of eighteenth-century fictions such as Burney's *Cecilia;* to overlook this persona is to overlook one significant contribution of this Bluestocking hostess to eighteenth-century elaborations of female capacity.

Complementing this analysis of Montagu as businesswoman are Emma Major's study of the millennial model of public engagement represented by

Montagu's and Vesey's assemblies, and Betty Rizzo's comparison of Montagu's model of community with that of her sister Sarah Scott. In these two essays, social theory and practice coexist in the sometimes uneasy tension implied by Child's emphasis on Montagu's self-portrayals. Major suggests that the self-definition of Montagu's circle as a peaceable union of competing political, linguistic, class, and private interest is founded upon an upper-rank, Anglican exclusivity that defines the "other" as a treasonous, dissenter-led, vulgar mob. This strategic marriage of religious language and political theory reveals that the discourse of "the Bluestocking millenium . . . represents nothing less than the most civilized and most patriotic public: the Anglican elite of God's chosen nation."

In Rizzo's discussion, the urban and privileged character of Montagu's salon and charitable activities is brought into a somewhat different focus through the contrastive lens of her sister Sarah's provincial and economically modest, but more fully theorized and idealistic, communal life and writings. This frame affords a provocative new reading of Montagu's letters to her sister in the time leading up to Scott's attempt to establish a female community at Hitcham House, "Scott's great effort to prove the Utopian scheme of *Millenium Hall* practicable." Rizzo suggests that Montagu's self-portrayal as charitable businesswoman and reformer of dissipated sociability is part of "the sisters' attempt at reconciliation during the Hitcham experiment," an attempt whose failure ultimately allows them to pursue more individualized and class-specific self-characterizations, "Montagu demonstrating her supremacy in the areas of taste, wit, and the best society; Scott demonstrating that the best society was really in some other place, among the provincial clerical sort at Norwich, for example, and that she, not her sister, was on the high road."

With Deborah Heller's essay "Subjectivity Unbound: Elizabeth Vesey as the Sylph in Bluestocking Correspondence," collaborative projects of identity construction shift to a third party, as Montagu and Carter develop for Vesey the persona of the "Sylph," characterized as "an unpredictable, mysterious, and indeterminate being who enjoyed almost magical powers of invention, energy, and freedom." Heller argues that Montagu and Carter were invested in this persona as a symbolic means of transcending defined gender roles, while nevertheless invoking for Vesey a more disciplinary discourse of ethical subjectivity that paralleled their own self-disciplines. While pointing to the modern ideal of the autonomous, experiential self, therefore, the figure of the Sylph simultaneously prefigures the relegation of this self to the developing realm of the aesthetic.

The final two essays in this volume turn to interrelated aspects of Bluestocking collective identity that have received little attention, perhaps because of this contemporary and subsequent focus on the disciplined female self: the

Bluestocking body and Bluestocking desire. As Susan Lanser puts it, when it is noted that the term "Bluestocking Circle" was and has been used to signify "a coalition of femininity, philanthropy, Anglican piety, English propriety, and intellectual pursuit, all integrated into a public identity that could promote women's participation in literary culture as decorous, salutary, and safe," it becomes clear that "Bluestocking feminism was also a project of constraint." Jane Magrath argues that, contrary to both a conventional mind-body dualism that gendered the mind as male and the body as female, and the corollary imperative of transcending the body to pursue a life of the mind, Carter and Montagu's correspondence reveals selves that are "complexly and intricately embodied," whereby the body sometimes impedes, but also cooperates, conspires with, and absolves the mind, providing "a certain degree of agency" to the writer. Most strikingly, the mind-body distinction at times collapses altogether in the medium of the letter, as physical separation is compensated for by vivid images of bodily connection.

Lanser pursues this attention to the body in language in a discussion of "Bluestocking Sapphism and the Economies of Desire" that raises the possibility that "scholarly decisions about who is true Blue" have been based on "scholarly identification with our objects of inquiry, reverence for their public images, or the need to resist the denigration of learned women that has continued through the years." As a corrective, Lanser suggests that "we stop seeking sex acts and examine the formations within which women's desires were expressed, restrained, and managed" as a means of "open[ing] different dimensions of Bluestocking lives and works." Using a comparative method to consider "a range of sexualities" for Montagu, Carter, Scott, Hester Chapone, and Catherine Talbot, Lanser identifies "signs of same-sex desire" in the published and private writings of all but Chapone, and particularly in Carter. She outlines as well the textual strategies used to "economize" this desire through spatial and temporal imagery, the use of signs and tokens, and figures of the body in distress. Lanser speculates that the much discussed Bluestocking conservatism that has seemed incompatible with sapphic desire might in fact be viewed as a "'compensatory conservatism' for managing not only intellectual interests but erotic and affectional interests as well."

The work represented in this volume, then, encourages us to widen and complicate our understanding of the Bluestockings' intervention in eighteenth-century culture and society, whether by probing the meaning of Bluestocking sociability as conservative feminism or compensatory conservatism, by pushing the boundaries of Bluestocking membership to include provincial gentlewomen and theological reformers, or by enlarging the Bluestocking sphere of action to encompass business, social experimentation, self-fashioning, and bodily expression. More fundamentally, reconsidering the Bluestockings invites us to reflect more generally on the different modes of women's lives in the eighteenth century, as writers and scholars indeed, but also as entrepreneurs and philanthropists, visionaries and reformers, theologians and lovers.

❧ ❧

We wish to express our gratitude to all those who organized and participated in the three recent Bluestocking conferences or conference sessions that provided the impetus for this volume—in March 2001 at the Centre for Eighteenth Century Studies at the University of York (U.K.), at the April 2001 American Society for Eighteenth-Century Studies Conference in New Orleans, and at the Huntington Library in May 2001. Particular thanks go to Harriet Guest, Jane Rendall, Emma Major, Kate Davies, Betty Rizzo, and Felicity Nussbaum. The support of the Social Sciences and Humanities Research Council of Canada in the early stages of this project, and later, of Dr. Bruce Clayman, Vice-President for Research at Simon Fraser University, and of the SFU Publications Fund, were instrumental. We are grateful to Janice Blathwayt and Anna Miegon for their help in putting the volume together in its final stages. Our contributors will join us, we are certain, in thanking Mary Robertson as well as the Reader Services staff at the Huntington Library for their unvarying patience and expert assistance. Susan Green's grace and professionalism as editor of the *Huntington Library Quarterly* made normally tedious editorial processes a pleasure. And as co-editors of this volume, our greatest debt of thanks is to our hard-working contributors, whose commitment to fine scholarship has been a continual inspiration.

*University College, Northampton; Simon Fraser University*

# The Elizabeth Robinson Montagu Collection at the Huntington Library

MARY L. ROBERTSON

A rich and incomparable archive of nearly seven thousand letters to and from Elizabeth Robinson Montagu was purchased in 1925 by Henry E. Huntington for his newly founded research library from the rare-book and manuscript dealer A. S. W. Rosenbach. The acquisition was perfectly consistent with Huntington's policy of collecting original materials for advanced scholarly research in English and American history and literature, and the Montagu papers are now, as they have been from the beginning, a mainstay of the Library's important holdings from eighteenth-century England.

In addition to 3,500 letters by Montagu herself (including 691 addressed to her husband Edward Montagu, 737 to her sister Sarah Robinson Scott, 754 to Elizabeth Carter, and 254 to Elizabeth Vesey), the collection contains letters written to her by a wide circle of friends and acquaintances, providing a valuable cross-section of elite English literary, social, and political life. Here are Margaret Bentinck, duchess of Portland (62 letters), Fanny Boscawen (73), George, Lord Lyttelton (116), Messenger Monsey (71), William Pulteney, earl of Bath (283), Elizabeth Vesey (96), Gilbert West (54), and William Wilberforce (26). Here too are letters from Montagu's family: from her husband Edward (439), her sister Sarah (367), her nephew Matthew Montagu[1] (129), and Dorothy Montagu, countess of Sandwich (50). And finally, there are single or a few pieces penned by other prominent figures in her world: Edmund Burke, Hester Chapone, Thomas Clarkson, David Garrick, Samuel Johnson, Hannah More, Hester Thrale Piozzi, Sir Joshua Reynolds, Laurence Stern, James Stuart, and Horace Walpole.

The collection is fairly evenly distributed over the years 1740 through 1800, although the decade of the 1760s is particularly well represented. Topics covered in the collection—which, unlike most preserved archives, often contains both sides of a correspondence—are wide-ranging, encompassing the literary, political, and social world of Montagu and her friends and acquaintances in London,

---

1. In 1776, following the death without direct male issue of Mrs. Montagu's husband, Edward, her nephew Matthew Robinson adopted the surname Montagu; in 1829 he inherited his elder brother Morris's barony and succeeded as fourth baron Rokeby.

Bath, Tunbridge Wells, and her home at Sandleford Priory in Berkshire; accounts of travel in England and abroad; and the financial matters and management of family coal mines in Northumberland.[2]

Montagu's papers have long been recognized as an important source for the history of England in the second half of the eighteenth century. Between 1809 and 1813 her nephew and executor Matthew Montagu solicited the return of her letters from many of their recipients (or their descendants) and published a selection of correspondence down to 1761,[3] but the editorial work fell far short of modern standards and the chronological arrangement (since Montagu seldom fully dated her correspondence) was highly questionable. His granddaughter Emily J. Climenson edited and published in 1906 a second selection of Montagu's letters,[4] also to 1761, and left the archive to a friend, Reginald Blunt, with the hope that he would continue her work. In 1923 Blunt published two further volumes of extracts of selected letters, covering the years 1762 through 1800, once again arranged in a chronological order based on conjecture from internal evidence.[5]

Within two years of the publication of Blunt's edition the Montagu papers were sold to the Huntington, where they were then more comprehensively arranged, and more than one Library cataloguer continued to struggle with the problems of fragmentary and undated or only partially dated letters. Full cataloguing was not completed until June 1952, although the Library had opened the material to research in the later 1920s, assisting readers on site, microfilming selected items for scholars, and answering research inquiries as time allowed. A summary report about the archive,[6] prepared by the Huntington cataloguer who completed the processing, presents a nice snapshot of mid-twentieth-century interests: he stressed information about Montagu's everyday life at London, Sandleford Priory, Bath, and Tunbridge Wells, with water-drinking and bathing, lectures, balls, assemblies, and tea parties; references to current books and plays; medicine (principally discussions of various ailments such as stomach trouble, headaches, eyestrain, influenza, and Montagu's smallpox inoculation); Montagu's

2.  The content is summarized briefly in the *Guide to British Historical Manuscripts in the Huntington Library* (San Marino, Calif., 1982), 333–37.

3.  *The Letters of Mrs. Elizabeth Montagu, with Some of the Letters of her Correspondents* (London, 1809 and 1813).

4.  *Elizabeth Montagu, the Queen of the Blue-Stockings: Her Correspondence from 1720 to 1761 . . . by Emily J. Climenson*, 2 vols. (London, 1906).

5.  *Mrs. Montagu, "Queen of the Blues": Her Letters and Friendships from 1762 to 1800*, ed. Reginald Blunt, 2 vols. (London, 1923).

6.  Huntington Library, in-house finding aid for the Elizabeth Robinson Montagu Collection, unpublished typescript [1952].

various travels to Newcastle-upon-Tyne, Bath, Sandleford Spa in 1763, Paris in 1776, and Scotland in 1766 and 1770; "local social and political gossip;" and references to current political affairs such as the Jacobite Rebellion of 1745, the Seven Years' War, the Coronation of George III, the John Wilkes affair, and the trial of Warren Hastings. There were "but very few references to American colonial affairs and the Revolutionary War," the cataloguer noted with disappointment. The Library has also been able to augment the main archive by purchasing, from time to time, a few additional Robinson and Montagu family letters from other sources; among these were a selection of letters between Elizabeth Montagu, Sarah Scott, William Robinson, and Mary Richardson Robinson that had been edited and published in 1873 by John Doran.[7]

Since that time the correspondence has been studied extensively by several generations of historians and literary scholars. The Huntington's exhibition programs and scholarly symposia have further publicized the importance of the archive to audiences in both America and the U.K., and circulation records going back to 1952 show that several hundred scholars have consulted the collection. Both single letters and series of correspondence have been edited, quoted, cited, and analyzed in a wide range of scholarly books and articles, yet for an archive mined so thoroughly the Montagu papers remain remarkably fruitful, fresh, and new. When Rosenbach described the archive for Huntington in 1925 he stressed its value for the study of kings, battles, high politics, and prominent men, but mentioned virtually nothing of the various topics for which the papers are read today; nor was he much interested in Montagu herself. By 1952, social history and the world of letters documented by the collection were attracting scholarly attention, but women's studies, public spheres, and material culture had not yet appeared on the horizon. The questions we ask now, as illustrated by the essays in this volume, will inevitably be replaced by new and different areas of investigation, for experience suggests that the Montagu archive is an infinitely renewable resource, always able to shed new light on the past.

*Huntington Library*

7.    John Doran, *A Lady of the Last Century (Mrs. Elizabeth Montagu); Illustrated in her Unpublished Letters, Collected and Arranged, with a Biographical Sketch, and a Chapter on Blue Stockings* (London, 1873).

# Biographical Sketches of
# Principal Bluestocking Women

Compiled by Anna Miegon

**Barbauld, Anna Laetitia** (1743–1825) was born Anna Laetitia Aikin at Kibworth Harcourt, Leicestershire, a "provincial Bluestocking" who was among the second generation of the group. She published in a range of genres, including poetry, essays, and literary reviews; she also published political works and didactic prose for children. She held notably liberal views on the French Revolution and on issues such as abolition and the freedom of religious and political expression.

Barbauld was the child of Jane Jennings and John Aikin, Presbyterian dissenters. Educated by her father, she learned Latin and Greek as well as modern languages. After age fifteen she lived in Warrington, Lancashire, where her father taught at Warrington Academy. In 1774 she married Rochemont Barbauld, a French dissenting clergyman. In 1777 they adopted her nephew, Charles Rochemont Aikin. The Barbaulds managed a boys' school in Palgrave, Suffolk, until 1785. They traveled on the Continent for a year and then settled in Hampstead. In 1802 they moved to Stoke Newington, where her brother, John Aikin, lived; there her husband died in 1808 after a lengthy mental illness. After his death, Barbauld focused on literary activity. Her circle included Joseph Priestley, Samuel Johnson, Joseph Johnson, Joanna Baillie, Hester Chapone, Maria Edgeworth, Hannah More, and Elizabeth Montagu, as well as leading dissenters and political liberals.

Barbauld's works include *Poems* and *Miscellaneous Pieces in Prose*, the latter coauthored with her brother (both 1773); *Hymns in Prose for Children* (1781), often reprinted and translated; *An Address to the Opposers of the Repeal of the Corporation and Test Acts* (1790); *Epistle to William Wilberforce* (1791); and *Sins of the Government, Sins of the Nation* (1793), published in response to England's declaration of war against the French Republic. She edited William Collins's *Poetical Works* (1794); *The Correspondence of Samuel Richardson* (1804); and *The British Novelists* (1810), which included biographical essays and critical reviews. She also compiled a collection of works for girls, *The Female Speaker*, in 1811. In 1812 her satirical poem *Eighteen Hundred and Eleven*, which forecasts the fading of the power of the British Empire, was negatively received. Her works were admired by her literary contemporaries, including Oliver Goldsmith, Samuel Taylor Coleridge, William Wordsworth, Frances Burney, and Sir Walter Scott.

**Boscawen, Frances** (1719–1805), born Frances Glanville, a first-generation Bluestocking, was a prominent hostess. Her correspondence reveals important aspects of her domestic and social life and contributed to her contemporary reputation as the ideal wife and mother to the "man of the Empire."

Boscawen was the only child of Frances Bromehall Glanville and William Evelyn of St. Clere, who took his wife's name on their marriage. In 1742 Frances married Edward Boscawen, who later became Admiral of the Blue, General of Marines, Lord of the Admiralty, with whom she had five children. Her early letters were written during her husband's absences. After her husband's death in 1761 she became famous for her evening parties. In 1766 her daughter Elizabeth married the duke of Beaufort, and in 1769 her son William, who was in the navy, was drowned in Jamaica. In 1774 her eldest son also died abroad. In 1784 her remaining son, George, now Lord Falmouth, married Miss Crewe, granddaughter of Frances Greville. Boscawen befriended Elizabeth Montagu and was admired by Hannah More.

Many of Boscawen's letters remain unpublished. Some are preserved in the biography of Hannah More (*Memoirs of the Life and Correspondence of Mrs. Hannah More,* by William Roberts [1834]) or in the correspondence of Mary Delany. Some of her letters to Elizabeth Montagu appear in *Bluestocking Letters,* edited by R. Brimley Johnson (1926). Boscawen's letters to her husband, preserved by her family, were published in *Admiral's Wife* (1940), and her later letters appeared in the companion volume, *Admiral's Widow* (1943).

**Carter, Elizabeth** (1717–1806), born in Deal, Kent, was a close friend of Catherine Talbot, Elizabeth Montagu, and Hester Mulso Chapone. Pious and notably conservative politically, she was along with Sarah Scott the most productive writer among the Bluestockings of the first generation, publishing poetry, essays, and a translation of Epictetus and maintaining an extensive correspondence. For a woman of her time, her achievement in classical scholarship was outstanding.

Carter was the daughter of Margaret Swayne and the Reverend Nicholas Carter, a clergyman who taught her Latin, Greek, and Hebrew. She also studied French, German, Italian, Portuguese, Arabic, astronomy, ancient geography, history, and music. After her mother's death in 1727 she ran the household until her father married again; after her stepmother's death, Carter took care of her father until his death in 1774. Her father was a friend of Edward Cave, the editor of the *Gentleman's Magazine,* to which she started contributing in 1734 as "Eliza." Cave introduced her to Samuel Johnson and other prominent figures and also published many of her works. Carter rejected the attentions of Thomas Birch, a scholar and clergyman, and elected single life. With the financial support she received from Montagu, the earl of Bath, and Talbot's mother, she was able to travel. She often visited London and her friends' country houses but maintained her permanent residence in Deal. In 1763 she went with the earl of Bath and Elizabeth Montagu to France, the Low Countries, and the Rhineland; she visited France once more in 1782 with Montagu. Her circle also included Elizabeth Vesey, Frances Boscawen, Samuel Richardson, Edmund Burke, Horace Walpole, Hannah More, Richard Savage, Mary Delany, Thomas Secker, and Mary Hamilton. Johnson praised her linguistic abilities and asked her to contribute to his *Rambler*. Hers are numbers 44 (18 August 1750) and 100 (2 March 1751).

Carter's works also include *Poems on Particular Occasions* (1738); *An Examination of Mr. Pope's Essay on Man*, translated from the French work by Jean Pierre de Crousaz, (1739); and *Sir Isaac Newton's Philosophy Explain'd for the Use of the Ladies* (1739), a translation from Francesco Algarotti. In 1749 she undertook a translation from the Greek, *All the Works of Epictetus that Are Now Extant*, which was published in 1758 and met with great success. She is the probable author of *Remarks on the Athanasian Creed* (1753). Her *Poems on Several Occasions* was published in 1762. Richardson included her "Ode to Wisdom" in *Clarissa*, originally without acknowledgment. In 1808 Carter's nephew Montagu Pennington published *A Series of Letters between Mrs. Elizabeth Carter and Miss Catherine Talbot*, which additionally includes letters to Vesey. He also published Carter's poetry, shorter prose, and several letters as *Memoirs of the Life of Mrs. Elizabeth Carter* (1816) and edited *Letters from Mrs. Elizabeth Carter, to Mrs. Montagu* (1817). Carter suffered from headaches throughout her life, and health was often the subject of her correspondence. Pennington claimed that Carter ceased to write forty years before her death, withdrawing from the public and publishing worlds.

**Chapone, Hester** (1727–1801), born Hester Mulso at Twywell, Northamptonshire, was among the first generation of the Bluestockings. A number of her publications went into multiple editions, particularly her epistolary work on female conduct, written from a position of middle-class morality. She is distinguished from the other Bluestockings by her early claim that women's domestic lives, as socially dictated, could be intellectually and emotionally satisfying. Her writings addressed such topics as religion, education, and economy as well as character, friendship, and female accomplishments. She attended the Bluestocking assemblies, giving modest receptions occasionally.

Chapone was a daughter of Hester Thomas and Thomas Mulso, a gentleman farmer. She educated herself in French, Italian, Latin, music, and drawing after her mother's death in 1750. In 1760, after a six-year struggle against her father's disapproval, she married John Chapone, a lawyer, who died ten months later. After the death of her father in 1763, she resided with various friends and family, staying often at Farnham Castle with her uncle, the bishop of Winchester. There, in 1778, the queen complimented Chapone's *Letters on the Improvement of the Mind*, modeling the education of the Princess Royal on it. Finally, until her death, Chapone lived in a hired house at Hadley with her youngest niece. Her circle included Elizabeth Carter, Mary Delany, William Duncombe, Samuel Richardson,

Thomas Edwards, Susanna Highmore, Elizabeth, Amy, and the Reverend Burrows, and Mary Prescott.

Chapone's first short romance, "The Loves of Amoret and Melissa," written when she was nine, together with other early literary efforts, were disapproved of by her mother. At Samuel Johnson's invitation, she contributed fictional letters to the *Rambler;* and "The Story of Fidelia," a fictional autobiography, appeared in the *Adventurer* (1753). She also wrote a Pindaric ode on Carter's *Epictetus* (1758). Her didactic works include *Letters on the Improvement of the Mind* (1773), the most noteworthy; *Miscellanies in Prose and Verse* (1775); and *A Letter to a New-Married Lady* (1777). *The Posthumous Works of Mrs. Chapone* (1807), published by her family, contains mainly letters.

**Delany**, **Mary** (1700–1788), a first-generation Bluestocking, was born Mary Granville at Coulston, Wiltshire. She was a frequent guest of Elizabeth Montagu and Frances Boscawen and a favorite of the royal family. Delany carried on notable correspondence and was concerned with the issue of companionate marriage. She invented an art form that she called "paper mosaic."

Delany was the daughter of West Country Tory and Royalist parents, Mary Westcombe and Bernard Granville. She was sent to court at an early age, but the death of Queen Anne ruined the family's plans for her advancement. By contemporary standards, she was well educated, reading French and some Italian. Her uncle, the poet and diplomat Lord Lansdowne, arranged a marriage of his seventeen-year-old niece to his nearly sixty-year-old political crony, a Cornish landholder, Alexander Pendarves. The couple lived mostly in Cornwall. When her husband died in 1724, she turned to painting and handiwork. She moved to London, where she became a member of court and aristocratic social circles. In the early 1730s she visited Ireland and met Jonathan Swift, who became one of her correspondents. In 1743 she married Swift's friend Patrick Delany, an Irish Anglican clergyman. The couple lived mainly in Ireland, visiting London and Bath. In 1785 George III granted the widowed Delany a pension and a house at Windsor, where she resided until her death. Her circle embraced Lady Margaret Cavendish Harley, her closest friend; and Sarah Chapone, Frances Burney, Mary Barber, John Wesley, Jonathan Swift, Hannah More, Edmund Burke, Horace Walpole, and George Frederick Handel.

Delany's works include a libretto from *Paradise Lost* for Handel (untraced, 1744); a moral romance, "Marianna" (unpublished, 1759); a translation of a Latin flower treatise (1762); letters to Swift (1766); advice on propriety to a great-niece (1777); *Letters from Mrs. Delany (Widow of Doctor Patrick Delany,) to Mrs. Frances Hamilton, from the Year 1779, to the Year 1788* (1820); and *The Autobiography and Correspondence of Mary Granville (Mrs. Delany), with Interesting Reminiscences of King George the Third and Queen Charlotte,* (1861–62), edited by Lady Llanover. The British Museum houses her *Flora Delanica,* "paper mosaic" flower pictures, made between 1772 and 1782.

**Fielding, Sarah** (1710–1768), born in East Stour, Dorset, a first-generation Bluestocking, was a member of the Bath community that included Sarah Scott. Her works were widely published and translated. She elaborated a theory of education and character as well as the scheme of a community for gentlewomen, and she was especially interested in the issue of equality among the sexes. She pioneered in the genre of didactic school stories and endorsed the sentimental mode, particularly exploring women's social, psychological, and intellectual issues, including domestic tyranny and self-deception.

The daughter of Sarah Gould, who died in 1718, and Edmund Fielding, Sarah, together with her three sisters and two brothers, was mainly raised by Lady Gould, her maternal grandmother, who was awarded custody of the children in 1722. Though her Salisbury boarding school education was less than scholarly, Fielding later learned Greek, French, and Latin and was well read in both English and European literature. After Lady Gould's death in 1733 she lodged with her sisters until 1739, when her eldest sister inherited a house in Westminster, where they resided throughout the 1740s. Shortly after all three of her sisters' deaths between July 1750 and January 1751, Fielding lived with Jane Collier. From 1754 she resided in or near Bath. Apart from her brother Henry Fielding, her circle included Arthur, Jane, and Margaret Collier, James Harris, Samuel Richardson, Elizabeth Carter, Frances Sheridan, Joseph Warton, Ralph Allen, David Garrick, Lady Barbara Montagu, Elizabeth Montagu, and Sarah Scott.

Fielding probably contributed to Henry's *Joseph Andrews* (1742) and to the second volume of his *Miscellanies* (1743). Her first book was a novel, *The Adventures of David Simple in Search of a Faithful Friend* (1744), which included a preface by her brother in its second edition of that year; and it was followed by a sequel, *Familiar Letters between the Principal Characters in "David Simple" and Some Others* (1747). In 1749 the first full-length children's fiction in English appeared, her *The Governess; or, the Little Female Academy*. Her other works include *Remarks on Clarissa, Addressed to the Author* (1749); *Volume the Last* (1753), a further sequel to *David Simple; The Cry: A New Dramatic Fable* (1754), written probably in collaboration with Jane Collier; *The Lives of Cleopatra and Octavia* (1757); *The History of the Countess of Dellwyn* (1759); probably *The History of Ophelia* (1760); and a translation of Xenophon's *Memoirs of Socrates* (1762).

**Macaulay** (later **Graham**), **Catharine** (1731–1791), born Catharine Sawbridge at Wye, Kent, was among the first generation of the Bluestockings. Her political voice was central to the formation of modern feminist politics in Britain, and her advocacy of equality between the sexes in education was especially significant. Though her republican politics were dismissed by her contemporaries among the Bluestockings, they admired her achievements as a historian. She was the first prominent female historian in England, and she recorded the inaugural republican account of British history, which gained her support from both political radicals in England and revolutionaries in France and the

United States. She was the first woman admitted to the reading room of the British Museum, and was a leader in the use of primary sources for history writing.

Macaulay was the second daughter of Elizabeth Wanley and John Sawbridge. After her mother's death in 1733 she was educated by her father; both were staunch Whigs. In 1760 she married George Macaulay, an obstetrician, and they settled in London. Her husband died in 1766, leaving her with a six-year-old daughter. In 1774 Macaulay moved into the house of the elderly Dr. Thomas Wilson in Bath. In 1778, to the dismay of the Bluestockings, she married William Graham, twenty-six years her junior. By the 1780s her politics garnered general public disapproval in England. The Grahams traveled to the United States in 1784, where they were guests of the future American president, George Washington, as the result of Macaulay's support for the colonists in the American Revolution. Before settling in London in 1787 the couple probably spent some time in France. In addition to her brother, John Sawbridge, Macaulay Graham associated with Tobias Smollett, William Hunter, Thomas Hollis, John Wilkes, John and Abigail Adams, Mercy Otis Warren, Benjamin Rush, and Ezra Stiles.

Her works include an influential scholarly history of England during the Civil War and the Restoration, *The History of England from the Accession of James I to that of the Brunswick Line*, published between 1763 and 1783; the political pamphlets *Loose Remarks on Certain Positions to be Found in Mr. Hobbes' Philosophical Rudiments of Government and Society* (1767), and *An Address to the People of England, Ireland, and Scotland, on the Present Important Crisis of Affairs* (1775); and *Letters on Education, with Observations on Religious and Metaphysical Subjects* (1790), social commentary that influenced Mary Wollstonecraft.

**Montagu, Elizabeth** (1720 or 1718–1800), born Elizabeth Robinson at York, recognized as the "Queen of the Blues," was a leader of the first generation of the Bluestockings and a frequent hostess of the group. She carried on extensive correspondence, especially with her sister Sarah Scott and with Elizabeth Carter. She encouraged young authors and writers in need such as Anna Williams and James Beattie, and she directed large-scale philanthropy toward the laboring poor. In her critical work on Shakespeare, she successfully challenged Voltaire's authority. She was also praised for her conversational skills and wit.

Montagu was the eldest daughter of Elizabeth Drake and Matthew Robinson, a squire of Edgeley and West Layton in Yorkshire. Much of her childhood was spent with her grandparents. She was educated under her grandfather, Conyers Middleton, librarian of Cambridge University. As a child she was fond of dancing and was nicknamed "Fidget." She read widely in English, French, and classical literature. After turning away several suitors she married Edward Montagu in 1742, the grandson of the earl of Sandwich. With her husband she visited the Continent and Scotland and accompanied him to his estates and coal mines in the north of England. After the death of their son in 1744 she also devoted herself to the literary salons that she hosted at her London houses, first in her famous Chinese Room in Mayfair's Hill Street and later in Portman Square. After the death of her husband in 1775 she inherited a fortune and estates that contained collieries. Her wealth allowed her to employ the leading architects and painters of her time, including Robert Adam and Angelica Kauffmann, to decorate her town and country houses. In 1781 she rebuilt Sandleford Priory, near Newbury, and built Montagu House, now 22 Portman Square, London. Her nephew, Matthew Robinson, was her favorite companion after her husband's death; he took the name of Montagu in 1776, and he was her principal heir upon her death. Her circle included Lady Margaret Harley (later duchess of Portland), Elizabeth Vesey, Frances Boscawen, Mary Delany, Hester Chapone, Hester Thrale, Lord Lyttelton, Dorothea Gregory, Horace Walpole, Samuel Johnson, David Garrick, Edmund Burke, and Sir Joshua Reynolds, who painted her portrait. She was a patron to such writers as James Beattie, Anna Barbauld, and Hannah More.

With the exception of three anonymous dialogues that Montagu contributed to the poet Lord Lyttelton's *Dialogues of the Dead* (1760), her only published work was *An Essay on the Writings and Genius of Shakespear, Compared with the Greek and French Dramatic Poets. With some Remarks upon the Misrepresentations of Mons. de Voltaire* (1769). After her death, Montagu's nephew published four volumes of her correspondence covering the years until 1761. Many of the letters remain unpublished.

**More, Hannah** (1745–1833), born in Stapleton, Gloucestershire, was among the second generation of the Bluestockings but was befriended by those of the first. More's poem, *Bas Bleu, or Conversation* (1786), describes the charm and social life of these literary women. A more productive author than the women of the first generation, she was also an educator of the poor and a prominent abolitionist, Christian moralist, and philanthropist. She expressed notably conservative views on the education and advancement of women.

More was one of the five daughters of Mary Grace and Jacob More, a schoolmaster who taught mainly Latin to his daughters. Her elder sisters opened a boarding school in Bristol, Gloucestershire, where she was educated further and where she later became a teacher. There she also studied Latin, French, Italian, and Spanish, improving her style by means of translations and imitations of the odes of Horace and the dramatic compositions of Metastasio. At around twenty-two she became engaged to a Mr. Turner; when the engagement was dissolved in 1773 he gave her an annuity of £200 in reparation. Between 1774 and 1775 she visited London, where David Garrick introduced her to the important literary figures of the day and produced her plays. In 1776 the Garricks offered More a suite of rooms in their house, and from that time she stayed with them whenever she came to London. After Garrick's death in 1779 she ceased writing for the stage. In 1784 More and Montagu became patrons of the working-class poet Anne Yearsley, publishing by subscription Yearsley's *Poems, on Several Occasions* (1785). More developed a friendship with the abolitionist philanthropist William Wilberforce, who urged her to set up a school at Cheddar. From 1789 More, together with Church of England clergymen, Hester Chapone, and Sarah Trimmer, set up Sunday Schools to fight illiteracy among working-class children. More persevered in her efforts in spite of much opposition from country neighbors, who claimed that even the most limited education of the poor would destroy their interest in farm labor; and from the clergy, who accused her of Methodism. More died in Bristol, leaving £30,000 chiefly to charities and religious societies. Her circle included John Langhorne, Benjamin Kennicott, Robert Lowth, Sir Joshua Reynolds, Samuel Johnson, Edmund Burke, David and Eva Marie Garrick, Elizabeth Montagu, Thomas Percy, Elizabeth Carter, Frances Boscawen, Hester Chapone, Horace Walpole, Edward Gibbon, James Beattie, and Sarah Trimmer.

More started writing verse at an early age. Her dramatic works include *The Search after Happiness* (1773); *The Inflexible Captive* (1774); *Percy* (1777), which was highly successful; and *The Fatal Falsehood* (1779). She also wrote *Sir Eldred of the Bower* (1776), a ballad; and *Thoughts on the Importance of the Manners of the Great to General Society* (1788), an anonymous essay that went into multiple editions. In the 1780s More wrote a series of ethical and religious tracts. *An Estimate of the Religion of the Fashionable World* (1790) was followed by *Village Politics, by Will Chip* (1792) and *Cheap Repository Tracts* (1795–98), which included *The Shepherd of Salisbury Plain* and sold over two million copies in four years, leading to the formation of the Religious Tract Society in 1799. She also wrote on the education of girls in *Strictures on the Modern System of Female Education* (1799). Her last works include the novel *Coelebs in Search of a Wife* (1809) and *Moral Sketches* (1819).

**Reeve, Clara** (1729–1807), born in Ipswich, Suffolk, can be considered a Bluestocking on the basis of her learning and literary activity, even though she lived in the provinces and had no contact with the members of the London circle. She upheld classical republican and old Whig ideals, and she argued for the abolition of slavery and for self-sustaining female community. She published domestic and gothic fiction devoted to these themes. She also advocated the didactic potential of biography and historical fiction and the value of "romance" in representing the interests of women. She maintained that the female role in domestic and public spheres was an agent of reform.

Little is known of Reeve's life. She was the eldest daughter of a prosperous upper-middle-class family. Her mother, Hannah Smithies, was the daughter of a goldsmith who was jeweler to George I. Reeve's father, William Reeve, was rector of Freston and of Kerton, Suffolk, and perpetual curate of St. Nicholas, Ipswich. Described by Reeve as "an old Whig," he required her at an early age to read parliamentary debates, the *History of England* by Paul de Rapin de Thoyras, Greek and Roman histories, and Plutarch's *Lives*. She also learned Latin and later translated John Barclay's *Argenis*, published as *The Phoenix* (1772). Reeve admired Marie-Jeanne Riccoboni, Sarah Fielding, Charlotte

Lennox, Frances Sheridan, Frances Brooke, Sarah Scott, Elizabeth Griffith, Katherine Philips, and Elizabeth Carter. After her father's death in 1755 she moved with her mother and sisters to Colchester, Essex. In the 1790s she settled on her own in Car Street.

Reeve wrote *Original Poems on Several Occasions* (1769); and *The Champion of Virtue: A Gothic Story* (1777), republished as *The Old English Baron* (1778). A Gothic romance modeled on Horace Walpole's *The Castle of Otranto, The Old English Baron* went through ten editions before 1800, was translated into French and German, and is notable for its measured use of supernatural elements. Her other works include *The Two Mentors: A Modern Story* (1783); *The Progress of Romance* (1785); *The Exiles; or, Memoirs of the Count de Cronstadt* (1788); *The School for Widows* (1791); *Plans of Education* (1792); *Memoirs of Sir Roger de Clarendon* (1793); and *Destination; or, Memoirs of a Private Family* (1799).

**Scott, Sarah** (1721–1795), born Sarah Robinson, baptized at York and raised in Kent, was among the first generation of the Bluestockings, and with Carter, was the most prolific writer of the circle. She was the sister and correspondent of Elizabeth Montagu, through whom she was connected to most of the Bluestockings only indirectly. She is distinguished for her fiction and historical writing, particularly for *A Description of Millenium Hall*, a manifesto of Bluestocking feminism incorporating an idealized and feminist model of gentry capitalism and a critique of courtly culture. She belonged to the Bath community of writers in the 1760s and expressed great interest in politics and public issues.

Scott was the daughter of Elizabeth Drake and Matthew Robinson, wealthy and well-connected members of the landed gentry. Educated at home, she was well read in French and English fiction, history, and belles-lettres. After Montagu's marriage in 1742, Scott traveled in England both with her sister and alone. In 1751 she was married to George Lewis Scott, a mathematician, musicologist, and subpreceptor to the Prince of Wales, later George III. The marriage ended with a legal separation in 1752. After this, Scott settled with her close friend Lady Barbara Montagu in Bath. Together with Elizabeth Cutts, Scott's brother's illegitimate daughter Miss M. Arnold, and perhaps Sarah Fielding, they became involved in various philanthropic activities such as the education of poor children. Scott's fullest utopian experiment, however, was carried out after Lady Barbara's death, when she attempted to establish a female community at Hitcham together with Cutts, Arnold, her sister Elizabeth Montagu, and a cousin, Grace Robinson Freind. Similar to that of Scott's Millenium Hall, though more modest, the community failed within months. Never well off, Scott moved her residence several times afterward. She died at Catton, near Norwich. Little is known of her life since she ordered her papers destroyed after her death.

Scott's works include *The History of Cornelia* (1750); *Agreeable Ugliness; or, The Triumph of the Graces* (1754), a translation of *Le Laideur aimable* by Pierre Antoine, Marquis de La Place; *A Journey through Every Stage of Life* (1754); a set of cards to teach geography to children (1758–59); *The History of Gustavus Ericson, King of Sweden* (1761); *The History of Mecklenburgh* (1762); *A Description of Millenium Hall* (1762); *The History of Sir George Ellison* (1766), a sequel to *Millenium Hall;* and *The Life of Theodore Agrippa d'Aubigné* and *The Test of Filial Duty* (both 1772).

**Seward, Anna** (1742–1809), born at Eyam, Derbyshire, known as the "Swan of Lichfield," was among the second generation of the Bluestockings. She expressed notably radical views on marriage and politics, and she is known for her criticism of conduct books that lauded marriage above all else, for her opposition to empire and slavery, and for her support of American independence.

The eldest daughter of Elizabeth Hunter and Reverend Thomas Seward, Anna was raised in a family known for its literary gatherings. She was educated at home and read French, Italian, and Latin. She spent most of her life in Lichfield, Staffordshire. When she was fourteen, the Sewards adopted Honora Sneyd, for whom Seward developed a passionate friendship that influenced her life and writing. When Honora and Richard Lovell Edgeworth married in 1773 Seward strongly disapproved of the relationship. After her stepsister's death in 1780 Seward met Lady Miller and took part in her well-known Batheaston poetry contests and assemblies. Seward's grandfather, the Reverend Mr. John Hunter, was Samuel Johnson's schoolmaster, and she informed James Boswell of many details of his early life. Her circle included Erasmus Darwin, Richard Lovell Edgeworth, Thomas Day, William Hayley, Honora Sneyd, Elizabeth Cornwallis, the Ladies of Llangollen (Eleanor Butler and Sarah Ponsonby), Hester Thrale Piozzi, Helen Maria Williams, and Sir Walter Scott.

Seward began to write verses at an early age, partly because of the encouragement of Erasmus Darwin. Her first published poems appeared in Lady Miller's *Batheaston Miscellany.* Her works include elegiac poems on David Garrick and Captain Cook (1780), Major André (1781), and Anne Miller (1782); the sentimental *Louisa, a Poetical Novel* (1784); an anonymous newspaper commentary on Samuel Johnson, whom she perceived as misogynist (1784); *Ode on General Eliott's Return from Gibraltar* (1787); *Llangollen Vale, with Other Poems* (1796); *Original Sonnets on Various Subjects; Odes Paraphrased from Horace* (1799); and *Memoirs of the Life of Dr. Darwin* (1804). She bequeathed to Sir Walter Scott the copyright to her poetry, which was published by him with a memoir in 1810. Her letters were published by Archibald Constable in 1811.

**Talbot, Catherine** (1721–1770), among the first generation of the Bluestockings, was probably the most reluctant of them to be known as a writer. She argued for the equality of the sexes and the dignity of female celibacy and was concerned with women's social position. She explored the aesthetic, domestic, ethical, economic, and educational concerns of women, and she contributed to a feminized genre of didactic piety and to a new female subjectivity entrenched in the practices of introspection and mannerly conduct. She developed a close friendship and an extensive correspondence with Elizabeth Carter.

Talbot came from a family of Church of England clerics. Her father, Edward Talbot, died before her birth, and Talbot and her mother, Mary Martyn, shared a household with Catherine Benson, sister of a bishop. When Benson married Thomas Secker, Talbot's father's former colleague, the Talbots joined the Secker household, and Secker taught the young Catherine the Scriptures, astronomy, and languages. The Secker household was involved in social and literary circles in London. In 1741 Talbot met Elizabeth Carter, who became her most intimate friend. When Secker became archbishop of Canterbury in 1758 the Talbots moved into Lambeth Palace with his family. Talbot rejected a proposal of marriage from George Berkeley in 1758 on the grounds that the relationship would be disapproved of by the friends of both sides. The Talbots continued to live with the archbishop after his wife's death; after his death in 1768 they inherited a large legacy. In 1770 Talbot died in London after a lengthy struggle with cancer. She had developed ties with Martin Benson, Joseph Butler, Jemima, Lady Grey and her husband Philip Yorke, the countess of Hertford, Elizabeth Montagu, Elizabeth Carter, Samuel Richardson, and Samuel Johnson.

Apart from letters, Talbot wrote chiefly poetry, essays, allegories, dialogues, pastorals, and imitations. She published little during her lifetime apart from some pieces in the *Athenian Letters* (1741 and 1743), the *Rambler,* and probably the *Adventurer*. After her death, her mother gave Talbot's manuscripts to Carter, who published her *Reflections on the Seven Days of the Week* (1770) and *Essays on Various Subjects* (1772). Talbot's collected *Works* were edited by Montagu Pennington (1808). In the same year Pennington also published *A Series of Letters between Mrs. Elizabeth Carter and Miss Catherine Talbot.*

**Thrale** (later **Piozzi**), **Hester Lynch** (1741–1821), born Hester Lynch Salusbury at Bodvel, Caernarvonshire, Wales, was a prominent Bluestocking hostess of the second generation whose friendship with Elizabeth Montagu brought together both generations of the group. However, she broke with the Bluestockings over her views on second marriages and also differed from them in her wish to gain an income from her work. She was one of the first women to publish in the biographical, anecdotal, and travel genres. She strongly believed in the moral force of literature and distrusted innovation in learning and politics.

Thrale Piozzi, the only child of Hester Maria Cotton and John Salusbury, was educated in several modern languages and was taught Latin, logic, and rhetoric by Arthur Collier. In 1763 she married Henry Thrale, a prosperous brewer. She had twelve children with him, but only four daughters attained adulthood. In 1765 Samuel Johnson became a close friend of the Thrales, and she frequently served as hostess to Johnson and other professional and business acquaintances. When her husband died in 1781, Mrs. Thrale was left a wealthy widow. Much to the dislike of Johnson and her other friends, in 1784 she married her daughter's music master, Gabriel Piozzi. Between 1784 and 1787 the couple traveled in France, Italy, and Germany. After her husband's death in 1809 she lived mainly in Bath until her death at Clifton, Bristol. As Mrs. Thrale, her circle included, in addition to Samuel Johnson, Giuseppi Baretti, Edmund Burke, Frances and Charles Burney, David Garrick, Oliver Goldsmith, and Sir Joshua Reynolds. In 1775 she became acquainted with Elizabeth Montagu and her circle, and from 1806 to 1820 she also corresponded with Marianne Francis.

Thrale had embarked on her writing by 1762, submitting short pieces and poems to newspapers. In 1785 she contributed to the *Florence Miscellany*. Her works include *Anecdotes of the Late Samuel Johnson, LL.D., During the Last Twenty Years of his Life* (1786), which thrust her into rivalry with his friend and biographer Boswell; *Letters to and from the Late Samuel Johnson* (1788); *Observations and Reflections Made in the Course of a Journey through France, Italy and Germany* (1789); *British Synonymy* (1794), a dictionary of English usage; *Three Warnings to John Bull before He Dies* (1798), a political pamphlet; and *Retrospection* (1801), a world history. Her diary, *Thraliana*, kept from 1776 to 1809 as a record of her private, intellectual, and public life, was edited by Katharine C. Balderston (1942).

**Vesey, Elizabeth** (1715?–1791), born probably in Ireland, was among the first generation of the Bluestockings. She initiated the tradition of Bluestocking parties at which the entertainment consisted of conversation on literary subjects. Her closest friend was Elizabeth Montagu. Vesey was indirectly responsible for the title of the Bluestocking group, for when she invited Benjamin Stillingfleet to one of her parties and he declined for lack of the appropriate dress, she told him to come in the blue stockings that he was wearing at the time. He did as advised, and his informal attire gave rise to the nickname.

Vesey was the daughter of Mary Muschamp and Sir Thomas Vesey, bishop of Ossory. Her first husband, William Handcock of Willbrook in Westmeath, a member of Parliament, died in 1741. His sister became her companion thereafter. By 1746 Vesey was married to her cousin Agmondesham Vesey, an Anglo-Irish landowner and politician. When her husband was in Dublin, Vesey enjoyed her time at her estate at Lucan; although she spent time in Dublin, its society did not appeal to her. The couple suffered from poor health, and her husband's death in 1785 left her impoverished.

Vesey had strong interests in architecture and in the poetry of "Ossian" and the ballad tradition; she left some verse and letters, a few of which were published in *Bluestocking Letters*, edited by R. Brimley Johnson (1926). Her writings are characterized by an imaginative, fantastical style in the treatment of the everyday, a style that, along with her personal characteristics, led her Bluestocking friends to call her "the Sylph." Her circle included Samuel Johnson, Edmund Burke, David Garrick, Edward Gibbon, Sir Joshua Reynolds, Thomas Warton, Adam Smith, Thomas Percy, Richard Sheridan, the dowager duchess of Portland, the duchess of Beaufort, Frances Boscawen, Lady Lucan, Lady Clermont, Lord Althorp, and Lord Macartney.

*Simon Fraser University*

# A Bluestocking Bibliography

COMPILED BY JANICE BLATHWAYT

T his bibliography is not comprehensive but is intended to provide a starting point for studying the Bluestockings' own publications and their reception history as well as recent criticism. The list is divided into three sections, "Manuscript Sources," "Published Works by the Bluestockings," and "Secondary Works."

## Manuscript Sources

Burney, Frances. Manuscript journals and letters. Correspondence with Dr. Charles Burney, Susan Burney, Hester Thrale, Dorothea Gregory Alison, Hester Thrale, Elizabeth Vesey. Henry W. and Albert A. Berg Collection, New York Public Library.

Carter, Elizabeth. Letters to Edward Cave. British Library, Stowe 748.
—— 1737–39, 1763, 1787. Miscellaneous letters and papers. British Library.
—— Miscellaneous correspondence and papers, including facsimiles. Bodleian Library, MS. Facs c 44.
—— 1767–ca. 1799. Letters from Elizabeth Montagu. Henry E. Huntington Library.
—— 1767–ca. 1799. Letters from Elizabeth Montagu (copies). Bodleian Library, MSS Film 1615–1617.
—— Latin letters, probably copied by Thomas Birch. British Library, MS. Add. 456.
—— 1773–1800. Letters to Countess Spencer, 26 items. British Library.
—— Prayer (1778). Bodleian Library, MS. Eng. th.e. 163.

Chapone, Hester. Letters, mostly to Frances D'Arblay (Frances Burney). British Library, MS. Egerton 3698, fols. 107–126b; 3700A, fols. 32, 45–48b, 232–234b.

Delany, Mary. Correspondence and papers. National Library of Wales.
—— 1751, 1770–86. Letters to the first earl of Guilford. Bodleian Library, MSS North.
—— Correspondence. Lewis Walpole Library.
—— 1718–33. Letters from Lord Lansdowne, 13 items. Newport Central Library, Delany Letters, vol. 4.

Montagu, Elizabeth Robinson. Correspondence and papers, 6,923 items. Henry E. Huntington Library.
—— Family Correspondence. British Library, MS. Add. 40663.
—— Letter to Sarah Robinson Scott. Bodleian Library, MS. Autography b. 10. no. 1059.
—— Letters to Hester Thrale. John Rylands Library, MS. Eng. 551.

More, Hannah. Letters and papers. British Library, MS. Add. 42511.

—— Letters and literary MSS. Yale University Libraries, Beinecke Library.

—— 1779–1827. Letters, 11 items. Bodleian Library, MS. Montagu d 19.

—— 1802. Letter to Bishop Beadon. Cambridge University, St. John's College Library.

—— 1805–11. Letters to Cadell and Davies, 13 items. Oxford University, Christ Church Archives, Evelyn Collection 4, vol. 3.

—— 1816–31. Letters to Dr. Carick. Bodleian Library, MS. Eng. lett d 2.

—— 1775–79. Letters to David Garrick, 23 items. Victoria and Albert Museum, F 48 F 5/vol. I.

—— 1776. Letters from David Garrick and his wife, 13 items. Bristol Reference Library, B7976.

—— 1813–17. Letters to Anne Gladstone. St. Deiniol's Library, Glynne-Gladstone MSS, 396.

—— 1811–25. Letters to C. Hoare (copies). British Library, RP 140.

—— 1800–1803. Letters to the bishop of Lincoln. Center for Kentish Studies, U1590/S5/03/6.

—— Letters to Zachary Macaulay, 58 items. Henry E. Huntington Library.

—— 1817–22. Letters from the duchess of Manchester. Cambridgeshire County Record Office, Huntington, DDM.

—— Letters to Elizabeth Montagu, 22 items. Henry E. Huntington Library.

—— 1813–27. Letters to Charles Ogilvie, 27 items. Bodleian Library, MS. Eng. lett d 124.

—— 1774–80. Letters to Frances Reynolds (copies). British Library, RP186.

—— ?1814–25. Correspondence with Thornton Family, 22 items. Cambridge University Library, Add. 7674/1/E1–9, F1–13.

—— 1815–27. Letters to Marianne Thornton, 14 items. Cambridge University Library, Add. 7951.

—— 1789–1830. Correspondence with William Wilberforce. Bodleian Library, Wilberforce MSS, c3, 48, d 14–17; Don e 164–65.

—— 1776–1830. Letters, 148 items. Henry E. Huntington Library.

—— 1779–1833. Letters and literary MSS, Bristol Record Office.

—— 1800–32. Letters, 36 items. Bristol Reference Library, B22448–22456, 28276, 288307–28308, 31226–31249.

—— Correspondence and papers, 12 items. Boston Public Library.

—— Papers. Historical Society of Pennsylvania.

—— Papers. Duke University, William R. Perkins Library.

—— Papers. Knox College.

—— 1825. Memoir of More. Gloucestershire Record Office, D3931/2/12/6.

Piozzi, Hester Lynch. Correspondence, literary MSS, and papers. John Rylands Library, Eng MSS 530–660; 891–893.

—— 1808–12. Diaries, miscellaneous correspondence. National Library of Wales, Brynbella Piozziana; NLW MSS 11099–11102.

—— Correspondence with her daughter, 367 items, and others (copies). British Library, RP 812, 5318.

—— 1778–84. Letters to Charles Burney, 13 items, and his family (copies). British Library, M/440).

—— 1780–82. Correspondence with Frances Burney. British Library, MS. Egerton 3695; RP 5318.

—— 1789–92. Correspondence with Hugh Griffith. National Library of Wales, Llanfair and Brynodol.

—— 1769–89. Letters from Samuel Johnson, 15 items. Samuel Johnson Birthplace Museum, MS. 21.

—— 1812–16. Lctters, about 110 itcms, to Alexander Leak (copies). British Library, M/572; RP766.

—— 1790–1809. Letters to John Lloyd, 18 items. National Library of Wales, NLW MS. 12421.

—— ca. 1812–20. Letters, mainly to Mr. and Mrs. Edward Mangin, 22 items. Harvard University, Houghton Library, MS. Eng 231.

—— 1812–14. Letters to Clement Mead, 22 items (copies). British Library, RP293.

—— 1818–19. Letters to Sophy Pugh, 23 items. Bath Central Library, AL 1873, 2081–2085.

—— 1773–76. Letters to Rice family of Tooting, 21 items. Hertfordshire Archives and Local Studies, misc. vol. X, D/EX 44, D/EX98, D/EBy.

—— 1800–1802. Letters to Sanford family. Somerset Archive and Record Service, DD/SF 4561.

—— 1796–1821. Letters to Williams family of Bodelwyddan, about 570 items. John Rylands Library.

—— 1796–1821. Letters to Williams family, 116 items. Victoria and Albert Museum, Forster Collection.

—— 1780–21. Letters, 39 items. Henry E. Huntington Library.

—— Letters, about 300 items. Princeton University Library, NUC MS. 60-1389.

—— Letters, 58 items. Yale University Libraries, Beinecke Library.

Reeve, Clara. 1790–1804. Letters to Joseph Walker, 11 items. Trinity College Dublin, MS. 1461.

Scott, Sarah Robinson. 1741–95. Family correspondence, 389 items. Henry E. Huntington Library.

—— Letters to Samuel Richardson. Cornell University Library.

—— Letters to Elizabeth Montagu. Lewis Walpole Library, MISC. MSS.

Seward, Anna. 1762–1804. Literary MSS and papers (copies). National Library of Scotland, MSS 879–880.

—— ca. 1770–1808. Correspondence and literary MSS. Samuel Johnson Birthplace Museum.

—— 1791–1804. Letters, 12 items. Birmingham University, Special Collections.

—— 1784–88. Correspondence with James Boswell. Yale University Libraries, Beinecke Library, L1142–53, C2467–75.

—— 1788–96. Letters from Henry Francis Cary, 15 items. Harvard University, Houghton Library, NUC MS. 83-908.

—— 1791–1804. Letters to the Dowdeswell family, 15 items, Birmingham University, Special Collections, AS.

—— 1781–85. Letters from William Hayley, 81 items. Cambridge University, Fitzwilliam Museum, Hayley XII.

—— 1785–1801. Letters to John Nichols, 11 items. Samuel Johnson Birthplace Museum, MS. 45/2–12.

—— 1782–1806. Letters to Sophia Pennington, 20 items. Yale University Libraries, Beinecke Library, C202.

—— 1787–90. Letters to Hester Lynch Piozzi, 11 items. John Rylands Library, MS. Eng. 565.

—— 1788–1807. Letters to Anne Parry Price, 15 items. British Library, MS. Add. 46400.

—— 1779–1809. Correspondence with Sir Walter Scott. National Library of Scotland.

—— 1802–8. Letters from Sir Walter Scott. British Library, MS. Add. 37425, fols. 97–115.

—— 1765–1807. Letters, 29 items. Henry E. Huntington Library.

—— 1764–1807. Letters, 21 items, and literary MSS. Lichfield Record Office, D262/1.

Talbot, Catherine. 1739–70, Correspondence. Bedfordshire and Luton Archives and Record Office, L30/21.

—— Journals and correspondence and verses. British Library, Add. MSS 4291, 39311–39312, 39316, 46688–46690.

—— Berkeley Papers: letters to George, Anne, and Elizabeth Berkeley. British Library, Add. MSS 39311; 39312; 39316.

—— Miscellaneous letters. Lambeth Palace Library, MSS 1719; 1349.

Vesey, Elizabeth. Letters to Elizabeth Montagu, 96 items. Henry E. Huntington Library.

—— Letters received, 260 items. Henry E. Huntington Library.

## PUBLISHED WORKS BY THE BLUESTOCKINGS

Aspinall-Ogland, Cecil Faber. *The Admiral's Widow, Being the Life and Letters of the Hon. Mrs. Edward Boscawen . . . 1761–1805*. London, 1942.

Carter, Elizabeth. *Letters from Mrs. Elizabeth Carter to Mrs. Elizabeth Montagu*. Edited by Montagu Pennington. 3 vols. London, 1817.

—— *Memoirs of the Life of Mrs. Elizabeth Carter*. Edited by Montagu Pennington. 2 vols. London, 1807.

—— *Remarks on the Athanasian Creed*. London, 1752.

—— *A Series of Letters between Mrs. Elizabeth Carter and Miss Catherine Talbot . . . to which Are Added, Letters from Mrs. Elizabeth Carter to Mrs. Vesey*. Edited by Montagu Pennington. 4 vols. London, 1809.

——, trans. *Sir Isaac Newton's Philosophy Explained for the Use of the Ladies*. Original author Francesco Algarotti. London, 1759.

Chapone, Hester. *A Letter to a New-Married Lady*. London, 1777.

—— *Letters on the Improvement of the Mind: Addressed to a Lady*. 2 vols. London, 1773.

—— *Miscellanies in Prose and Verse*. London, 1775.

—— *The Posthumous Works of Mrs. Chapone*. Edited by her family. 2 vols. London, 1807.

Delany, Mary. *The Autobiography and Correspondence of Mary Granville, Mrs. Delany: With Interesting Reminiscences of King George the Third and Queen Charlotte*. Edited by Lady Llanover. 3 vols. London, 1862.

—— *A Catalogue of Plants Copied from Nature in Paper Mosaick, Finished in the Year 1778, and Disposed in Alphabetical Order, According to the . . . Names of Linnaeus*. n.p., n.d.

——, trans. Epictetus. *Moral Discourses; Enchiridion and Fragments* (1757). London, 1955.

—— *Letters from Georgian Ireland: The Correspondence of Mary Delany, 1731–68.* Edited by Angelique Day. Belfast, 1991.

Ewert, Leonore H. "Elizabeth Montagu to Elizabeth Carter: Literary Gossip and Critical Opinions from the Pen of the Queen of the Blues." Ph.D. diss., Claremont Graduate School and University Centre, 1968.

Fielding, Sarah. *The Adventures of David Simple.* 2 vols. Dublin, 1744.

—— *The Adventures of David Simple* (1744). Edited by Peter Sabor. Lexington, Ky., 1998.

—— and Henry Fielding. *The Correspondence of Henry and Sarah Fielding.* Edited by Martin C. Battestin and Clive T. Probyn. Oxford, 1993.

—— and Jane Collier. *The Cry: A New Dramatic Fable.* 3 vols. London, 1754.

—— *Familiar Letters between the Principal Characters in David Simple and Some Others.* London, 1747.

—— *The Governess; or Little Female Academy.* London, 1749.

—— *The History of Ophelia.* London, 1760.

—— *The Lives of Cleopatra and Octavia.* London, 1757.

—— *The Lives of Cleopatra and Octavia* (1757). Edited by R. Brimley Johnson. London, 1928.

——, trans. *Xenophon's Memoirs of Socrates. With the Defence of Socrates, before His Judges.* London, 1762.

Griffith, Elizabeth. *The Delicate Distress.* 2 vols. Dublin, 1775.

—— *The Delicate Distress* (1775). Edited by Cynthia Ricciardi and Susan Staves. Lexington, Ky., 1997.

—— *Essays Addressed to Young Married Women.* London, 1782.

—— *Elizabeth Griffith.* Edited by Betty Rizzo. Vol. 4 of *Eighteenth-Century Women Playwrights.* Edited by Derek Hughes. 6 vols. London, 2001.

—— *The History of Lady Barton, a Novel, in Letters.* 3 vols. London, 1771.

—— *The Platonic Wife. A Comedy.* Dublin, 1765.

—— *The School for Rakes.* Dublin, 1769.

—— *The Story of Lady Julian Harley. A Novel, in Letters.* 2 vols. London, 1776.

Johnson, R. Brimley, editor. *Bluestocking Letters.* London, 1926.

Macaulay, Catharine. *An Address to the People of England, Scotland, and Ireland, on the Present Important Crisis of Affairs.* London, 1783.

—— *The History of England from the Accession of James I to That of the Brunswick Line.* London, 1763–83.

—— *Letters on Education with Observations on Religious and Metaphysical Subjects.* London, 1790.

—— *Letters on Education with Observations on Religious and Metaphysical Subjects* (1790). Edited by Gina Luria. New York, 1974.

—— *Observations on the Reflections of the Right Hon. Edmund Burke on the Revolution in France.* London, 1790.

—— *A Treatise on the Immutability of Moral Truth.* London, 1783.

Montagu, Elizabeth. *An Essay on the Writings and Genius of Shakespear, Compared with the Greek and French Dramatic Poets, with some Remarks upon the Misrepresentations of Mons. de Voltaire.* London, 1769.

—— *The Letters of Mrs. Elizabeth Montagu, with Some of the Letters of Her Correspondents.* 4 vols. London, 1810–13.

—— *Elizabeth Montagu, the Queen of the Bluestockings, Her Correspondence from 1720 to 1761 . . . by Emily J. Climenson.* New York, 1906.

—— *Mrs. Montagu, "Queen of the Blues": Her Letters and Friendships . . . 1762–1800.* Edited by Reginald Blunt. 2 vols. London, 1923.

More, Hannah. *Essays on Various Subjects, Principally Designed for Young Ladies.* London, 1777.

—— *Florio: a Tale, for Fine Gentlemen and Fine Ladies: and, The Bas Bleu; or, Conversation: Two Poems.* London, 1786.

—— *The Letters of Hannah More.* Edited by R. Brimley Johnson. London, 1925.

—— *Memoirs of the Life and Correspondence of Mrs. Hannah More.* 4 vols. Edited by William Roberts. London, 1834.

—— *Search after Happiness: a Pastoral . . . By a Young Lady.* Dublin, 1773.

—— *Strictures on the Modern System of Education.* London, 1799.

—— *Works.* 11 vols. London, 1853.

—— *The Works of Miss Hannah More in Prose and Verse.* Cork, Ireland, 1778.

Piozzi, Hester Lynch. "Anecdotes of the Late Samuel Johnson, LL.D., During the Last Twenty Years of His Life." In *Memoirs of the Life and Writings of the Late Samuel Johnson (by William Shaw) and Anecdotes of the Late Samuel Johnson, LL.D., During the Last Twenty Years of His Life.* Edited by Arthur Sherbo. London, 1974.

—— *Memoirs of the Life and Correspondence of Mrs. Hannah More.* Edited by William Roberts. 4 vols. London, 1834.

—— *Thraliana: The Diary of Mrs. Hester Lynch Thrale (Later Mrs. Piozzi) 1776–1809.* Edited by Katharine C. Balderston. 2 vols. Oxford, 1942.

Reeve, Clara. *The Champion of Virtue* (later *The Old English Baron*). Colchester, England, 1777.

—— *The Champion of Virtue* (1777). Edited by James Trainer. Oxford, 1967.

—— *Original Poems on Several Occasions.* London, 1769.

—— *The Exiles or Memoirs of Count de Cronstadt.* 3 vols. London, 1788.

——, trans. *The Phoenix, or the History of Polyarchus and Argenis.* Original author John Barclay. London, 1772.

—— *Plans of Education; with Remarks on the Systems of Other Writers.* London, 1792.

—— *Plans of Education; with Remarks on the Systems of Other Writers* (1792). Edited by Gina Luria. New York, 1974.

—— *The Progress of Romance through Times, Countries, and Manners.* 2 vols. Colchester, England, 1785.

—— *The Progress of Romance through Times, Countries, and Manners* (1785). Edited by Murtad iban al-Khafif and Ester McGill. New York, 1930.

—— *The Two Mentors.* 2 vols. Dublin, 1783.

Scott, Sarah. *Agreeable Ugliness; or, The Triumph of the Graces*. London, 1754.
—— *A Description of Millenium Hall and the Country Adjacent*. London, 1762.
—— *A Description of Millenium Hall and the Country Adjacent* (1762). Edited by Gary Kelly. Peterborough, Ont., 1995.
—— *The History of Cornelia*. London, 1750.
—— *The History of Mecklenburgh*. London, 1762.
—— *The History of Sir George Ellison*. 2 vols. London, 1766.
—— *The History of Sir George Ellison* (1766). Edited by Betty Rizzo. Lexington, Ky., 1996.
—— *A Journey through Every Stage of Life . . .* 2 vols. London, 1754.
—— *The Life of Theodore Agrippa d'Aubigné*. London, 1772.
—— *Memoirs of Sir Roger de Clarendon*. London, 1793.
—— *A Test of Filial Duty. In a Series of Letters Between Miss Emilia Leonard and Miss Charlotte Arlington*. 2 vols. London, 1772.

Seward, Anna. *The Poetical Works of Anna Seward, with Extracts from her Literary Correspondence*. Edited by Walter Scott. 3 vols. Edinburgh, 1810.
—— *Letters of Anna Seward written between the years 1784 and 1807*. Edited by A. Constable. 6 vols. Edinburgh, 1811.
—— *Monody on Major André. By Miss Seward . . . To which are added, Letters addressed to her by Major André, in the year 1769*. Lichfield, England, 1781.

Talbot, Catherine. *Essays on Various Subjects*. London, 1772.
—— *The Works of the Late Miss Catharine Talbot, First Published by the Late Mrs. Elizabeth Carter*. Edited by Montagu Pennington. London, 1809.

Trimmer, Sarah. *Some Account of the Life and Writings of Mrs. Trimmer with Original Letters, and Meditations and Prayers, Selected from Her Journal*. London, 1825.

## SECONDARY WORKS

Agorni, Mirella. "The Voice of the 'Translatress,' from Aphra Behn to Elizabeth Carter." *Yearbook of English Studies* 28 (1998): 181–95.
—— "Women Manipulating Translation in the Eighteenth Century: The Case of Elizabeth Carter." In *The Knowledges of the Translator: From Literary Interpretation to Machine Classification*, edited by Malcolm Coulthard and Patricia Anne Odber de Baubeta, 135–44. Lewiston, N.Y., 1996.

Aldis, Mrs. Harry Gilney. "The Bluestockings." In the *Cambridge History of English Literature*, 11:80. Edited by Sir Adolphus W. Ward and A. R. Waller. Cambridge, 1914.

Allibone, Samuel. *A Critical Dictionary of English Literature and British and American Authors*. Philadelphia, Pa., 1891.

Astell, Mary. *The First English Feminist: Reflections upon Marriage and Other Writings.* Edited by Bridget Hill. New York, 1986.

Balfour, Clara Lucas. *A Sketch of Mrs. Hannah Moore and Her Sisters.* London, 1854.

Balfour, Ross. *The Library of Mrs. Elizabeth Vesey, 1715–1791, with a Biographical Note, by Ross Balfour.* Newcastle-on-Tyne, England, 1926.

Ballard, George. *The Memoirs of Several Ladies of Great Britain.* London, 1752.

Barbauld, Anna Laetitia, editor. *Correspondence of Samuel Richardson.* 6 vols. London, 1804.

Barbey D'Aurevilly, Jules. *Les Bas-Bleus.* Paris, 1878.

Bentham-Edwards, Matilda. *Six Lives of Famous Women* (1880). Reprint ed., Freeport, N.Y., 1972.

Blain, Virginia, Patricia Clements, and Isobel Grundy, editors. *Feminist Companion to Literature in English.* London, 1990.

Blathwayt, Janice. "More than Distinguished for 'Piety and Virtue': New Perspectives on Elizabeth Carter." Ph.D. diss., York University, 2002.

Bodek, Evelyn Gordon. "Salonières and Bluestockings: Educated Obsolescence and Germinating Feminism." *Feminist Studies* 3 (1976): 185–99.

Bree, Linda. *Sarah Fielding.* New York, 1996.

Brewer, John. *The Pleasures of the Imagination: English Culture in the Eighteenth Century.* Chicago, 1997.

Brink, J. R., editor. *Female Scholars: A Tradition of Learned Women before 1800.* Montreal, 1980.

*British Lady's Magazine.* "Memoirs of Eminent Women of Great Britain." Vol. 3 (1816): 104–13.

—— "Portraits of Woman, Her Conduct, Character and Attainments." Vol. 1, no. 3 (1817): 101–5.

Brown, Laura. *Ends of Empire: Women and Ideology in Early-Eighteenth-Century Literature.* Ithaca, N.Y., 1993.

Brown, Martha G. "Fanny Burney's 'Feminism': Gender or Genre?" In *Fetter'd or Free? British Women Novelists, 1670–1815,* edited by Mary Anne Schofield and Cecilia Macheski, 29–39. Athens, Ga., 1986.

Brownley, Martine Watson. "'Under the Dominion of Some Woman': The Friendship of Samuel Johnson and Hester Thrale." In *Mothering the Mind: Twelve Studies of Writers and Their Silent Partners,* edited by Ruth Perry and Martine Watson Brownley, 64–79. New York, 1984.

Burney, Frances. *The Early Diary of Frances Burney*. 2 vols. Edited by Annie Raine Ellis. London, 1889.

—— *The Early Journals and Letters of Fanny Burney*. 3 vols. Edited by Lars E. Troide. Montreal and Kingston, 1994.

—— *Memoirs of Doctor Burney, Arranged from His Own Manuscripts, from Family Papers, and from Personal Collections*. 3 vols. London, 1832.

—— *The Streatham Years, Part II, 1780–1781*. Edited by Betty Rizzo. Vol. 4 of *The Early Journals and Letters of Fanny Burney*. Edited by Lars Troide. Montreal and Kingston, 2002.

Calhoun, Craig, editor. *Habermas and the Public Sphere*. Cambridge, Mass., 1996.

Carretta, Vincent. "'Utopia Limited': Sarah Scott's *Millenium Hall* and *The History of Sir George Ellison*." *The Age of Johnson* 5 (1992): 305–25.

Clarke, Norma. *Dr. Johnson's Women*. London, 2000.

—— "Soft Passions and Darling Themes: from Elizabeth Singer Rowe (1674–1737) to Elizabeth Carter (1717–1806)." *Women's Writing* 7 (2000): 353–71.

Cohen, J. M. *English Translators and Translations*. London, 1962.

Crittenden, Walter M. *The Life and Writing of Mrs Sarah Scott, Novelist (1723–1795)*. Ph.D. diss., University of Pennsylvania, 1931.

Darby, Barbara. *Frances Burney, Dramatist: Gender, Performance, and the Late-Eighteenth-Century Stage*. Lexington, Ky., 1997.

Davidoff, Leonore, and Catherine Hall. *Family Fortunes: Men and Women of the English Middle Class, 1780–1850*. London, 1992.

Deal Historical Society. "Letters to a Famous Daughter." In *Deal and Its Place in Architectural Heritage*, 7–9. N.d.

D'Monté, Rebecca, and Nicole Pohl, eds. *Female Communities, 1600–1800: Literary Visions and Cultural Realities*. New York, 2000.

Dobson, Austin. "The Learned Mrs. Carter." In *Later Essays*, 97–123 (1921). Reprint ed., Freeport, N.Y., 1968.

Dolan, Brian. *Ladies of the Grand Tour: British Women in Pursuit of Enlightenment and Adventure in Eighteenth-Century Europe*. London, 2001.

Doody, Margaret Anne. "Women Poets of the Eighteenth Century." In *Women and Literature in Britain, 1700–1800*, edited by Vivien Jones, 117–37. Cambridge, 2000.

Donoghue, Emma. *Passions between Women*. London, 1993.

Doran, John. *A Lady of the Last Century: Illustrated in Her Unpublished Letters*. London, 1873.

Dorn, Judith. "Reading Women Reading History: The Philosophy of Periodical Form in Charlotte Lennox's *The Lady's Museum.*" *Historical Reflections/Réflexions Historiques* 18, no. 3 (Fall 1992): 7–27.

Duncombe, John. *The Feminiad* (1754). Edited by Jocelyn Harris. Los Angeles, 1981.

Duncombe, Susanna. "A Sketch of the Character of the Author of *Reflections on the Seven Days of the Week.*" *Gentleman's Magazine* 42 (June 1772): 257–58.

Dunne, Linda. "Mothers and Monsters in Sarah Robinson Scott's *Millenium Hall.*" *Utopian and Science Fiction by Women: Worlds of Difference*, edited by Jane L. Donawerth and Carol A. Kolmerten, 54–72. Syracuse, N.Y., 1994.

Easton, Celia. "Were the Bluestockings Queer? Elizabeth Carter's Uranian Friendships." *Age of Johnson* 9 (1998): 257–94.

Edwards, Janet Ray. "Singing the Blues: the Voices of Eighteenth-Century Bluestockings and Later Literary Women." *Review* 14 (1992): 45–56.

Eger, Elizabeth. "Luxury, Industry, and Charity: Bluestocking Culture Displayed." In *Luxury in the Eighteenth Century: Debates, Desires and Delectable Goods*, edited by Maxine Berg and Elizabeth Eger, 190–206. Basingstoke, England, 2002.
——, Charlotte Grant, Cliona Ó Callchoir, and Penny Warburton, eds. *Women, Writing, and the Public Sphere, 1700–1830.* Cambridge, 2001.

Elliott, Dorice Williams. "Sarah Scott's *Millenium Hall* and Female Philanthropy." *Studies in English Literature, 1500–1900* 35 (1995): 535–53.

Eshleman, Dorothy Hughes. "Elizabeth Griffith: A Biographical and Critical Study." Ph.D. diss., University of Pennsylvania, 1949.

Ezell, Margaret. *Social Authorship and the Advent of Print.* Baltimore, 1999.
—— *Writing Women's Literary History.* Baltimore, 1993.

Faderman, Lillian. *Surpassing the Love of Men: Romantic Friendship and Love between Women from the Renaissance to the Present.* New York, 1981.

Ferguson, Moira, ed. *First Feminists: British Women Writers, 1578–1799.* Bloomington, Ind., 1985.

Fiquet du Boccage, Marie-Anne. *Letters Concerning England, Holland, and Italy.* 2 vols. London, 1770.

Ford, Charles Howard. *Hannah More: A Critical Biography.* New York, 1996.

Freeman, Lisa A. "'A Dialogue': Elizabeth Carter's Passion for the Female Mind." In *Women's Poetry in the Enlightenment*, edited by Isobel Armstrong and Virginia Blain, 50–63. London, 1999.

Freeman, R. *Kentish Poets, a Series of Writers in English Poetry.* Canterbury, England, 1821.

Frye, Susan and Karen Robertson, editors. *Maids and Mistresses, Cousins and Queens: Women's Alliances in Early Modern England*. Oxford, 1999.

Gardner, Catherine. "Catharine Macaulay's Letters on Education: Odd by Equal." *Hypatia* 13 (1998): 137–58.

Gardiner, Dorothy. *English Girlhood at School*. London, 1929.

Gaussen, Alice. *A Woman of Wit and Wisdom*. London, 1906.

Gilbert, Sandra M. and Susan Gubar. *The Madwoman in the Attic: The Woman Writer and the Nineteenth-Century Literary Imagination*. New Haven, Conn., 1979.
—— *No Man's Land: The Place of the Woman Writer in the Twentieth Century*. New Haven, Conn., 1988.

Goodman, Dena. "Public Sphere and Private Life: Toward a Synthesis of Current Historiographical Approaches to the Old Regime." *History and Theory* 31 (1992): 1–20.
—— *The Republic of Letters: A Cultural History of the French Enlightenment*. Ithaca, N.Y., 1994.

Greenfield, Susan C. "'Oh Dear Resemblance of Thy Murdered Mother': Female Authorship in *Evelina*." *Eighteenth-Century Fiction* 3 (July 1991): 301–20.

Grosz, Elizabeth. *Volatile Bodies: Toward a Corporeal Feminism*. Bloomington, Ind., 1994.

Grundy, Isobel. *Lady Mary Wortley Montagu: Comet of the Enlightenment*. Oxford, 1999.
—— "Samuel Johnson as Patron of Women." *Age of Johnson* 1 (1987): 59–77.
—— "(Re)discovering Women's Texts." In *Women and Literature in Britain, 1700–1800*, edited by Vivien Jones, 179–96. Cambridge, 2000.

Guest, Harriet. "Eighteenth-Century Femininity: 'A Supposed Sexual Character.'" In *Women and Literature in Britain, 1700–1800*, edited by Vivien Jones, 46–68. Cambridge, 2000.
—— *Small Change: Women, Learning, Patriotism, 1750–1810*. Chicago, 2000.

Habermas, Jürgen. *The Structural Transformation of the Public Sphere: An Inquiry into a Category of Bourgeois Society* (1962). Translated by Thomas Burger. Cambridge, 1996.

Haggerty, George E. "'Romantic Friendship' and Patriarchal Narrative in Sarah Scott's *Millenium Hall*." *Gender* 13 (Spring 1992): 108–22.
—— *Unnatural Affections: Women and Fiction in the Later Eighteenth Century*. Bloomington, Ind., 1998.

Hampshire, Gwen. "An Edition of Some Unpublished Letters of Elizabeth Carter, 1717 to 1806." Master's thesis, Oxford University, 1971.

Hansen, Marjorie. "Elizabeth Montagu: A Biographical Sketch and a Critical Edition of Her Writings." Ph.D. diss., University of Southern California, 1982.

Harth, Erica. "The Salon Woman Goes Public . . . or Does She?" In *Going Public: Women and Publishing in Early Modern France*, edited by Elizabeth C. Goldsmith and Dena Goodman, 179–93. Ithaca, N.Y., 1995.

Hay, Douglas, and Nicholas Rogers. *Eighteenth-Century English Society*. Oxford, 1997.

Hayley, William. *Philosophical, Historical, and Moral Essay on Old Maids*. London, 1785.

Heller, Deborah. "Bluestocking Salons and the Public Sphere." *Eighteenth-Century Life* 22 (1998): 59–82.

Hesse, Carla. *The Other Enlightenment: How French Women became Modern*. Princeton, N.J., 2001.

Hill, Bridget. "The Course of the Marriage of Elizabeth Montagu: An Ambitious and Talented Woman without Means." *Journal of Family History* 26 (2001): 3–17.
——— "The Links between Mary Wollstonecraft and Catharine Macaulay: New Evidence." *Women's History Review* 4 (1995): 177–92.
——— *The Republican Virago: The Life and Times of Catharine Macaulay, Historian*. Oxford, 1992.

Hyde, Mary. *The Thrales of Streatham Park*. Cambridge, 1977.

Huchon, René. *Mrs. Montagu and Her Friends, 1720–1800: A Sketch*. London, 1907.

Irving, Henry. *Province of Wit in the English Letter Writers*. Durham, N.C., 1955.

Jacob, Margaret C. "The Mental Landscape of the Public Sphere: A European Perspective." *Eighteenth-Century Studies* 28 (1994): 95–113.

Johns, Alessa. "Journeying towards Identity: Sarah Fielding, Sarah Scott, and Feminist Utopianism in Eighteenth-Century England." In *Vite di Utopia*, edited by Vita Fotunati and Paola Spinozzi, 319–25. Ravena, Italy, 1996.
——— "Realizing Fiction: Sarah Scott's Utopian Biography." In *Vite di Utopia*, edited by Vita Fortunati and Paola Spinozzi, 199–207. Ravena, Italy, 2000.
——— *Women's Utopias of the Eighteenth Century*. Urbana, Ill., 2003.

Jones, Ann Rosalind. *The Currency of Eros: Women's Love Lyric in Europe, 1540–1620*. Bloomington, Ind., 1990.

Jones, Vivien, editor. *Women and Literature in Britain, 1700–1800*. Cambridge, 2000.
——— *Women in the Eighteenth Century: Constructions of Femininity*. London, 1990.

Kelly, Gary, general editor. *Bluestocking Feminism: Writings of the Bluestocking Circle, 1738–1785*. 6 vols. With a general introduction, "Bluestocking Feminism and Writing in Context," by Gary Kelly, 1:ix–liv. London, 1999.
 Eger, Elizabeth, editor. *Elizabeth Montagu*. Vol. 1 of *Bluestocking Feminism*.
 Hawley, Judith, editor. *Elizabeth Carter*. Vol. 2 of *Bluestocking Feminism*.
 Zuk, Rhonda, editor. *Hester Chapone and Catherine Talbot*. Vol. 3 of *Bluestocking Feminism*.
 Kelly, Jennifer, editor. *Anna Seward*. Vol. 4 of *Bluestocking Feminism*

Kelly, Gary, editor. *Sarah Scott*. Vol. 5 of *Bluestocking Feminism*.

Kelly, Gary, editor. *Sarah Fielding and Clara Reeve*. Vol. 6 of *Bluestocking Feminism*.

—— "Bluestocking Feminism." In *Women, Writing, and the Public Sphere, 1700–1830*. Edited by Charlotte Grant, Cliona Ó Callchoir, and Penny Warburton, 163–80. Cambridge, 2001.

—— "Women's Provi(de)nce: Religion and Bluestocking Feminism in Sarah Scott's *Millenium Hall* (1762)." In *Female Communities, 1600–1800: Literary Visions and Cultural Realities*, edited by Rebecca D' Monté and Nicole Pohl, 166–83. New York, 2000.

—— *Women, Writing, and Revolution, 1790–1827*. Oxford, 1993.

Keutsch, Wilfried. "Teaching the Poor: Sarah Trimmer, God's Own Handmaiden." *Bulletin of the John Rylands University Library of Manchester* 76 (1994): 43–57.

King, Heather. "Catharine Trotter, Charlotte Lennox, and Frances Burney: Fictions and Foundations of Female Virtue in the Eighteenth Century." Ph.D. diss., University of Wisconsin, 1999.

Kirkpatrick, Kathryn. "Sermons and Strictures: Conduct-Book Propriety and Property Relations in Late-Eighteenth-Century England." In *History, Gender, and Eighteenth-Century Literature*, edited by Beth Fowkes Tobin, 198–226. Athens, Ga., 1994.

Klein, Lawrence E. "Gender and the Public/Private Distinction in the Eighteenth Century: Some Questions about Evidence and Analytical Procedure." *Eighteenth-Century Studies* 29 (1995): 97–109.

Knight, Helen Cross. *A New Memoir of Hannah More; Or, Life in Hall and Cottage*. New York, 1851.

Kowaleski-Wallace, Elizabeth. "A Night at the Opera: The Body, Class, and Art in *Evelina* and Frances Burney's Early Diaries." In *History, Gender, and Eighteenth-Century Literature*, edited by Beth Fowkes Tobin, 141–58. Athens, Ga., 1994.

—— *Their Fathers' Daughters*. New York, 1990.

—— "Two Anomalous Women: Elizabeth Carter and Catherine Talbot." In *Eighteenth-Century Women and the Arts*, edited by Frederick M. Kenner and Susan E. Lorsch, 19–27. New York, 1988.

—— "Milton's Daughters: The Education of Eighteenth-Century Women Writers." *Feminist Studies* 12 (1986): 275–93.

Kucich, Greg. "'This Horrid Theatre of Human Sufferings': Gendering the Stages of History in Catharine Macaulay and Percy Bysshe Shelley." In *Lessons of Romanticism: A Critical Companion*, edited by Thomas Pfau and Robert F. Gleckner, 448–65. Durham, N.C., 1998.

"Memoirs of Mrs. Carter." *Lady's Magazine* (February, 1809): 61–65.

Landes, Joan B. *Women and the Public Sphere in the Age of the French Revolution*. Ithaca, N.Y., 1994.

Lanser, Susan. "Befriending the Body: Female Intimacies as Class Acts." *Eighteenth-Century Studies* 32 (1998–99): 179–98.
—— *Fictions of Authority: Women Writers and Narrative Voice.* Ithaca, N.Y., 1992.

Larson, Edith Sedgwick. "A Measure of Power: The Personal Charity of Elizabeth Montagu." *Studies in Eighteenth-Century Culture* 16 (1986): 197–210.

Le Breton, Anna Laetitia. *Memoir of Mrs. Barbauld, Including Letters and Notices of Her Family and Friends.* London, 1874.

Leranbaum, Miriam. "'Mistresses of Orthodoxy': Education in the Lives and Writings of Late Eighteenth-Century English Women Writers." *Proceedings of the American Philosophical Society* 121 (1977): 281–301.

Lerner, Gerda. *The Creation of Feminist Consciousness.* Oxford, 1993.

Linney, Verna. "The Flora Delanica: Mary Delany and Women's Art, Science, and Friendship in Eighteenth-Century England." Ph.D. diss., York University, 1999.
—— "A Passion for Art, A Passion for Botany: Mary Delany and her Floral 'Mosaiks.'" *Eighteenth-Century Women: Studies in Their Lives, Work, and Culture* 1 (2001): 203–35.

London, April. *Women and Property in the Eighteenth-Century Novel.* Cambridge, 1999.

Lonsdale, Roger, editor. *Eighteenth-Century Women Poets: An Oxford Anthology.* Oxford, 1989.

Lowenthal, Cynthia. *Lady Mary Wortley Montagu and the Eighteenth-Century Familiar Letter.* Athens, Ga., 1994.

Lutz, Alfred. "Commercial Capitalism, Classical Republicanism and the Man of Sensibility in *The History of Sir George Ellison*." *Studies in English Literature, 1500–1900,* 39 (1999): 557–74.

Magrath, Jane. "Corporal Punishment: Women's Bodies and Their Eighteenth-Century Readers." Ph.D. diss., University of Alberta, 1997.

Martin, Reginald. "Elizabeth Carter: 'Found' Poet of the Eighteenth Century." *Publications of the Arkansas Philological Association* 11, no. 2 (1985): 49–64.

Mavor, Elizabeth. *The Ladies of Llangollen.* Harmondsworth, England, 1971.

Mazzucco-Than, Cecile. "'As Easy as a Chimney Pot to Blacken': Catharine Macaulay 'The Celebrated Female Historian.'" *Prose Studies: History, Theory, Criticism* 18 (1995): 78–104.

McAllister, Marie E. "Gender, Myth, and Recompense: Hester Thrale's Journal of a Tour to Wales." *The Age of Johnson* 6 (1993): 265–82.

McCarthy, William. *Heter Thrale Piozzi, Portrait of a Literary Woman.* Chapel Hill, N.C., 1985.
—— "The Repression of Hester Lynch Piozzi; Or, How We Forgot a Revolution in Authorship." *Modern Language Studies* 18 (1988): 99–111.

—— "A Verse Essay on Man by H. L. Piozzi." *The Age of Johnson* 2 (1989): 375–420.

—— "The Writings of Hester Lynch Piozzi: A Bibliography." *Bulletin of Bibliography* 45 (1988): 129–41.

Meehan, Johanna, editor. *Feminists Read Habermas: Gendering the Subject of Discourse.* New York, 1995.

Mellor, Anne K. *Mothers of the Nation: Women's Political Writing in England, 1780–1830.* Bloomington, Ind., 2000.

"Memoirs and Remains of Eminent Persons: Original Letters of Miss E. Carter and Mr. Samuel Richardson." *Monthly Magazine* 33 (1812): 533–43.

Moore, Lisa. *Dangerous Intimacies: Towards a Sapphic History of the British Novel.* Durham, N.C., 1997.

Myers, Sylvia Harcstark. *The Bluestocking Circle.* Oxford: 1990.

—— "Learning, Virtue, and the Term 'Bluestocking.'" *Studies in Eighteenth Century Culture* 16 (1986): 279–88.

Noble, Mark. *A Biographical History of England.* 3 vols. London, 1806.

Nussbaum, Felicity A. *The Limits of the Human Fictions of Anomaly, Race, and Gender.* Cambridge, 2003.

—— "Women and Race: A Difference of Complexion." In *Women and Literature in Britain, 1700–1800,* edited by Vivien Jones, 69–88. Cambridge, 2000.

—— "The Pleasures of Deformity in Mid-Eighteenth-Century England." In *Body and Physical Difference: Discourses of Disability,* edited by David T. Mitchell, Sharon L. Snyder, and James I. Porter, 161–73. Ann Arbor, Mich., 1997.

—— *Torrid Zones: Maternity, Sexuality, and Empire in Eighteenth-Century English Narratives.* Baltimore, 1995.

—— *The Autobiographical Subject.* Baltimore, 1989.

—— "Eighteenth-Century Women's Autobiographical Commonplaces." In *The Private Self: Theory and Practice of Women's Autobiographical Writings,* edited by Shari Benstock, 147–71. Chapel Hill, N.C., 1988.

Opie, Amelia. *Detraction Displayed.* London, 1828.

Ostade, Ingrid Tieken Boon van. "A Little Learning Is a Dangerous Thing? Learning and Gender in Sarah Fielding's Letters to James Harris." *Language Sciences* 22 (2000): 339–58.

Owre, Jacob Riis. "Hester Mulso Chapone: A Typical Eighteenth-Century Feminist." Master's thesis, University of Minnesota, 1932.

Parke, Catherine. "Vision and Revision: A Model for Reading the Eighteenth-Century Novel of Education." *Eighteenth-Century Studies* 16 (1982–83): 162–74.

Pawl, Amy J. "'And What Other Name May I Claim?' Names and Their Owners in Frances Burney's *Evelina*." *Eighteenth-Century Fiction* 3, no. 4 (July 1991): 283–99.

Pearson, Jacqueline. *Women's Reading in Britain, 1750–1835*. Cambridge, 1999.

Perry, Ruth. "Bluestockings in Utopia." In *History, Gender, and Eighteenth-Century Literature*, edited by Beth Fowkes Tobin, 159–78. Athens, Ga., 1994.
—— *The Celebrated Mary Astell*. Chicago, 1986.

Pohl, Nicole. "'Sweet Place, Where Virtue Then Did Rest': The Appropriation of the Country-House Ethos in Sarah Scott's *Millenium Hall*." *Utopian Studies* 7 (1996): 49–59.

Polwhele, Richard. *The Unsex'd Females*. London, 1798.

Poovey, Mary. *The Proper Lady and the Woman Writer*. Chicago, 1984.

Reynolds, Myra. *The Learned Lady in England, 1650–1760*. Boston, 1920.

Ribeiro, Alvaro, SJ. "The 'Chit-Chatway': The Letters of Mrs. Thrale and Dr. Burney." In *Tradition in Transition: Women Writers, Marginal Texts, and the Eighteenth-Century Canon*, edited by Alvar Ribeiro, SJ, and James G. Basker, 25–40. Oxford, 1996.

Richetti, John J. "Voice and Gender in Eighteenth-Century Fiction: Haywood to Burney." *Studies in the Novel* 19 (1987): 263–72.

Riely, John. "Johnson and Mrs. Thrale: The Beginning and the End." In *Johnson and His Age*, edited by James Engell, 55–81. Cambridge, 1984.

Rivers, Isabel, editor. *Books and the Readers in Eighteenth-Century England*. Leicester, England, and New York, 1982.

Rizzo, Betty. *Companions without Vows: Relationships among Eighteenth-Century British Women*. Athens, Ga., 1994.
—— "'Depressa Resurgam': Elizabeth Griffith's Playwriting Career." In *Curtain Calls: British and American Women and the Theatre, 1660–1820*, edited by Mary Anne Schofield and Cecilia Macheski, 120–42. Athens, Ga., 1991.

Rogers, Katherine M. *Feminism in Eighteenth-Century England*. Urbana, Ill., 1982.

Rogers, Pat. "Richardson and the Bluestockings." In *Samuel Richardson: Passion and Prudence*, edited by Valerie Grosvenor Myer, 147–64. Totowa, N.J., 1986.

Ross, Ian. "A Bluestocking over the Border: Mrs. Elizabeth Montagu's Aesthetic Adventures in Scotland." *Huntington Library Quarterly* 28 (1965): 213–33.

Ruhe, Edward. "Birch, Johnson, and Elizabeth Carter: An Episode of 1738–39." PMLA 73 (1958): 491–500.

Rousseau, Jean-Jacques. *Discours sur les sciences et les arts; Lettre à d'Alembert* (1758). Edited by Jean Varloot. Paris, 1987.

Runge, Laura L. *Gender and Language in British Literary Criticism, 1660–1790*. Cambridge, 1997.

Russel, Gillian, and Clara Tuite, eds. *Romantic Sociability: Social Networks and Literary Culture in Britain, 1770–1840*. Cambridge, 2002.

Schellenberg, Betty A. "Making Good Use of History: Sarah Robinson Scott in the Republic of Letters." *Studies in Eighteenth-Century Culture* 32 (forthcoming, 2003).
—— "From Propensity to Profession: Authorship and the Early Career of Frances Burney." *Studies in Eighteenth-Century Fiction* 14 (2002): 345–70.

Schnorrenberg, Barbara Brandon. "A Paradise Like Eve's: Three Eighteenth-Century English Female Utopias." *Women's Studies* 9 (1982): 263–73.

Scott, Walter S. *The Bluestocking Ladies*. London, 1947.

Senna, John F. "The Melancholy in Anne Finch and Elizabeth Carter: The Ambivalence of an Idea." *The Yearbook of English Studies* 1 (1971): 108–19.

Shaffer, Julie. "Not Subordinate: Empowering Women in the Marriage Plot—The Novels of Frances Burney, Maria Edgeworth, and Jane Austen." In *Reading with a Difference: Gender, Race, and Cultural Identity*, edited by Arthur F. Marotti and Renata R. Mauntner, 21–43. Detroit, 1993.

Shoemaker, Robert. *Gender in English Society, 1650–1850*. London, 1998.

Siebert, Donald T. "Catharine Macaulay's History of England: Antidote to Hume's History?" *Studies on Voltaire and the Eighteenth Century* 303 (1992): 393–96.

Simons, Judy. "Invented Lives: Textuality and Power in Early Women's Diaries." In *Inscribing the Daily: Critical Essays on Women's Diaries*, edited by Suzanne L. Bunkers and Cynthia A. Huff, 252–63. Amherst, Mass., 1996.
—— "The Unfixed Text: Narrative and Identity in Women's Private Writings; Erasmus Project on Women's Studies." In *The Representation of the Self in Women's Autobiography*, edited by Vita Fortunati and Gabriella Morisco, 1–16. Bologna, 1993.

*Sketch of the Character of Mrs. Elizabeth Carter*. London, 1806.

Spacks, Patricia Meyer. "Female Rhetorics." In *The Private Self*, edited by Shari Benstock, 177–91. Chapel Hill, N.C., 1988.

Spencer, Jane. *Rise of the Woman Novelist: From Aphra Behn to Jane Austen*. Oxford, 1986.

Staves, Susan. "'The Liberty of a She-Subject of England': Rights and Rhetoric and the Female Thucydides." *Cardozo Studies in Law and Literature* 1 (1989): 161–83.

Stabile, Susan. "Salons and Power in the Era of Revolution: From Literary Coteries to Epistolary Enlightenment." In *Benjamin Franklin and Women*, edited by Larry E. Tise, 129–48. University Park, Pa., 2000.

Stockstill, Ashley. "Better Homes and Gardens: The Fairy World(s) of Sarah Fielding and Sarah Scott." *Feminist Studies in English Literature* 6 (1998): 137–58.

Stoddard, Eve W. "A Serious Proposal for Slavery Reform: Sarah Scott's *Sir George Ellison*," *Eighteenth-Century Studies* 28 (1995): 379–96.

Suzuki, Mika. "The 'Words I in Fancy Say for You': Sarah Fielding's Letters and Epistolary Method." *Yearbook of English Studies* 28 (1998): 196–211.

Taylor, Jane. *Display: A Tale*. London, 1815.

Taylor, Derek. "Clarissa Harlowe, Mary Astell, and Elizabeth Carter: John Norris of Bemerton's Female 'Descendants.'" *Eighteenth-Century Fiction* 12 (1999): 19–38.

Thaddeus, Janice Farrar. *Frances Burney: A Literary Life*. London and New York, 2000.
—— "Mary Delany, Model to the Age." In *History, Gender, and Eighteenth-Century Literature*, edited by Beth Fowkes Tobin, 113–40. Athens, Ga., 1994.

Thomas, Claudia. "'Th'Instructive Moral and Important Thought': Elizabeth Carter Reads Pope, Johnson, and Epictetus." *Age of Johnson* 4 (1991): 137–69.

Tinker, Chauncey Brewster. *The Salon and English Letters: Chapters on the Interrelations of Literature and Society in the Age of Johnson*. New York, 1915.

Titone, Connie. "Catharine Macaulay: Feminist Philosopher on Education: From Beliefs to Practice." Ph.D. diss., Harvard Graduate School of Education, 1995.

Tobin, Beth Fowkes, editor. *History, Gender, and Eighteenth-Century Literature*. Athens, Ga., 1994.

Todd, Janet. *The Sign of Angellica*. New York, 1989.
—— *A Dictionary of British and American Women Writers, 1660–1800*. London, 1985.
—— *Women's Friendship in Literature*. New York, 1980.

Vickery, Amanda. *The Gentleman's Daughter: Women's Lives in Georgian England*. New Haven, Conn., 1998.

Walpole, Horace. *A Catalogue of the Royal and Noble Authors of England, Scotland and Ireland*. 5 vols. London, 1806.

Wendorf, Richard, and Charles Ryskamp. "A Bluestocking-Friendship: The Letters of Elizabeth Montagu and Frances Reynolds in the Princeton Collection." *Princeton University Library Chronicle* 41 (1980): 173–207.

Wheeler, Ethel Rolt. *Famous Blue-Stockings*. London, 1910.

Williams, Carolyn. "Poetry, Pudding, and Epictetus: the Consistency of Elizabeth Carter." In *Tradition in Transition: Women Writers, Marginal Texts, and the Eighteenth-Century Canon*, edited by Alvaro Ribeiro and James G. Basker, 3–24. Oxford, 1996.
—— "Fielding and Half-learned Ladies." *Essays in Criticism* 38 (1988): 22–34.

Williams, Jane. *The Literary Women of England*. London, 1861.

Williamson, Marilyn L. "Who's Afraid of Mrs. Barbauld? The Bluestockings and Feminism." *International Journal of Women's Studies* (Janurary/February 1980): 89–101.

Wills, Deborah. "Sarah Trimmer's Oeconomy of Charity: Politics and Morality in the Sunday School State." *Lumen: Selected Proceedings of the Canadian Society for Eighteenth-Century Studies* 12 (1993): 156–66.

Wilner, Arlene Fish. "Education and Ideology in Sarah Fielding's *The Governess*." *Studies in Eighteenth-Century Culture* 24 (1995): 307–27.

Wilson, Kathleen. "Citizenship, Empire, and Modernity in the English Provinces, c. 1720–1790." *Eighteenth-Century Studies* 29 (1995): 69–96.

Yadlon, Susan M. "The Bluestocking Circle: The Negotiation of 'Reasonable' Women." In *Communication and Women's Friendships: Parallels and Intersections in Literature and Life*, edited by Janet Doubler Ward and JoAnna Stephens Mink, 113–31. Bowling Green, Ohio, 1993.

Zonitch, Barbara Anne. "Familiar Violence: Gender and Social Upheaval in the Novels of Frances Burney." Ph.D. diss., Rutgers University, 1993.

# Bluestocking Feminism

HARRIET GUEST

The group of women writers we now think of as the Bluestockings were, on the whole, a conservative group—conservative in their political inclinations as well as in their attitudes to class and to sexuality. Like many other women writing in the eighteenth century before the 1790s, these women did not obviously or vociferously attempt to reform the condition or treatment of women. They spent much of their time socializing with men—the Bluestocking circle included men as well as women, and mostly men who were also conservative. It is perhaps because of that character—in conjunction with the failure of most of them to show any inclination to write novels—that they did not become prominent as a result of the drive to unearth hidden ancestors and to meet the pre-feminist family of the past that energized so much feminist enquiry in the 1970s.

The nature of feminist interest in women writers of the past has of course changed considerably in the last decade or so. Participating as it must in the questions we ask of the present, enquiry into the past has become more tolerant of what could seem disappointing about women—more curious about women whose sense of their own relation to the public social and political issues of their day seems vague, uncertain, sometimes absent, and who display little confidence that discourses of political or economic theory will articulate a coherent or persuasive account of their circumstances. I am not of course suggesting that there is any simple sense in which we map the present onto the past, finding image or likeness of ourselves in eighteenth-century women who did not employ a language of rights and whose sense of themselves as potential agents of cultural or political change was at best oblique. But perhaps we are now more prepared to hear in exchanges between these women ways of thinking about their own lives and social roles that are echoed in later forms of extraparliamentary political activity—a sense of what constitutes them as a group that may be at least a precondition for the development of feminist political self-awareness. In this essay I want to consider the extent of this Bluestocking feminism-before-the-fact as well as some of the implications of its conservatism, in light of Habermas's notion of the public sphere.[1]

1. This essay revisits and refocuses some of the arguments of my book, *Small Change: Women, Learning, Patriotism, 1750–1810* (Chicago, 2000).

59

The Bluestocking group has a fairly flexible definition. In its broadest sense, the term refers to women who are socially prominent not because they are aristocratic, and not always because they are wealthy, but because of their learning, because they are women of letters. More narrowly, the group can be taken to include most of the well-educated but not aristocratic women linked through correspondence as well as social interaction in London, Edinburgh, and perhaps Dublin, from around 1750 to the early decades of the nineteenth century. I have chosen to adopt the latter, more focused definition, which accords with the account of the group given by Sylvia Myers in her invaluable study *The Bluestocking Circle* (1990).[2] The women of what Myers calls the first generation of Bluestockings (and with whom this essay will primarily be concerned) are Hester Chapone, Elizabeth Carter, Catherine Talbot, and Elizabeth Montagu, a group distinguished in their own lifetimes for their successful publications, but now also for the letters they produced and exchanged with each other and with a wide range of correspondents that also included Elizabeth Vesey and Frances Boscawen.

The publications of the Bluestocking women were widely read and celebrated in the second half of the eighteenth century. Myers records that Talbot's *Reflections on the Seven Days of the Week*, published after her death in 1770, sold more than twenty-five thousand copies before 1809. Chapone's *Letters on the Improvement of the Mind* (1773), addressed to her young niece, became a standard text for issue to young ladies, a handbook on the acquisition of respectable middle-class femininity. These were contributions to genres appropriate to women writers—essays and manuals of advice that might be thought of as private and feminine versions of the collections of sermons published by clergymen. Chapone's publications did not seriously disrupt her capacity to live in private (and impoverished) seclusion, though they must have gained her more of the invitations to other people's houses on which her domestic economy depended (she unwisely sold the copyright of her book outright). Carter's translation of the *Works of Epictetus* (1758), in comparison with these more feminine publications, was perceived as a much more direct and dramatic intervention in public life. It involved a degree of classical scholarship to which few women had any access, and it made available texts central to political discourse. As a result, Carter achieved a different kind of fame, a fame that made her in some sense public property. Montagu's *Essay on the Writings and Genius of Shakespear* (1769) was widely praised. She was perceived as a sort of critical defender of faith in the national bard, and therefore in the nation itself, as Horace Walpole acknowledged (however mockingly) in referring to her as "Mrs Montagu of Shakespeareshire."[3]

2.   Sylvia Harcstark Myers, *The Bluestocking Circle: Women, Friendship, and the Life of the Mind in Eighteenth-Century England* (Oxford, 1990). This essay is indebted to Myers's pioneering scholarly research.

3.   See Myers, *Bluestocking Circle,* 233. Walpole cited in R. Huchon, *Mrs. Montagu and Her Friends, 1720–1800: A Sketch* (London, 1907), 208.

These women are not as obscure or as isolated as most of the untitled women writers that preceded them. Catherine Talbot in 1751 lamented the fate of Catherine Trotter Cockburn—a poet, playwright, and philosopher active earlier in the century—whose writings had recently been republished in a posthumous collected edition: "She was a remarkable Genius, & Yet how Obscure her Lot in Life! . . . such Straitness of Circumstances as perplexes & Cramps the Mind, is surely a Grievance. . . . methinks those who knew such Merit did not do their Duty in letting it remain so Obscure." Talbot feared that Carter might "live & die perhaps as Obscurely."[4] But Carter's fate was nothing like Cockburn's. Carter's remarkable scholarship meant that she was singled out for praise as an icon of national progress, and she and her friends, as the exemplary vanguard of women writers of the day, were celebrated as a group by poets, essayists, and reviewers. The cultural significance attributed to the group by their contemporaries sets them apart from earlier women writers, but celebrations of them frequently emphasized that their appearance as published authors was sanctioned by their reputation for conventional feminine skills—by, for example, Montagu's fashionable elegance or Carter's (rather more dubious) culinary expertise. These women present themselves as models of acceptable or traditional notions of feminine virtue: the wealthy Montagu represents herself as a dispenser of hospitality, patronage, and philanthropy, while less affluent women such as Carter and Chapone defend the privacy of their lives.

Carole Pateman has recently cautioned against what she calls the narrow view that sees "feminist political thought . . . as beginning with Wollstonecraft." But it is the case that by the 1790s, and within the lifetimes of most of the first-generation Bluestockings, Catharine Macaulay and Mary Wollstonecraft had achieved a kind of political articulacy and a degree of public audibility that are central to the emergence of modern feminist politics in Britain.[5] Wendy Gunther-Canada points out that the responses of Macaulay and Wollstonecraft to Burke's *Reflections on the Revolution in France* were "interjections to the historical debate [that] proved that women could forcefully defend republican political principles." She argues that Macaulay's *Observations on the Reflections* demonstrate that "she was no political outsider," while Wollstonecraft's *Vindication of the Rights of Men* "led directly to the articulation of a theory of the rights of woman."[6]

4.    Catherine Talbot, Journals, 13 May 1751; cited in Myers, *Bluestocking Circle,* 164 (BL, MS. Add. 46690, fol. 7r–v).

5.    Pateman, "Conclusion: Women's Writing, Women's Standing: Theory and Politics in the Early Modern Period," in Hilda L. Smith, ed., *Women Writers and the Early Modern British Political Tradition* (Cambridge, 1998), 367.

6.    Wendy Gunther-Canada, "The Politics of Sense and Sensibility: Mary Wollstonecraft and Catharine Macaulay Graham on Edmund Burke's *Reflections on the Revolution in France,*" in Smith, *Women Writers,* 145, 141.

Figure 1. *The Nine Living Muses of Great Britain*, by Richard Samuel
(fl. 1768–86); courtesy of the National Portrait Gallery, London.

Celebrations of the Bluestocking women in newspapers and periodicals and in catalogues of eminent women published before the 1790s link their publications with those of Macaulay, and she appears among them as one of their number in Richard Samuel's now famous painting, *The Nine Living Muses of Great Britain* (1779; figure 1). Wollstonecraft wrote in her *Vindication of the Rights of Woman* in praise of Chapone's *Letters*, and though she acknowledged that she could not "always coincide in opinion with" Chapone, she passes easily enough from expressing her respect for this "worthy writer" to remembering Macaulay as the "woman of the greatest abilities, undoubtedly, that this country has ever produced."[7] The relation between Bluestocking women writers and the emergence of a feminist political voice is perhaps too easily dismissed as an odd contiguity, a merely curious historical juxtaposition.

A helpful framework for thinking about this relation can perhaps be gleaned from Habermas's comments on the relation between two forms of public: the

7.   Mary Wollstonecraft, *A Vindication of the Rights of Woman* (1792), in *The Works of Mary Wollstonecraft*, ed. Janet Todd and Marilyn Butler, with Emma Rees-Mogg, 7 vols. (London, 1989), 5:174. On catalogues of learned women, see Guest, *Small Change*, chaps. 2 and 7.

"world of letters," where "privatized individuals in their capacity as human be-ings communicated through critical debate"; and the "political realm," where "private people in their capacity as owners of commodities communicated through rational-critical debate." Habermas explains that "the circles of people who made up the two forms of public were not … completely congruent. Women and dependents were factually and legally excluded from the political public sphere," but they "often took a more active part in the literary public sphere than the owners of private property and family heads themselves." Despite this incongruity, Habermas emphasizes that "*the fully developed bourgeois public sphere was based on the fictitious identity of the two roles assumed by the privatized individuals who came together to form a public: the role of property owners and the role of human beings pure and simple.*" Habermas attributed to the "educated classes," who are responsible for the "self-understanding of public opinion," this fiction of the identity of property owners who have a political voice, and human beings who are merely literary subjects.[8] It is these educated classes that I am concerned with, and I suggest that it is the very need to recognize and preserve the distinction between the literary and the political publics—in conjunction with the fiction that the same individuals play the same roles in both—that produces the possibility of Bluestocking feminism, with its ambivalently politi-cal edge. In order to explore this possibility I sketch a rather over-schematized diachronic narrative about the Bluestocking world of letters, or Bluestock-ing sociability.

~ ~

In the 1760s and early 1770s, Bluestocking assemblies were valued because they seemed to exclude the factionalisms of politics. Sir John Macpherson, who was later to become governor-general of India, wrote to Montagu in 1772 remem-bering visits to her house in 1769 and 1770. He commented that "George the third does not know how much he is indebted to the chearful and Classic Assemblies of your Chinese Room." He explained that the pleasures of her as-semblies "gave that sweetness and refinement to the thoughts of our Statesmen which could alone counteract the acid and gloom of their Dispositions" in the period of the Wilkite riots. He thought that Montagu's influence had lent debates

---

8. Jürgen Habermas, *The Structural Transformation of the Public Sphere: An Enquiry into a Category of Bourgeois Society*, trans. Thomas Burger with Frederick Lawrence (London, 1989), 55–56; italics in original. Habermas specifies those who take part in the literary public sphere as "female readers as well as appren-tices and servants."

between leading politicians urbanity and even good humour, and he concluded: "we are all indebted to you; and that without your being sensible of it."[9] Montagu's role in his account is ambiguously poised between active intervention and the more indirect diffusion of polished manners that is a more traditional feminine skill. And it is a role that clearly depends, to a large extent, on her enormous wealth. When she moved into her grand London house in Portman Square in 1781, she was able to imagine it as a cross between a public building and a private house, combining a "certain dignity of appearance to the publick, and elegant accommodations for ones private enjoyment."[10] Montagu did not participate actively in politics in the way that some aristocratic women did—she did not canvas in elections, visit military camps, or purchase battleships.[11] Her assemblies effect political ends because they *remove* men from their political context, reconfirming their identities as what Habermas calls "*human beings pure and simple*," as private men who participate in the literary public sphere.

Montagu wrote with admiration, in 1772, of her friend Elizabeth Vesey's talent for bringing together "all the heterogeneous natures in the World" in the Tuesday assemblies in her Blue Room, which, Montagu thought,

> indeed in many respects resembles Paradise, for there the Lion sits down by the Lamb, the Tyger dandles the Kid; the sly scotchman and the etourdi Hibernian, the Hero and Maccaroni, the Vestal and the demi rep, the Mungo of Ministry and the inflexible partisans of incorruptible Patriots, Beaux esprits and fine Gentlemen all gather together under the downy wing of the Sylph, and are soothed into good humour[.]

Vesey's most famous parties were held in London, but she probably also entertained in Dublin, where she spent much of her time (her husband represented two Irish constituencies in Parliament and was appointed accountant-general for Ireland). Here she is praised for bringing about an ideal of harmonious national identity, smoothing over political and national differences. Montagu writes that were Vesey "to withdraw her influence a moment, discord would reassume her reign, and we should hear the clashing of swords, the angry flirting of fans, and

---

9.   Sir John Macpherson to Elizabeth Montagu, Madras, 15 October 1772; *Mrs. Montagu, "Queen of the Blues": Her Letters and Friendships from 1762 to 1800*, ed. Reginald Blunt, 2 vols. (London, n.d.), 1:266.
10. Elizabeth Montagu to Elizabeth Carter, Sandleford, 14 July 1781; ibid., 2:112.
11. On these activities of the duchess of Devonshire and the marchioness of Granby (who became the duchess of Rutland in 1779), see Amanda Foreman, *Georgiana: Duchess of Devonshire* (London, 1998), chaps. 4 and 9; and Guest, *Small Change*, chap. 4.

Sr Andrew and Sr Patrick gabbling in dire confusion of the different dialects of the Erse tongue."[12]

Hannah More a decade later celebrated Vesey's talents as a hostess in her poem *The Bas Bleu; or, Conversation* (written in 1783). More asserts, in her advertisement to the poem, that the Bluestocking assemblies or "little Societies" had been "sometimes misrepresented" as exceptional social occasions. She recalls with nostalgic pleasure that they were "composed of persons distinguished, in general, for their rank, talents, or respectable character, who met frequently at Mrs. *Vesey's* and at a few other houses, for the sole purpose of conversation, and were different in no respect from other parties, but that the company did not play at cards." Mores goes on to claim, in both the advertisement and the poem, that conversation in these gatherings was exceptional only because it was free of the "censurable errors with which it is too commonly tainted."[13] By 1783 she clearly believed that in the past, perhaps in the early 1770s in particular, there had been a kind of social world of the educated and polite that could cut across differences of gender and politics—a world that was not peculiar to Bluestocking gatherings, and constituted something resembling Habermass's notion of the literary public formed by the educated class.[14]

James Beattie's diary, recording the trip he made to London in 1773 in hopes of garnering praise and preferment as a result of the success of his recently published refutation of David Hume's philosophy, suggests that he encountered the kind of harmonious sociability for which More was nostalgic. At the beginning of his account, Beattie notes that "when traduced by my enemies," he has "found relief in recollecting the kindness & favourable opinions of my friends," and he now wants to store up salvific memories by recording all those "flattering circumstances, in regard to publick or private approbation, as may hereafter prove a Cordial"; he makes a note of almost everyone he met. Elizabeth Montagu took a strong interest in Beattie's career, and he visits her regularly. She introduces him to much of the diverse range of people that made up London polite society, and

12. Elizabeth Montagu to Elizabeth Carter, Sandleford, 4 September 1772; quoted in Leonore Helen Ewert, "Elizabeth Montagu to Elizabeth Carter: Literary Gossip and Critical Opinions from the Pen of the Queen of the Blues" (Ph.D diss., Claremont Graduate School and University Center, 1968), 113 (citing Huntington Library, Montagu Collection, MO 3304). For a fuller discussion of this letter, see Emma Major's essay in this volume.

13. Hannah More, *The Bas Bleu; or, Conversation. Addressed to Mrs. Vesey*, "Advertisement," in *The Works of Hannah More*, 8 vols. (London, 1801), 1:12.

14. Deborah Heller suggests that by the 1780s Bluestockings wistfully recalled the earlier days of easy sociability. Her important essay does not, however, consider the political implications of sociability or of public life; see "Bluestocking Salons and the Public Sphere," *Eighteenth-Century Life* 22.2 (1998): 59–82, esp. 59–60, 76–78.

perhaps the most striking feature of his lists of dining companions and new acquaintances is the inclusiveness of the metropolitan social world in these years. Beattie hopes to secure a pension from the government or perhaps the king, and is told that Lord North will be more inclined to look on him favorably because of the "lucky circumstance . . . that I am on so good terms with some of the opposition."[15] He socializes with Whigs and Tories, bishops and dissenters, radicals and conservatives. At Montagu's house he frequently encounters Richard Price, who introduces him to other dissenters. He dines with Catharine Macaulay and spends an evening consuming bread and cheese and porter with Alexander Jardine—who, Mary Hays later suggested, had discussed the condition of women so ably in his *Letters from Barbary* of 1790 that it seemed unnecessary for her to publish, or indeed write, her own *Appeal*.[16] Beattie, Price, and Macaulay share, of course, a common hostility to Hume's work, but Beattie's diary of 1773 is, I think, typical of journals of this period in suggesting the extent to which the educated formed something like a class, a grouping that embraced differences of politics or religious belief.

A more famous and striking example of sociability, between men at least, is provided by Boswell's comments on Samuel Johnson's encounter with John Wilkes at a dinner in 1776 at the house of the dissenting bookseller Edward Dilly. Boswell thought the encounter "had the agreeable and benignant effect of reconciling any animosity, and sweetening any acidity, which in the various bustle of political contest, had been produced in the minds of two men, who though widely different, had so many things in common—classical learning, modern literature, wit, humour, and ready repartee."[17] His comments emphasize that the pleasure Wilkes and Johnson apparently take in each other's company in 1776 is remarkable—not least of course because Boswell is so pleased with his own success in setting the occasion up, but also because by the mid-1770s, when Dilly's dinner party took place, it had become unusual for political differences between men to be set aside for the sociable pleasures of a shared taste in classical learning and modern literature. By the mid-1770s, as Kathleen Wilson has argued, "the complexities and sheer novelties of waging a war against the colonies, and the fractious and contradictory demands it placed upon the claims of patriotism and citizenship," had polarized the nation and divided opinions in ways that did not necessarily follow party lines, yet increased what Wilson identifies as the "rad-

15. Ralph S. Walker, ed., *James Beattie's London Diary, 1773*, Aberdeen University Studies no. 122 (Aberdeen, 1946): 33, 37.

16. Mary Hays, *Appeal to the Men of Great Britain in Behalf of Women* (1798). On Jardine, see Guest, *Small Change*, 246–47.

17. 15 May 1776, in James Boswell, *Life of Johnson*, ed. R. W. Chapman (Oxford, 1980), 776.

ical potential" of opposition to the war and to the ministry.[18] Historians differ in their characterizations of the fault lines that opened up in British society during the early years of the American conflict, but they agree that the rifts were dramatic and deep.

The women of the Bluestocking group were, I suggest, not so rapidly or divisively polarized as were educated men in their attitudes to the major issues of the mid-1770s—the conduct of the ministry, the increasing power of the monarch, and the developing crisis in the American colonies—partly because most of them apparently did not want to imagine themselves as having a role to play in a political world, as opposed to a world of letters. Before the 1770s, many of the women of the Bluestocking group seem to have seen little or no overlap between their own lives and the political events of the time. They exchange news about court and parliamentary politics, but they usually handle it as a spectator sport, as something in which they do not participate and that they view with some detachment. For instance, Elizabeth Carter comments in 1767 on a possible change in the administration:

> Indeed it seems of no great consequence what particular person goes out or comes in, as there seems to be nothing in the general system of politics likely to produce any great good. Of that only true policy, the aim of which is to make a nation virtuous and happy, there does not appear to be any idea existing, through all the various changes of men and of measures that have happened among us. All the rest is mere party and faction, and the opposition of jarring interests among individuals.[19]

Carter clearly welcomes the news about political events in London that Montagu's letters bring her, and which she discusses energetically. Her comments do not indicate lack of interest, and the disillusion with parliamentary politics that she voices from early in the 1760s echoes and endorses views that were widespread and that could quicken extraparliamentary political activity. But for her, dismay at the state of party politics and public affairs confirms and strengthens her belief in the values and virtues of private life. For example, she writes in 1763: "How thankful ought they to be whom the obscurity of private life shelters from the turbulence of ambition, and preserves from the temptations of power!"[20]

18. Kathleen Wilson, *The Sense of the People: Politics, Culture, and Imperialism in England, 1715–1785* (Cambridge, 1998), 247.
19. *Letters from Mrs. Elizabeth Carter to Mrs. Montagu, between the years 1755 and 1800*, ed. Montagu Pennington, 3 vols. (London, 1817), letter 95, Deal, 4 July 1767, 1:337.
20. *Carter to Montagu*, letter 55, Deal, 5 October 1763; ibid., 1:202.

Repeatedly, throughout the six decades between 1741 and 1800 covered by her published correspondence, discussions of political affairs lead Carter to meditate on the joys of the private life to which she sees herself as confined.

Hester Chapone, who corresponded with Carter for over fifty years, agreed with her friend that "there is very little virtue, and a great deal of iniquity and corruption to be found among those who are engaged in public life," adding that "those are not the people in whom we ought to look for virtue, . . . human nature is not to be judged of by the most corrupted part of it." Like Carter, she valued the positive benefits enjoyed by women as a result of their exclusion from public life, writing that: "Private life is without doubt the most innocent, and I will never seek friendships out of it; therefore I hope I shall not be a great sufferer from the corruptions of the grande monde, nor lose my benevolence in the resentment of injuries."[21] This commitment to a life excluded from politics may, by the late 1770s, reinforce the sense in which this group of educated women define themselves increasingly as a distinctively gendered collective, and not only as members of the educated class. With increasing frequency and explicitness, I think, they value the work of other women because it was produced by women, and judge it in terms of notions of literary value rather than political opinion.

Women readers in turn seem to have taken a strong interest in promoting and patronizing their work. Talbot liked to joke to Carter about the interest that "fine ladies" would take in her translation of *Epictetus*, but in the event more than a quarter of the subscribers to the first edition were women—a figure that may be most significant as an indication of the willingness of women readers to be seen to be patronizing women writers (many of the women subscribers are listed alongside their husbands, which suggests that they had other motives beside their eagerness to get their hands on a copy). Talbot urged Carter, with more seriousness, to take pride in the notion that her *Epictetus* would "do honour to Epictetus, yourself, your country, and womankind."[22] In their correspondence, all of the women eagerly discuss publications by women. Carter "felt a triumph" in the successes of new women writers, such as Joanna Baillie; she commented positively on Macaulay's *History*; and in the 1790s she praised Helen Maria Williams's *Letters from France* and Charlotte Smith's poetry, despite her disagreement with democratic politics. As her nephew explained, Carter "had a

21. *The Posthumous Works of Mrs. Chapone. Containing her correspondence with Mr. Richardson, A series of letters to Mrs. Elizabeth Carter, and some fugitive pieces*, 2 vols. (London, 1808), letter 13 to Elizabeth Carter, 1751, 1:57–58, 60.

22. Montagu Pennington, *Memoirs of the Life of Mrs. Elizabeth Carter, with a new Edition of her Poems*, 2d ed., 2 vols. (London, 1808), 1:196, 187. Of approximately 910 subscribers to Carter's *Epictetus*, about 640 identified themselves as male, about 270 as female.

decided bias in favour of female writers, and always read their works with a mind prepared to be pleased." She believed that "women had not their proper station in society, and that their mental powers were not rated sufficiently high."[23] She and Chapone corresponded about their disapproval of what they saw as "the contemptuous manner" in which Johnson "generally speaks of women" in the *Rambler*. Chapone noted, in the context of this discussion, that "you carry your partiality to your own sex farther than I do. Indeed you have the strongest reason to think highly of it; and have the best right of any woman in the world to expect others to do so too."[24] What is interesting about this is that these women clearly think of their gender in terms of collective identity and are strongly aware of the representative status that they and other women writers have in relation to that collectivity. It seems to be this consciousness of a gendered group identity, and of their capacity to represent its interests, that informs the powerful sense of their duty or obligation to be socially and publicly useful.

〜 〜

Though representations of these learned women often emphasized what they had in common, their group identity was of course inflected and diversified by differences of wealth and social rank, which to some extent determined what they each made of that identity and how each understood its public or political implications. In the mid-1760s, both Carter and Macaulay sat to the fashionable women's portrait painter Catherine Read, and were both depicted in silky and vaguely classical drapery and equipped with the tools of their expertise—Carter with her quill and a copy of her *Epictetus*, Macaulay with a historical scroll and volumes of her *History* (figures 2 and 3). The similarity between the two images suggests the way catalogues of learned or eminent women grouped their subjects together, allowing their exceptional learning and gender to obscure differences between them. In this case, it was not so much explicit political differences that were masked—for, as I have mentioned, Carter approved the spirit of Macaulay's *History*—but disparity in social station: Carter was the relatively impecunious

<hr />

23. Women writers mentioned in Carter's correspondence include Sarah Fielding, Katherine Philips, Lady Mary Wortley Montagu, Frances Sheridan, Catharine Macaulay, Madame de Sevigny, Mary Collier, Elizabeth Rowe, Catherine Trotter Cockburn, Charlotte Lennox, Hester Mulso, Teresa Constantia Phillips, Mary Jones, Frances Burney, Charlotte Smith, Jane West, Anne Radcliffe, Joanna Baillie, Mary Wollstonecraft, Hannah More, Anna Laetitia Aikin/Barbauld, Sarah Scott, Hester Thrale Piozzi, Ann Thicknesse, Ann Yearsley, Sarah Trimmer, Mrs Kiers [Kerr?], and Helen Maria Williams; ibid., 1:447–48.
24. Ibid., 1:442; Chapone, *Posthumous Works*, letter 14 to Carter, 64.

Figure 2.  Portrait of Elizabeth Carter by Catherine Read;
reproduced by kind permission of Dr. Johnson's House Trust.

daughter of a provincial perpetual curate; to her, Catharine Sawbridge Macaulay, the daughter of a wealthy city family, was "a fine fashionable well-dressed lady whose train was longer than anybody's train."[25]

Read seems to have approached Montagu with the intention of producing a companion portrait of her, but Montagu wrote that "I cannot see what can give me admission to the set of distinguished Ladies." She claimed that she could not appear as one of the "select & sacred number nine," as there were "in this Land nine thousand such sort of good women as I." It is interesting that Montagu should refer to the portraits as the beginnings of a set of what seem to be national muses. She took strong exception to Macaulay's work and politics, and

25.  *A Series of Letters between Mrs. Elizabeth Carter and Miss Catherine Talbot, from the year 1741 to 1770*, ed. Montagu Pennington, 3d. ed., 2 vols. (London, 1819); Carter to Talbot, Deal, 27 August 1757, 2:121–22. See Bridget Hill, *The Republican Virago: The Life and Times of Catharine Macaulay, Historian* (Oxford, 1992), 11.

Figure 3. J. Spilsbury engraving (1764) after Catherine
Read's portrait of Catharine Macaulay.

seems to have been surprised by Carter's tolerance, but she is reported to have
commissioned Read's portrait of Carter, presumably in the knowledge that it
would appear to be one of a set that included Macaulay. Her reasons for not
wanting to be portrayed in that set herself are also interesting. She wrote to
Carter: "I know even your partiality never could distinguish me for any thing but
making good marmalade," and claimed that she could only "be drawn with a
pot of orange sweetmeat honourably label'd in ye stile of receipts, *Orange
Marmalade the best way.*" She adds, perhaps more revealingly, that "I believe
all the Men on the other side Temple Bar, & some on ours, will worship the
Marmalade Muse, & you Sappho will be neglected."[26] Perhaps she suggests that
men, and particularly city merchants, are most interested in their stomachs; but

---

26. Montagu to Carter, Sandleford, 30 June 1765; quoted in Ewert, "Literary Gossip and Critical Opinion,"
57; and in Myers, *Bluestocking Circle*, 246 (Huntington Library, Montagu Collection, MO 3146).

she also implies that the glamour of her wealth from her husband's land and collieries may outshine in their unphilosophical eyes the luster of her friend's learning and poetic skill, and perhaps she prefers to think of the inspiration she provides as that of a wealthy patron rather than a living muse.

The classical style of dress worn by Carter and Macaulay in Read's portraits became a characteristic feature—almost a trademark—of representations of Macaulay throughout the 1770s. In the portraits engraved as frontispieces to the volumes of her *History*, in the infamous statue of the historian commissioned by her friend Thomas Wilson in 1778, in the ceramic figurines of her, and in the two oil portraits painted by Robert Edge Pine in the mid-'70s, her dress and hair style cast her as a Roman matron, a figure reminiscent of the severe ideals of the early Roman republic (for some of these see figures 4, 5, and 6). Images of Macaulay in classical dress indicate her authority as a historian and political commentator informed by the ideals of classical republicanism. Later images of Carter, however, present a more softened and private image. In Lawrence's pastel portrait of 1790, for example, her modesty and retirement are indicated by her downward gaze and mob cap, though her scholarship is hinted at in her high brow and in the suggestion of an academic gown in the black material around her shoulders (figure 7). She is still studious, perhaps stoical, but she seems to turn away from the public role that Read's portrait could suggest. In the mid-1770s, after the publication of her *Essay on Shakespear*, Montagu's portrait was painted by Sir Joshua Reynolds (see figure 8). There is no reference in this image to the success of Montagu's *Essay;* instead, she is shown sitting with her hands folded in her lap, apparently listening and attending to some unseen figure, with an expression that I imagine is meant to suggest patience and benevolence. In the print of the image, the splendor of her clothes is pronounced. There is no sign of the ascetic simplicity associated with the Roman republic here, and if there is self-denial it is in the forbearance indicated by her expression, not in plainness of material adornment. Set alongside Read's portrait of Carter, Reynolds's image suggests Montagu's wealth and powers of patronage rather than her personal productivity or literary fame.

Montagu, occasionally at least, endorsed this image of herself as a patron rather than an author. When she cultivated an acquaintance with Anna Aikin (later Barbauld) in 1774, she introduced herself with this explanation:

> You must not expect to find in me, the talents which adorn the friends around me, I shall not think myself disgraced in your opinion if you find something in me to love, tho' nothing to admire. The genuine effect of polite letters is to inspire candour, a social spirit, and gentle manners; to teach a disdain of frivolous amusements,

Figure 4. Frontispiece from Catharine Macaulay's *History of England,* volume 3 (1767).

> injurious censoriousness, and foolish animosities. To partake of
> these advantages and to live under the benign empire of the muses,
> on the conditions of a naturalized subject, who, not having any
> right to a share of office, credit, or authority, seeks nothing but the
> protection of the society is all I aim at.[27]

Montagu's comments here echo her response to Read nearly a decade earlier. In both, she denies that she has any direct claim to identification with the muses. In this letter, she is perhaps being disingenuous about her reputation, but she nevertheless confirms that she prides herself on her powers of social organization and patronage, for the emphasis here is on the consumption of polite letters and the distinctive forms of sociability enjoyed by the well educated.

27. Anna Letitia Le Breton, *Memoir of Mrs. Barbauld, including Letters and Notices of Her Family and Friends* (London, 1874); letter from Montagu, Hill Street, 22 February 1774, 38–39.

Figure 5. Portrait of Catharine Macaulay (1774) by Robert Edge Pine (ca. 1730–88); courtesy of the National Portrait Gallery, London.

The women of the Bluestocking group may be to a limited extent comparable with the French *salonnières,* about whom Dena Goodman has written so persuasively, in that they do instill notions of polite, enlightened behavior as opposed to aristocratic decorum through their sociability, through the conversational practices the importance of which they so frequently emphasize.[28] Enlightenment theories of the civilized polish diffused by the sociability of women seem to inform representations of Montagu that portray her importance not so much as the author of the *Essay on Shakespear*—defending him from what were perceived as the Anglophobe strictures of Voltaire—but as a philanthropist and patron.

28. See Dena Goodman, "Public Sphere and Private Life: Toward a Synthesis of Current Historiographical Approaches to the Old Regime," in *History and Theory* 31. 3 (1992): 1–20; and *The Republic of Letters: A Cultural History of the French Enlightenment* (Ithaca, N.Y., and London, 1994).

Figure 6. Statue of Catharine Macaulay as "History," Warrington Public Library; courtesy of Warrington Borough Council, Libraries and Information Services.

James Barry, for example, gave her the central position in his huge image, *The Distribution of the Premiums in the Society of the Arts* (figure 9). This painting is fifth in a series of six murals on *The Progress of Human Culture,* which Barry painted for the Society of Arts between 1777 and 1784. In the center Montagu presents a protégé, while on the right Samuel Johnson urges her example on the duchesses of Rutland and Devonshire. Barry's mural points up the uneasy relation between Montagu as the exemplary patron of what appears to be a poor but deserving girl and the duchesses, both of whom were of course actively and even scandalously involved in national politics in these years. Montagu, like the duchesses, is exceptional because of her wealth, but Montagu's philanthropic interests are not represented as setting her apart from other women, as do the rank and public prominence of the duchesses. Montagu is here the patron or sponsor of women rather than of politicians.

Figure 7. Portrait of Elizabeth Carter (1790) by Sir Thomas Lawrence
(1769–1830); courtesy of the National Portrait Gallery, London.

❧ ❧

I do not of course want to suggest that the interests of the Bluestocking women
were exclusively absorbed in or centered on their gendered identities, though
femininity becomes a more prominent and to some extent defining characteristic of their group as part of the process of historical change that produces polarized divisions in polite and educated British society of the mid-1770s. Carter
wrote to Montagu in 1778, when the fame of her classical scholarship was well
established, commenting that she had recently

> received much more literary information among politicians than I
> did … from a company of scholars and authors. As if the two sexes
> had been engaged in a state of war, the gentlemen ranged them-
> selves on one side of the room, where they talked their own talk,
> and left us poor ladies to twirl our shuttles, and amuse each other,

Figure 8. John Raphael Smith after Sir Joshua Reynolds, *Elizabeth Montagu* (1776); reproduced by kind permission of Dr. Johnson's House Trust.

by conversing as we could. By what little I could overhear, our op-
posites were discoursing on the old English poets, and this subject
did not seem so much beyond a female capacity, but that we might
have been indulged with a share in it.[29]

Carter seems surprised and disappointed by the gendered division she encounters.
Her remarks suggest that at dinner with male politicians, "literary information"
had provided common ground, had been available as a conversational space
in which gendered identities could be set aside in favor of something like
Habermas's pure humanity. But in the company of scholars and authors, she
implies, the women have been excluded from literary discussion that is properly
their conversational resource, and consigned to the world of things rather than

29.  *Letters from Carter to Montagu*, letter 210, Clarges Street, 10 May 1778, 3:67–68.

ideas—left to twiddle their shuttles. The feminine right to Habermas's public world of letters seems to be confirmed by its juxtaposition with the political realm, where masculine "owners of commodities communicated through rational-critical debate." Carter's comments seem both to confirm and to deny what Habermas describes as "*the fictitious identity of the two roles assumed by the privatized individuals who came together to form a public: the role of property owners and the role of human beings pure and simple.*" For here politicians seem able to discuss literature with women because the sense in which the world of literature is private and intimate—is purely human—is thrown into relief by its juxtaposition with the possibility of political discussion, the possibility of the conversation the politicians would have if they were not relaxing in the company of women. The men of literature, on the other hand, when in the company of women, may need to preserve more firmly the fiction that their professional role in the intimate but public world of letters is identical with their more explicitly manly role as property owners in the public world of political debate. They need to insist on their gender perhaps because it is not confirmed by active engagement in the political arena.

Carter's dismay at her exclusion from literary discussion indicates the strength of her sense of her right to take part, and in Habermas's terms that might imply a right to at least a fiction of participation in political discussion. When Catherine Macaulay and Mary Wollstonecraft intervene in the debate over the politics of the French Revolution in the 1790s, their intervention is perceived to be unsexing. Wollstonecraft writes about Macaulay that she "was an example of intellectual acquirements supposed to be incompatible with the weakness of her sex. In her style of writing, no sex appears, for it is like the sense it conveys, strong and clear. I will not call hers a masculine understanding, because I admit not of such an arrogant assumption of reason; but I contend that it was a sound one."[30] Both Macaulay and Wollstonecraft seem at least occasionally to find it necessary or convenient to set gendered identity to one side in order to engage in political argument. But the character in which the first-generation Bluestockings gain access to the public "world of letters" is unambiguously feminine, its gendered character reinforced by their support for the work of women and their distance from political involvement.

Earlier I suggested that Bluestocking forms of sociability in the 1760s and early 1770s could be understood as having an ambivalently political character precisely because of the ways in which their assemblies turned away from or smoothed over political differences. After the mid-1770s, that ambivalently political character becomes perhaps more distinctively associated with the gender of Bluestocking women than with their status as members of the educated

30. Wollstonecraft, *Vindication* (1792), in *Works*, 5:175.

Figure 9. *The Distribution of Premiums in the Society of Arts* (detail), fifth in the series *The Progress of Human Culture and Knowledge*, ca. 1777–84, by James Barry (1741–1806); oil on canvas. R.S.A, London; UK/Bridgeman Art Library.

classes; at the same time, male members become, because of their role in the "world of letters," more clearly distinct from the unambiguously masculine world of political participation. After the mid-1770s, as men became caught up in the "fractious and contradictory demands" of extraparliamentary political debate, the Bluestocking sociability available to some women may have identified them (rather than men of letters) with the literary public sphere of "*human beings pure and simple.*" The educated classes responsible for public opinion, Habermas suggests, needed to perceive this literary sphere as enjoying a "*fictitious identity*" with the "*privatized individuals*" who came together to form a bourgeois political public. Bluestocking sociability may thus have made available the fiction or fantasy of a feminine political voice—or at least may have made it possible for more explicitly political writers such as Macaulay, Wollstonecraft, and later Hays to think about gender as a collective identity in ways that were more directly and explicitly political.

*Centre for Eighteenth Century Studies*
*University of York*

# Church of England Clergy and Women Writers

Clergymen of the Church of England had a privileged monopoly on the prestigious forms of literary learning cultivated at the universities. Given that this was so for the entire period, 1660–1800, it is not surprising that intellectually ambitious women, themselves excluded from university study, sought out Church of England clergymen for various kinds of educational and literary assistance. Although such women would have been called "Bluestockings" only in the second half of the century, the kind of high-minded, morally and intellectually ambitious literary woman to which it referred predated the term. Here I want to consider Anglican Bluestockings from Mary Astell (1666–1731) to Hannah More (1745–1833). Examples of Church of England clergymen who assisted women writers in the period from 1660 to 1800 come readily to mind. During the Restoration, the Rev. William Elstob helped his sister, Elizabeth Elstob, to learn ancient languages and Anglo-Saxon. Mary Astell is thought to have been educated by her uncle, the Rev. Ralph Astell, in philosophy and logic. A striking percentage of intellectually ambitious women publishing serious non-fiction had clergy fathers (or sometimes uncles or brothers) who contributed substantially to their educations. The Rev. Nicholas Carter, Doctor of Divinity, Elizabeth Carter's father, is only one of the most dramatic examples. Anna Seward's father, the Rev. Thomas Seward, was not only a learned clergyman but also the author of "The Female Right to Literature" (1748).[1]

Of at least equal importance, Church of England clergymen who were not relatives also assisted Bluestocking women writers. The famous nonjuror and Anglo-Saxon scholar, the Rev. George Hickes, encouraged and assisted Elizabeth Elstob. When Astell went to London in her twenties, William Sancroft,

---

1. For biographies that address the intellectual formation of these women, see Ruth Perry, *Mary Astell: An Early English Feminist* (Chicago, 1986); Sarah Huff Collins, "Elizabeth Elstob: A Biography" (Ph.D. diss., Indiana University, 1970); Sarah H. Collins, "The Elstobs and the End of the Saxon Revival," in Carl T. Berkhout and Milton McC. Gatch, eds., *Anglo-Saxon Scholarship: The First Three Centuries* (Boston, 1982), 107–18; Sylvia Harcstark Myers, *The Bluestocking Circle: Women, Friendship, and the Life of the Mind in the Eighteenth Century* (Oxford, 1990), including Carter; and on Seward, John Brewer, *The Pleasures of the Imagination: English Culture in the Eighteenth Century* (New York, 1997), 573–612.

archbishop of Canterbury, assisted her, she testified, "when even my Kinsfolk had failed, and my familiar Friends had forgotten me."[2] Her friendship with the Rev. John Norris, beginning with her letters to him posing theological and philosophical questions, led him to publish their correspondence as *Letters Concerning the Love of God* (1695). This published correspondence between Astell and Norris suggested what potential there was in a new kind of non-sexualized, non-familial relationship between an intellectually ambitious, religiously serious woman and a learned clergyman willing to take her seriously as a mind and as a soul.

Hannah More's correspondence demonstrates her friendships with a staggering number of learned bishops and scholarly clergymen. Among More's notable clerical friends and encouragers were Benjamin Kennicott, an Oxford fellow who devoted his career to collating Hebrew manuscripts of the Old Testament, published as *Vetus Testamentum Hebraicum cum Variis Lectionibus* (1776, 1780); and Robert Lowth, variously Oxford Professor of Poetry, bishop of Oxford, and bishop of London.[3] Judith Hawley, Elizabeth Carter's recent editor, remarks that her correspondence "often has the appearance of a protracted seminar, or salon discussion of literary and artistic concerns"; the same might be said of other Bluestocking correspondence.[4] Suggestions for the reading lists of such "seminars" often came from friendly clergymen, and Anglican clergymen wrote many of the works read by intellectually ambitious women. Thus, we find Hannah More writing to Frances Boscawen that she is reading her friend Robert Lowth's *Isaiah. A New Translation. With Notes* (1778). In the same letter, More recommends Lowth's *De Sacra Poesi* as "a treasure," reporting, it "has taught me to consider the Divine Book it illustrates under many new and striking points of view; it teaches to appreciate the distinct and characteristic excellence of the sacred poetry and historians, in a manner wonderfully entertaining and instructive."[5]

2.   Perry, *Astell,* 68.

3.   On Kennicott and Lowth and the general state of Hebrew study, see D. Patterson, "Hebrew Studies," in L. S. Sutherland and L. G. Mitchell, eds., *The History of the University of Oxford: The Eighteenth Century* (Oxford, 1986), 535–50. Patterson describes Kennicott's as "perhaps the most familiar name in Hebrew scholarship in the period" (p. 540). On Lowth, celebrated by More as "Illustrious Lowth" in "Sensibility," see also Brian Hepworth, *Robert Lowth* (Boston, 1978).

4.   Gary Kelly, gen. ed., *Bluestocking Feminism: Writings of the Bluestocking Circle, 1738–1785,* 6 vols. (London, 1999); vol. 2, ed. Judith Hawley, 376.

5.   William Roberts, *Memoirs of the Life and Correspondence of Hannah More,* 2 vols. (New York, 1834), 1:137. More refers to *Prælectiones de Sacra Poesi Hebræorum,* Latin (1753); English trans., *Lectures on the Sacred Poetry of the Hebrews* (1787). If Roberts's dating of this letter to 1782 is correct, More would seem to have had access to an English translation before one was published.

The traditional version of the history of the Church of England in the eighteenth century stressed its torpor and its worldliness. *The English Church in the Eighteenth Century* (1878), an influential and still valuable two-volume tome by Charles Abbey and John Overton, proclaimed that in the eighteenth-century Church of England:

> Long-standing disputes and the old familiar controversies were almost lulled to silence, but in their place a sluggish calm rapidly spread over the Church.... It might seem as if there were a certain heaviness in the English mind, which requires some outward stimulus to keep alive its zeal. For so soon as the press of danger ceased, and party strife abated, with the accession of the House of Brunswick, Christianity began forthwith to slumber.[6]

Their long chapter on "Church Abuses" is concerned with political power, pluralities and nonresidence, excessive love of preferment, chaplains as "hangers-on" in great families, and prejudice against emotionalism. E. P. Thompson claimed that if the Church of England had not been ineffective, then Methodism "would have been neither necessary nor possible."[7] Even a 1989 history of the eighteenth-century Church is entitled *The Church in an Age of Negligence.*[8] Similarly, the universities in the eighteenth century, responsible for the scholarly training of the Church's clergy, have been seen as also torpid and worldly. Everyone remembers Gibbon's famous complaints in his autobiography about the laziness and uselessness of his Oxford teachers and about the clergy's governing Oxford and Cambridge: "The legal incorporation of these societies by the charters of popes and kings had given them a monopoly of the public instruction; and the spirit of monopolists is narrow, lazy and oppressive.... From the toil of reading or thinking or writing they had absolved their conscience."[9]

Nevertheless, much recent historiography has challenged this older picture to argue that the Church of England in the eighteenth century was more spiritually

---

6.    Charles J. Abbey and John H. Overton, *The English Church in the Eighteenth Century*, 2 vols. (London, 1878), 1:2–3.

7.    E. P. Thompson, *Customs in Common* (New York, 1991), 49. See also John H. Overton and Frederick Relton, *The English Church, 1714–1800* (London, 1906); Leonard Elliott-Binns, *The Early English Evangelicals: A Religious and Social Study* (London, 1953); R. H. Tawney, *Religion and the Rise of Capitalism: A Historical Study* (Harmondsworth, England, 1984), 192–96; Robert W. Malcolmson, *Life and Labour in England, 1700–1800* (New York, 1981), 84–85.

8.    Peter Virgin, *The Church in an Age of Negligence: Ecclesiastical Structure and Problems of Church Reform* (Cambridge, 1989). For a critical review arguing that Virgin's view is outdated, see Frances Knight, "The Hanoverian Church in Transition: Some Recent Perspectives," *Historical Journal* 36 (1993): 745–52.

9.    Edward Gibbon, *Memoirs of My Life*, ed. Georges A. Bonnard (London, 1966), 49–54.

and intellectually healthy than historians like Abbey and Overton supposed. Jeremy Gregory joins other recent students of eighteenth-century ecclesiastical history in arguing that church leaders effectively raised standards for clergy, "both in the quality of those ordained, and in the behaviour and attitudes of the parish clergy." Gregory points out that even John Wesley, "usually seen as a stern critic of the eighteenth-century Anglican clergy," recognized this. According to Wesley, "in the present century, the behaviour of the clergy in general is greatly altered for the better.... Most of the Protestant clergy... have not only more learning of the valuable kind, but abundantly more religion."[10]

While politics and patronage certainly influenced clerical appointments and advancements—the Church of England was the state church and some rights to appoint clergy were attached to land ownership—it is now realized that clerical careers in the eighteenth century were significantly determined by talent, application to appropriate tasks, and piety, not merely by birth and family connection. Norman Ravitch, for example, has shown that even Anglican bishops represented "a type of cross-section of the entire literate, educated, and significant population."[11] William Gibson has shown how the older historical account of the eighteenth-century Church was shaped: first by eighteenth-century Evangelicals and dissenters attacking the Church as decadent and corrupt; then by nineteenth-century Whigs, including Thomas Macaulay, who darkened the picture in the name of reform; and lastly by the nineteenth-century Tractarians, with their own very different schemes for reform.[12]

I intend my own look at the relationship between Church of England clergy and women writers to open another chapter in this revisionist historiography of the eighteenth-century church, as well as a chapter in the history of women's writing. I note, looking back now at Gibbon's attack on the clergy of midcentury Oxford, that one of the two examples he gives as the climax of his picture of their utterly foolish ways of spending time is "an half-starved Chaplain, Ballard was his name, who begged Subscriptions for some Memoirs concerning the learned ladies of Great-Britain."[13] One could make useful distinctions between Bluestockings of the Restoration and early eighteenth century and those of the later eighteenth

10.   Jeremy Gregory, *Restoration, Reformation, and Reform, 1660–1828: Archbishops of Canterbury and Their Dioceses* (Oxford, 2000), 100–101.

11.   Norman Ravitch, "The Social Origins of the French and English Bishops in the Eighteenth Century," *Historical Journal* 8 (1965): 324.

12.   William Gibson, *The Achievement of the Anglican Church, 1689–1800: The Confessional State in Eighteenth-Century England* (Lewiston, N.Y., 1995).

13.   Gibbon, *Memoirs*, 52–53. Gibbon was mistaken about Ballard's being a chaplain, although Ballard had been appointed one of the eight clerks of Magdalen.

century, but here I want to focus on similarities between Anglican Bluestocking writers from Astell to More. Much feminist scholarship has, understandably, emphasized ways in which patriarchal religion has repressed women's expression of their innate capacities. But here I want to analyze some ways in which this particular form of patriarchal religion fostered and celebrated women's expression of their intellectual and spiritual capacities. I will also explore some tensions that emerged in these relationships.

∿ ∿

What motivated Church of England clergy to help intellectually ambitious, virtuous women to cultivate their talents and to publish their work? First, and not trivially, pious clergy believed they had a Christian duty of charity. Charity prompted the Rev. Thomas Secker to take the widowed Mrs. Talbot and her child Catherine into his household after his colleague the Rev. Mr. Edward Talbot died. Secker's care for Catherine's education and his continuing the widow and the orphan as members of his household during their lives, his provision not only of material but also of intellectual and spiritual food, quite properly prompted Catherine to write to Elizabeth Carter in 1765 that she lifted up her heart "in serious thankfulness to that Providence which raised up for me, without any degree of relationship, such a parent; and has continued such a blessing from the dawn to the evening of life."[14] Secker's enduring charity toward Catherine Talbot was echoed by similar, if less remarkable, clerical kindnesses to other Bluestocking women—for example, the hospitality John Thomas, bishop of Winchester, offered to his niece Hester Chapone when she became a widow after ten months of marriage.[15]

Residence in or frequent visits to the palace of a learned bishop or archbishop meant access to a steady stream of learned guests and to a significant library. Virginia Woolf's room of one's own may suffice for a woman novelist or poet, but to produce works of more learning a woman needs access to a library. Catherine Talbot's living as a member of the family of Thomas Secker, successively bishop of Bristol, bishop of Oxford, and archbishop of Canterbury, gave her access to his libraries and to his learned clerical guests. More importantly, because Carter's scholarly accomplishments were greater, the friendship between Talbot and Carter allowed Carter access to these same scholarly resources. During the period when Secker was helping Carter with her translation of Epictetus, one is hardly surprised that Carter writes to Talbot expressing gratitude that her friendship

14. *A Series of Letters between Mrs. Elizabeth Carter and Miss Catherine Talbot, from the year 1741 to 1770*, ed. Montagu Pennington, 4 vols. (1807; reprint ed., New York, 1975), 3:130.
15. Myers, *Bluestocking Circle*, 229.

with Talbot has been "a means of introducing me to the acquaintance of a family whose regard I consider as one of the principal advantages of my life;… and from whose superior talents and excellent example I have had the means of so much improvement."[16] The letters of Talbot and Carter record the encouragement and assistance given by Secker and other clerical acquaintances in his circle. For example, while Carter is working on the Epictetus, Talbot sends her "some volumes of stoic philosophy which the Bishop of Norwich has lent me for our service, as he thinks there is the best account given in them of any he has any where met with."[17] John Brewer rightly emphasizes how important Anna Seward's lifelong residence in the Bishop's Palace in Lichfield was to her intellectual development and how the cultural life of this cathedral town and the surrounding towns "centered on the families of clerics and ecclesiastics."[18] Clerical charity of a less personal kind also was a major reason so many clergymen's names appear in the subscription lists of books published by Bluestocking women.

A second, also religious, motive further prompted clerical assistance to Bluestocking women: concern for providing pastoral care for children. Clergy often encouraged women to take special responsibility for the education and catechizing of children. This reflects the Protestant turn away from clerical intermediaries and toward a new emphasis on the responsibility of parents for the religious education of the members of their households. Thus, we find Susanna Wesley, the wife and mother of Church of England clergymen, writing "The Apostles' Creed Explicated in a Letter to her Daughter Susanna" and "A Religious Conference between Mother and Emilia"; these are clearly designed to give her daughters a firm philosophical and theological grounding in the reasons for faith and to protect them from the blandishments of atheism and other heresy. The manuscript "Conference between Mother and Emilia," dated 1711/12, allows the daughter to raise fundamental philosophical questions about natural versus revealed religion and about the role of reason in religion, and even to inquire whether the world could have been made by chance:

> E.… I have heard of a sect of philosophers that believed all things were reduced into the order we now behold them by a 'fortuitous concourse of atoms.' That the various innumerable particles of which this world is composed, being in a vigorous motion, did at last by a lucky hit strike on this goodly system of things. Now, pray, what have you to object against this notion?[19]

16. *Letters between Carter and Talbot*, 2:90, 12 August 1752.
17. Ibid., 2:194, 23 January 1755.
18. Brewer, *Pleasures of the Imagination*, 591.
19. *Susanna Wesley: The Complete Writings*, ed. Charles Wallace Jr. (New York and Oxford, 1997), 430.

The mother replies invoking a range of philosophers and theologians including Nicholas Malebranche, John Norris, and John Locke—all also had been part of Astell's reading.

Encouragement of women's attending to the religious education of their own children developed into encouragement of genteel churchwomen's founding schools to educate poor children. The Sunday School movement—so important both as opening opportunities for literacy to working-class children and as laying a foundation for women's public social activism—was very much a cooperative pastoral project of Church of England clergymen and energetic, pious laywomen, notably Sarah Trimmer and Hannah More. Despite some tendency to associate the Sunday School movement exclusively with the Evangelical revival, support for Sunday Schools "came from across the clerical spectrum."[20] For example, George Horne, dean of Canterbury and a High Churchman, preached a sermon recommending Sunday Schools at Canterbury in 1785, raised money for the cause, and had his own Sunday School at Canterbury.[21] Trimmer was an early activist in the Sunday School movement, founded her own Sunday School, and urged other women to do the same in her *Oeconomy of Charity* (1787). She began her writing career with *An Easy Introduction to the Knowledge of Nature and Reading the Holy Scriptures adapted to the Capacity of Children* (1780), followed by her children's *Sacred History* (1782), and *Abridgement of the Old and New Testaments* (1793), and commentaries on the catechism and Prayer Book. Trimmer applied to have her children's books for charity schools approved and circulated by the church's Society for the Propagation of Christian Knowledge, the SPCK.[22] Her correspondence shows the encouragement she received from Samuel Horsely, bishop of St. David's, her belief that without the support of the SPCK "my schemes will fall to the ground," and her joy at the news of the society's adoption of her books: "I have the greatest reason in the world to believe they will be widely circulated."[23] More's Sunday School activism was supported by many of her clerical friends, including Beilby Porteus, known as sympathetic to the Evangelicals and frequently mentioned as an habitué of Bluestocking salons. As bishop of

20. Gregory, *Restoration, Reformation, and Reform*, 252.

21. Gregory notes the sermon and his general support; ibid., 252–53. A Mrs. Denward in a letter to Trimmer, 1 September 1786, reports that he "has a very large Sunday School at Canterbury, to which he gives vast attention"; *Some Account of the Life and Writings of Mrs. Trimmer with original letters, and meditations and prayers, selected from her Journal*, 3d ed. (London, 1825), 142.

22. Sean Gil, *Women and the Church of England from the Eighteenth Century to the Present* (London, 1994), 51.

23. *Life of Trimmer*, 294, 296, 317.

Chester, Porteus published in 1786 a long letter recommending the establishment of Sunday Schools in his diocese.

With the encouragement of some clergymen, churchwomen also addressed themselves particularly to women on the subjects of women's spiritual and intellectual development. Works ranging from Astell's *Serious Proposal to the Ladies* (1694, 1697) and *The Christian Religion as Profess'd by a Daughter of the Church of England* (1705) through Hester Chapone's *Letters on the Improvement of the Mind* (1773) to Hannah More's *Strictures on the Modern System of Female Education* (1799) all insisted that true religion was the basis for sound knowledge and that women had a religious duty to develop their intellects. Charles Ford has usefully pointed out that More chose to reserve "the womanly penchant for sensibility" for religious feeling and to claim that this "facilitated the teaching of religion to girls." A female instructor of girls was to "interest their feelings, by lively images, and by a warm practical application of what they read to their own hearts and circumstances."[24]

A third reason that Church of England clergy encouraged women intellectuals and writers mixed pastoral concerns with apologetics: clergy wished to exhibit to the world sound models of Anglican female belief and piety. Clergy wrote lives of virtuous women and promoted the publication of their works, including their prayers, devotional meditations, journals, and letters. They intended such models to inspire imitation by other Anglican women. Moreover, they offered them to serve as evidence that the Church of England was an effective Christian church. T. Goodwyn, archdeacon of Oxford, for example, wrote an account of the life of Elizabeth Burnet, wife of Bishop Gilbert Burnet, prefaced to the 1713 edition of her *Method of Devotion, or Rules for Holy and Devout Living*. This life emphasizes Burnet's piety, her serious study of Scripture, and her charity both to the poor and to needy clergymen.[25]

Protestant clergy were well aware of the long tradition of the publication of Roman Catholic saints' lives, including female saints' lives; they considered that this tradition had to be replied to by what amounted to a countertradition of lives and works of exemplary Protestant women. This is perhaps most obvious in the publication of the lives of so-called Methodist women. I say so-called because in the eighteenth century most of these women later claimed by Methodism were actually members of the Church of England, as, of course, were

24. Charles Howard Ford, *Hannah More: A Critical Biography* (New York, 1996), 221. Ford quotes from *Strictures*.
25. Elizabeth Burnet's *Methods of Devotion* was first published in 1708, anonymously. After her death in 1709, it appeared in further editions (1709, 1713, 1738) with her name and the life. In addition to this life, see C. Kinchberger, "Elizabeth Burnet, 1661–1709," *Church Quarterly Review* 148 (April–June 1949 ): 17–51.

Samuel and John Wesley themselves.[26] These Evangelical lives sometimes make explicit reference to published lives of Catholic women saints or Catholic women of extraordinary piety. For example, the introduction to the life of Jane Cooper remarks that the life of Armelle Nicholas, a seventeenth-century Catholic lay-woman known as Armelle the Good, has been widely read, but claims that the life of Cooper offers a superior model for imitation. The introducer to the life of the Protestant Cooper remarks that Armelle had a confessor, a director of her conscience, but "[a]ll here is *genuine*: which I fear is not the case in the account given us of *Armelle*"; in the life of Cooper, the introducer boasts, we will find "no extravagant flights, no mystic reveries, no unscriptural enthusiasm."[27]

Anglican clergy untainted by Methodism also promoted publication of the writing and lives of women they wished to offer as models of Christian virtue and sound doctrine. Early in the century, George Hickes wrote to the Master of University College urging him to support Oxford University Press's publishing Elstob's Anglo-Saxon homilies: "The university hath acquired much reputation and honour at home, and abroad by the Saxon books printed there … the publication of the MSS she hath brought (the most correct I ever saw or read) will be of great advantage to the Church of England against the papists…. and the credit of our country, to which Mrs Elstob will be counted abroad, as great an ornament in her way, as Madam Dacire is to France."[28]

26. At midcentury some warned that the conduct of the Wesleys threatened to produce schism. In the 1780s John engaged in a series of acts that were the beginning of institutional schism, including permitting some registration of chapels and preachers as dissenting under the Toleration Act, permitting Methodist services during the hours of Church of England worship, and ordaining clergy for America and Scotland. It must be remembered, though, that John died in 1791 at the age of eighty-eight insisting that he was still within the Church of England. His ecclesiastical superiors never even attempted to defrock him. An excellent account of the life of Wesley and the development of the movement may be found in Henry D. Rack, *Reasonable Enthusiast: John Wesley and the Rise of Methodism*, 2d ed. (Nashville, Tenn., 1992). A sense of how extensively documented the lives of eighteenth-century evangelical women were may be gained from "Appendix A: Biographical Outlines of Methodist Women Preachers," in Paul Wesley Chilcote, *John Wesley and the Women Preachers of Early Methodism* (Metuchen, N.J., and London, 1991). Further evidence abounds in the bibliographies of the entries for women in Samuel J. Rogal, *A Biographical Dictionary of Eighteenth-Century Methodism*, 10 vols. (Lewiston, Me., 1997–99).
27. *Life of Jane Cooper, of Bristol*, 3d ed. (Bristol, 1770), [iii], iv. Two English translations of Armelle's life went through many editions, the most popular entitled *Daily Conversations with God, exemplified in the holy life of Armelle Nicholas*.
28. George Hickes to Arthur Charlett, 23 December 1712, quoted by David Fairer, "Anglo-Saxon Studies," in *The History of Oxford*, 822. Dacier began life as a Huguenot but had converted to Roman Catholicism. Why Elstob was not as celebrated as Carter was later is a complex question. A general development of media for publicity in the later period is part of the explanation. I think the decline of Anglo-Saxon studies after 1715, described by Fairer, and the deaths in 1715 of both William Elstob and George Hickes, Elstob's intellectually involved champions, were contributing causes.

Similarly, Anglican clergy promoted Talbot and Carter as models of sound Anglican practice and doctrine. The Rev. George Berkeley encouraged Catharine Talbot to compose her *Reflections on the Seven Days of the Week* (pub. 1770). The Rev. Montagu Pennington, Carter's nephew, published many volumes of Carter's correspondence and her *Memoirs*. A letter from Carter to Elizabeth Vesey in 1768, describing Talbot's reaction to the death of Archbishop Secker, offers Talbot as a model of Christian resignation under suffering: "Her behaviour under the present trial is conformable to every other part of her conduct, and worthy of the principles by which she has ever been so uniformly guided. With the weakest health and the quickest sensibility of her loss, she discovers the noblest fortitude and the most unrepining resignation, of which she gives the best, and, during the struggles of recent grief, the most difficult proof, by constantly endeavouring to set every remaining blessing in the most comfortable and cheerful point of view."[29] In an earlier letter to Vesey, in 1766, Carter remarks on the famous quarrel between Hume and Rousseau, commenting on Rousseau: "Natural infirmities of temper are to be treated with tenderness and compassion: but when people work up perverseness into a philosophical system, and contrive to make themselves as troublesome as they possibly can, they forfeit all claim to indulgence, and every encouragement to their unreasonable humours is an injury to society." The Rev. Mr. Pennington cannot resist crowing in a note: "Mrs. Carter seems to have formed a very just idea of Rousseau's character, though she always refused to read his, Voltaire's, or any other works of a similar tendency; which might, she said, do her hurt, and could do her no good. Perhaps it might be well if other persons whose faith and practice were not established upon so firm a foundation as her's had made a similar resolution."[30]

It is worth remarking that the so-called Methodist women's lives often contained long journal extracts and copies of letters written by their subjects and that they were often written or introduced by clergymen. Carter and Talbot may have felt that having their own life-writing published would make them look too much like the Evangelical or Methodist women.

Clergy of all denominations took pleasure in being able to offer accounts of intelligent women who had abandoned other denominations for the superior truth of their own; Church of England clergy were no exceptions. Like Astell herself, the Rev. George Hickes supported better education for women partly on the ground that it would help to root out enthusiasm and schism. In his *A Second Collection of Controversial Letters Relating to the Church of England and the Church*

---

29. *Letters between Carter and Talbot*, 3:347–48, 2 September 1768.
30. Ibid., 3:305, 304, 30 August 1766.

*of Rome* (1710), Hickes proudly published Susanna Hopton's letter to Father Turberville in which she developed her reasons for converting from Roman Catholicism to the Church of England. Addressing the book to a lady who has been unsettled in her own religious belief, Hickes expresses a hope that the publication of Hopson's reasons "may have good Effect upon all those of her Sex, who are so ready to be drawn away by the subtle Artifices, the Slight, and Craftiness of the Roman Missiners."[31]

Goodwyn's life of Elizabeth Berkeley Burnet, previously mentioned, gains suspense when the young Elizabeth is married at seventeen to Robert Berkeley and goes to live with his mother, "a zealous Papist." Elizabeth turns to the study of "the Controversy between our Church and the Church of Rome, so that she might be able to preserve her Husband, and her self, from the Artifices and Insinuations of the Popish Priests, and the Influence of his Mother, who had great Interest in him." When Catholicism later tempts her husband in James II's reign, she persuades him to go on a tour of Holland. His family provides her with letters of introduction on the Continent, recommending her "as one, that had she been, as they call it, of the Catholick Church, her Piety and Virtue were great enough to entitle her to the Character of a Saint."[32]

✧ ✧

It seems to be the case that women religious writers were more likely than male religious writers to avoid doctrinal controversies; however, especially in light of the new emphasis on the greater intellectual and theological activity in the eighteenth-century Church, more investigation of this would be worthwhile.

31. George Hickes, *A Second collection of Controversial Letters Relating to the Church of England and the Church of Rome, As they passed between an Honourable Lady, and Dr. George Hickes. To which is added, A Letter by a Gentlewoman of Quality to a Romish Priest upon her Return to the Church of Rome to the Church of England* (London, 1710), "Dedicatory Epistle," viii; "The Eighteenth Century" (Research Publications, Woodbridge, Conn.), microfilm; reel 432, no. 16. On Hopton, see also Gladys I. Wade, "Mrs. Susanna Hopton," *English Review* 62 (1936): 41–46; and Julia I. Smith, "Susanna Hopton: A Biographical Account," *Notes and Queries* 38 (June 1991): 165–72. Catherine Trotter sent a copy of her *Defence of Mr. Locke's Essay on Human Understanding* to Burnet. The Locke-Burnet correspondence shows Burnet's distress that Trotter was apparently then still a Roman Catholic, her surprise that someone so rational "can be of a religion that puts such shackles on the exercise of thought and reason," and her asking Locke to make an effort to free Trotter from her theological errors. That, writes Burnet, would be "a kindness in itself," and "make her more capable of the assistence and encouragement of her friends"; Burnet to Locke, 20 June 1702, *The Correspondence of John Locke*, ed. E. S. de Beer, 8 vols. (Oxford, 1976–89), 7:638.

32. T. Goodwyn, "An Account of the Life and Character of the Author," in Elizabeth Burnett, *Method of Devotion, or rules for Holy and Devout Living* (London, 1709), viii; "Eighteenth Century," reel 4104, no. 8; quotations at vi and vii.

Clergymen, of course, had a professional obligation to defend their doctrines, an obligation from which laywomen were free. Much of the hagiographic writing about pious women stresses that they avoided theological controversy, and women writers themselves often claimed to eschew speculative theology for practical piety. Yet serious study of religion and firm adherence to well-understood principles of one theological camp could easily lead to controversy. The recent discovery that Susannah Wesley was the author of *Some Remarks on a Letter From the Rev. Mr. Whitefield To the Rev. Mr. Wesley, In a Letter from a Gentlewoman to her Friend* (1741) makes one wonder how many other women came forth as proxy champions of particular doctrinal positions. In this pamphlet, her only work published during her lifetime, Wesley attacks Whitefield's Calvinism. She shows herself quite able to attack Calvin himself and to quote the *Institutes*, arguing that if predestination were true, then "preaching the Gospel" would be "a cruel ordinance": "if, as Calvin says, 'God speaketh by his Ministers to Reprobates that they may be deafer; he gives Light to them that they may be the blinder; he offers Instruction to them that they may be the more ignorant; and uses the Remedy that they may not be healed,' what good man would not rather choose to be a hangman than a minister of the gospel?" Commenting on the persona Wesley adopts for this pamphlet, her recent editor Charles Wallace observes: "In *Some Remarks* she is, if not licensed to kill, at least authorized as a controversialist, expected to make trenchant points against an opponent; and this she clearly enjoys."[33] Judith Hawley, in her recent edition, agrees with the attribution to Elizabeth Carter of an anonymous pamphlet on a doctrinal dispute, *Remarks on the Athanasian Creed; on a Sermon Preached to the Parish Church of Deal, Oct. 15, 1752*.[34] Just as Wesley supported her husband in a doctrinal dispute, so Carter supported her father.

With more indirection, Talbot and Carter write against the supposed errors of the Evangelicals and Methodists, who they think have revived and elaborated upon the theological errors of the Puritans. Gently, in *Reflections on the Seven Days of the Week*, Talbot diagnoses, pities, and implicitly rebukes the errors of the overly zealous:

> Another Sort of People, much to be esteemed, and greatly to be pitied, are scrupulous about every Thing; and frighted by a Misapprehension of some alarming Texts, dare not allow themselves the most innocent Conveniences, and most harmless, and on many accounts useful and commendable Pleasures. Their minds are

33. Wesley, *Complete Writings,* 469; Wallace, in Wesley, *Complete Writings,* 462.
34. *Bluestocking Feminism,* 2:409.

so truly pious, that they are far from deliberately thinking of the infinitely great and good God, as a hard and rigid Master: But they act with such a slavish Fear, as must needs make those, who are less well disposed, frame such horrible false Imaginations of Him; and their well meant Strictness is the most dangerous Tendency in the World.[35]

Talbot's *Rambler* 30 on Sunday and Carter's *Rambler* 140, pitting gloomy Superstition against a more rational and cheerful Religion, similarly offer covert apologetics for the kind of Anglicanism approved of by their circle.

Twentieth-century feminist scholars were often struck, as I noted earlier, by a sense of how patriarchal authority limited the ambitions of women writers and inhibited them from seeking publication. Sylvia Myers makes this a theme of her analysis of the relationship between Secker and Talbot, agreeing with Susanna Duncombe that Talbot "was awed by the deference she paid" to Secker.[36] Yet I would argue that some of these clergy, including Secker, used their patriarchal authority to overcome women writers' diffidence. The positive urging of a bishop or an archbishop, after all, conveniently trumps scruples that a diffident Anglican woman might have about publication, and these clergy were forthcoming with expressions of their own wishes that the women publish. I doubt Carter would have completed a translation of the works of Epictetus without the stimulus and support of Secker and his circle; I am surer that she would not have published *All the Works of Epictetus* in the absence of Secker's and Nicholas Carter's urging and without the practical assistance of Secker and his circle. Carter refused to solicit subscriptions for the publication, but Secker and other clergy very effectively bestirred themselves for this purpose.[37] Less retiring than Talbot or Carter, Hannah More nevertheless regales her correspondents with constant news that one or the other of her distinguished clerical friends is pressing her to publish something she has in manuscript, urging her to wield her pen in the cause of

35. Catherine Talbot, *Reflections on the Seven Days of the Week* (London, 1770), 38–39; "Eighteenth Century," reel 11699, no. 9.

36. Myers, *Bluestocking Circle*, 228. Talbot's most recent editor, Rhoda Zuk, agrees in finding Talbot's "excessive diffidence" in part a consequence of "a subtle and complex quasi-filial relationship" with Secker; *Bluestocking Feminism*, 3:4. Susanna was the wife of John Duncombe, author of *The Feminiad* (1754), a poem praising virtuous women writers. He was an Anglican clergyman who went on to be vicar of Horne in Kent and one of the six preachers at Canterbury Cathedral.

37. The *Letters between Carter and Talbot* give some account of the history of composition and publication, but a fuller account appears in Montagu Pennington, *Memoirs of the Life of Mrs. Elizabeth Carter,* 4th ed., 2 vols. (1825; reprint ed., New York, 1974). Because Talbot's letters communicate to Carter suggestions from Secker, from herself, and perhaps from others (and include enclosures from Secker that have not survived), there is ambiguity about the extent to which Carter was resisting Secker or Talbot. I read more of these suggestions as Secker's, rather than as Talbot's own, than Hawley does.

virtue and religion, or warmly congratulating her on having done so. In 1781, for example, an eager More writes to her sister: "Mrs. Kennicott tells me Bishop Lowth insists upon my publishing 'Sensibility,' and all my other poems together, immediately, that people may have them all together."[38]

The relationship between these Church of England clergy and these Bluestocking writers was one of mutual promotion, mutual patronage. On the one hand, the clergy assisted the women and promoted their work; on the others, the women praised the clergy and studied and promoted their work, including their books. Deprecating the light reading of novels and empty entertainments like cards, Bluestocking women characteristically advocated that other women also study religious and improving books, often books written by Church of England clergy. Astell in *A Serious Proposal* sends women to read the Rev. Mr. Norris, More in *Strictures* instructs them to study Bishop Joseph Butler's *Analogy of Religion, Natural, and Revealed, to the Constitution and Course of Nature*. Each number of Trimmer's *Family Magazine* contained an abridged sermon, usually one by "some learned Divine of the Church of England."[39]

~ ~

To summarize the argument so far, Church of England clergy assisted Bluestocking writers because they were charitable, because they saw ways that these women could assist in pastoral efforts, and because they wanted to offer models of Anglican female piety and learning that were worthy of imitation and that would enhance the reputation of the Anglican Church. These clergymen and these Bluestocking writers engaged in mutual patronage. Yet relations between clergymen and such women could become tense, even explosive. Let us now turn to a consideration of some of the sources of such tensions.

Perhaps most obviously, high-minded intellectual and spiritual relationships between male clergymen and women writers could become suffused with eros and degenerate into illicit love affairs. Although this was a favorite topos of satirists and, especially, became a cliché of attacks on the Methodists, it seems to have happened with perhaps surprising infrequence. One notable instance of an alleged *amour* between a Church of England clergyman and a Bluestocking woman writer—herself not an Anglican—is worth brief consideration: the relationship between the Rev. Thomas Wilson, son of the Bishop of Sodor and Mann

---

38.  "More to one of her Sisters," Roberts, *Memoirs of More,* 1:123. Anne Kennicott, who learned Hebrew to assist her husband, may be considered a Bluestocking herself.
39.  *Life of Trimmer,* 55–56.

and rector of a church in Bath, and Catharine Macaulay. Eight years after the death of her first husband, Macaulay accepted Mr. Wilson's invitation that she and her daughter move into his house in Bath and that she use his extensive library. At this time, Macaulay was forty-five and Wilson seventy-three, which perhaps explains why they seem to have thought this living arrangement immune from criticism. Unusually for an Anglican vicar, Wilson was a supporter of Macaulay's radical politics; he was one of the founding members of the Society of the Supporters of the Bill of Rights. While living with Wilson, Macaulay published the first volume of her *History of England from the Revolution to the Present Time in a Series of Letters to a Friend* (1778), the friend being the Rev. Mr. Wilson. Wilson famously—or infamously—celebrated Macaulay's accomplishments as an historian on her forty-sixth birthday with the ringing of bells, six odes read aloud to her by six gentlemen, and his presentation to her of "'a large and curious gold medal … accompanied with a speech strongly expressive of her merit, and of his friendship and veneration.'"[40]

The extravagance of the Rev. Mr. Wilson's devotion and Macaulay's apparent acceptance of it made her ridiculous to many, including other clergy friends. One of them, the Rev. Augustus Toplady, hearing of the event from the Rev. Dr. Baker, observed that it "contributed to reduce my opinion of her magnanimity and good sense." "Such contemptible vanity," he thought, "and such childish affectation of mock majesty, would have disgraced a much inferior understanding."[41] Not long after, Wilson commissioned and erected a marble statue of Macaulay, represented as Clio, a pen in her hand, leaning on five volumes of her *History of England*. He placed it in the chancel of his church. Although Macaulay appears not to have fallen in love with the Rev. Mr. Wilson, he does seem to have felt something very like love for her. Perhaps also, as Toplady observed when he wrote to warn her that she should avoid behavior apt to attract the notice of the malicious, Wilson desired to "derive luster" from his association with Macaulay. Once Macaulay left Wilson's house and married Dr. Graham, Wilson behaved like a spurned lover and excoriated her. Satirists rejoicing in the scandal of the middle-aged widow marrying the young Graham vacillated between suggesting that Wilson was too feeble sexually to hold onto a woman so lusty and claiming that he was "one of those gay old gentlemen, who, the older they grow, the more wicked they are."[42] Perhaps grown a trifle senile, Wilson provoked scandal by

40.  Quoted in Bridget Hill, *The Republican Virago: The Life and Times of Catharine Macaulay, Historian* (Oxford, 1992), 95.
41.  Quoted ibid., 97.
42.  Quoted ibid., 116–17.

demonstrating so publicly his admiration for Macaulay in a language suffused with a rhetoric of courtly love, not to say idolatry. He thus abandoned what was supposed to be the superior position of a Church of England clergyman in a relationship with a woman, however learned or accomplished. This was an error soberer divines such as Archbishop Secker or Bishop Porteus did not make.[43]

Yet, even absent the disruptive power of eros, relationships between Church of England clergy and Bluestocking women could be tense. Problems arose because the clergy encouraged women to study seriously and even, sometimes, to publish. For example, as mentioned above, Archbishop Secker strongly encouraged Elizabeth Carter to translate Epictetus, assisted her with cruxes in the translation, and then very strongly encouraged her to publish *All the Works of Epictetus*. One of his reasons for so doing was that he wanted the world to see that England could produce a woman of as much learning as Madame Dacier. Yet Secker and Carter did not entirely agree. The archbishop and Catherine Talbot pressed Carter to use her *Epictetus* as an occasion for displaying the superiority of Christianity to pagan stoicism, suggesting that she use parallel passages "chosen and made in such a manner as evidently to manifest that superiority of divine to human, which so many, alas, are endeavouring as fast as they can to forget."[44] Resisting one of the suggested notes, Carter replies: "I find myself obliged sometimes in mere charity to undertake the cause of the poor heathen against you, upon whom, I think, you are in general too severe.... In general I believe it is scarcely ever of any use, and perhaps very seldom right, to depreciate the heathen morality."[45]

When women were encouraged to study the Bible and Christian doctrine, to take a degree of independent responsibility for their religious principles, and to perform active works of charity, it was inevitable that they would sometimes be in conflict with the male ministers of the established Church. The common eighteenth-century view that Evangelicalism and Methodism were reincarnations of seventeenth-century Puritanism and that they had similar potential for producing unruly women, prophetesses, heretics, schism, and even civil war was not without some justification. Although Protestant prophetesses are most frequently

---

43.  More was aware that clerical enthusiasm over her talent might prove embarrassing. In 1781 she worried that publication of Lowth's Latin poem celebrating her would make her look ridiculous and presuming (Roberts, *Memoirs of More,* 1:119–20). Peter Pindar did mock the warmth of Porteus's enthusiasm for More in "Nil admirari; or a smile at a bishop; occasioned by an hyperbolical eulogy on Miss Hannah More."
44.  *Letters between Carter and Talbot,* 2:211, 29 November 1755. Talbot refers to an enclosed copy of Secker's remarks, not printed.
45.  Ibid., 2:228–29, 3 May 1756.

associated with the period of the Civil War, at least two remarkable prophetesses appeared in the Church of England during the Restoration and eighteenth century, Jane Lead (1624–1703) and Joanna Southcott (1750–1814). Both were simple women, barely literate, lacking the gentility and education of women writers we usually think of as Bluestockings. Alarmingly, from the perspective of the Anglican establishment, Lead nevertheless drew Frances Lee, an Oxford clergyman and fellow, into her movement; he became her scribe.[46] The real fear, however, was not that pious Anglican women would turn into prophetesses but that they would succumb to the errors of Roman Catholicism or, increasingly as the eighteenth century went on, to "enthusiasm."

When an educated Anglican woman believed that she had carefully arrived at a religious position and that she had a religious duty to maintain that position, she might think herself obliged to maintain it despite clerical objections. Although Anglican women from Astell to Wesley to More wrote fervently of the duty to obedience, they qualified that duty with Protestant caveats. Astell insisted that women do not owe blind obedience to ecclesiastical authority and that God "has not only allow'd, but requir'd" women to judge for themselves.[47] She regularly wrote against the positions of Church of England clergymen she considered in error, for example in her attack on the politics of Bishop White Kennett's sermon, *A Compassionate Enquiry into the Causes of the Civil War.*[48]

Susanna Wesley challenged the authority not only of Whitefield but also of the Church of England clergyman who was her own husband. Both Susanna and her husband, the Rev. Samuel Wesley, began life as dissenters, then converted to the Church of England. Samuel conducted the sort of laymen's meetings that had been introduced into the Church of England, then Susannah transformed them into more public meetings that foreshadowed the Methodist classes and field preaching later authorized by Charles and John. Susanna's meetings, attended by over two hundred people, were a source of tension between her and her husband. She wrote to him that she would cease if he ordered her to do so, but wrote in such a way that he determined to acquiesce: "If you do after all think fit to dissolve this assembly, do not tell me any more that you desire me to

---

46. See Catherine Smith, "Jane Lead: Mysticism and the Woman Clothed in the Sun," in Sandra M. Gilbert and Susan Gubar, eds., *Shakespeare's Sisters: Feminist Essays on Women Poets* (Bloomington, Ind., 1979), 3–18.

47. Mary Astell, *The Christian Religion as Profess'd by a Daughter of the Church of England* (London, 1705), 3, 36; American Theological Library Microfiche at Harvard-Andover Divinity School.

48. One of Astell's principal targets in *The Christian Religion* is a book entitled *The Lady's Religion*, published as by a "Divine of the Church of England" (1697). Astell's attack on Kennett's sermon was *An Impartial Enquiry into the Causes of Rebellion and Civil War in this Kingdom* (London, 1704).

do it, for that will not satisfy my conscience; but send me your positive command, and in such full and express terms as may absolve me from all guilt and punishment for neglecting this opportunity of doing good to souls, when you and I shall appear before the great and awful tribunal of our Lord Jesus Christ."[49]

Mary Bosanquet, a well-educated Anglican gentlewoman, underwent an Evangelical conversion in 1762 and left her wealthy family to live a life of Christian charity to the poor. She was part of John Wesley's connection; many letters between them survive. In 1766 she published *Jesus, altogether Lovely*. Considering obedience, she instructs the women she addresses that they owe "a willing and ready Submission to the directions, or desires of those, who are in authority over us," but immediately adds the caveat, "as far as the light of God in our own souls does not contradict."[50] Although Wesley recognized his mother as having had an authentic calling, he did not at first approve of women's preaching. Nevertheless, in June 1771 Bosanquet persuaded him that she and selected other women should be authorized to preach. In a famous letter to John Wesley, Bosanquet agreed that women ought not to "teach... by usurping authority" nor "meddle in Church discipline," yet she argued that a woman might nevertheless "entreat sinners to come to Jesus" and say, "Come, and I will tell you what God hath done for my soul." Bosanquet's biblical hermeneutics are not too far from the Quaker Margaret Fell's in *Women's Speaking Justified*, although Bosanquet relies a bit more on logical argument. Bosanquet casts part of her letter to Wesley in the form of objections made to women's preaching, to which she then responds.

> Obj.... will not some improper woman follow your example?
>
> An. This I acknowledge I have feared; but the same might be said of preachers that come out, will not some improper man follow them?
>
> Obj. But if an improper man comes out, the Church has power to stop his mouth, but you will not let yours be stopped.
>
> A. Yes, on the same condition I will. You would not say to him, no *man* must speak, therefore be silent; but only, *You* are not the proper man.[51]

49. Wesley, *Complete Writings*, 13.
50. Mary Bosanquet, *Jesus, altogether Lovely; Or, a letter to some of the single women in the Methodist Society* (Bristol, 1766), 10. "Eighteenth Century," reel 3960, no. 7.
51. Appendix D in Chilcote, *Women Preachers*, 301, 302.

With Wesley's support, Bosanquet then preached publicly; in September 1776 she spoke on the text "The Lord is our Judge, the Lord is our Lawgiver, the Lord is our King, he will save us" to an outdoor congregation apparently numbering between two and three thousand.

Sometimes Church of England clergy looked to women of wealth and high social class for patronage. The eighteenth century was the age of the fashionable sermon and the "fashionable public service attended by elite families"; the attention of elite women could help advance a clerical career.[52] But a relationship in which a woman was the patron and the clergyman the client could also be treacherous. In such a relationship, class threatened to trump both gender and ordained religious authority.

The most important example of an aristocratic woman patron of Church of England clergy who turned out to be impossible for the clergy to control is probably the countess of Huntingdon. The countess was an important source of funds for Evangelical clergy and, under her patronage, Whitefield gained importance by preaching to the aristocracy "at her famous 'spiritual routs.'"[53] In the early days of her conversion to Evangelicalism, she was influenced by John Wesley, who continued to try to treat her with tact. As the widow of a peer, Lady Huntingdon could legally appoint chaplains of her own; she used these appointments to advance and to protect Evangelical Church of England clergy. In 1768 she established a new college in Wales for the training of preachers, inviting the Rev. John Fletcher, ordained in the Church of England, to be its superintendent, and intending its graduates to supply more clergy for the Church.[54] Not wishing to promote schism, she disowned a group of her Dublin followers when they showed signs of becoming Independents.

Nevertheless, London Evangelicals in the countess's connection provoked a crisis in 1777 when they bought a former theater in Clerkenwell and opened it as Spitalfield's Chapel. Lady Huntingdon did not consider herself a dissenter and did not want to register this chapel as a dissenting chapel. All over the country, Evangelicals were worshipping in new chapels that they did not consider dissenting chapels and hence did not register under the provisions of the Toleration Act. Some clergy, including Bishop Porteus, were sympathetic in the 1770s to the old pre–Act of Uniformity dream of a comprehensive Protestant Church of England. Far from being eager to clamp down on possible instances of Anglican

52. William Gibson, *A Social History of the Domestic Chaplain, 1530–1840* (London and Washington, 1997), 178.
53. Rack, *Reasonable Enthusiast,* 165.
54. Fletcher accepted, but he never left the church. He married Bosanquet, they became virtually co-pastors, and she preached and ministered for many years after his death.

Evangelicalism turning into dissent, some liberal clergy were supporting petitions to Parliament to drop the requirement of subscription to the Thirty-nine Articles as a requirement for admission to Oxford or Cambridge.[55] But how comprehensive the Church ought to be and how vigorously it should pursue its legal prerogatives were contested matters in the 1770s. The London rector of the parish in which Spitalfield's Chapel lay sued Lady Huntingdon in the courts and forced her to decide whether to close the chapel or to declare it a dissenting chapel. She chose to register it as a dissenting chapel in 1782, formally left the Church of England in 1783, and also in 1783 allowed her preachers to ordain laymen. She thus became the leader of a new dissenting sect. For the many Englishmen who believed that women were peculiarly subject to religious enthusiasm and peculiarly likely to become lost in heresy if not properly directed by male learning and reason, Lady Huntingdon's career fulfilled their worst nightmares of what might happen when religious women decided to become their own ultimate authorities.

Eighteenth-century Anglican clergymen were, of course, committed to maintaining an ecclesiastical order in which women were supposed to lack the capacity to perform as ordained priests; yet clerical encouragement of women's serious and thoughtful engagement with religion threatened to blur the line between the capacities of ordained men and the capacities of laywomen. The women of the Bowdler family, most notably Elizabeth Stuart Bowdler, offer interesting examples of this. Elizabeth Bowdler, who probably knew Hebrew, published in 1779 a translation of the Song of Solomon with a commentary, then in 1787 published, anonymously, her *Practical Observations on the Book of Revelation*. The *Monthly Review* thought the author of *Practical Observations* was a "man of sense, who had an acquaintance with his subject."[56] Given the problematic intelligibility of *Revelation*, it offers formidable challenges to any commentator; the idea of "practical observations" on *Revelation* initially seems oxymoronic. Bowdler begins by insisting that while some books of the Bible may be of more general use

55.  V. H. H. Green, "Religion in the Colleges," in *History of Oxford*, 465–66. See also B. W. Young, "'Subscribe or Starve': The Subscription Controversy and its Consequences," *Religion and Enlightenment in Eighteenth-Century England: Theological Debate from Locke to Burke* (Oxford, 1998), chap. 2, 45–80. Porteus's chaplain and biographer is concerned to insist that Porteus did not sign a petition against subscription but acknowledges that his efforts to revise the articles, especially the one on predestination, were attempts "to diminish schism and separation by bringing over to the National Church all the moderate and well-disposed of other persuasions"; the Right Rev. Robert Hodgson, *The Works of the Right Reverend Beilby Porteus, D.D.... With his Life*, 6 vols. (London, 1816), 1:40.

56.  Janet Todd, ed., *A Dictionary of British and American Women Writers: 1660–1800* (Totawa, N.J., 1985), s.v. "Bowdler, Elizabeth Stuart."

than *Revelation*, no book of the Bible ought to be considered useless to any Christian: "It is not sufficient reason for neglecting any part of scripture to say we do not fully understand it."[57] She devotes over one hundred pages of her book to a patient, historicist, close-reading that attempts to establish the literal sense of *Revelation*. While she refers explicitly to a seventeenth-century Latin commentator on *Revelation*, Joseph Mede, rather than to the more recent scholarship of Kennicott and her contemporaries, Bowdler has grasped something of the modern method of biblical scholarship. "I am … inquiring," she writes, "as an antiquarian might do, into an ancient writing, and by comparing it with itself, and with other books of the same age, am endeavouring to fix the literal sense, the relation of the parts to each other, and the meaning of its peculiar expressions."[58] This approach leads her to reject as historically spurious an established Protestant interpretation of the Beast as the Church of Rome and other Protestant interpretations of the two witnesses as Calvin and Luther. She makes her allegiance to the Church of England clear, but she will not accept Protestant readings uncritically. Many Protestant commentators, she points out, seem to ignore the fact that "the scene of action" in *Revelation* is the Roman Empire of St. John's period. The "practical applications" of her reading stress the need for vigilance against apostasy and for courage in the face of religious persecution. Elizabeth's daughter, Henrietta Maria, published, anonymously, *Sermons on the Doctrines and Duties of Christianity* (1801). According to the *Gentleman's Magazine*, Bishop Porteus was so impressed with these *Sermons* that he offered their author, through the publisher, a living in his diocese.[59]

A demonstration of women's capacity to perform the intellectual work of clergymen by publishing scriptural commentary or sermons might blur the line between the capacities of laywomen and university-educated clergy, yet it seems to me that women's religious practices were more profoundly threatening to the gender hierarchy of the church than was women's religious writing. Anglican Bluestockings liked to claim that they confined themselves to the humbler spheres of practice and forbore meddling with theology and theory, but critics often found this a distinction without a difference. And their claims of religious duty

---

57. Elizabeth Bowdler, *Practical Observations on the Revelation of St. John. Written in the Year 1775. By the late Mrs. Bowdler* (Bath, 1800); "Eighteenth Century," reel 2781, no. 9. This edition is edited by a woman, probably by her daughter Henrietta Maria. The preface quotes Elizabeth's ingenious, if tortuous, defense of having cultivated her biblical learning and writing on the ground that her duty as a mother required it. I have not been able to see a copy of the 1787 edition.

58. Ibid., 39.

59. *Gentleman's Magazine*, n.s., 23 (1830), pt. 1, p. 567.

to act were harder to resist than Wollstonecraft's rights claims. As Harriet Guest has shown, Carter's religion made available to her a "sense of social duty" that overrode "the modesty appropriate to femininity."[60] A similar religious belief that led to action animated Susanna Wesley, Lady Huntingdon, and Hannah More. When More hired Sunday School teachers and set school curricula, she provoked reaction from clergymen who considered, not unreasonably, that a woman was taking over some of their clerical functions.

It is instructive to compare the careers of Lady Huntingdon and Hannah More. Both arrived at a crisis when they engaged in practices construable as fostering unlicensed conventicles, Lady Huntingdon with the Spitalfield's Chapel, More in the Blagdon controversy. Charlotte Yonge, the nineteenth-century novelist and imitator of More, author of a biography of More, saw that More and her Sunday School teachers were publicly appearing as successful rivals to the local clergy, women who as pastors outdid the licensed incumbents. Yonge rather glories in this. She lets More narrate the opening of a new Mendip School that attracts 170 pupils, "many [of them] thieves," some "tried at the last assizes": "and when the clergyman, a hard man, who is also the magistrate, saw these creatures kneeling around us, whom he had seldom seen but to commit or punish in some way, he burst into tears."[61] At the funeral of Mrs. Baker, the Mores' principal schoolmistress, hundreds followed her to the grave. The clergyman's sermon, More's sister relates, "was affecting and bold; as a proof of the latter, though the vicar was there and he himself was curate, he said, with an emphasis in his voice and a firmness in his look, "'This eminent Christian first taught salvation in Cheddar.'"[62] It should not be surprising that the Rev. Thomas Bere, curate at Blagdon and a justice of the peace, charged More's schoolmaster with running an

60. Harriet Guest, *Small Change: Women, Learning, Patriotism, 1750–1810* (Chicago, 2000), 146.
61. Charlotte Yonge, *Hannah More* (Boston, 1888), 112. Useful studies of the Blagdon controversy include Mitzi Myers, "'A Peculiar Protection': Hannah More and the Cultural Politics of the Blagdon Controversy," in Beth Fowkes Tobin, ed., *History, Gender, and Eighteenth-Century Literature* (Athens, Ga., 1994), 227–57, stressing More's behind-the-scenes activism, including her giving suggestions to friendly clergy who lobbied and wrote on her behalf; chap. 5 of Ford, *Hannah More*; and chap. 5 of Patricia Demars, *The World of Hannah More* (Lexington, Ky., 1996). Yonge does not give her source for this quotation, but a recent study by Ann Stott reveals it to be a letter from More to Wilberforce, 14 October 1795. Stott gives a refined account of the Blagdon controversy focused on differences within the Church over theology and ecclesiology. Developing Myers's point, she argues that More ultimately survived the Blagdon ordeal "less because of the 'secret influence' wielded by her Evangelical friends (though they used such influence as they had as effectively as they could) than because her enemies failed to enlist the main body of High Churchmen to their side." They failed, Stott reasonably contends, because More had earlier built effective alliances with High Churchmen as well; "Hannah More and the Blagdon Controversy," *Journal of Ecclesiastical History* 51 (2001): 319–46 at 321.
62. Yonge, *More*, 137.

unlicensed conventicle or that More got called a "Bishop in Petticoats" or "the Imperial Juno of Methodism."

Here I cannot hope to do much more than suggest that all those bishops and clergymen in attendance at Bluestocking routs were more than mere ornamental wallpaper, that they are worth careful study. The very fact that so much Bluestocking writing has been transmitted to us by Anglican clergymen acting as editors and biographers has helped me to make my case, since they were eager to highlight the importance of these relationships. If we were more able to see original Bluestocking documents before this editorial intervention, I suspect we would see more intellectualism and perhaps more signs of the tensions I have described. On the one hand, the Anglican clergy bestowed on Bluestocking women many kindnesses, much respectful attention, and encouragement to take up lives of serious thought and vigorous practical Christian action. Such attentiveness—not only because of the prestige attached to it but also because of its intrinsic value— more closely bound women like Astell, Elstob, Carter, Talbot, Trimmer, and More to the Church. It thus, ironically, contributed to maintaining the Church's gender hierarchy. The closer contact they enjoyed with learned divines like Seeker, Kennicott, and Lowth also made evident to most of these women that there was a real difference between the divines' professional learning and their own amateurism, again reinforcing the hierarchy. On the other hand, the degree of spiritual and intellectual autonomy that this version of Protestantism encouraged in Bluestocking women could challenge hierarchy, as we have seen it did in significant ways in Susanna Wesley, Mary Bosanquet, Lady Huntingdon, and Hannah More. In the case of Lady Huntingdon, it produced schism; in the case of More, negotiated accommodation. In our own lifetimes, the Church of England at last agreed to the ordination of women themselves as clergy. Susanna Wesley and Mary Bosanquet would no doubt rejoice. And, I like to believe, even the conservative Elizabeth Carter would not now object.

*Brandeis University*

# Clara Reeve, Provincial Bluestocking: From the Old Whigs to the Modern Liberal State

— Gary Kelly

As far as we know, Clara Reeve (1729–1807) had no direct contact with the Bluestocking circle. Reeve was not a Bluestocking in the sense that the term first conveyed in the 1750s and 1760s and still does when capitalized—that is, belonging to the social network of the original Bluestockings led by Elizabeth Montagu and her friends from about 1750 to the 1790s.[1] She was, however, a bluestocking in the sense the term acquired by the 1790s when uncapitalized—a literary or learned woman. Literary she certainly was, publishing at least twenty-four volumes over thirty-three years. Learned she also was, being knowledgeable in music, science, Latin, history, political theory, and belles-lettres. Reeve was a near contemporary of the "Bluestocking ladies" of Montagu's circle and may be regarded as parallel to but apart from them. Like some of her other contemporaries, such as Anna Seward, Reeve was rooted in provincial life, but unlike Seward and the Bluestockings such as Elizabeth Carter and Sarah Scott who lived mostly outside London, Reeve had few and tenuous connections with the metropolitan literary and intellectual world, let alone with the wealthy and fashionable world of Montagu's Portman Square and London's West End. In fact, since "provincial" meant "not of the capital," and hence "countrified" and "lacking the culture or polish of the capital"—the second sense emerging during Reeve's lifetime—the phrase "provincial Bluestocking" might seem an oxymoron. Nevertheless, in this essay I will argue that Reeve was a Bluestocking with specifically provincial experience, viewpoint, and politics, and that these gave her much in common with the metropolitan Bluestockings.

Who the Bluestockings were has long been known, although fully described only recently.[2] Who Clara Reeve was has long been obscure, though more has

---

1. These definitions adapted from the *Oxford English Dictionary*.
2. See, for example, Sylvia Harcstark Myers, *The Bluestocking Circle: Women, Friendship, and the Life of the Mind in Eighteenth-Century England* (Oxford, 1990); and Harriet Guest, *Small Change: Women, Learning, Patriotism, 1750–1810* (Chicago and London, 2000).

☙ 105

been discovered recently.[3] She was born in 1729 in Ipswich, Suffolk, about seventy miles from London. She was proud of these provincial roots and boasted to Joseph Cooper Walker that her family had resided there for "several Centuries" and "been free Burgesses ever since the first Charter."[4] This charter was granted in 1200 by King John, who also granted the Magna Charta of 1215, celebrated by classical republicans and "old Whigs" as a milestone in Britain's constitutional development. Until the Municipal Reform Act of 1835, "burgess" was an official title in certain towns, indicating a magistrate or member of the borough's governing body. In many places, the burgesses were also those with the right to vote for the borough's representatives in Parliament—Ipswich elected two. Historians with Reeve's political views accorded these burgesses a leading role in the "progress" from feudalism to modernity, and from monarchic tyranny to the "liberties" that supposedly distinguished Britain from other nations. The burgesses were the core of what later became the bourgeoisie—the middle classes who everywhere founded modern constitutional states in the nineteenth and twentieth centuries. In Reeve's day, however, these middle classes were divided into two broad groups: the professions, led by the "learned" professions of the clergy, law, and medicine; and the commercial and manufacturing middle class, or those in "trade." The former were considered genteel; the latter, no matter how wealthy, were generally considered to be respectable but not genteel.

Reeve's parents came from upper echelons of both groups. Her father, William, was rector of Freston, just south of Ipswich, and of Kerton in Suffolk and perpetual curate of St. Nicholas, Ipswich. Reeve's maternal grandfather was at the pinnacle of "tradesmen" as goldsmith and jeweler to King George I. Reeve's brothers were educated for professions; one became a clergyman and another went into the navy, a profession famously open to merit at that time. Because they were practitioners of intellectual service industries, their incomes ceased or became greatly diminished upon retirement or death. This may have been so with William Reeve, for after his death in 1755 his widow moved to the nearby genteel market town of Colchester, Essex, with three daughters, including Clara, though the sisters later moved back to Ipswich. From statements in her published works and her letters, it seems that Clara took up writing from an early age, but her family disapproved of her publishing, according to a reference in her first book, *Poems* (1769), and much later she told Walker that her "own family" were

3.  For more detail, see my entry on Reeve in the forthcoming *New Dictionary of National Biography*.
4.  Clara Reeve to Joseph Cooper Walker, Ipswich, October 1804; letter in the collection of Reeve's correspondence in the library of Trinity College, Dublin, MSS 1461/3 (Walker was a public servant and amateur antiquarian living in Dublin). Unless otherwise noted, all subsequent references to Reeve's correspondence, given in the text, are to this collection.

"not partial" to her or her works (letter of 1 December 1792). One sister married, two others remained unmarried. Reeve preferred living on her own, and in the 1790s she had a "cottage" in Car Street, Ipswich, with what she called "a tolerable Collection of Books" (Reeve to Walker, October 1804). She died at Ipswich on 3 December 1807 and was buried in St. Stephen's churchyard.

Reeve was a provincial writer, then, in the sense that she lived out her life in the provinces, and indeed was proud of the fact. Nevertheless, her output was prolific, especially for a single self-supporting woman residing in a provincial town, apparently without metropolitan connections. In 1804 Reeve told Walker, "I have written 21 Volumes, beside pamphlets"; work known to be hers totals twenty-four volumes. In addition, Reeve wrote a novel, probably in three volumes, entitled *Castle Connor: An Irish Story* (1787), but it was lost on the Ipswich to London coach. Reeve also told Walker in 1804 that she had many "beginnings" of works, "many works unfinished," and "several drawers of MSS-s" (letters dated 25 April 1791, 1 December 1792, October 1804).

She seems to have managed this extensive publishing career herself, at a time when sexist social conventions and the property laws made it advisable for a woman author to have a husband or male relative deal with publishers. Reeve seems to have acted for herself, though in the 1790s she asked Walker—a correspondent she had never met—to intercede with a dilatory and condescending London publisher and to act as her agent with one in Dublin. Most of her work was published in London, by prominent metropolitan firms, but with two of her earlier works she fell back on a provincial publisher.

These two works constitute her claim to fame as a bluestocking, or literary and learned woman. *The Champion of Virtue: A Gothic Story*, based on historical and antiquarian knowledge, was published by W. Keymer at Colchester in 1777 and republished a year later in London as *The Old English Baron: A Gothic Story*. It proved to be her most enduring work, republished as a popular classic to the end of the nineteenth century. *The Progress of Romance, through Times, Countries, and Manners; with Remarks on the Good and Bad Effects of It, on Them Respectively; in a Course of Evening Conversations*, two volumes stuffed with literary and bibliographical scholarship, was published by W. Keymer at Colchester in 1785. Though long overlooked, it is not only a pioneering history and defense of "romance" from antiquity to the mid-eighteenth century but also a groundbreaking work of literary scholarship by a woman.

Reeve was, then, a provincial writer in the sense that she published these two central works of her œuvre, perhaps reluctantly, in the provinces. Yet, as recent historians of publishing have shown, the period of Reeve's literary career saw great advances in provincial publishing, especially after 1775.[5] Provincial bookseller-publishers were a major force in what was referred to at the time as "the rise of the reading public," or the spread of the fashion for reading through the professional middle classes, to which Reeve belonged. Furthermore, as Cheryl Turner points out, provincial publishers contributed particularly to women's writing by publishing "a wide range" of their work that would not otherwise have reached the reading public.[6] This was certainly the case with the two works central to Clara Reeve's career as a provincial Bluestocking. A brief survey of this publisher's output illuminates Reeve's provincial Bluestocking context.

## W. KEYMER, PROVINCIAL PUBLISHER

W. Keymer's business served southern East Anglia. He was related to other Keymers publishing in Essex and Suffolk from early in the eighteenth century[7] and seems to have passed his business to a W. Keymer Jr. about 1792. Most of the Keymers' publishing was through congers, and they sold works published by others in London and elsewhere in East Anglia. W. Keymer had ties with the prestigious London trade, especially the Robinsons' publishing concern. Firms like the Keymers' helped both to constitute a provincial reading public and to connect it to others and to a metropolitan and national reading public. Indeed, London publishers served both the metropolitan and national level, largely through widening business relations with provincial booksellers and circulating libraries after 1774. Provincial bookseller-publishers such as W. Keymer operated within this network and at the same time served their own market with books and pamphlets of predominantly local interest.

W. Keymer was an active publisher of miscellaneous items, but certain categories dominated. There were utilitarian publications of entirely local interest, such as household sale catalogues, handbooks for grain merchants, and prospectuses for infrastructure projects, for example a canal from London to Norwich. East Anglian social conditions and political events were a recurring theme. As elsewhere, bribery and violence marred parliamentary elections and patronage was a powerful economic and political force, so there was a good market in election poll-books. There was also interest in reforming this system, expressed

5. See John Feather, *The Provincial Book Trade in Eighteenth-Century England* (Cambridge, 1985).
6. Cheryl Turner, *Living by the Pen: Women Writers in the Eighteenth Century* (London and New York, 1994), 85.
7. S. Keymer was involved in bookselling and/or publishing in London in the early eighteenth century; R. Keymer was publishing at Hadleigh, Essex, from the 1740s to the mid-1760s; and W. Keymer was publishing at Colchester in the early 1760s.

especially around the election of 1784, addressed for example in the anonymous satire *Memoirs of Sir Simeon Supple, Member for Rotborough* (1785), published by the London bookseller George Kearsley and by W. Keymer at Colchester. Other national and international issues received attention from Keymer, including the American war and the campaign against the slave trade. Another strong publishing interest was religion; some publications served local clergy, congregations, and choirs in practical matters, such as anthologies of church music, keys to psalmody, and guides to confirmation. Other publications illustrate the deeply politicized nature of religion at that time, with locally authored theological speculation, controversy, and sermons by both Anglicans and Dissenters—W. Keymer prudently published for both sides.

The French Revolution, because it disclosed how closely politics and religion were intertwined, exacerbated local social, religious, and political differences. Reeve read publications devoted to these matters, telling Walker in March 1793, "We have had many squibs of the political kind, fired off here in the course of this winter for two pence, three pence, and six pence on all sides, and [I] gather information from the whole" (letter of 14 March 1793). The outbreak of the Revolution caused both rejoicing and consternation, but the tone changed in the mid-1790s as famine and wartime economic dislocation increased local conflicts. The reading public, nationally and locally, became increasingly anti-Revolutionary, as indicated by the Rev. John Kelly's sermon, *The Duty of Submission to Established Government, as Founded in Nature, Reason, and Revelation, Particularly Necessary in Modern Times* (1795), published by W. Keymer Jr. and also sold by the London firms of the Robinsons, Joseph Johnson, and Cadell and Davies.[8] By the late 1790s opinion was strongly anti-Revolutionary, as reflected in the Rev. James Round's *English Loyalty the Best Antidote against French Perfidy: A Sermon, Preached before the Loyal Colchester Volunteers* (1798), published by W. Keymer Jr. and sold by the London firms of Robinson and Rivington.

If politics and religion had both metropolitan-national and provincial readerships, so too did the belles-lettres, arts, and sciences. London remained the center for such publishing, but provincial publishers had their own markets, usually in publications by local authors, often sold by subscription or paid for by the authors themselves. For example, W. Keymer published *Observations and Conjectures on the Nature and Properties of Light, and on the Theory of Comets* (1777) by William Cole, who lived at Colchester, with participation of booksellers at

---

8.  This was perhaps a surprising collaboration, since the Robinsons published many "English Jacobins," such as William Godwin, and Johnson was the leading publisher of the English Nonconformist Enlightenment and other reformist writers, including Mary Wollstonecraft.

Oxford, Cambridge, and London; Keymer also published William Hurn's *Heath-Hill: A Descriptive Poem, In Four Cantos* (1777) "for the author," with participation by the London firm of Robinson. There was much publishing associated with provincial theater and music. The Keymers also joined in publishing belles-lettres by authors from elsewhere in the region, such as Charles Collington's *Messiah: A Poem* (1763) and *An Enquiry into the Structure of the Human Body, Relative to Its Supposed Influence on the Morals of Mankind* (1764). *Poems* (1799) by the Rev. John Black of Butley, Suffolk, was published in Ipswich and sold by Keymer in Colchester and others in London, Edinburgh, Yarmouth, Norwich, Bury, Chelmsford, and Woodbridge. *Poems, Chiefly on Religious Subjects* (1797) by John Forster, shoemaker, was published at London, Colchester (Keymer), Hull, and York, with a "recommendatory preface" by a Suffolk clergyman—encouraging "respectable" plebeian writers was a middle-class (and a Bluestocking) philanthropic avocation. Finally, W. Keymer published the first edition of *The Champion of Virtue* and the only edition of *The Progress of Romance*, and the firm maintained an interest in Reeve's publications: a prospectus for Reeve's *Destination; or, Memoirs of a Private Family* (1799) stated that the novel was "printed for Longman and Rees . . . London" and "sold by W. Keymer, Colchester, and by P. Forster, Ipswich."

Certainly there were disadvantages to provincial publication. Keymer's edition of *The Champion of Virtue* has many more errors than the version republished at London as *The Old English Baron*.[9] Reeve herself believed that *The Progress of Romance* had "ill success" because it was published in the provinces. She told Walker, "I printed it in the country, and my Printer relied upon his correspondent in town"—that is, the firm of Robinsons, in London—"to give it the proper circulation," but "London Publishers will not push a work so printed, because they wish to keep the trade entirely in their own hands" (letter of 19 April 1790). According to the publishing historian John Feather, this was a sound belief.[10] As the loss of Reeve's novel *Castle Connor* on the London coach indicates, even communicating with London publishers from the provinces was risky. Being a woman made things more difficult still. Reeve told Walker, "A woman lies under many disadvantages in treating with the London Publishers." She found them "the most insolent, greedy, & oppressive set of men that can be met with" (letter of 19 April 1790) and "inclined to treat our sex en Cavalier" (letter of 21 September 1792) and consequently inattentive, dilatory, and careless.

9.   See textual notes to the edition of *The Champion of Virtue*, in *Varieties of Female Gothic*, ed. Gary Kelly, 6 vols. (London, 2002), vol. 1.

10.  Feather, *Provincial Book Trade*, 4–11.

## POLITICS AND CULTURE IN IPSWICH

Seemingly worse for a Bluestocking than these hazards of provincial publishing and authorship, however, was Reeve's particular situation at Ipswich. Britain's provincial towns grew and prospered through the eighteenth century, but there were distinct differences between them based on their economic structure and resulting social and cultural character. London, the metropolis, was uniquely multifaceted, but otherwise there were county and market towns, manufacturing centers, port and dockyard towns, and spas and resorts.[11] Anna Seward (1742–1809), for example, spent her life in provincial Lichfield, but it was a cathedral town and crossroads for the Midlands Enlightenment, which comprised writers, intellectuals, scientists, inventors, and entrepreneurs from Birmingham to Warrington. Sarah Scott, sister of the "queen of the Bluestockings," grew up on an estate in Kent, holidayed in various spa towns, visited her sister's London Bluestocking circle, and lived in Bath for much of her literary career.[12] As the most fashionable spa in England, Bath was a center for elegant society, with an active literary and intellectual life.

Reeve's Ipswich was very different—mercantile, industrial, and naval. Suffolk's county town was Bury St. Edmunds, where the county gentry and elite professional people assembled during the assizes. Nearby Colchester, in Essex, where Reeve's provincial publisher was located, had a similar position. Bungay, where Reeve's clergyman brother was master of the respected grammar school from 1777 to 1795,[13] became a center of genteel culture in the eighteenth century, having a theater, spa services, and fashionable assemblies. For centuries Ipswich's leading commercial and professional people had actively developed its infrastructure and public amenities, but it would not have the fashionable cachet or the genteel intellectual and literary society of Bath, Lichfield, or even Colchester.

Yet Ipswich provided the context and the inspiration for Reeve as a provincial Bluestockings. In fact, as a seaport, it provided materials for one of her learned, and at Ipswich cheap, pursuits—conchology.[14] And it had more to offer: good shopping by the standards of the time, newspapers, coffee houses, a bowling green, two theaters, fortnightly concerts and a musical society, and horse-race

---

11.  P. J. Corfield, *The Impact of English Towns, 1700–1800* (Oxford, 1982).

12.  See Betty Rizzo, "Introduction," Sarah Scott, *The History of Sir George Ellison*, ed. Rizzo (Lexington, Ky., 1996), ix–xlii; and Gary Kelly, entry on Sarah Scott, forthcoming in the *New Dictionary of National Biography*.

13.  *Victoria History of the County of Suffolk*, ed. William Page (London, 1907), 345, 288.

14.  A letter to Thomas Percy (Bodleian Library, MS. Percy c. 3, fols. 32–33) thanks him for additions to her shell collection, arranged following Emanuel Mendes da Costa's *Elements of Conchology* (1776).

meetings.[15] Its energetic and diverse bourgeoisie and skilled tradespeople were closely connected to its rich agricultural vicinage. In the seventeenth century and later, many middle-class townspeople owned land in that hinterland, which they also served by food processing, manufacturing, and port facilities for a coastal shipping trade.[16] Ipswich, then, was no social or cultural backwater. Writing a few years before Reeve was born, Daniel Defoe found it "an airy, clean, and well gov-ern'd Town," with "Good Houses, at very easie Rents," "all manner" of cheap provisions, and easy passage to London. He found twelve Anglican parish churches, a Presbyterian chapel, an Independents' meeting house, and "as large and fine" a Quaker meeting house as could be found in eastern England. Accordingly, Defoe found that, though there were not as many gentry as at Bury, Ipswich's "very good Company" were "Persons well informed of the World," with "something very Solid and Entertaining in their Society."[17] Ipswich retained this character throughout Reeve's lifetime. Just two decades after she died, William Cobbett visited the town and found it a "fine, populous and beautiful place" of about twelve thousand people, surrounded by lovely hills picturesquely crowned by windmills grinding the East Anglian grain shipped as flour through Ipswich to London.[18] Cobbett's description, a panoramic view, suggests what Reeve must have liked about her native town:

> Ipswich is in a dell, meadows running up above it, and a beautiful arm of the sea below it. The town itself is substantially built, well paved, everything good and solid, and no wretched dwellings to be seen on its outskirts. From the town itself you can see nothing; but you can, in no direction, go from it a quarter of a mile without finding views that a painter might crave, and then the country round about it so well cultivated; the land in such a beautiful state, the farmhouses all white, and all so much alike; the barns, and everything about the homesteads so snug ... in short, here is everything to delight the eye, and to make the people proud of their country; and this is the case throughout the whole of this county.[19]

15. Peter Borsay, *The English Urban Renaissance: Culture and Society in the Provincial Town, 1660–1770* (Oxford, 1989), 35, 83, 145, 173, 329, 333, 364.

16. See Michael Reed, "Economic Structure and Change in Seventeenth-Century Ipswich," in *Country Towns in Pre-industrial England* (Leicester, 1981), 88–141; *Victoria History of . . . Suffolk*, 272; and John Glyde, *The Moral, Social and Religious Condition of Ipswich in the Middle of the Nineteenth Century* (1850; Wakefield and London, 1971), 22.

17. Daniel Defoe, *A Tour through the Whole Island of Great Britain*, letter 1, in *Writings on Travel, Discovery, and History by Daniel Defoe*, vol. 1 (London, 2001), 90–91.

18. William Cobbett, *Rural Rides*, 2 vols. (London and New York, 1957), 22 March 1830, 2:221–22.

19. Ibid., 2:225.

Cobbett loved solidly middle- and lower-class industry, prosperity, and independence, so it is not surprising that he loved Ipswich. By contrast, he saw London and spa towns such as Bath as nests of the "tax-eaters," from king through placeman to clergyman, who were corrupting the government, repressing the people, and ruining the country.[20]

Reeve loved Ipswich, too, and her social and political views were not that different from Cobbett's—in fact, views like hers were an important source for Cobbett and his generation of middle-class and artisan reformers.[21] In Reeve's day Ipswich was a bastion of "old Whig" politics,[22] and it is clear from her letters and published works that these were also Reeve's politics. The "old Whigs" (also referred to in contemporary writings as "real Whigs" and "true Whigs") adapted Renaissance political thought to eighteenth-century Britain and its empire.[23] In opposition to the "new Whigs," who consolidated their grip on power and patronage through the late seventeenth and early eighteenth centuries and supposedly regarded the Revolution Settlement of 1688 as sufficient, old Whigs sought to extend the implications of the settlement and were "quite often praised or blamed as Commonwealthmen," supposedly for looking back to the Puritan Commonwealth for their political model.[24] Old Whigs, Commonwealthmen, and "classical republicans" (admirers of the ancient Roman republic) supported the "Country interest," believing that the best constitution mixed the best aspects of of monarchy, aristocracy, and democracy." Supposedly this balance had been achieved by the Revolution Settlement, but there was continuing concern that it could be upset by the excessive wealth of the crown and the aristocracy.[25] Yet the old Whigs insisted, as H. T. Dickinson puts it, that "the liberties of the nation could not be entrusted to servants and labourers who were always dependent upon others." Therefore only "independent proprietors" who could

20. Ibid, 1:33.
21. Albert Goodwin, *The Friends of Liberty: The English Democratic Movement in the Age of the French Revolution* (London, 1979), chap. 2, "The Radical Tradition in the Eighteenth Century."
22. Nicholas Rogers, *Whigs and Cities: Popular Politics in the Age of Walpole and Pitt* (Oxford, 1989), 100.
23. J. G. A. Pocock, *The Machiavellian Moment: Florentine Political Thought and the Atlantic Republican Tradition* (Princeton, N.J., 1975), esp. chap. 14; see also J. G. A. Pocock, "The Varieties of Whiggism from Exclusion to Reform: A History of Ideology and Discourse," in *Virtue, Commerce, and History: Essays on Political Thought and History, Chiefly in the Eighteenth Century* (Cambridge, 1985), 215–310.
24. Caroline Robbins, *The Eighteenth-Century Commonwealthman: Studies in the Transmission, Development, and Circumstance of English Liberal Thought from the Restoration of Charles II until the War with the Thirteen Colonies* (Cambridge, Mass., 1959), 88.
25. During the debate on the French Revolution Edmund Burke tried to subvert the distinction between "old" and "new" by switching the labels, declaring himself an old Whig opposed to pro-Revolutionary new Whigs in his *Appeal from the New to the Old Whigs* (1791).

"withstand the corrupting embrace" of the rich and powerful should enjoy the "rights and privileges of citizenship." The old Whigs also maintained that this "ancient free constitution, which could be traced back to a Gothic [that is, Germanic] and Anglo-Saxon past, had always depended for its survival on the virtue of the community of independent freeholders."[26] Among such independent freeholders were Ipswich's "free Burgesses," from whom Reeve was proud to be descended.

Not surprisingly, then, Reeve's politics were old Whig, and they ran in the family. Reeve later declared that from her father "I have learned everything that I know; he was my oracle."[27] She termed him an "old Whig" and described how he made her read aloud from newspaper reports of parliamentary debates and study old Whig classics, such as Plutarch's *Lives*, an English translation of the history of England written by Paul Rapin de Thoyras (1661–1725), and *Cato's Letters* (1720–23) by John Trenchard and Thomas Gordon. Plutarch's parallel lives of Greeks and Romans—with its celebration of independent citizens resisting despots, pursuing civic virtue, and heroically opposing corruption and decadence—inspired opponents of court monarchy from the Renaissance to Rousseau, the French Revolution to the modern liberal state.[28] Rapin's history celebrates the ancient "Gothic" freedoms of England, supposedly suppressed by the Norman Conquest and steadily reinstated by generations of civic virtue and heroism.[29] *Cato's Letters* arose from the controversy over the South Sea financial scandal involving the new Whig government of Sir Robert Walpole, originally an East Anglian squire, who used crown patronage, government influence, and bribery to survive the scandal and maintain power. *Cato's Letters* covers a diverse range of political, social, moral, religious, philosophical, and cultural issues, as suggested by some of the essays' titles: "The Fatal Effects of the South-Sea Scheme, and the necessity of punishing the directors"; "Of Publick Spirit"; "Civil Liberty Produces All Civil Blessings, and how, with the baneful nature of tyranny"; "The Contemptibleness of Grandeur Without Virtue"; "Of the Proper Use of Words"; "Of Good Breeding"; "Against Standing Armies"; "Polite Arts and Learning Naturally Produced in Free States, and marred by such as are not free";

26.  H. T. Dickinson, *Liberty and Property: Political Ideology in Eighteenth-Century Britain* (London, 1979), 103, 104.
27.  Undated letter quoted in Walter Scott, "Prefatory Memoir to Clara Reeve," *Ballantyne's Novelist's Library*, vol. 5 (Edinburgh, 1823), lxxix.
28.  For example, Plutarch is a key text in the dæmon's republican and democratic political education in Mary Shelley's *Frankenstein*.
29.  Robbins describes Rapin's history as "Whig republican" in tone; *The Eighteenth-Century Commonwealthman*, 274.

"A Vindication of Brutus, for having killed Caesar"; and "Letter from a Lady, with an answer, about love, marriage, and settlements."[30] Among those who felt the impact of the letters, and who diffused it further, was Clara Reeve.

Thus, in the political sense, too, Reeve could be termed a provincial Bluestocking. For although old Whig, classical republican, or Commonwealthman politics could not be equated with the provinces, those politics were rooted and expressed there, in regional economies, like Ipswich's, and in the coalition of local landed gentry on the one hand, and town burgesses and professional people on the other, who served and intermarried with them. This alliance opposed the coalition of royal court, new Whig politicians, landed magnates, and City financiers based in and symbolized by the metropolis. At the same time, the metropolis was home to many who shared Reeve's politics. I have argued elsewhere that the Bluestockings, based in the metropolis but with strong provincial associations, also promoted classical republican, old Whig politics in their works, with a feminist inflection.[31] That inflection would be shared by Reeve and many women writers, for, very broadly, both provincial and metropolitan Bluestockings opposed a system—like the new Whig government of Walpole and his successors—sustained by the intertwined political and sexual intrigue and patriarchy of court government and oligarchy.

## POLITICAL ISSUES IN REEVE'S FICTION

Reeve's politics informed her works throughout her career.[32] Her second book and first fiction, *The Phœnix; or, The History of Polyarchus and Argenis* (4 volumes, 1772), translates and adapts John Barclay's Latin *Argenis* (1621), a political allegory on France's religious civil wars of the late sixteenth and early seventeenth centuries. English political writers often drew analogies between these wars and English political conflicts, especially to urge that constitutional restraints be placed on the monarchy.[33] Reeve's preface describes *The Phœnix* as "a romance, an allegory, and a system of politics" and declares that "in it various forms of

30.  John Trenchard and Thomas Gordon, *Cato's Letters; or, Essays on Liberty, Civil and Religious, and Other Important Subjects*, ed. Ronald Hamowy, 2 vols. (Indianapolis, 1995), xxxvii. According to Hamowy, throughout the eighteenth century their "impact on both sides of the Atlantic was enormous."

31.  See Gary Kelly, "Bluestocking Feminism," in *Women, Writing and the Public Sphere, 1700–1830* (Cambridge, 2001), 163–80; and "Introduction," Sarah Scott, *A Description of Millenium Hall*, ed. Gary Kelly (Peterborough, Ont., 1995), 11–43.

32.  For a more detailed examination of Reeve's works, see Gary Kelly, "Introduction: Clara Reeve," in *Bluestocking Feminism: Writings of the Bluestocking Circle, 1738–1785*, vol. 6 (London, 1999), xxiii–xlviii.

33.  J. H. M. Salmon, *The French Religious Wars in English Political Thought* (Oxford, 1959).

government are investigated, the causes of faction detected, and the remedies pointed out for most of the evils that can arise in a state." She both defends her right to intervene in public affairs and denounces the lower-class agitation over "Wilkes and Liberty":

> England is become a nation of politicians, and men of all ranks and degrees believe themselves capable of investigating the art of government, and since women have written with success upon the subject, the editor has thought herself at liberty to aim a blow at popular [that is, plebeian] error, from behind Barclay.

Members of the Bluestocking circle, including Montagu and Scott, addressed the same issues, the former in *An Essay on the Writings and Genius of Shakespear* (1769) and the latter in *The Life of Theodore Agrippa d'Aubigné, Containing a Succinct Account of the Most Remarkable Occurrences during the Civil Wars of France* (1772).

Reeve turned away from such explicitly political fiction until the 1790s, when old Whig politics were appropriated by new, middle-class and working-class reform campaigns. Meanwhile, she expressed her political views in the form many women writers chose—domestic fiction, or the novel of private life. As its title indicates, *The Two Mentors: A Modern Story* (2 volumes, 1783) is a novel of education, with a young protagonist torn between seductive courtly decadence and the virtues promoted by the old Whigs. In *The Progress of Romance* (2 volumes, 1785), Reeve argues that prose fiction, conventionally associated with women and devalued accordingly, is as useful in moral and civic education as the classical literature employed to form patriotic and virtuous young men. The work includes, as an example of such romance, "The History of Charoba, Queen of Ægypt," in which a clever, public-spirited woman defeats attempts by despotic neighboring kings to subdue her and her kingdom. Reeve's *The Exiles; or, Memoirs of the Count de Cronstadt* (3 volumes, 1788), another novel of private life, illustrates the dangerous consequences of upper-class social prejudice and courtly libertinism. *The School for Widows: A Novel* (3 volumes, 1791) represents female domestic heroism against vitiated courtly culture that reaches even into middle-class life. The connection with classical republicanism may seem tenuous but is indicated by the preface's quotation from "Cato the Elder" (Marcus Porcius Cato, 234–149 B.C.), a severe Roman republican critic of luxury and corruption in public and private life. Reeve did think less of her domestic fiction than of her other work, describing *The School for Widows* to Walker as "a lighter work, written for the circulating library, sprinkled however, with moral inferences" (letter of 12 April 1791).

The French Revolution severely tested Reeve's old Whig politics. The Bluestockings condemned the Revolution as a manifestation of the "leveling"

politics feared by old Whigs, but Reeve, like many others, first welcomed it as a
realization of old Whig principles of constitutional monarchy. In April 1791 she
told Walker that she had "been reading nothing but Politics for some time past,"
including Burke's *Reflections on the Revolution in France* (1790) and "all the answers to it." She made her political sympathies clear to Walker, declaring, "I am
a friend to liberty, and the security of property, and the rights of man. I wish
well to them & all those who defend them." She also made clear her classical republican roots, telling Walker that she had "read the Greek and Roman Histories,
and Plutarch's lives when quite a child, from them I imbibed principles that can
never be shaken.—A love of liberty, a hatred of Tyranny, an affection to the whole
race of mankind, a wish to support their rights and properties" (letter of 12 April
1791). She told Walker she would intervene in the Revolution debate herself
through the genre conventionally allowed to women—fiction—and that she had
high hopes of the result: "In my Gothic Story my principles will appear, it will
speak to men, to citizens, to Princes, & to the People; in the character of one bad
prince I have delineated thousands, in a good one, I fear very few." Aware of
growing animosity in the Revolution debate she also expected obloquy, confess-
ing, "I shall risk my reputation upon it," expecting that "it will probably be my
Vale to the public"(letter of 25 April 1791). The novel, *Memoirs of Sir Roger de
Clarendon,* did not appear until two years later.

A key point of Whig politics was distrust of "excessive" liberty, or influence
of the "mob"—the lower and lower–middle classes—in politics. Whereas Reeve
saw the Revolution, at first, as a triumph of liberty and of Whig politics, the metropolitan Bluestockings such as Montagu and Scott saw it as a dangerous unleash-
ing of the "mob." As the Revolution became more violent, Reeve's opinion of it
moved toward that of the metropolitan Bluestockings. After the September
Massacres at Paris in 1792 she wrote despondently to Walker, "What times do we
live in?—My politics are all overthrown." She felt that "France has ruined herself and hurt all the other countries of Europe" by turning to violence and mili-
tarism. Worse, France "has strengthened the hands of the enemies of liberty, who
will now boldly assert, that mankind are not to be trusted with it." Like a good
classical republican, she was against the extremes of both absolute monarchy and
plebeian leveling, declaring,

> All extremes are in the wrong, all the blessings of heaven must be
> enjoyed within certain limits,
> > For things of best and noblest uses
> > Convert to poison by abuses.
> > > (Letter of 7 September 1792)

This sentiment informs her *Plans of Education; with Remarks on the Systems of Other Writers; in a Series of Letters between Mrs. Darnford and Her Friends* (1792), which recent criticism has placed in a line of feminist utopian writing going back through Scott's *A Description of Millenium Hall* to Mary Astell's *A Serious Proposal to the Ladies for the Advancement of Their True and Greatest Interests* (1694).[34] Like Scott, Reeve proposes self-sustaining utopian female communities, independent of the male-dominated public sphere, as a way of gradually reforming that sphere. Like the Bluestockings' works, *Plans of Education* is informed by the classical republican idea of a patriot king and virtuous ruling class. An "Essay on Education," within Reeve's story, links education to encouragement of the public virtue and national reform necessary to avoid revolution in Britain, citing historical examples of the kind favored by classical republicans. Accordingly, Reeve's friends perhaps encouraged her to seek patronage from the Bluestockings themselves, for she told Walker that she had several copies of *Plans* bound for presentation "to the great Ladies" (letter of 1 December 1792).

Reeve also links her work, however, to feminist interventions in the Revolution debate. *Plans of Education* appeared two years after *Letters on Education* by the leading classical republican writer, Catharine Macaulay Graham (noticed briefly in Reeve's preface), and in the same year as Mary Wollstonecraft's *A Vindication of the Rights of Woman*. Reeve's purpose resembles theirs—education of women to resist courtly decadence and to support patriotic values in a national crisis. Reeve tells the reader, "The Revolution in France will be a standing lesson to Princes and to People of all countries; it is a warning to Kings, how they oppress and impoverish their people; it warns them to reform the errors and corruptions of their governments, and to prevent the necessity of a revolution" (p. 214). Like Wollstonecraft, Reeve envisages a major role for educated women in this patriotic crusade, but with a more conservative emphasis on discipline, order, and hierarchy:

> Nothing is of equal consequence to the health of a state, as the education of youth. When the manners are chaste and virtuous, we cannot doubt that education was so; when there is a general relaxation of manners and discipline, there must be great defects in the methods of education. (P. 29)

A year after publishing *Plans of Education* appeared, Reeve addressed the Revolution crisis in her "Gothic story," *Memoirs of Sir Roger de Clarendon, the Natural Son of Edward Prince of Wales, Commonly Called the Black Prince; with*

---

34. Barbara Brandon Schnorrenberg, "A Paradise Like Eve's: Three Eighteenth-Century English Female Utopias," *Women's Studies* 9:3 (1982): 263–73.

*Anecdotes of Many other Eminent Persons of the Fourteenth Century* (3 volumes, 1793). By now both the French Revolution and the debate in Britain had disclosed powerful new political forces in the lower classes. Plutarch was frequently invoked in the Revolution debate, by all sides, and Reeve's preface signals her old Whig allegiances by quoting his justification for applying history to contemporary political events in order to rouse patriotic spirit in national crisis. She also restates the classical republican rejection of both despotic government and leveling plebeian politics. Reeve denounces the prorevolutionary "new philosophy of the present day," represented by Tom Paine and the so-called "English Jacobins," for promoting "a levelling principle" against "order and regularity" (vol. 1, p. xvii). She situates her work as both antimonarchic and antirevolutionary, exclaiming:

> May despotism be for ever abolished!—May a just and benevolent system rise upon its ruins!—But a form of government founded upon levelling principles, never did, nor ever can continue. Rome had a gradation of ranks during her republican state. (Vol. 1, p. xviii)

Historical fiction was criticized at the time for misleading young readers with a mixture of fact and fabrication, but Reeve defends its potential for patriotic education of "young and ingenuous minds" that are still "uncontaminated by the vile indolence, effeminacy, and extravagance of modern life and manners" (p. xxii). Her novel concludes with a classical republican, old Whig manifesto for the revolutionary era:

> The historical anecdotes, interspersed through the whole of this work, are full of inferences to all orders and degrees of people: to princes, to avoid dissimulation, oppression, and injustice; to beware of evil counsellors, and fawning sycophants, and to listen to those who tell them truth, and to be certain that those men love them best, who hazard their displeasure to serve them: to the nobles, to respect themselves, if they expect others to respect them; and to beware of using deception and imposition on their king, lest they bring punishment upon him and themselves; and to make the good of their country their first object: to those in public offices, to practise strict integrity and assiduity, and not to embezzle the wealth of the nation: to men in private stations, that family harmony and peace is the greatest happiness mankind are permitted to taste in this world, and that it is found the most pure and unallayed in the lower stations of life, who enjoy a competency [that is, the middle classes]: to those who are obliged to practise useful

arts and trades, to avoid imitating the luxuries, follies and vices of their superiors, and to practise honesty, frugality, and content: to the people at large, submission to their lawful prince, to the laws, and to the magistrates, as to those who are placed in authority under them, "and to learn and labour to gain their own livelihood, and to do their duty in that state of life unto which it hath pleased God to call them;" and to shun all those who would seduce them to worship the idol *Equality*, which, if it could be introduced, would reduce them to indolence and despondency: that a true and regular subordination is what makes all orders and degrees of men stand in need of each other, and stimulates them to exercise their courage, industry, activity, and every generous quality, that supports a state and government. (Vol. 3, pp. 228–30)

## FICTION AND POLITICS AFTER THE REVOLUTION

Reeve did not publish again until the end of the decade, and then returned to the novel of domestic life and education. *Destination; or, Memoirs of a Private Family* (3 volumes, 1799) apparently ignores the Revolution debate, which included numerous "Jacobin" and "Anti-Jacobin" novels. Nevertheless, *Destination* addresses a major theme of the revolutionary aftermath. The complex narrative shows how an older, upper-class form of the family, based on ascribed social status, rentier gentry economy, conspicuous consumption, and patronage, can be refounded as a newer form of family, based on professional middle-class values of inward merit, self-discipline, accumulation of moral and intellectual capital, nurturing domestic intersubjectivity, and social responsibility and philanthropy. "Destination" here refers to profession, and the novel describes how various characters succeed or fail at the accumulation of the moral and intellectual capital required "to put them into a situation that will employ them to their own advantage, and to the good of the public" (3:207). Thus *Destination* represents nonviolent transition from the old order to a new one. This is a postrevolutionary lesson, as the novel's last paragraph indicates: "We have seen a new æra in the history of mankind. God send peace to Europe and to all the world."

Reeve's last known (and recently discovered) work was a departure for her—a fictionalized history for young readers entitled *Edwin, King of Northumberland: A Story of the Seventh Century* (1802), by "Clara Reeve, Author of the Old English Baron."[35] It follows a Plutarchan program for using lives of great men of the past to educate youth in civic virtues. As Preceptor states in the preface:

35.   Copy in Bruce Peel Special Collections, University of Alberta Library.

It is a mark of a well-disposed mind, to believe that your own country is the best and happiest of all others; to be well instructed in the
history of it; to know the advantages it possesses; the climate, the
soil, the produce; you ought also to know the commerce, the agriculture, and the resources it contains within itself; and more spe-
cially the great men it has produced, for this will give you the
greatest respect for it, and the true *amor patria*. (P. v)

With its insistence on the relations between local and national economic factors,
and between these and the national character and history, this passage reflects a
provincial—perhaps specifically of Ipswich—old Whig perspective and echoes
another in Reeve's *Memoirs of Sir Roger de Clarendon*. That work intervened in
the Revolution debate; *Edwin* intervenes in the great patriotic war against
Napoleon and the emergence of a new kind of nationalism, indebted to earlier
ideas of "patriotism," also associated with the old Whigs, here called *amor patria*
(properly *amor patriae*). *Edwin* also recurs to classical republican ideas of civic
virtue, as Preceptor insists that "[w]hen a people are declining in virtue, we ought
to fear every other kind of decline" (pp. xi–xii). *Edwin* implies that a similar kind
of danger faced England in the seventh century and in the early nineteenth.

Throughout her career, then, Reeve maintained the classical republican principles that she had learned as a child and that were intrinsic to her provincial situation, society, and culture. Those principles can be seen most clearly, however,
in the work by which she became best known. The political themes of *The
Champion of Virtue: A Gothic Story* suggest the reasons for its continuing popularity during the nineteenth-century transformation of old Whig politics into reformist and liberal ones. Republished as *The Old English Baron: A Gothic Story*,
the work is a critique, not only literary but also ideological, of new Whig politics
as represented particularly by the "founding" Gothic romance, *The Castle of
Otranto* (dated 1765; published December 1764), and its author, Horace Walpole.

Reeve's "Address to the Reader" engages immediately with *Otranto*. It
approves *Otranto*'s aim, stated in the preface to its second edition, to create a
new fictional genre by blending the "old" romance with the "new"—that is,
medieval and Renaissance verse and prose romance with the "modern novel" (or
eighteenth-century novel of contemporary life and manners), and the fantastic
and improbable with the realism of common life. The professed aim is to seize
the reader's interest for the purposes of entertainment and moral edification.
Reeve's "Address" criticizes *Otranto*, however, for favoring the "marvellous" over
the probable and claims that *The Champion* achieves a better balance.

Despite many similarities, *The Champion* goes far beyond "correcting"
*Otranto* by underplaying the miraculous; in fact, it argues old Whig values and

virtues on every level. Both, it is true, are set several centuries earlier—*Otranto* in the thirteenth century and *The Champion* in the fifteenth. Both present a plot of usurpation (occurring before the time of the story) and restoration (achieved in the course of the story). Both purport to be "translations"—*Otranto* of a sixteenth-century Italian book, *The Champion* of a manuscript in "the old English language." Both include supernatural occurrences and require providential intervention to obtain justice. Both feature trial by single combat accompanied by chivalric formalities, and both have a subplot of love and marriage in the younger generation. These strong similarities serve to highlight the differences, however. Walpole's text purports to be translated from a book originally designed to reinforce popular superstitions and thus resist intellectual enlightenment and religious Reformation. Reeve's text, on the other hand, purports to be translated from a fragmentary manuscript originally compiled by order of "the champion of virtue" as a "striking lesson to posterity"—an old Whig use of history. Walpole's novel is set in southern, Catholic Europe, supposedly distant from centers of social, cultural, and religious reform. Reeve's is set in an England remote in time but not space from that of the novel's writer and reader. Reeve's fictional world is purposely less alien, less "un-English," than Walpole's.

These differences are reflected in other formal elements, especially characterization. Whereas *Otranto*'s lower-class characters are loquacious, ignorant, vulgar, and unhelpful, *The Champion*'s are loyal and dignified and help the hero regain what is his right. Instead of *Otranto*'s stagy dialogues and numerous tirades, *The Champion* has informal and even colloquial, yet dramatic, dialogue and no tirades. Reeve's villain appears late and cannot compare to *Otranto*'s spectacularly evil Manfred, and Reeve generally replaces evildoers with benefactors, led by "the champion of virtue," Sir Philip Harclay, who defeats the usurper in single combat and restores Edmund to his birthright. Most important, *Otranto* foregrounds the feelings, thoughts, and motives of the villain and the two female protagonists, Isabella and Matilda, as extreme masculine and feminine subjectivities. Reeve's novel, unusually for a Gothic fiction, represents subjectivity much less, and less in terms of extreme feelings. In *Otranto*, excessive subjectivity arises from the drive for sexual power over another as a means to power over property, title, status. *The Champion*'s emphasis on ethical behavior and social civility accords with values of self-discipline and civic virtue. The differences in characterization are paralleled in incident and plot. Although there are some supernatural elements, there are fewer frights and no terrors. There are no female vessels of sensibility upset by threats, grotesqueries, and horrors. There *are* ghostly signals, faced by the self-commanding hero Edmund and his plebeian supporters, disclosing a secret crime and leading to justice. In *Otranto*, justice is achieved entirely by supernatural intervention; in *The Champion*, supernatural intimations move human agents to right wrongs and ensure justice.

In short, *Otranto* emphasizes—though ostensibly as a warning—the unbridled desire and transgressive subjectivity supposedly characteristic of a time and place that are "Gothic" in the sense of "barbarous, uncouth, unpolished." *The Champion* emphasizes—and expressly as a model—self-discipline, social loyalty, and civic virtue in a time and place that are "Gothic" in the sense used by old Whigs— "characterized by originally Germanic independence, liberty, and virtue." Significantly, elements of both *Otranto* and *The Champion of Virtue* are to be found in other fiction from the 1790s to the 1820s. Otranto's example was followed to a large extent by Gothic romancers and "English Jacobin" novelists of the late eighteenth and early nineteenth centuries, from M. G. Lewis through William Godwin and Percy Shelley to C. R. Maturin and James Hogg; *The Champion*'s example was followed, largely but not exclusively, by other Gothic romancers and reformist novelists, from Ann Radcliffe through Mary Shelley, and perhaps Jane Austen. There is no simple dichotomy here; both the novel of transgressive subjectivity and the novel of self-disciplined civility addressed central interests of the reading public during Reeve's old age, and after. More particularly, both kinds of fiction addressed the revolutionary middle-class readership's interest in subjectivity that could be dangerously excessive but should be educated and disciplined into a sovereign subject—the basis for economic individualism, social independence, and political rights in the long process of modernization. Those developments became increasingly evident, although after *The Champion of Virtue* was published.

*The Champion* can be interpreted in various ways but, set in its time, it can be read specifically as an anti-*Otranto*, for it purposely avoids *Otranto*'s excesses and sensationalism, suggesting a literary critique that is also political in implication. To an old Whig, *Otranto* could seem formally and thematically characteristic of its author, his family, his political associations, and his public character. Notoriously, Horace Walpole was son of the corrupt and corrupting new Whig politician Sir Robert Walpole. The elder Walpole had been strongly opposed at Ipswich, in particular when Reeve was growing up there,[36] and his character, associates, and political regime were condemned in *Cato's Letters* and other old Whig writings for, among other things, exhibiting in themselves and encouraging in others unbridled desire for power, wealth, and pleasure. Horace Walpole, too, corruptly enriched himself while holding public office arranged by his father; Horace Walpole, too, indulged himself largely, disposing of his wealth in

36. Over the election of Admiral Vernon, naval hero and outspoken opponent of Walpole's government; Rogers, *Whigs and Cities*, 235, 239.

infamously conspicuous consumption at his pseudo-Gothic mansion, Strawberry Hill, near London. To an old Whig like Reeve, Horace Walpole would epitomize his father's political system, uniting royal prerogative, government patronage, landed oligarchy, and City financial interests to subvert the "constitution" in their own interests. In fact, Horace Walpole, too, thought of himself as an old Whig, partly in revolt against his father.[37] Nevertheless, against *Otranto* and its author, Reeve constructs her novel, formally and thematically, as "the champion of virtue." Retitled *The Old English Baron: A Gothic Story*, it makes the same point differently. Old Whigs decried the corruption and decadence of the "modern" age and its rage for the "new," and they blamed the fashion system of conspicuous consumption for spreading social emulation and extravagance, along with the corruption necessary to sustain these. Old Whigs frequently recurred to the past, to the "old," and to the "Gothic" constitution. Retitled, Reeve's novel promotes replacement of the "new" or "modern" English baron, such as Walpole, by the "old."

This theme is reinforced by *The Champion*'s "chronotope," or spatial and temporal dimensions. It is set in the 1420s, during a long period of instability, conflict, and civil war, with a child on the English throne, baronial factionalism that would in time ignite the Wars of the Roses, threats of revolt in Wales, and looming English defeat in the Hundred Years War with France. The novel refers to all of these events, as well as the imminent collapse of the Eastern Roman Empire before Muslim armies. Well-informed readers of Reeve's novel could draw parallels to their own time. Led by William Pitt, Britain had recently defeated France in the Seven Years' War and augmented its empire, but seemed about to lose much of it in a widely unpopular war, imposed by royal will, against the rebellious American colonies, who were supported by France. At home there was continuing party factionalism in Parliament and riotous extra-Parliamentary reform agitation spearheaded by John Wilkes. "Junius" published a series of famous letters (1768–71) based on classical republican principles and attacking the growth of royal and oligarchic power. Classical republican politics as advocated by the old Whigs were being transformed into the broadly reformist politics that would, in the nineteenth century, refound Britain as a modern liberal state.

This transformation extended the popularity of Reeve's novel through the nineteenth century. In 1810 Anna Laetitia Barbauld, another provincial Bluestocking, included it in her "British Novelists," one of many series building a canon of "national" literature for the modern state. In 1811 a "ninth edition" of Reeve's novel was published, followed by many other, usually cheap editions, aimed at middle- and lower–middle class aspirants to literature as cultural capital. These included Walker's "British Classics" edition (1817), C. Whittingham's

---

37. W. S. Lewis, *Horace Walpole* (New York, 1961), 72–73.

elegantly printed "Cabinet Library" edition, and double-column editions in cheap part-form such as Walter Scott's Ballantyne's "Novelist's Library" (1823) and Limbird's "British Novelists" (1824). Appropriately, Reeve's novel was often paired with *Otranto*, as in J. Smith's down-market editions of popular fiction (1830), Bentley's volume-a-month "Standard Novels" (1853), Milner's "Cottage Library" of "books for the people" (1858), Warne's sixpenny "Notable Novels" (1872),[38] Nimmo and Bain's popular "Old English Romances" (1883),[39] and Cassell's "National Library" (1888), edited by Henry Morley, the Liberal, education reformer, and popularizer of "good" literature for a mass readership. Reeve's novel continued to be packaged as cultural capital, but Victorian publishers and critics also prescribed it to "improve" newly enfranchised middle- and lower-class readers and to displace other kinds of "popular" fiction that were perceived as corrupting and insidious, such as "Salisbury Square" Gothic fiction and the "sensation" novel.[40]

Like the old Whig politics and purpose that animated it, then, Reeve's novel proved adaptable to new political and cultural conditions, new political and cultural agendas, new tasks in state formation and maintenance—more so than any work by other eighteenth-century Bluestockings. Appropriately, the adaptability of Reeve's novel illustrated a central critical argument of her other major work, *The Progress of Romance*. Whereas Reeve's novel remained a popular classic long after her death, the other Bluestockings were taken up by the educated and well-to-do reading public of the nineteenth and early twentieth centuries as letter writers who were thought to combine feminine interests with intellectual ones. But all of them were appropriated in the formation of the modern liberal state, albeit in different ways, and they continue to be so used in the process of reforming it today, as feminist scholarship and criticism claim a greater place for women, past and present, in the lineages, institutions, culture, and politics of the modern state. The Bluestockings may not have had the modern liberal state in mind, any more than did other old Whigs, classical republicans, or eighteenth-century Commonwealthmen. They did have the task of reforming the state in mind, however, and they believed that "literary and intellectual women"— Bluestockings—could and should help to carry it out.

*University of Alberta*

38. Other "Notable Novels" were Elizabeth Helme's *St Clair of the Isles;* Regina Maria Roche's *The Children of the Abbey;* Maria Cummins's *The Lamplighter;* Jane Porter's *Thaddeus of Warsaw* and *The Hungarian Brothers;* and Anna Warner's *The Howards of Glen Luna.*

39. "Old English Romances" included Sterne's *Tristram Shandy*, 2 vols.; *The Arabian Nights*, 4 vols.; Beckford's *Vathek* with Johnson's *Rasselas;* Defoe's *Robinson Crusoe*, 2 vols.; Swift's *Gulliver's Travels;* and Sterne's *A Sentimental Journey* with Swift's *A Tale of a Tub.*

40. See Cannon Schmitt, *Alien Nation: Nineteenth-Century Gothic Fictions and English Nationality* (Philadelphia, 1997), chap. 4.

# "Out rushed a female to protect the Bard": The Bluestocking Defense of Shakespeare

> SOME ladies indeed have shewn a truly public Spirit in rescuing the ad-
> mirable, yet almost forgotten Shakespear, from being totally sunk in
> oblivion: —they have generously contributed to raise a monument to
> his memory, and frequently honoured his works with their presence on
> the stage: —an action, which deserves the highest encomiums, and will
> be attended with an adequate reward; since, in preserving the fame of
> the dead bard, they add a brightness to their own, which will shine to
> late posterity.
>
> — Eliza Haywood, *The Female Spectator*

Eliza Haywood's tribute to "some ladies" provides the twentieth-first-century literary scholar with a striking example of a reversal of roles.[1] Here we find a male writer being rescued from oblivion—one who today is the undisputed symbol of excellence at the heart of the canon of English literature, a staple ingredient in all curricula. It is hard to envisage a time when his reputation was not yet formed or to imagine that the work of a group of ladies was necessary to defend his cause. While Haywood may have been exaggerating in describing Shakespeare as on the point of sinking into oblivion, it is certain that the Shakespeare Ladies' Club did much to promote his work at an opportune moment in the history of his reputation. Formed in the late months of 1736, this

I would like to thank the Huntington Library for the award of a Michael J. Connell Foundation Fellowship in the spring of 2001, and I am extremely grateful to the librarians and staff for their help during the three months I spent reading the Montagu correspondence. I would also like to thank Felicity Nussbaum and Roy Ritchie for organizing the memorable Bluestocking Conference held at the Huntington in April 2001; Nicole Pohl, Betty Schellenberg, and Susan Green for their editorial wisdom and support; Nick Harrison for his extremely helpful readings of this essay; and all those who participated in seminars at the University of Warwick Eighteenth Century Centre, the Feminism and Enlightenment Project, and the Romantic Seminar at the University of Chicago, where earlier versions of this essay were read and discussed.

1.   *The Female Spectator* quoted in Michael Dobson, *The Making of a National Poet: Shakespeare, Adaptation, and Authorship* (Oxford, 1992), 197.

group of women was concerned to encourage London's theatrical managers to give Shakespeare a greater share in their repertories.[2] Haywood's optimistic prophecy that these ladies would enjoy "adequate reward" for their labors in the glories of posterity has unfortunately proved mistaken. Women's contribution to "preserving the dead bard" has largely been forgotten, despite their often pioneering role as agents of change in the history of his reputation.[3]

As early as 1753 Arthur Murphy commented, "With us islanders Shakespeare is a kind of established religion in poetry,"[4] and by the beginning of the nineteenth century a knowledge and love of Shakespeare was considered integral to the English character, a definitive aspect of national identity. In Jane Austen's *Mansfield Park* (1814), for example, Henry Crawford's facility with Shakespeare proves his most attractive attribute in the eyes of the pure-hearted Fanny. He refers to the bard as "part of an Englishman's constitution. . . . His thoughts and beauties are so spread abroad that one touches them everywhere, one is intimate with him by instinct."[5] Austen's description reveals the degree to which critics and theater managers of the previous century had been successful in cultivating a taste for his "natural genius" and "impetuous poetry."

Modern critics have often addressed the eighteenth-century revival of Shakespeare's reputation through reference to the developing phenomenon of textual revision and adaptation as well as the dramatic trends of the English stage.[6] Two recent studies of the creation of Shakespeare's reputation as a national poet in the eighteenth century refer fleetingly to women's role in spreading "his thoughts and beauties."[7] However, as critics, patrons, and readers of his work, women were strongly associated with Shakespeare during the eighteenth century, the pe-

2. Emmett L. Avery, "The Shakespeare Ladies Club," *Shakespeare Quarterly* 7 (1956): 153–58.
3. Feminist literary critics have started to explore women writers' responses to his work in terms of their processes of "re-vision." See Marianne Novy, ed., *Women's Re-visions of Shakespeare: On the Responses of Dickinson, Woolf, Rich, H.D., George Eliot, and Others* (Urbana and Chicago, 1990); and her *Cross-Cultural Performances: Differences in Women's Re-visions of Shakespeare* (Urbana and Chicago, 1993); Judith Hawley, "Shakespearean Sensibilities: Women Writers Reading Shakespeare, 1753–1808," in Joan Batchelor, Tom Cain, and Claire Lamont, eds., *Shakespearean Continuities: Essays in Honour of E. A. J. Honigman* (London, 1997), 290–304.
4. *Shakespeare: The Critical Heritage, Volume 4, 1753–1765*, ed. Brian Vickers (London and Boston, 1976), 1.
5. Jane Austen, *Mansfield Park* (London, 1988), 335.
6. See Simon Jarvis, *Scholars and Gentlemen: Shakespearean Textual Criticism and Representations of Scholarly Labour, 1725–1765* (Oxford, 1995); Fred Parker, *Johnson's Shakespeare* (Oxford, 1989); Magreta De Grazia, *Shakespeare Verbatim: The Reproduction of Authenticity and the 1790s Apparatus* (Oxford, 1991); and Dobson, *Shakespeare, Adaptation, and Authorship*.
7. Jonathan Bate, *Shakespearean Constitutions: Politics, Theatre, Criticism, 1730–1830* (Oxford, 1989); and Gary Taylor, *Reinventing Shakespeare: A Cultural History from the Restoration to the Present* (London, 1990).

riod in which his identity as hero of the national literary pantheon was first established.[8] While many contemporary critics have been concerned to add
women's writing to an existing canon of literature by men, few have considered
women's role in forming that canon at its first inception or acknowledged their
active critical presence as a historical fact that must be relearned. By considering
the qualities in Shakespeare's writings that appealed to women critics (or repelled
them), one can not only learn a great deal about their professional literary interests and allegiances but also form a richer and more nuanced picture of a period
in which women's cultural ascendancy coincided with the formation of the literary canon.

This essay will focus on Elizabeth Montagu's *Essay on the Writings and Genius
of Shakespear, Compared with the Greek and French Dramatic Poets: With Some
Remarks upon the Misrepresentations of Mons. de Voltaire* (London, 1769), drawing
comparisons with Elizabeth Griffith's *The Morality of Shakespeare's Drama Illustrated* (London, 1775). Montagu and Griffith of course appear among the group
of women portrayed in Richard Samuel's painting *The Nine Living Muses of Great
Britain* (1779), an image frequently used in recent years to demonstrate the cultural importance of Bluestocking activity to the British nation (and reproduced in
this volume on page 62).[9] In a less well known celebration of female achievement,
*The Female Geniad* (1791), the thirteen-year-old Elizabeth Ogilvie Benger specifically linked Montagu and Griffith as "female champions" of Shakespeare's cause:

> Well might great Shakespeare crowns of triumph wear,
> When female champions in his cause appear;
> E'en nature's bard's indebted to their aid,
> They gleam'd resplendent o'er his hoary shade:
> And whilst they his reviving laurels wreath'd,
> On both the spirit of the poet breath'd:
> Let then their mem'ries in ne'er fading bloom,
> Immortal flourish on their Shakespeare's tomb.[10]

Like Eliza Haywood before her, the precocious Benger celebrated the interdepen-
dent relation between "nature's bard" and the Bluestocking critics. Her heroines
included Elizabeth Carter, Anna Barbauld, Angelica Kauffman, Charlotte Smith,

---

8.   See Ann Thompson and Sasha Roberts, eds., *Women Reading Shakespeare, 1600–1900: An Anthology of
     Criticism* (Manchester and New York, 1997).
9.   See Elizabeth Eger, "Representing Culture: *The Nine Living Muses of Great Britain,* 1779," in Elizabeth
     Eger, Charlotte Grant, Cliona O'Gallchoir, and Penny Warburton, eds., *Women, Writing, and the Public
     Sphere, 1700–1830* (Cambridge, 2001), 104–32.
10.  Elizabeth Ogilvie Benger, *The Female Geniad* (London, 1791), canto 3, pp. 44–45.

and Charlotte Lennox.[11] Her sense of pride in her countrywomen unites them in their cultural mission, eliding differences in their critical approaches. Her attitude was in fact typical of contemporary interest in female literary activity, which often expressed ideas of national identity in complex and perplexing ways, as Harriet Guest has recently suggested in her illuminating and subtle study of women, learning, and patriotism in the period.[12] National interest in Shakespeare's genius provided female critics with an opportunity to gain a public platform not only for "female genius" but also for questions of gender and literary authority related to the place and future of women in society. In considering the dialectical relationship between Shakespeare's cultural authority and Bluestocking critical authority, I will consider not only how women positioned themselves in relation to masculine literary models of their own and previous eras but also how the Bluestockings made a distinctively feminine contribution to a critical tradition that focused on Shakespeare's powers of characterization and his status as a poet of the vernacular. Montagu's and Griffith's work paved the way for an emerging critical association between Shakespeare and national identity that was to gain strength and dominate literary criticism in the Romantic period and beyond.

11. Lennox was also a Shakespeare critic, of course. Her *Shakespear Illustrated* (1753–54) presented, for the first time, translations of Shakespeare's sources in French and Italian romances. Unlike her successors Montagu and Griffith, Lennox found Shakespeare inadequate in relation to his literary models, arguing that he was lacking in invention and originality. Her negative attitude to Shakespeare proved extremely unpopular in her lifetime, damaging her own reputation as a playwright, but her unusual stance, which presents a thinly veiled defense of the feminine genre of romance literature (and by extension, the novel), has proved of great interest recently. See Margaret Anne Doody, "Shakespeare's Novels: Charlotte Lennox Illustrated," *Studies in the Novel* 19 (1987): 296–310. For a reading of Lennox's text in terms of Kristeva's theory of abjection, see Susan Green, "A Cultural Reading of Charlotte Lennox's *Shakespear Illustrated*," in J. Douglas Canfield and Deborah C. Payne, eds., *Cultural Readings of Restoration and Eighteenth-Century English Theatre* (Athens and London, 1995), 221. See Jonathan Brody Kramnick, *Making the English Canon: Print-Capitalism and the Cultural Past, 1700–1770* (Cambridge, 1998), 115–29, for a discussion of Lennox's *Shakespear Illustrated* in relation to Enlightenment debates about the relative literary value of the novel and Shakespeare's drama.

    In *The Female Geniad* Benger described Lennox's "penetration" and her ability to "prune" Shakespeare's "flowers" in the following enthusiastic terms:

    > We thank great Shakespeare for his pleasing faults!
    > Since these employ'd a female critic's thoughts.
    > Long had proud man with an usurping pride,
    > The right of judgment to our sex denied;
    > But now no longer can exclude our claim;
    > Which finds protection in a Lennox's name
    > Nor more presume our just demand to slight,
    > When female genius beams such radiant light.

    (Canto 3, pp. 47–48)
12. Harriet Guest, *Small Change: Women, Learning, Patriotism, 1750–1810* (Chicago, 2000).

## Female Champions: Women, Shakespeare, and Critical Authority

Elizabeth Montagu's *Essay on the Writings and Genius of Shakespear* was first published, anonymously, by Dodsley in 1769. The run of a thousand copies quickly sold out. The *Essay* is a patriotic defense of Shakespeare and his English admirers that argues for his originality and natural genius. The work is exceptional both in taking on Voltaire's notorious criticisms directly and in mounting a blistering critique of the French neoclassical dramatists in return.[13] While her desire to publish anonymously conformed to contemporary practice and cannot be interpreted solely as a feminine act of modesty, it is certain that she harbored general doubts about being a "female Author" in a masculine field as well as specific concerns about the work's merit and her temerity in opposing Voltaire.[14] When she heard that her father had discovered her authorship, she wrote to him explaining her reasons "for the secrecy with which I acted":

> In the first place, there is in general a prejudice against female Authors especially if they invade those regions of litterature which the Men are desirous to reserve to themselves. While I was young, I should not have liked to have been class'd among authors, but at my age it is less unbecoming. If an old Woman does not bewitch her Neighbours Cows, nor make any girl in the Parish spit crooked pins, the World has not reason to take offence at her amusing herself with reading books or even writing them. However, some circumstances in this particular case advise secrecy. Mr Pope our great Poet, the Bishop of Gloucester our Great Critick, & Dr Johnson our great Scholar having already given their criticism upon Shakespear, there was a degree of presumption in pretending to meddle with a subject they had already treated tolerably well, sure to incur their envy if I succeded, their contempt if I did not. Then for a weak & unknown Champion to throw down the gauntlett of defiance in the very teeth of Voltaire appear'd too daring.... I was obliged to enter seriously into the nature of the Dramatick purposes, & the character of the best dramatick writings, & by sometimes differing from the Code of the great Legislator in Poeticks,

---

13. For a history of Voltaire's views on Shakespeare, see Thomas Lounsbury, *Shakespeare and Voltaire* (London, 1902); and Haydn Mason, "Voltaire versus Shakespeare: The Lettre à l'Académie française (1776)," *British Journal for Eighteenth-Century Studies* 18, no. 2 (1995): 173–85.

14. James Kennedy and W. A. Smith, eds., *Dictionary of Anonymous and Pseudonymous English Literature* (London and Edinburgh, 1926), xi–xxiii; and Catherine Gallagher, *Nobody's Story: The Vanishing Acts of Women Writers in the Marketplace, 1670–1820* (Berkeley, Calif., 1994).

Aristotle, I was afraid the Learned would reject my opinions, the unlearned yawn over my pages, so that I was very doubtfull of the general success of my work. (MO 4767, Montagu to Matthew Robinson, 10 September 1769)[15]

She was aware that her opinions were highly unconventional and might be unpopular, with both scholars and the general reader; she considers herself "very fortunate that the pert Newswriters have not sneered at the Lady Critick," as she says later in the same letter.

Montagu's fears proved unnecessary. Public admiration for her heroic and pioneering deed, which appealed to national pride, ensured that her identity as author was swiftly circulated. She soon received flattering letters from several of the leading male philosophers and critics of her day, including Edmund Burke, Lord Kames, Hugh Blair, James Beattie, and Sir Joshua Reynolds. The theater manager David Garrick, who had orchestrated a series of elaborate performances and popular entertainments to celebrate "Shakespeare's Jubilee" in 1769, first at Stratford-upon-Avon and then at Drury Lane in London, was one of Montagu's greatest admirers.[16] He published a poem praising her in *St. James's Chronicle* for 24–26 January 1771, in which he depicted Voltaire as "The Gallic God of literary War":

A Giant He, among the Sons of France
And at our Shakespear pois'd his glitt'ring Lance.
Out rush'd a Female to protect the Bard,
Snatch'd up her Spear, and for the fight prepar'd:
Attack'd the Vet'ran, pierced his Sev'n-fold Shield,
And drove him wounded, fainting from the field.
With Laurel crown'd, away the Goddess flew,
Pallas confest then open'd to our view,
Quitting her fav'rite form of Montagu.

Montagu appeared as a critical Amazon, slaying her opponent with fatal precision. By the time the fourth edition of the *Essay* appeared in 1777, she was confident enough to print her name on the title page, a year after a triumphant visit to Paris, where she had participated in a heated debate about the relative value of English and French literature at the Académie Française, which I discuss in

15. See Elizabeth Eger, ed., *Selected Works of Elizabeth Montagu*, vol. 1 of *Bluestocking Feminism: Writings of the Bluestocking Circle, 1738–1785*, gen. ed. Gary Kelly, 6 vols. (London, 1999), 170; cited henceforward in the text. "MO" numbers refer to letters in the Huntington Library's Montagu Collection, also cited in the text.

16. See Johanne M. Stochholm, *Garrick's Folly: The Shakespeare Jubilee of 1769 at Stratford and Drury Lane* (London, 1964).

more detail below. She also added her three *Dialogues of the Dead*, satirical comments on modern society, to the fourth and fifth editions. In 1783, Andrew Kippis, editor of the *Biographica Britannica*, wrote to Montagu to tell her that her work was "the best Defense of Shakespeare ever written, and that it is one of the most complete pieces of poetical Criticism which any Age or Country has produced" (MO 1211, 27 December 1783). Robert Potter encouraged her, telling Montagu that "whoever writes for the public ought to have a proper confidence in himself and this the public authorizes you to have; you have therefore a right to feel and express a consciousness of the merit of that admirable work" (MO 4165, 1 July 1783).

While the figures of the Scottish Enlightenment welcomed Montagu's brilliance, Samuel Johnson proved harder to impress. The moral philosopher James Beattie probably gives a reliable assessment of Johnson's reaction to her work; he was writing under her patronage and was therefore inclined to flatter, but his sentiments were shared by Montagu's circle of eminent literary friends:

> Johnson's harsh and foolish censure of Mrs Montagu's book does not surprise me, for I have heard him speak contemptuously of it. It is, for all that, one of the best, most original, and most elegant pieces of criticism in our language, or any other. Johnson had many of the talents of a critic; but his want of temper, his violent prejudices, and something, I am afraid, of an envious turn of mind, made him often a very unfair one. Mrs Montagu was very kind to him, but Mrs Montagu has more wit than anybody; and Johnson could not bear that any person should be thought to have wit but himself.[17]

Montagu's relationship with Johnson, whose edition of Shakespeare had appeared in 1765, was inevitably competitive. As two of the most powerful figures of London literary life, they sometimes courted and flattered each other but were generally suspicious and wary.[18] Montagu began her *Essay* before his edition appeared, but she was anxious about the comparisons people would inevitably make. She herself found the preface to his edition disappointing, as she expressed in no uncertain terms to her sister in 1766:

> I find people so dissatisfied with Mr Johnson's performance that I can hardly displease more & indeed must do it less as he has disappointed a great expectation. While he was following the syllables

---

17. *Life of Beattie*, ed. Sir William Forbes, 2 vols. (London, 1807), 2:375.
18. See Norma Clarke, *Dr. Johnson's Women* (London, 2000), 138–45.

of verbal criticism he neglected the scope of the Author, & if he has cleared some passages he has rather thrown an obscurity over the genius of the great Tragedian. (MO 5836, Montagu to Sarah Scott, 11 January 1766)

Single-minded in her views and self-consciously differing from previous critics of Shakespeare, Montagu wanted to distance herself from Johnson in particular, although this is clearer from the correspondence than from the *Essay* itself. While Johnson's preface dealt with a number of pressing methodological questions in the history of Shakespeare criticism, he failed in Montagu's view to address "the peculiar excellencies of Shakespear as a Dramatick poet." As she protested in a letter to Elizabeth Carter, "this point I shall labour as I think he therein excells everyone" (MO 3176, 19 July 1766; Eger, 170). Montagu mounted a passionate defense of Shakespeare's dramatic powers, particularly original in her focus on his supernatural beings.[19]

Montagu's correspondence with Carter at this time conveys the emerging strength of her confidence as she proceeds to take on the venerable sages of dramatic criticism, past and present:

> I am quite of your opinion that our last Commentator of Shakespear [Johnson] found the piddling trade of verbal criticism below his genius and I am much at a loss when I would account for his persisting in it, through ye course of so many volumes. It has been lucky for my amusement, but unfortunate for the publick, that he did not consider his author in a more extensive view. I have so much veneration for our Poet, & so much zeal for the honour of our Country, & I think the Theatrical entertainments capable of conveying so much instruction, & of exciting such sentiments in the people, that if I am glad he left the task to my unable hand, I dare hardly own it to myself. Our rank in the Belles lettres depends a good deal on that degree of merit which is allow'd to Shakespeare, who is more than any other writer read by foreigners. (MO3187, 21 October 1766; Eger, 173)

Once again, Montagu identifies England's reputation with that of Shakespeare. She expresses her belief in his plays' potential for "conveying instruction" and "exciting sentiments in the people." She goes on to criticize Johnson's negative

19. Jonathan Bate's claim that her *Essay* "is wholeheartedly Johnsonian, often uncritically dependent on the 1765 preface" is misleading, to say the least (*Shakespearean Constitutions*, 14).

attitude to previous commentators, again lamenting his inability to praise Shakespeare's "dramatick genius":

> [H]e should have said more or have said nothing. If he had given attention to the dramatick genius of Shakespear he might have done him justice, & I wonder he did not enter with pleasure into a task that seem'd peculiarly suited to him, he has taste & learning, therefore is a capable critick; he wants invention, he wants strength & vigour of genius to go through a long original work. I will own he gives smart correction to former commentators, but ye last Commentator deserves the least indulgence, as he had most opportunity of seeing the futility of the thing. (MO 3187, 21 October 1766; Eger, 173–74)

It is in the semi-public realm of her correspondence with a fellow female author, rather than in her published works, that Montagu's critical energy and ambition are most apparent and that she formulated pungent criticisms of the strongest male literary voices of her age. In the published version of the *Essay*, Montagu was more respectful to her male forebears and peers and to the tradition of eighteenth-century scholarship:

> Mr Pope, in the preface to his edition of Shakespear, sets out by declaring, that, of all English poets, this tragedian offers the fullest and fairest subject for criticism. Animated by an opinion of such authority, some of the most learned and ingenious of our critics have made correct editions of his works, and enriched them with notes. The superiority of talent and learning, which I acknowledge in these editors, leaves me no room to entertain the vain presumption of attempting to correct any passages of this celebrated author; but the whole, as corrected and elucidated by them, lies open to a thorough enquiry into the genius of our great English classic. Unprejudiced and candid judgement will be the surest basis of his fame. (*Essay*, 1–2; Eger, 1)

While her epistolary commentary was often competitive and aggressive, then, her public critical demeanor was characterized by a shrewd adherence to a feminine model of literary decorum. Nevertheless, her appeal to "Unprejudiced and candid judgement" was one calculated to suggest her own particular qualification for the task in hand. She was, it appeared, happy to neglect the dry labors of masculine critical scholarship in order to assert a more naturalistic and particularly feminine understanding of Shakespeare's genius.

## SHAKESPEARE'S FEMININE VIRTUES: SYMPATHY, CHARACTER, AND MORAL PHILOSOPHY

In both her criticism and her correspondence, Montagu emphasized Shakespeare's capacity to dramatize a moral language. She wrote to George Lyttelton in 1760, "I must observe too that the moral reflections of Shakespeare are not the cold and formal observations of a Spectator, but come warm from the heart of an interested person" (MO 4531; Eger, 160). Montagu saw the social potential of such an instinctive form of morality, writing to William Pulteney, "Dramatick writings may be of the greatest service to the Morals of the people, if written as naturally as Shakespeare writes" (MO 3084; Eger, 162). Writing in the wake of Montagu's success, Elizabeth Griffith dedicated her *Morality of Shakespeare's Drama Illustrated* (1775) to David Garrick, friend to both women. In her preface she referred to Montagu's work as her inspiration:

> To the further honour of the Author, be it said, that a Lady of distinguished merit has lately appeared a champion in his cause, against the minor critic, this minute philosopher, this fly upon the pillar of St. Paul's [Voltaire]. It was her example which has stirred up my emulation to this attempt; for I own that I am ambitious of the honour of appearing to think, at least, though I despair of the success of writing, like her.[20]

Griffith found Montagu's confidence and critical combativeness worthy of emulation, and both writers communicate a profound respect for their contemporary sister authors.[21] Furthermore, I would suggest that Bluestocking critical solidarity revolved around a shared belief in the feminine virtues that Shakespeare's drama brought to life.

20. Elizabeth Griffith, *The Morality of Shakespeare's Drama Illustrated* (London, 1775), vii; cited henceforward in the text.

21. While Montagu was more willing to criticize her male contemporaries than was Griffith, both women shared a debt to women writers and aligned themselves with their sister authors. In her discussion of the follies of love in *As You Like It*, Griffith mentions fellow muse Anna Barbauld (then still Aikin): "There is a very pretty poem of the same subject, and which seems to have taken its hint from this same passage in Shakespeare, though the instances are different and more in number, written by Miss Aikin, among a collection of her's lately published, which I would insert here, but that I suppose every reader of taste must be in possession of the work which so well deserves a place in the most select libraries; as doing equal honour to literature, and her sex (see page 66 of her Poems)" (Griffith, *Morality of Shakespeare,* 77). Montagu regularly solicited the opinion of Elizabeth Carter in preparing for the task of writing the *Essay;* Carter sent her translations of Greek drama and extended essays on tragedy and comedy. They corresponded frequently during the time of the *Essay's* composition and it appears that Carter checked and authorized the revisions that appear in the fifth edition (1785).

However, while Griffith and Montagu shared a concern for the morally instructive quality of Shakespeare's work, their approaches are very different.
Montagu's *Essay* begins with a general chapter on the quality of Shakespeare's
"Dramatic Poetry" and then presents detailed discussions of his historical drama
(particularly *Henry IV*); "Preternatural Beings"; and his tragedies, concentrating
on *Macbeth* and *Julius Caesar*, including an aggressive attack on Corneille's *Cinna*.
Her analysis has the formal sophistication of traditional defenses, such as those
of Sidney and Pope. Griffith's work is closer in style to an educational anthology,
in which she reprints long excerpts from thirty-two of Shakespeare's plays, in-
terspersed with her moral commentary. She explains her purpose thus:

> In these remarks and observations I have not restricted myself to
> morals purely ethic, but have extended my observations and re-
> flections to whatever has reference to the general oeconomy of life
> and manners, respecting prudence, polity, decency, and decorum;
> or relative to the tender affections and fond endearments of human
> nature; more especially regarding those moral duties which are the
> truest source of moral bliss—domestic ties, offices and obligations.
> (*Morality of Shakespeare,* xii–xiii)

Here Griffith is developing a theme suggested by Montagu, as she owns in her
"General Postscript":

> Mrs Montagu says, very justly, that "We are apt to consider
> Shakespeare only as a poet; but he is certainly one of the greatest
> moral philosophers that ever lived." And this is true; because, in his
> universal scheme of doctrine, he comprehends manners, propri-
> eties, and decorums; and whatever relates to these, to personal char-
> acter, or national description, falls equally within the great line of
> morals. Horace prefers Homer to all the philosophers,
>
> Qui, quid sit pulchrum, quid turpe, quid utile, quid non, Plenius
> et melius Chrysippo et Crantore dicit.
>
> And surely Shakespeare *plenius et melius* excels him again, as much
> as the living scene exceeds the dead letter, as action is preferable to
> didaction, or representation to declamation. (*Morality of Shake-
> speare,* 526)

Like Montagu's, Griffith's work formed a zealous defense of Shakespeare's dramatic power, particularly focusing on his ability to create believable and compelling characters. Both Montagu and Griffith considered example better than

precept, and they praised Shakespeare's ability to represent virtue on stage. As Griffith wrote, "Plato wished that Virtue could assume a visible form. Dramatic exhibition gives one, both to Virtue and to Vice" (p. 526).

It was Shakespeare's powers of imaginative sympathy and of characterization that made his lessons so compelling, for Montagu and Griffith. These, Montagu argued, gave his work a realism superior to the allegorical conceits of neoclassical drama: "In delineating characters he must be allowed far to surpass all dramatic writers, and even Homer himself; he gives an air of reality to everything, and in spite of many and great faults, effects, better than any one has done, the chief purpose of the theatrical representation" (*Essay*, 20; Eger, 7–8). As she explained:

> For copying nature as he found it in the busy walks of human life, he drew from an original, with which the literati are seldom well acquainted. They perceive his portraits are not of the Grecian or of the Roman school: after finding them unlike to the celebrated forms preserved in learned museums they do not deign to enquire whether they resemble the living persons they were intended to represent. Among these connoisseurs, whose acquaintance with the characters of men is formed in the library, not in the street, the camp, or village, whatever is unpolished and uncouth passes for fantastic and absurd, though, in fact, it is a faithful representation of a really existing character. (*Essay*, 17–18; Eger, 7)

Both Griffith and Montagu thus praised Shakespeare's psychological astuteness as derived not from formal training but from everyday experience and for that reason able to reach the inner depths of the human imagination.[22] Montagu wrote of his *Julius Caesar:*

> Great knowledge of the human heart had informed him, how easy it is to excite a sympathy with things believed real.... He wrote to please an untaught people, guided wholly by their feelings, and to those feelings he applied, and they are often touched by circumstances that have not dignity and splendor enough to please the eye accustomed to the specious miracles of ostentatious art, and the nice selection of refined judgement. (*Essay*, 276–27; Eger, 108)

In the eyes of Montagu and Griffith, Shakespeare's knowledge of the "human heart" made him especially successful in his characterization of the female sex.

22.  Cf. Griffith, *Morality of Shakespeare:* "[The Greeks' plays] were performed in the morning; which circumstance suffered the salutary effect to be worn out of the mind, by the business or avocation of the day. Ours are at night; the impressions accompany us to our couch, supply the matter for out latest reflections, and may sometimes furnish the subject of our very dreams" (p. 526).

Montagu's assessment of Macbeth and Lady Macbeth praises Shakespeare's sensitivity to the difference between male and female emotions:

> The difference between a mind naturally prone to evil, and a frail one warped by force of temptations, is delicately distinguished in Macbeth and his wife. There are also some touches of the pencil that mark the male and female character. When they deliberate on the murder of the king, the duties of host and subject strongly plead with him against the deed. She passes over these considerations; goes to Duncan's chamber resolved to kill him, but could not do it, because, she says, he resembles her father while he slept. There is somthing feminine in this, and perfectly agreeable to the nature of the sex; who, even when void of principle, are seldom entirely divested of sentiment; and thus the poet, who, to use his own phrase, had overstepped the modesty of nature in the exaggerated fierceness of her character, returns back to the line and limits of humanity, and that very judiciously, by a sudden impression, which has only an instantaneous effect. As her character was not composed of those gentle elements out of which regular repentance could be formed, it was well judged to throw her mind into the chaos of madness; and, as she had exhibited wickedness in its highest degree of ferocity and atrociousness, she should be an example of the wildest agonies of remorse. As Shakespear could most exactly delineate the human mind in its regular state of reason, so no one ever so happily caught its varying forms in the wanderings of delirium. (*Essay*, 200–202; Eger, 77)

This is an unusually tolerant interpretation of Lady Macbeth's conduct, which proved notoriously unpalatable to eighteenth-century audiences. But it is consistent with Montagu's admiration for Shakespeare's powers of identification with his characters, his facility to inhabit their minds, which she describes thus:

> Shakespear seems to have had the art of the Dervise, in the Arabian tales, who could throw his soul into the body of another man, and be at once possessed of his sentiments, adopt his passions, and rise to all the functions and feelings of his situation.[23] (*Essay*, 37; Eger, 13)

23.  This language appears in an earlier form in a letter to Lord Lyttelton of 10 October 1760, in which Montagu also compares Sophocles to Dryden, Cowley, and Shakespeare: "Shakespear; he alone, like the Dervise in the Arabian tales, can throw his soul into the body of another man; feel all his sentiments, perform his function, & fill his place. . . . Every passing sentiment is caught by this great genius; every shade of passion, every gradation of thought is mark'd" (MO 1402).

It could be argued that Shakespeare's sympathetic portrayal of his heroines was particularly admired by female critics. Margaret Cavendish wrote that "one would think that he had been Metamorphosed from a Man to a Woman, for who could describe Cleopatra Better than he hath done, and many other Females of his own Creating."[24] However, both Montagu and Griffith seem to highlight Shakespeare's most impressive female characters in fact to emphasize his depiction of a common humanity that transcends the boundaries of gender, praising his capacity to educate and reform both sexes in their knowledge of each other. Griffith referred to Shakespeare's chameleon-like ability to display a range of characters thus: "What age, what sex, what character, escapes the touches of Shakespeare's plastic hand!" (*Morality of Shakespeare*, 169).

The Bluestocking emphasis on the didactic potential of Shakespeare's plays was taken up by several nineteenth-century women, from Mary Lamb to Anna Jameson, whose *Characteristics of Women, Moral, Poetical and Historical,* first published in 1832, later became known as "Shakespeare's Heroines." "It appears to me," she wrote in the introduction, "that the condition of women in society, as at present constituted is false in itself, and injurious to them,—that the education of women is at present founded in mistaken principles, and tends to increase fearfully the sum of misery and error in both sexes." Rather than write "essays on morality, and treatises on education," however, Jameson used Shakespeare's heroines

> to illustrate the manner in which the affections would naturally display themselves in women—whether combined with high intellect, regulated by reflection, and elevated by imagination, or existing with perverted dispositions or purified moral sentiments. I found all these in Shakespeare . . . his characters combine history and real life; they are complete individuals, whose hearts and souls are laid open before us—all may behold and all judge for themselves.[25]

Jameson was attracted to Shakespeare's plays precisely because they appeared to invite what Montagu had termed "unprejudiced and candid judgement." Bluestocking criticism can be seen, then, to foreshadow a nineteenth-century feminist interest in Shakespeare's strength as a moral teacher and humane judge of female character.

24. From Margaret Cavendish, duchess of Newcastle, Letter CXXIII in *CCXI Sociable Letters* (London, 1664); quoted in Thompson and Roberts, eds., *Women Reading Shakespeare*, 13.
25. Quoted ibid., 67.

However, while it might be tempting to define Montagu's and Griffith's works in terms of a female tradition of writings on Shakespeare's uses as a moral teacher, it is important to recognize their ambitions in a broader critical context. Both were keen to reach a general audience of both sexes and to be treated as critical equals with their male counterparts. Griffith's work is addressed both to men and women, who are in equal need of reform: "Vice is neither masculine, nor feminine; 'tis the common of the two" (*Morality of Shakespeare*, 169).

Montagu wished to share her commitment to Shakespeare's genius with as many of her contemporaries as possible; she took great satisfaction in the idea of her *Essay*'s spreading influence as reflected in reviews of her works, as she notes in a letter to Elizabeth Vesey:

> You will be glad to hear that doughty Corporation of Criticks who call themselves ye Critical Reviewers have most graciously extoll'd a certain essay, indeed far beyond its desert, & indeed far beyond the Authors conceit of its merit. As many good people in all the towns in England regulate their opinions by this review it is lucky. The rich Grocer, the substantial Manufacturer sits & reads this litterary gazette with implicit faith, & ye Curate (who dictates in matters of learning to ye Farmers Heiress, who at boarding school learnt to read Novels) takes his opinions & derives his knowledge from ye Monthly papers. (MO 6398, 5 June 1769)

In the same letter, she fantasizes about the instructive benefits to be received from her work by "ye Farmers Heiress, who at boarding school learnt to read Novels." She intended to educate readers of all social ranks in Shakespeare's genius. With this purpose in mind, she ensured that her own expository style was clear and simple, accurate and accessible. In the following section of this essay I will explore the question of women's particular investment in the status of the English language.

## FEMALE CRITICS AND THE "MOTHER-TONGUE"

The defense of Shakespeare by women writers was inevitably political in the context of broader eighteenth-century debates about the relative status of the classical and modern languages.[26] But Bluestocking Shakespeare critics were in particular conscious of following in a line of female scholars who had made serious arguments for their sex's privileged relation to English itself. As Aphra Behn wrote

26.  Joseph M. Levine, *The Battle of the Books: History and Literature in the Augustan Age* (Ithaca, N.Y., 1991).

in the preface to her play *The Dutch Lover* (1673), the genre of drama provided particularly good evidence of the pleasures of plain speaking:

> Plays have no great room for that which is men's great advantage over women, that is Learning; we all well know that the Immortal Shakespeare's Plays (who was not guilty of much more than often falls to women's share) have better pleas'd the World than Jonson's works, though, by the way 'tis said that Benjamin was no such Rabbi neither, for I am inform'd that his Learning was but Grammar high; (sufficient indeed to rob poor Salust of his best Orations.)[27]

Part of Shakespeare's attraction for his earliest female commentators and imitators, then, was the quality of "unlearnedness." Anxieties about the effects of scholarship on the fair sex tended to focus on the dangerous disciplines of classical learning and science, in which women's demonstration of learning was potentially transformative, unsettling their role in practical life. Appreciation of the national poet was ostensibly less objectionable, not appearing to represent a threat to the patriarchal foundations of higher knowledge and in fact complying with contemporary restrictions of women's access to the classical languages. Women who knew the classical languages, such as Carter, were considered curious exceptions, and Anna Barbauld had to plead with her father to allow her access to Latin and Greek lessons at Warrington Academy. It can be no accident that some of the most powerful early defenses of the native tongue were written by women, who emphasized the scholarly achievement of the study of English grammar and literary history.

Elizabeth Elstob was one of those stoutly committed to lauding the Northern tongues. An ambitious scholar from an early age, she mastered eight languages but considered Germanic studies more open to women than "the Greek and Latin store." Her eventful life included a spell working as consultant to George Ballard, author of the pioneering and scholarly *Memoirs of Several Ladies of Great Britain Celebrated for their Writings* (1752).[28] Toward the end of her life she became governess to the children of the duchess of Portland, who was a great friend of Montagu's. Montagu's letters are said to have passed through Elstob's hands on

27. Aphra Behn, preface to *The Dutch Lover*, in *The Works of Aphra Behn*, ed. Montague Summers (London, 1915; reprint ed., New York, 1967), 224.
28. See Ruth Perry, "George Ballard's Biographies of Learned Ladies," in J. D. Browning, ed., *Biography in the Eighteenth Century* (New York, 1980), 85–111.

occasion and it is quite possible that they met when Montagu visited the family home at Bulstrode.[29]

Elstob's *The Rudiments of Grammar for the English Saxon Tongue, first given in English: with an apology for the study of the Northern Antiquities. Being very useful for the study of our ancient English poets and other writers* (1715), dedicated to the Princess of Wales, included on the title page an explicit defense of the critical capacities of her sex:

> Our Earthly Possessions are truly enough called a PATRIMONY, as derived
> to us by the Industry of our FATHERS; but the Language that we
> speak is our MOTHER-TONGUE; And who so proper as play the Crit-
> ticks in this as the FEMALES.

Here is one of the earliest and most forthright apologies for the female critic. Her grammar book was written in English especially for women rather than in Latin, which was standard for such works. She took issue with the political stance of a Tory classicist such as Swift, whose *Proposal for Correcting, Improving and Ascertaining the English Tongue* (1712) promoted the social structure as well as the linguistic excellence of the classical world. Elstob attacked his "anti-Gothic" stance in her brilliant prefatory "Apology," a polemic directed against Swift and his fellow grammarians. She praised the utility, even the necessity, of Old English studies, arguing that the Anglo-Saxon language is the spring of modern English and therefore the epitome of national identity, law, and religion. In answering Swift's charge that monosyllabic languages were harsh and grating to the ear, she marshaled counterexamples from the world's great poets, from Homer and Virgil to Chaucer, Waller, Dryden, and Swift himself. She concluded by adding "a few Instances from some of our Female Poets," including extracts from the work of Katherine Philips, Anne Wharton, and Anne Finch, countess of Winchelsea.[30] Swift never directly acknowledged Elstob's preface but, according to Richard Morton, it appears to have influenced his subsequent views both of language and of women's education.[31] The two issues were linked, of course—the higher the status that the native language achieved in the world of learning, the higher the position that women could occupy within its precincts.[32]

---

29.  See *Elizabeth Montagu, The Queen of the Bluestockings: Her Correspondence from 1720 to 1761, by Emily J. Climenson,* 2 vols. (London, 1906), 1:133. See also Perry, "Ballard's Biographies of Learned Ladies," 85–111.

30.  See the Folger Collective on Early Women Critics, ed., *Women Critics, 1660–1820* (Bloomington and Indianapolis, 1995), 58–66.

31.  Richard Morton, "Elizabeth Elstob's *Rudiments of Grammar* (1715): Germanic Philology for Women," *Studies in Eighteenth-Century Culture* 20 (1990): 267–87.

32.  See Mitzi Myers, "Domesticating Minerva: Bathsua Makin's 'Curious' Argument for Women's Education," *Studies in Eighteenth-Century Culture* 14 (1985): 173–92.

The celebration of Shakespeare's genius was coeval with the rise of interest in the vernacular language and its stylistic complexities, as well as coinciding with the increasing visibility of the professional woman writer. In opposition to the rigid rules of orthodox classical drama, writers increasingly invoked concepts of Shakespeare's genius, nature, and imagination. As Brian Vickers has demonstrated, changing concepts of genius and inspiration produced both a more direct response to his poetry and a new spirit of detailed and systematic analysis of his text. Edward Upton's *Critical Observations of Shakespeare* (1748), for example, an important critique of Shakespeare's language and style, argued for the musical powers of his poetic expression. These qualities were seen to be aided by his lack of learning; only "inferior wits" needing formal training. Accordingly, when Montagu defended Shakespeare from charges of barbarism raised by Voltaire, among others, she based her argument on his spontaneity and originality:

> Great indulgence is due to the errors of original writers, who, quitting the beaten track which others have travelled, make daring incursions into unexplored regions of invention, and boldly strike into the pathless sublime: it is no wonder if they are often bewildered, sometimes benighted; yet it is surely more eligible to partake in the pleasure and the toil of their adventures, than still to follow the cautious steps of timid imitation through trite and common roads. (*Essay*, 8; Eger, 3)

She further exonerated his reputation on the grounds of his belonging to "the people," an observation to be echoed by Madame de Staël.[33] This argument accounted for his faults as well as his brilliance:

> If the severer muses, whose sphere is the library and the senate, are obliged in complaisance to this degeneracy, to trick themselves out with meretricious and frivolous ornaments, as is too apparent from the composition of the historians and orators in declining empires, can we wonder that a dramatic poet, whose chief interest is to please the people, should, more than any other writer, conform himself to their humour. (*Essay*, 9; Eger, 4)

Bluestocking investment in Shakespeare's use of the vernacular turned in part, then, on its accessibility. Plays in English could be understood by everyone and discussed even by those lacking classical learning. On another level, of course, the

---

33.  "In England, all classes are equally attracted by the pieces of Shakespeare. Our finest tragedies, in France, do not interest the people"; Anne Louise Germaine de Staël, *De L'Allemagne* (1810–13)—published in English in 1813—quoted in Jonathan Bate, ed., *The Romantics on Shakespeare* (London, 1992), 82.

distinctive modern role of English as a *national* language was crystalizing in this period. In this respect, too, the Bluestocking defense of Shakespeare played its part.

## THE BLUESTOCKINGS AND A NATIONAL CANON OF LITERATURE

Montagu opens her chapter "Upon the Cinna of Corneille" with a spirited defense of the unique strengths of English blank verse. She argues that while iambic pentameter might appear easily achieved because of its affinity with the patterns of speech, it was extremely difficult for the poet to master. She accuses the French neoclassicists of insensitivity to the sophistication of English verse, mocking their arrogant dismissal of its technical complexities. Before exposing the particular errors of Voltaire's translations of Shakespeare, she celebrates the natural beauty of Shakespeare's poetry, which, she argues, has an affinity with music:

> It rises gracefully into the sublime; it can slide happily into the familiar; hasten its career if impelled by vehemence of passion; pause in the hesitation of doubt; appear lingering and languid in dejection and sorrow; is capable of varying its accent, and adapting its harmony, to the sentiment it should convey, and the passion it would excite, with all the power of musical expression.
>
> Even a person, who did not understand our language, would find himself very differently affected by the following speeches in that metre. (*Essay*, 210–11; Eger, 80)

Griffith conveys an even greater pride in the beauty of the vernacular, praising Shakespeare as superior to "the whole collective host of Greek or Roman writers, whether ethic, epic, dramatic, didactic or historic." She described his idiosyncratic use of words thus:

> [O]ur Author shall measure his pen with any of the antient *styles*, in their most admired compound and decompound epithets, descriptive phrases, or figurative expressions. *The multitudinous sea, ear-piercing fife, big war, giddy mast, sky-aspiring, heaven-kissing hill, time-honoured name, cloud-clapt towers, heavenly-harnessed team, rash gunpowder, polished perturbation, gracious silence, golden care, trumpet-tongued, thought-executing fires;* with a number of other words, both epic and comic, are instances of it. (*Morality of Shakespeare*, 525)

Griffith particularly praises Shakespeare's bold use of English—for example, in her comment on the use of the word "Sightless": "Shakespeare often places the negative at the end of the adjective, instead of the beginning. This varies his phrases, and enriches his language. Modern writers are too much *dictionary bound*" (*Morality of Shakespeare*, 177). In her commentary one can detect an implicit argument for the superiority of the native tongue. Her discussion of *Henry IV* takes a side-swipe at "the learned":

> [T]hey deny Shakespeare to have been a classic scholar, but one would fancy that he was both a master and admirer of Ovid by the manly and puerile stile he frequently mixes together in the same passage; . . . There is hardly a line in the above speech of the king, that is not worth the whole of what Sophocles makes Oedipus say to his son in the same circumstance. But I don't expect *the learned* will ever give up this point to me, *while one passage remains in Greek, and the other only in English.* (*Morality of Shakespeare*, 221–22)

In her concluding defense of English tragedies she cites Montagu's critical example with patriotic ardor.

Montagu's enthusiasm for the native tongue influenced the higher ranks of intellectual institutions as well as achieving popular appeal, and it is arguable that her *Essay* contributed to the early development of the idea of "English Literature" as an object of university study. In a letter to Montagu, Hugh Blair, who was a founding figure in the history of literary studies, noted that she had placed the works of Shakespeare "in a light that is New & Just; and have defended them . . . on the most rational principles of Criticism," declaring that he would "refer my Students to your Essay for proper ideas concerning so Capital an Author in our Language" (MO 483, 3 June 1769). Alastair Fowler has recently charted the influential contribution to the birth of literary studies made by Adam Smith, Lord Kames, and Blair, all of whom Montagu corresponded with. She was especially close to Lord Kames, who asked her for literary advice on several occasions.[34] Blair's enthusiasm for Montagu's "masterly" *Essay* as a didactic work founded on the "most rational principles of Criticism" suggests the impact of her work on education in particular, where it enhanced curricular emphasis on the native tongue.[35]

---

34. As Fowler has recently written, "By the middle of the eighteenth century, instruction in vernacular literature was in demand throughout Britain. The Scottish Enlightenment (a movement so consequential for Britain that England has tried to forget it) was generating enthusiasm for 'improvement' of various sorts. And the improvers turned to history and literature as agencies for change" ("Leavis of the North: The Role of Hugh Blair in the Foundation of English Literary Studies" [*Times Literary Supplement*, 14 August 1998, 3–4]).

35. Griffith also stressed the importance of a literary education in her treatment of Shakespeare's plays, urging readers to perform "the dissection of its parts to his own judgement, taste and feeling" (*Morality of Shakespeare*, 217).

Montagu had always thought of her literary identity in nationalist terms, of course, openly pitting her arguments against Voltaire's "misrepresentations" in the title of her *Essay*, for example. From an early age she had admired Voltaire's wit and legendary intelligence but was profoundly irritated by his attacks on Shakespeare's genius. In 1755, having just read his *Orphelin de Chine*, she wrote to her sister that she did not care for it: "When I compare this indifference with the interest, the admiration, the surprise with which I read what the saucy Frenchman calls *les farces monstreuses* of Shakespeare, I could burn him and his tragedy.... Oh! that we were as sure our fleets and armies could drive the French out of America as that our poets and tragedians can drive them out of Parnassus. I hate to see these tame creatures, taught to pace by art, attack fancy's sweetest child."[36] Montagu's equation of military with literary power reveals the profoundly nationalist and competitive cultural context in which she wrote. As Haydn Mason has recently pointed out, Voltaire himself came to see Shakespeare more and more in symbolically patriotic terms, the playwright increasingly connected in his mind with British success in the Seven Years' War. In 1760 he attacked Shakespeare in his *Appel à toutes les nations de l'Europe*, which, as the title suggests, attempted to court the whole of Europe against the Englishman.[37]

The opening pages of Montagu's *Essay* establish the grounds of her antipathy to Voltaire:

> —Our Shakespear, whose very faults pass here unquestioned, or are perhaps consecrated through the enthusiasm of his admirers, and the veneration paid to long-established fame, is by a great wit [Voltaire], a great critic, and a great poet of a neighbouring nation, treated as the writer of monstrous farces, called by him tragedies; and barbarism and ignorance are attributed to the nation by which he is admired. Yet if wits, poets, critics, could ever be charged with presumption, one might say there was some degree of it in pronouncing, that, in a country where Sophocles and Euripedes are as well understood as in any in Europe, the perfections of dramatic poetry should be as little comprehended as among the Chinese. (*Essay*, 1–3; Eger, 1)

While Montagu may present herself as humble in relation to the great English Shakespeare editors, such as Pope, she confidently attacks the presumption and inaccuracy of Voltaire. She launches a withering attack on his knowledge of

---

36.  *The Letters of Mrs. Elizabeth Montagu, with Some of the Letters of Her Correspondents,* 4 vols. (1908–13; New York, 1974), 4:7, 18 November 1755.

37.  Haydn Mason, "Voltaire versus Shakespeare," *British Journal for Eighteenth-Century Studies* 18 (1995): 173–84.

English. On his misinterpretation of the word "course," she remarks drily, "It is very extraordinary, that a man should set up for a translator, with so little acquaintance in the language, as not to be able to distinguish whether a word, in a certain period signifies a race, a service of dishes, or a mode of conduct" (*Essay*, 213; Eger, 81). She even retranslates Voltaire's French back into a crude form of English to try to demonstrate his faults to those who do not understand French. Her aim is to "deter other beaux esprits from attempting to mar works of genius by the masked battery of an unfair translation" (*Essay*, 218; Eger, 83). Her piercing criticisms of Corneille's "weak effeminacies" and "awkwardly conducted" drama are intended as a direct retaliatory gesture, and they demonstrate not only her scholarly attention to the details of the English language but also the superiority of the greatest English dramatist, specifically in a linguistic register. The argument was nationalist on both counts.

No male critic dared to take on Voltaire with as much ferocity as did Montagu. In fact, Voltaire was not refuted so roundly and frankly by any other English writer during his lifetime. Thomas Lounsbury has described Johnson's refusal to reply to his criticisms, despite the encouragement of Boswell.[38] Montagu's knowledge of French, though she spoke it badly, was seemingly superior to Voltaire's of English. Her demonstration was conclusive. The "faithful translator stood convicted of presumption and ignorance."[39]

Montagu's work attracted a good deal of attention in Europe. It was translated into German in 1771 by Johann Eschenburg, whose translation of Shakespeare's works appeared a few years later, an important influence on the German Romantic movement. The *Essay* was also translated into French in 1777 and into Italian in 1828. Meanwhile, Letourneur's translation of three plays— *Othello*, *The Tempest*, and *Julius Caesar*—foreshadowed the first complete edition of Shakespeare's works in French. As Mason notes, the edition of the three plays contained notes and commentaries, prefatory fanfare including a dedicatory epistle to Louis XVI, a life of Shakespeare, and a subscription list with over a thousand names, and a refutation of criticisms on Shakespeare.[40] Voltaire was extremely offended by the fact that he was not invited to contribute, perceiving a calculated insult. He decided to address these matters by writing a letter in response to the translation, to be read by his friend and ally D'Alembert at a meeting of the Académie Française. He saw this as his patriotic duty, and his letter is peppered with the defensive language of a man at war: "Je plaide pour la France"; "je combats pour la nation"; "je ne veux point être l'esclave des Anglais."[41]

38.   Thomas Lounsbury, *Shakespeare and Voltaire* (London, 1902), 288.
39.   René Louis Huchon, *Mrs. Montagu and Her Friends, 1720–1800: A Sketch* (London, 1907), 141.
40.   Mason, "Shakespeare versus Voltaire," 175.
41.   Ibid., 176.

When Montagu visited Paris in 1776, she was fêted by polite society. Her status as a literary and cultural ambassador, already present in her capacity as patron and salon hostess, was considerably strengthened by her appearance as a published author. She was invited to the meeting of the Académie Française where Voltaire's retaliatory letter was to be read out to the assembled members, followed by a discussion of the merits of Letournour's translation. In a letter to her friend Mrs. Vesey, Montagu reported the scene:

> Then rose Monsr D'Alembert to read a most blackguard abusive invective of Monsr de Voltaire's against Shakespear the translation of whose works he apprehended wd spoil ye taste of ye French Nation. He attributed to Shakespear many things he never said, he gatherd together many things the rudeness of the age allowd him to say, & with a few mauvaises plaisanteries season'd ye discourse with as much mauvaise foy. He gave an account of ye Tragedy of Gorboduc, & represented it as ye taste of yea Nation in Drama though not ten people have for these hundred years read Gorboduc. This trash of Monsieur Voltaires answered the great purpose of his life, to raise a momentary laugh at things that are good, & a transient scorn of Men much superior to himself, but I must do that justice to the Academy & Audience they seemd in general displeased at ye paper read. I was askd by an Academician if I wd answer this piece of Voltaires & did not doubt but I could do it very well. I said Mr l'Abbé Arnauld had done it much better than I could, in ye praises he had give to Original genius, & ye benefits arising from the study of them, that I remembered 60 years ago in the same Academy, Old Homer had met with ye same treatment with Shakespear, that they now did justice to Homer, I did not doubt but they wd do so to Shakespear, for that great Geniuses survived those who set up to be their Criticks, or more absurdly to be their Rivals. (MO 6486, 7 September 1776; Eger, 196–97)

While D'Alembert's report of the meeting is more positive, he nevertheless admitted to Voltaire that the overall reaction to his letter had been mixed: "Je n'ai pas besoin de vous dire que les Anglois qui étoient là sont sortis mécontens, & même quelques François qui ne se contentent pas d'être battus par eux sur terre st sur mer, & qui voudroient encoire que nous le fussions sur le théâtre."[42] Montagu had become enmeshed in a controversy of national importance, provoking the interest of all the "beaux esprits" in Paris. Her sense of critical superiority in this

42. *Voltaire: Correspondence*, ed. T. Besterman (Paris, 1968–77), D20272, D'Alembert to Voltaire, August 1776.

context is striking. Her letter to Vesey conveys her self-satisfaction in rising above the demeaning squabbles of contemporary literary society, calling for her audience to submit to a longer view of literary history in determining Shakespeare's value to the literary canon. On her return to England she was welcomed as a national heroine.

The success of Montagu's intervention in a public and nationalist literary debate demonstrates the power of the female intellect in the public sphere of letters. The *Essay* remained popular at the beginning of the nineteenth century. The sixth edition appeared in 1810, a decade after her death, and was still well known as an authoritative celebration of the national poet's genius. Maria Edgeworth referred to the Bluestocking defense of Shakespeare against the French assault in her novel *Patronage*, published in 1814, the same year that Austen's *Mansfield Park* appeared. The French and English heroes of Edgeworth's novel argue about the merits of Shakespeare:

> "I have every edition of Shakespeare, that ever was printed or published, and every thing that ever was written, good, bad, or indifferent, at Clay-Hall.—I made this a principle, and I think every Englishman should do the same.—Your Mr Voltaire," added this polite Englishman, turning to Count Altenberg, "made a fine example of himself by *dashing* at *our* Shakespeare?"
>
> "Undoubtedly, Voltaire showed he did not understand Shakespeare, and therefore, did not do him justice," replied Count Altenberg. "Even Voltaire had some tinge of national prejudice, as well as other men. It was reserved for the women, to set us in this instance, as in many others, an example at once of superior candor, and superior talent."[43]

Edgeworth's reference to the women who came to Shakespeare's aid suggests that her readers would have been familiar with the Bluestocking defense of their national playwright. However, one can detect a slightly patronizing tone in Count Altenberg's acknowledgment that "the women" have set "us" an example. The sexes remain apart, members of different systems of aesthetic judgment. Edgeworth gently suggests that there is more than national pride at stake in laying the groundwork for the future of literary reputations.

Adopting a reverential attitude to Shakespeare's work, Montagu and Griffith participated in a literary debate that remained conservative and nationalist in many respects. So while they legitimized themselves as writers by addressing the

43. Maria Edgeworth, *Patronage*, ed. Dale Spender (London and New York, 1986), 328. I would like to thank Cliona O'Gallchoir for alerting me to this reference.

issue of Shakespearean excellence, it might be argued that their work did not ultimately challenge masculine authority in the context of an emerging national literary canon; one cannot help wondering whether Montagu's *Essay* would have been quite so popular had she openly criticized Johnson in the manner that she attacked Voltaire. The Bluestocking defense of Shakespeare negotiated a difficult balance of gender politics in relation to the hierarchy of literary genres—and languages—that was being established as part of Britain's cultural identity. One particular female tradition of writing laid claim to the previously masculine arena of critical judgment, paradoxically by using what were considered feminine attributes, "candor" and "talent," and a certain "unlearnedness." While Montagu, and to a lesser extent Griffith, had bolstered their own status as female critics by contributing to the creation of Shakespeare's reputation, in the longer term their writings slipped from view and out of the literary tradition, even as Shakespeare's became ever more prominent. Thus while students are familiar with the critical elaboration of Shakespeare's powers of sympathy, characterization, and moral philosophy in the work of Coleridge, Keats, and Hazlitt, and while key elements of the Bluestocking defense of Shakespeare became part of subsequent critical orthodoxy, few have heard of Montagu or Griffith, whose work undoubtedly contributed to the Romantic fascination with Shakespeare's particular genius and to the nature of his modern reputation.

*University of Liverpool*

# Elizabeth Montagu, Bluestocking Businesswoman

ELIZABETH CHILD

In her voluminous correspondence, Elizabeth Montagu cultivated many personas: flirtatious belle, adoring bride, long-suffering wife; ambitious hostess, anxious author, influential critic. Montagu's passion for reading and literary criticism in particular permeates her letters, most of which include at least a passing literary allusion. Her own epistolary insistence on the importance of letters and learning has helped shape her enduring reputation as a leading member of the Bluestockings, that informal circle of learned, literary eighteenth-century English women and men who gathered in person at London salons hosted by Montagu and her friend Elizabeth Vesey, and who also maintained an epistolary network that cultivated both intellectual interests and friendships.[1] Montagu's celebrity as a literary hostess in her own day, along with her major published work, *An Essay on the Writings and Genius of Shakespear* (1769), has until recently encouraged most editors and scholars to receive her on these rather narrowly defined Bluestocking terms—as a writer, *salonnière,* and patron.[2] This essay explores, in contrast, a sphere of Montagu's life to which she herself devoted a great

A generous fellowship from the Huntington Library supported my initial research for this essay. I am also grateful to Trinity College of Washington, D.C., for additional funding. The Bluestockings panel arranged by Betty Schellenberg and Nicole Pohl for the American Society for Eighteenth-Century Studies conference of 2001 helped me to conceptualize and write this paper—many thanks to both of them. Finally, I am indebted to Jacqueline Padgett, Sharon Groves, and Karen Nelson for their comments on this essay.

1.    See Sylvia Harcstark Myers's *The Bluestocking Circle* (Oxford, 1990); and *Bluestocking Feminism*, gen ed. Gary Kelly, 6 vols. (London, 1999), specifically Kelly's "General Introduction," vol. 1.
2.    Montagu's editors tend to emphasize her letters discussing the arts, politics, and personalities. See, for example, *The Letters of Mrs. Elizabeth Montagu, with Some of the Letters of her Correspondents*, 4 vols. (London, 1810–13); Emily J. Climenson, *Elizabeth Montagu, the Queen of the Blue-Stockings: Her Correspondence from 1720 to 1761* (London, 1906); and *Mrs. Montagu, "Queen of the Blues": Her Letters and Friendships from 1762 to 1800,* ed. Reginald Blunt, 2 vols. (London, n.d.). For more recent accounts of Montagu's role in the Bluestocking circle, see Myers, *Bluestocking Circle*; Betty Rizzo, *Companions without Vows: Relationships among Eighteenth-Century Women* (Athens, Ga., 1994); and Elizabeth Eger, ed., *Bluestocking Feminism*, vol. 1.

deal of attention, as evidenced by her correspondence, but that has been all but ignored by subsequent accounts: Montagu as a Bluestocking businesswoman.[3]

As Betty Rizzo has noted, "One might well ask why, when Montagu functioned for years as a captain of commerce, she should be known only as a hostess."[4] From the time of her marriage in 1742, Montagu managed two large properties, a house in London and an estate (Sandleford) in Berkshire. In the 1750s the Montagus inherited substantial additional estates in the north of England, and by the time she was forty Elizabeth was beginning to take an active role in the burgeoning, highly lucrative business of coal mining and distribution. Upon her husband's death, Montagu inherited sole control of his estate, but well before then she had become one of only a handful of women known to have owned collieries in the eighteenth and early nineteenth centuries, and was perhaps unique in her managerial capacity. Her actual success as a colliery owner was considerable.

Montagu's immersion in the role of "captain of commerce" through her involvement in the coal industry sheds new light on the Bluestockings' sphere of influence in mid- to late-eighteenth-century England. The abortive attempt of Montagu, her sister Sarah Scott, and others in her intellectual circle to establish a community of women at Hitcham has received considerable critical attention in recent years as the preeminent example of a Bluestocking attempt to translate ideological agendas from fiction into practice.[5] Meanwhile, less visibly, in her evolving business attitudes and practices, Montagu pursued an alternative "real-life" outlet for her Bluestocking ideals. In describing her ideas and agendas for developing the family coal interests, Montagu suggests that benevolence, sensibility, altruism, and imagination can be the governing values not only for domestic economies or cottage industries, described in novels such as Sarah Fielding's *David Simple* and Scott's *Millenium Hall,* but also for large-scale industrial enterprises. Her vision for the Montagu mining community is obviously not female-centered like the community at Hitcham (except in the sense that Montagu came to see herself as the managerial center of the family mining operations). However, her epistolary blueprint for Denton colliery and other smaller mines imagines a carefully structured community, hierarchical but based

3.   In *Bluestocking Feminism*, for example, the chronology of Montagu's life does not mention coal mines until after her husband's death in 1775 (1:lxxxv). Myers mentions Montagu's business interests only in passing: "She also found an absorbing interest in helping with the management of her husband's lands and coal-mines, finally doing much of the management herself"; see Myers, *Bluestocking Circle,* 187.

4.   Rizzo, *Companions without Vows,* 111.

5.   For accounts of the Hitcham experiment, see Linda Bree, *Sarah Fielding* (New York, 1996), 27–28; Rizzo, *Companions without Vows,* 317–19; and Rizzo's introduction to *The History of Sir George Ellison* (Lexington, Ky., 1996), xvi–xxix.

on principles and practices that she believed beneficial to both workers and owners. Bluestocking ideas about social organization and Christian activism, aligned
with Montagu's own natural aptitude for business, form a cornerstone of her
rhetorical self-invention as a businesswoman, helping her to construct an entrepreneurial authority grounded in tropes of female ability, duty, and education.[6]

In her letters, Montagu writes freely and frequently about her own entrepreneurial talents. In so doing, she has to juggle the psychological rewards of self-
representation as a model of female energy and accomplishment with the risk
that she will compromise her own class and gender status by affiliating herself
with the marketplace economy—particularly the nonagrarian economy of coal
mining and distribution. In that economy, the familiar hierarchies of quasi-
feudal estate farming gave way to unfamiliar, and sometimes unwelcome, new
relationships with labor representatives, agents from competing mines, lawyers,
hostile colliery owners, and so on. In balancing propriety with profit, Montagu
uses ideas promulgated by Bluestocking women such as Scott, Fielding, and
Elizabeth Carter both to publicize and to legitimize her status as an entrepreneur.
Her letters emphasize the hard work of making money. But they also domesticate "business" by aligning capitalist production, at least rhetorically, with cultural
production, the mining of coal a metonymy for the mining of the imagination.
Montagu's epistolary rhetoric feminizes and gentrifies her own financial success
even further by couching her mercantilism in terms of social altruism and benevolence. Simultaneously, Montagu allies herself with conservative social politics that
reify her class loyalties even as she assumes the unusual female role of an active
industrialist. Montagu emerges, in both her own letters and those of her friends,
as a veritable Bluestocking invention, combining the cultured altruism of a
Millenium Hall lady with the benevolent patriarchy of a Sir George Ellison, all
packaged in the witty, polished prose of an accomplished letter writer. In this entrepreneurial persona, Montagu thus makes the implicit claim that the business
of a Bluestocking life might as profitably be coal mines as verse.

This essay will argue that Montagu sought rhetorical goals just as eagerly as
material gains through the painstaking cultivation of an industrialist persona in
her letters. I analyze Montagu's epistolary rhetoric vis-à-vis coal mining from the
time of her first trip to Newcastle in 1758 through the mid-1770s, when she came
into full ownership of the mines after her husband's death. I have not attempted
to evaluate her role in the eighteenth-century British coal trade or in British
industry as a whole. My study is based on the Montagu Collection at the
Huntington Library, which contains dozens of letters mentioning coal but very
few between Montagu and her colliery agents or her fellow mine owners, a lacuna

6.   For a comprehensive discussion of Bluestocking feminism, see Kelly's "General Introduction," *Bluestocking
     Feminism*, vol. 1.

that makes it difficult to assess her business practices and acumen.[7] The letters discussed below also offer only a limited scope for reassessing Montagu as a "feminist," given that her claims about female executive ability are almost exclusively claims about herself rather than women in general.

However, Montagu's colliery-related letters do suggest some perspectives beyond the role of Bluestocking philosophy in authorizing her industrialist persona. For example, her accounts of her travels and experiences in the north of England—particularly her attribution of civility and genteel accomplishment to the southern counties and her representation of the northern counties as a dark and savage province—illuminate the fractures, as well as the diversity, within English national identity as it was evolving in the eighteenth century. Her letters also remind us in general of the urgent need to attend to letters, diaries, and other manuscript writings as we continue to explore women's experiences in eighteenth-century England. Montagu devoted literally hundreds of pages of correspondence to the challenges of owning and managing a big and complex industrial enterprise. By comparison, there is no female "captain of industry" in eighteenth-century women's (or men's) published fiction. Finally, Montagu's entrepreneurial zeal, and the comfort with which she situated herself in a competitive industrial arena, adds further evidence to recent studies that have challenged the usefulness of "separate spheres" ideology as a monolithic theoretical framework for women's lives and writings in eighteenth-century England, especially for elite women.[8] Montagu actively intervened in the public, overwhelmingly masculine, sphere of large-scale coal mining and chafed at the restrictions on her autonomy imposed by her husband. Her letters suggest that she saw her own executive authority as a businesswoman as constrained primarily by the particularities of her specific marital relationship rather than by larger societal imperatives.

❧ ❧

It could be said that Elizabeth Montagu, née Robinson, married money. When her husband Edward died in 1775, he left extensive properties in Berkshire, Yorkshire, Northumberland, and Durham: "in Yorkshire alone she oversaw five hundred miners toiling in her pits, sixty reapers in her cornfields, and a brick, tile, and tar manufactory."[9] Elizabeth herself had brought to the marriage only a small

---

7.   It seems indisputable, however, that the mining concerns increased greatly in profitability after passing to Elizabeth and her husband. According to Eger, "By the end of her lifetime, 'Montagu Main' was the second-most popular coal on the market, and her bank account at Hoare & Co. was transferred to the category reserved for the richest members of the aristocracy"; see *Bluestocking Feminism*, 1:lxiii.

8.   I refer in particular to Amanda Vickery's *The Gentleman's Daughter: Women's Lives in Georgian England* (New Haven, Conn., 1998).

9.   Rizzo, *Companions without Vows*, 117.

dowry.[10] The couple had one child, a son, who died in 1744 before age two. By the time Edward died, relations between husband and wife had long been strained, and Scott worried that Montagu might even be disinherited, but Montagu's own letters express her conviction that in default of a male heir direct, she herself had earned control of the family wealth and that her husband's decision to leave his estate to her almost in its entirety concluded an unwritten but binding contract between them.

Elizabeth's status as the de facto head of the family enterprises in the later years of her marriage was an open secret. Upon Edward's death, family friend and business partner William Archdeacon wrote Elizabeth that her husband had "in return made you ample Amendment in his Will, wch. was most Certainly highly Incumbent upon him to do, and was all he Could do in gratitude for the long & Tedious Number of years you have been Obliged to Support his Ill State of health, Age, & Infirmities, with the very extensive trouble you've had in managing his Affairs" (MO 146, 27 May 1775).[11] Archdeacon represents Elizabeth's role as a burdensome one that was imposed upon her. Elizabeth's own letters from Newcastle and the Northumberland estate of Denton indeed sound a note of "very extensive trouble" at times. While the Montagus employed agents to oversee and manage their northern properties, many decisions required the owners' physical presence. Edward seems to have made the trip at least once a year after he inherited the Denton estate in 1758. Elizabeth joined him somewhat less frequently, but nonetheless traveled north at least once every two or three years between the late 1750s and the mid-1770s.

Montagu's letters at times describe her expeditions north as a kind of exile. She harps on the physical distances entailed by these trips, the harshness of northern life, the strangeness of local customs, and her own intellectual and cultural isolation. The journey was long and arduous, consuming a week or longer and posing a constant threat to the health and well-being of the traveler. As Montagu wrote to Sarah Scott in 1763, "Six days travelling without intermission & without amusement is a laborious thing" (MO 5804, 22 October 1763). A year later she reported to her husband that she had arrived safely in Grantham en route back to London, but that other travelers had been less fortunate: "Our Coach is fortunately hung very high, all ye people who passd Newark today got a great deal

---

10. For an in-depth exploration of Montagu's marriage, including her dowry, see Bridget Hill, "The Course of the Marriage of Elizabeth Montagu: An Ambitious and Talented Woman without Means," *Journal of Family History* 26, no. 1 (January 2001): 3–17.

11. Unless otherwise noted, all quotations from letters in this essay are based on my own transcription of materials in the Huntington Library's Montagu Collection, cited in the text. I have generally followed the original spelling and abbreviations but have occasionally amended punctuation for greater clarity, indicated in brackets; full stops added to the ends of block quotations are not bracketed.

of water into their carriages but I had very little. The waters were impassable till this morning & it is now raining hard" (MO 2473, 18 December 1763).

The distance between London and Denton meant long separations between Montagu and her friends, only partially bridged by a constant stream of letters. Scott frequently visited Elizabeth in both London and Sandleford and had gone with the Montagus to their house in Yorkshire immediately after their wedding, but she seems never to have made the trip to Denton. Nor did any of Montagu's other intimates from the southern counties; her closest friend in the north was to be Dr. John Gregory of Edinburgh. In November 1763, Montagu wrote to Scott in tropes suggesting that the Montagus' flourishing coal enterprises were sometimes cold comfort for the deprivations entailed: "I am forced to warm my imagination at my coal fire. I live here in more hurry than at London, business in the morning or visits from the Northumberland Ladies & gentlemen in the morning, & Newcastle dames & Messieurs in the evening, leave me hardly leisure to write letters to my absent friends & alas all my friends are absent" (MO 5805). Scott too felt the separation, writing Montagu that "I should love your Mines better if You were not to go to them. I hate the thought of that distant abode for you. While we are both on the same Turnpike road we are almost Neighbors, but that prodigious distance between Newcastle & Bath appears to me a horrid gulf" (MO 5308, 1763). Several years later, a letter to Elizabeth Carter casts the northern journey as punitive, the price Montagu must pay for her own materialism and pleasure in worldly goods: "I assure you there is something desolate & melancholly in these remote regions, but I hope after many rolls of Phoebus's car & my post chaise to be restored to the persons & places I grieved to abandon. The love of *things* [Montagu's emphasis] of which you accuse me seem here to meet with condign punishment, as I am in this situation condemn'd to ugly things, & disagreable things, & troublesome things, & tiresome things." Montagu adds, however, that her own proprietary interests offer a considerable incentive to make the requisite sacrifices: "The reasonableness & fitness of things, which urges a Coal owner to be near the coal mines, gives me spirit to go through all the desagremens I meet with" (MO 3171, 31 May 1766).

Nonetheless, Montagu found the local company mostly uncongenial, writing acerbically to Carter: "I wish we had the noble sport of bear hunting in the Country, for any thing would amuse me better than the Visiting conversation" (MO 3021, August 1758). Nor did she find much consolation in the cultural amenities of Newcastle, where she and her husband lived during their earliest northern trips before the manor house at the Denton estate was renovated and refurbished. She wrote to Scott that "the Country about Newcastle is not displeasing to the eye," but the town itself came in for Montagu's severest disapprobation (MO 5772, 12 August 1758). Although by the mid-eighteenth century Newcastle boasted such cultural venues as theaters, assembly rooms, circulating libraries, and public baths, Montagu on first visiting the city characterized it as almost Stygian in its darkness and claustrophobic atmosphere:

> The Town of Newcastle is horrible like the ways of Night[;] it is narrow dark & dirty, some of ye streets so steep one is forced to put a drag chain on ye wheels[.] ... The streets are some of them so narrow that if ye tallow chandler ostentatiously hangs forth his candles you have chance to sweep them into your lap as you drive by, & I do not know how it has happened that I have not yet caught a coach full of red herrings for we scrape the citty wall on which they hang in great abundance. (MO 5772, 12 August 1758)

Two years later, she reported to Carter that she was entering into the "diversions" of Newcastle to avoid giving offense, but added acidly: "The desire of pleasure & love of dissipation rages here as much as in London. Diversions here are less elegant, & conversation less polite, but no one imagines retirement has any comforts" (MO 3030, 24 October 1760).

Her letters on the primitivism of Newcastle and its environs conjure a fractured national geography in which all the amenities of civilized life—beautiful landscapes, pleasant company, pleasing architecture—accrue to the south, leaving Montagu as a kind of Robinson Crusoe, cast away in the desolate regions of the north and its "barbarous" (to use her own oft-invoked adjective) inhabitants:

> The people here are little better than Savages, they are dirty, their dwellings are sordid, & their Countenances bear the marks of hard labour & total ignorance. Our Pittmen are litterally black as a coal. They earn much more than labourers, their children get a shilling a day at 9 or 10 years old, but they are so barbarous & uncultivated they know no use of money but to buy much meat & liquor with it. (MO 3171, 31 May 1766)

Yet the very distance and isolation lamented in some of her letters may actually have helped enable Montagu's entrepreneurial success. Harriet Guest has recently suggested that in her role as London hostess and literary critic, Montagu became a national symbol, a position that "brought Montagu both respect and ridicule as on the one hand a shining spectacle for the civilized progress of the nation, and on the other a figure of vanity whose learning is tainted by the doubtful glitter of fashionable display."[12] Once in Northumberland, however, Montagu

---

12.   Harriet Guest, *Small Change: Women, Learning, Patriotism, 1750–1810* (Chicago, 2000), 131.

was far less visible, at least in terms of being in the mist of a fashionable throng, allowing her to craft a role for herself on the margins of the nation different from the one she enjoyed in London. Her northern forays brought her into the midst of a populace offensive to her aesthetic sensibilities, but the "barbarous" inhabitants also served as attractive discursive subjects through whom Montagu could pursue Bluestocking themes of social activism, altruism, and reform. Eventually, Montagu even came to identify the industrial landscape as a fit subject for the moral imagination, deserving of extensive description both in its novelty and in its capacity to prompt moral reflection.

At the same time, the "savage" state of the northern populace depicted in the letters throws into relief Montagu's own class status. In this juxtaposition, Montagu's birth, wealth, and cultivation ground her claims to authority in both rhetorical and material ways: she masters the local terrain through both the skill of her pen and her skill with money. She never lets her correspondents forget that while she might be *in* the north, she is never *of* the north. Her mercantile talents blossom in Northumberland, but her voice is that of the London drawing room. Montagu's complaints about the rigors of the north and the travails of coal ownership are often highly self-conscious, highlighting in droll turns of phrase the oddity of the "Queen of the Blues" landed so far from London salons and London pleasures, her "fish-out-of-water" plight the source as much of irony as of real distress. "Indeed we have here the same cause of Confusion as at Babel which is a diversity of tongues," she wrote to Carter in 1770. "I was much entertain'd ye other day at hearing my footman Thomas cd not make Jenny ye kitchen maid understand him nor could understand her, an Interpreter was call'd or never had ye tea kettle been set on ye fire" (MO 3276, 19 July 1770). These kinds of remarks, undoubtedly intended to amuse the recipients, also remind her correspondents that she has not abandoned her feminine accomplishments as a clever letter writer, even as those "feminine" letters detail the practices and profits of a savvy entrepreneur.

❧ ❧

Montagu's initial alienation from northern society and landscapes was tempered in part by immersion in new work she clearly found engaging and rewarding. Virtually from the moment of her arrival in Newcastle, Montagu tackled with relish the complex, competitive business of coal extraction and distribution. Husband and wife traveled together to Newcastle for the first time in August 1758, and her earliest letters south indicate that Elizabeth was already assuming an active role both in the transfer of the Denton agricultural estate and colliery to her husband, which involved a long probate process, and in provisions for the future management of the properties. "What gives Mr Montagu most pleasure is the opinion of many that some will offer to take Denton Colliery on a lease for 20 years paying a thousand pound a year clear," she wrote Sarah a few days after her arrival. "We apply with great alacrity to his business," she adds with a telling choice of pronoun (MO 5772, 12 August 1757). Her "alacrity" included investigation of the mechanics of the business at hand. "Now that I have uttered some of my miseries I must tell you I have some amusement in seeing a Country so different from any I have ever been in," she wrote to friend and confidant Benjamin Stillingfleet, adding:

> Riches here lye very deep, but avarice would dive to the center for them, by engines of different sorts, some of which draw off ye water[.] Coals are brought up from an immense depth, other inventions obviate the difficulty of carriage & by means of what are call'd the Waggon-ways, great burthens of Coals are moved with little force & easily carried to the sea side. (MO 5110, 22 August 1758)

She wrote in a similar vein to Thomas Lyttelton, telling him, "The mechanisms of the engines & their operations in the Coal pitts are well worth observation, & before I leave this Country I design to make myself acquainted with them" (MO 1498, 27 August 1758).

Montagu's letters reveal a quick grasp of the challenges facing the would-be coal magnate. The minerals had to be extracted, the coal transported, prices set, and markets established. As Kathleen Wilson notes in her detailed study of Newcastle in the eighteenth century, coal was a popular but risky and competitive enterprise; it required considerable capital investment, and success could be easily derailed, exploitation of mineral wealth "being subject to a range of geological, meteorological and political vagaries, from shallow seams, bad weather and interruptions in trade caused by war or labor disputes to the endless and expensive legal haggling about wayleaves (permission to pass over a neighboring landowner's ground)."[13]

By the mid-eighteenth century coal had become the great business of northern counties such as Northumberland and Durham.[14] Montagu wonders in her early letters at the abandonment of agriculture by the local gentry: "The gentlemen here who have coal mines find such profit in working them they neglect the

---

13. Kathleen Wilson, *The Sense of the People: Politics, Culture, and Imperialism in England, 1715–1785* (Cambridge, 1998), 290.
14. See T. S. Ashton and Joseph Sykes, *The Coal Industry in the Eighteenth Century* (Manchester, 1964): "Coal-mining was the main business of the landed proprietor, ... not merely one of many preoccupations" (p. 9).

surface of their estates.... Every Gentleman in the County, from the least to the greatest, is as solicitous in the pursuit of gain as a tradesman in Cheapside," she wrote to Lyttelton (MO 1499, 20 October 1758). However, she quickly threw herself into the spirit of the local economy, remarking to Lyttelton that "as we are as possess'd with the Northumberland Demon covetousness, I find there is no resisting the contagion. I thought myself secured from it by many fine sentiments but I am now as deeply infected as the natives themselves."

Montagu brought to this new undertaking a considerable managerial prowess. Through her responsibilities for managing the couple's London house and Sandleford estate, she was thoroughly experienced in both domestic management and the oversight of agricultural matters. Montagu's wealth distinguished her from most of her Bluestocking friends—Scott and Carter, for instance, managed only small households and relatively modest incomes from their writings. Because of her marriage, Montagu was in a different social stratum from most of her friends; however, her management roles before the Denton inheritance were in fact fairly typical for an elite eighteenth-century woman, if on a somewhat larger scale than was usual. As Amanda Vickery has argued, "the household and family were not the limit of an elite woman's horizon" in the eighteenth century, "nor was the house in any simple sense a private, domestic sphere.... Genteel families were linked to the world in a multiplicity of ways, as kinsfolk, landowners, patrons, employers and as members of the elite."[15] Montagu's involvement in the business of coal, on the other hand, represents a real anomaly. The only other well-known female colliery owner of the premodern era is Anne Lister, a Halifax heiress who assumed control of a family coal mine in the 1830s. According to the editor of Lister's diaries, only one percent of colliery owners in England and Wales in Lister's era were women.[16] Presumably the numbers for Montagu's era were no higher.

Undeterred by the lack of female role models, however, Montagu demonstrates in her letters a quick grasp of the possibilities and challenges of trying to profit from coal as well as the confidence to persuade her husband to act on her opinions, sometimes at enormous capital expenditure. In the most in-depth investigation of Montagu's career as a manager to date, Rizzo refers to Montagu as her husband's "executive arm" rather than an independent agent. Certainly, as Rizzo notes, Elizabeth deferred to her husband's financial judgments, especially

---

15. Vickery, *Gentleman's Daughter*, 9.
16. Jill Liddington, *Female Fortune: Land, Gender, and Authority* (London, 1998), 263 n. 46; this book includes excerpts from the diaries of Anne Lister and a discussion of the challenges facing her as a female colliery owner.

in the late 1750s and early 1760s, and he had exclusive legal authority to make decisions about the couple's property. More questionable is her claim that Montagu owed much of her business success to the assistance of her companion and protégée Dorothea Gregory, who joined the Montagu household as a teenager in 1770.[17] Elizabeth began making long-range decisions about the collieries long before Gregory came on the scene, although implementing those decisions sometimes entailed subterfuge and indirection. For example, the Montagus faced an immediate decision in 1758 about whether to continue leasing the mineral rights to their new properties or to develop, or "win," the mines for themselves. Elizabeth pushed hard for the latter course, despite apparent reservations on the part of both her husband and her father. By the early 1760s Elizabeth was writing confidently about her own grasp of the business, telling the earl of Bath in 1763 that "the affair is by no means the mystery people not conversant in these things imagine" (MO 4599, 15 November 1763). Frequently she contrasts her own managerial prowess with her father's tendency toward hasty and ill-informed business decisions:

> I know my young and lively Father would in one instant determine that I might get somebody to lett our coalmine and come away to London: but the Affair is pretty serious[.] It would be very easy to get a thousand guineas a year on a lease for between twenty and thirty years to come for the colliery, and a thousand guineas a year is a very pretty thing; but if by such a hasty bargain we are assured by the most skillfull persons in the country…we should lose above as much more, it would not be very wise to do it merely to avoid a little trouble. (MO 4599, 15 November 1763)

In the early years of mine ownership, Montagu is less explicitly critical of her husband than she is here of her father, but she contrasts Edward's cautiousness and sometime dilatory attention to pressing matters with her own energy and foresight. "I am as necessary as the smiths bellows to a forge," she wrote to Scott. "I keep a continual pressing when I am there that the business may go on, & I may go off" (MO 5827, 21 October 1765). Edward obviously relied on her, taking her to business meetings ("I went out at half an hour after eight today with Mr Montagu to a Mr Brown's six miles from hence, we spent the whole day in business with him concerning our colliery") and forwarding business reports to her in the south (MO 4607, 4 December 1763). At times it was Edward who left Denton during its busy season (summer and fall) and Elizabeth who was left

---

17. Rizzo, *Companions without Vows*, 115.

to manage their affairs. "The coal trade seems to be rising again," she wrote to
Edward on 1 September 1767:

> We were obliged to refuse 5 ships this week, not having coal ready
> for them, for while the new boyler was pulling in, the Belly Pit was
> laid off, but will be at work again in a week.... Mr Carr... had a
> balance in his hands of near 900L, the 600d due to Atkinson...
> is discharged, the straith mans house is paid for, & Atkinson is also
> in your debt. This is a pleasanter account of things than you had
> last year. When the new bindings come in we shall save a guinea a
> day in the hewing. (MO 2262)[18]

Her comments suggest that she had the outright authority to make certain
decisions—about shipping arrangements, for example—as well as oversight of the
mine accounts. She also got her way on larger issues, such as the decision to work
the Northumberland collieries directly rather than lease them.

Ultimately, the risks urged by Elizabeth paid off. Once the main coal mine
had been successfully enlarged and put into full-scale operation, she wrote glee-
fully to several friends about the enormous profits beginning to accrue:

> I believe you heard me say, that Mr Montagu was offerd 2000 L pr
> ann for 1000 tunns of Coal, & my Father wonderd I wd not take
> it.... We could not tell what profit exactly ye Mine wd work to till
> we had made all things perfect, & fix'd expences at a certainty, &
> Mr Montagu who is too great a mathematician to deal in proba-
> bility would not give the least attention to the Colliery, but be-
> cause he had had a bad agent was so out of humour he desired
> never to hear it named[.] [W]hen the Coal trade becomes brisk
> he may easily vend enough to clear him 9000 pr ann: but that is
> a secret with which I wd not trust any one but yrself. (MO 3205,
> 12 September 1767)

In other words, Montagu expected her superior work ethic and ability to calcu-
late return on capital to result in about a four-fold increase in profits.

As Montagu's involvement with the mines grew, so did her enthusiasm. She
actively intervened in all aspects of running the collieries, from the training of pit
boys to the design of new mining equipment to ambitious plans for shipping
and distribution. Her work required considerable effort, and she took pains to
perfect her executive abilities, writing, "With inferior agents I enter into every

---

18.  A straith is a pier from which the coal is loaded onto ships; "bindings" refer to employment contracts with
     the miners.

detail that I can be made to comprehend, for I think if a master does not seem to Servants to attend to every article, & to interest himself in ye prosperity of every branch of his undertakings, they will grow remiss. I reward, I exhort, I command, I endeavour to do by art & study what a Miser would do by instinct" (MO 5859, 27 September 1767). Her letters reveal the hard work required to master the family's commercial interests as well as her own willingness to invest her personal labor in that enterprise. Her expertise is at times hard won, but nowhere does she admit defeat in her undertakings; rather, the epistolary persona of Montagu the businesswoman is in general confident—even triumphant.

❧ ❧

The epistolary persona of Montagu the author and critic is more vexed. While obviously proud of her own success in the difficult and competitive coal business, she frequently expresses qualms about the constraints her business obligations place on her other roles, particularly her literary projects. At times she distances herself from her business interests by emphasizing the reluctance with which she relinquishes her "real" work: cultivation of the literary imagination. In the fall of 1770, she writes self-deprecatingly to Lyttelton from Denton: "Your Lordship asks why I don't write verses. Did you ever hear of a Coal owner that was a Poet? Phoebus to his favorites gives golden verses; and gold mines, Prose and coal mines to those he despises."[19] Here Montagu skirts the tricky subject of gender and labor by equating the working of coal with work in the lesser literary genres; not totally banished from Parnassus, she finds her place away from the lofty heights of epic verse in the lowlier, but still rewarding, terrains of coal and prose.

Even under the greatest press of business demands at Denton, Montagu never entirely relinquished her literary projects, although she frequently noted the difficulties of balancing literary projects with more immediate demands on her time and attention. "As to Shakespear poor Gentleman he has not been thought of since I went to Denton," Montagu wrote to Sarah in 1767. "From ten in ye morning till 9 at night I was engaged in business…& then there were letters to write very often & I was so fatigued I could not think of Shakespear" (MO 5864, 28 October 1767). Eventually, however, she seems to have come to terms with her industrialist role, privileging her colliery work almost as much as her intellectual labors. A 1767 letter to Sarah lists her "coal owner" role alongside other roles: "a Critick, a Coal Owner, a Land Steward, a sociable creature" (MO 5871, 26 December 1767).

19.   Blunt, *Queen of the Blues,* 240.

Through it all she continued to be engaged by the *Essay on Shakespear*. In her letters, the literary persona commenting on Shakespeare seems to have the superior claim on Montagu's energy: "Seeing my Shakespear & my Colliery both call on me beside ye daily duty of letters & billets, (not billets doux for which ye season certainly is as much over for me as ye month of July for primroses) indeed I dont see how a sociable Being can live without writing" (MO 5875, 25 January 1768). However, the frequency with which she wrote her friends about her collieries and the enormous length and detail of many of those letters suggest that she found in her life as a coal capitalist a deeply satisfying discursive topic. If not as elevated a topic as literature, coal mining nonetheless proved worthy of the labor of a well-turned phrase. In a sense, the letters mirror the technical processes of mining and distribution: Montagu mines her experiences as an industrialist, making technological and economic production the subject of cultural production. Some of her mine-related letters are almost novelistic in their narrative and descriptive qualities; their writing perhaps offered a pleasant refuge from the authorial anxiety that made writing the *Essay* such an agonizing task for her.[20]

Shakespeare clearly represented cultural capital for Montagu, her *Essay* the currency with which she might trade in the marketplace of ideas on an equal basis with such literary luminaries as Voltaire and Samuel Johnson. On the other hand, coal mines brought her real capital, currency that could fund the precepts of social usefulness and benevolence so important to her circle of friends. In that sense, profit becomes for Montagu a kind of moral agent that supersedes imagination:

> You may be ask'd by some if I have told you at what advantage we work ye Colliery, & shd you tell half ye truth only, I shd be call'd a Castle Builder. I never had ye talent in my life. I have always wishd I had for in the first place Castles in ye air certainly pay no ground rent, there are no Masons, Carpenters, or Bricklayers bills, & the owner of ye Castle, while he resides is not only well lodged, but has a fine table, a brilliant equipage, agreable guests.... but I was never good at this kind of architecture. My imagination is apt to sport in the regions of poetry but every one knows no harvests are reaped there. (MO 5859, 27 September 1767)

Here, profit displaces poetry from its lofty Parnassian perch in favor of the kind of material labor that yields tangible proceeds. Part of the "harvest" that Montagu reaped from her managerial success was an increasing power to act as a benefactor,

20. See Myers, *Bluestocking Circle:* "The Essay's greatest fault is the lack of a strong, controlling prose style. Here timidity may have been the underlying cause" (p. 205).

both to her "subjects" in the mines and to her Bluestocking friends. She wrote at length about the moral obligations of wealth, particularly in terms of the opportunities afforded for social usefulness. "Mr Montagu tells me things promise beyond our expectation before we came hither, & the appearance gives him spirit on the subject, so that I hope to get him to undertake what is necessary and right.... Whatever the bounty of providence has bestow'd on me, I hold it my duty towards God, my family, and my large Brotherhood mankind, to make a proper use of," she wrote to the earl of Bath in a letter that reveals her dependency on her husband in terms of enacting her plans for a harmonious working community, as well as her sense of her own moral agency (MO 4589, 16 October 1763).

References to "use" and "usefulness" redound when Montagu discusses her flourishing business interests. "If I had not inherited coal mines I should not have coveted them, but as they are fallen to me I am desirous to make use of them," she writes in 1763 (MO 5804, 22 October 1763). A few years later, a long letter on the importance of working mines rather than leasing them cites social utility as an important concern: "By keeping the Mine in our hands we have too the pleasure of being usefull to many people" (MO 3205, 12 September 1767). It is no accident that both of the letters cited above were addressed to Elizabeth Carter. In the sentiments she expresses here, Montagu aligns herself philosophically with Carter, Scott, and the other Bluestocking women who espoused the idea in their writings that an important aspect of female virtue lies in a woman's social usefulness rather than only her private learning or morals.[21]

In reconciling her mercantilism with her aspirations to virtue, Montagu calls on imagination and sensibility as transformative agents. Her imagination transforms coal from dirty lumps into a catalyst for neoplatonic reflection:

> Imagine an old Gothick house in the worst style of Gothick, gloomy without sublimity, the prospect much confined by Trees & buildings. My best object the mouth of a coal mine, round which a horse is continually pacing in order to draw up the coals, the said coals look to the common eye as very ugly black objects but my imagination sees them taking various shapes: the hand of bounty may bestow them in seasonable assistance to distress, the hand of taste transform them to beautiful forms, they may purchase sometimes pleasure sometime ease, & indeed will procure many vulgar comforts, but health, friendship, chearfullness, content... & the nobler joys are not to be dispensed but by the more

---

21.  For a more extensive discussion of the Bluestockings' attitudes toward women and social usefulness, see the chapter on Elizabeth Carter in Guest, *Small Change*.

immediate communication of the great Giver of good gifts, who imparts them as rewards for what has been well done. These coarser things are only opportunities to do well. (MO 3178, 28 July 1766)

Here, she appropriates the "ugly" industrial landscape as raw material for a utopian vision in which the landowner's "taste" in a sense mirrors God's work. She is unable to dispense the "nobler" gifts of health and happiness, but as a benefactor, an enlightened employer can certainly provide "coarser" material benefits, even as she educates the recipients about those greater rewards yet to come from the "great Giver." Thereby she also earns herself those "nobler gifts," by using her own material gifts well.

Montagu's concept of "proper use" for her coal-generated wealth included more than flights of spiritual fancy. She advocated fair hiring practices for miners and opposed attempts by her fellow mine owners to fix prices. She also planned charities designed to promote a happier, better educated, and more moral work force, both through schools and through material assistance to the working poor. Her northern charities began hypothetically: "As the children are so early sent into ye mines I am afraid it will be impossible ever to civilize them, but if I lived here I should attempt it by establishing some little school amongst them" (MO 3171, 31 May 1766). Later, Montagu's charitable projects take a more concrete form: "I have orderd a large room to be built for ye girls school, they are to be taught to read knit & spinn. Ye boys & girls are to go to Church every Sunday which I hope with others care in that point will give them more knowledge of their Religion than they have now" (MO 5864, 28 October 1767).

❧ ❧

Montagu's rhetoric in describing her educational projects clearly evokes Scott's *Millenium Hall*, a work in which Montagu was popularly thought to have figured in the unflattering role of socially ambitious, vain, and useless Lady Brumpton. In developing her own reformist schemes at Denton, which she appears to have undertaken without any active involvement by her husband, Montagu may be deliberately (re)writing herself into *Millenium Hall* in a new, more admirable persona, the moral peer of protagonists Lady Mary, Miss Mancel, and Mrs. Morgan. Like those ladies, Montagu endorses education, especially religious training, for girls as well as boys. She emphasizes the teaching of useful skills that will help females to succeed as wives and perhaps also to earn a living. Like those ladies, she plans to offer little incentives to encourage virtue and proficiency in the young:

I intend to give a salary to a schoolmaster to teach ye Pittmens sons the Lord prayer, the catechism, & to read the bible. To endeavour to smooth their manners shall also be a part of his business. If I can get a good mistress I will have spinning school for ye girls. I will distribute prizes quarterly to those who spin most & best. A coloured silk handkerchief to some, a coloured linen one to inferior merit. To the boy who comes most regularly to school a certain reward, to him who reads best another, to him who best says ye creed Lords prayer & ten commandments another and if I live to come here again, I will then myself examine them in all these articles. If my school thrives, I will after a while desire the Minister of ye Parish to catechize the children. The school master shall carry all his children to Church every Sunday. (MO 3173, 16 June 1766)[22]

Montagu unquestionably enjoyed the role of Lady Bountiful, basking in the public returns on her philanthropies, and sometimes her accounts strike an unpleasantly self-congratulatory note: "I had sent often meat & broth to the poorer Pittmens families, & done kindness to the sick. When I appear'd in the field where they were assembled for ye feast many of ye poor Women fell on their knees, & they assured me there was never no such Woman in Northumberland" (MO 5840, 17 July 1766). However, her letters also consistently reveal a sincere devotion to Bluestocking philanthropic principles: the importance of educating girls as well as boys, the need to reach out to a local community through well-organized philanthropic institutions, and the reciprocal benefits that flow between benefactor and beneficiary in a well-ordered society.[23] In the following letter to Scott, Montagu explicitly cites pleasures both philosophical and aesthetic derived from the reciprocal commerce between her and the colliery:

I often walk down to ye Colliery & at sometimes round my grounds, if all summer[s] were like this, so dry & warm, I shd spend great part of them with much satisfaction here for the reciprocal benefit flowing from the Colliery to me, & from me to the Colliery, and make a very pleasant commerce. There are poor

22. Montagu's plans for her school for miners' children echo the various educational schemes imagined by Sarah Scott for Millenium Hall, as in this passage: "Here we found about 50 girls, clad in a very neat uniform, and perfectly clean, already seated at their respective businesses. Some writing, others casting accounts, some learning lessons by heart, several employed in various sorts of needle-work, a few spinning, and other knitting…. [T]hey are bred up in the strictest piety; the ladies by various schemes, and many little compositions of their own, endeavour to inculcate the purest principles in their tender minds" (*A Description of Millenium Hall*, ed. Gary Kelly [Toronto, 1995], 196–97).
23. See Kelly, *Bluestocking Feminism*, 1:xlv–xlviii.

everywhere & money given to them will be a comfort to him who receive, & him who gives it, but amongst my own workpeople it seems an act of justice, of all ye poor they have certainly ye first right. The order & oeconomy of my concerns here is to me what musick is to a good ear. (MO 5977, 22 July 1775)

Montagu's desire to create a hierarchical yet reciprocal community of mutual benefit extended into the colliery workplace. She was far from being a radical labor reformer, but her letters express a real concern for the exploitation of the local miners by "cabals" of mine owners and unscrupulous agents. Nonetheless, she could wax sentimental over child labor without making any move to abolish it in her own mines. At times she is simply callous, as in a letter describing a visit to one of her mines: "A gin which is continually going round & while the horse are in a gallop a little boy is in a manner slung to them made me shudder, but this I am told is rarely productive of mischief" (MO 5858, 19 September 1767). Montagu was also capable of rendering scenes of exhausting, unpleasant manual labor into picturesque narratives for her friends: "The Ladies that belong to the Colliery, & work in picking out slates, seem to be of a different species from ye Sacharissas & Chloes celebrated by the poets; fit Cupid for ye coalmine Venus are ye little boys poor things black as imps" (MO 5858, 19 September 1767). At the same time, she did endorse, at least rhetorically, a standard of fair pay for fair work. In her concern for fair hiring practices and her opposition to price fixing, Montagu seems to have broken ranks with her peers in the northern community of mine owners, despite their shared class status, and she even persuaded her husband to espouse her principles in public.[24] Montagu's sympathies frequently lay with the workers. For example, she opposed efforts to restrict the workers' ability to move from mine to mine on a seasonal basis:

I am sorry to hear the Coal owners are so much in fault in regard to ye poor Pitmen. These poor creatures apprehended a scheme which they had much reason to resent, it was rumoured that ye Coal owners had enterd into an association to keep all the men to the Mine to which they were enterd, by which they wd be made slaves, the power of changing Masters being as necessary to them as to Servants, & if the Coal owners agreed not to take any Pitman the one from the others how basely wd they enfringe the liberty of

24.  Northern coal owners in the eighteenth century consisted largely of representatives from England's elite families, and while not homogeneous politically, "if their common interests were endangered they could act with … vigour and unanimity"; Ashton and Sykes, *Coal Industry in the Eighteenth Century,* 2.

these men? They are hired for half a year which is reasonable, but to attempt to bind them for longer is shocking. (MO 5824, 22 September 1765).

Montagu makes clear her debt to Bluestocking philosophy in her attitudes toward organized labor when she specifically invokes, in the context of wicked coal owners, that model figure of benevolent capitalism, her sister's Sir George Ellison from the eponymous novel: "I wish our friend Mr Ellison had an estate in Northumberland or the County of Durham," she wrote to Scott when describing the cabal for binding the miners (MO 5824, 22 September 1765). For propriety's sake, she abdicates the Ellisonian role to her husband, noting "I thank god my honest Gentleman will never be guilty of any of these base encroachments on the poor men." Scott, however, deciphering a plea underneath these accounts of high principles and charitable endeavors, responds as she was surely intended to; she praises unstintingly Montagu's efforts at fair labor practices. In one letter, responding to a long account of a public feast for the benefit of the local miners and their families, Scott even identifies her sister as a transgendered Ellison, enabled through her wealth to transcend the seeming limitations of her sex:

> To make them [the colliers] in some measure sharer in your good fortune is politic as well as humane; they will learn to look on your success with an eye of self-interest, & we know that principle is no small spur to industry. Having on some occasions a sort of enthusiastic warmth in my nature, I can fancy that I see you among the Colliers what I made Sir George Ellison among his Blacks; your Subjects are little inferior either in untowardness or gloominess of complexion. (MO 5333, 20 July 1766)

Scott comments in another letter, "You are fortunate in being thrown into a sphere as extensive as your benevolence, & the comparison between you & the rest of the Coal owners will render your conduct more conspicuous & more endearing" (MO 5334, July 1767).

Montagu's business acumen also enabled acts of altruism less self-aggrandizing than the huge and boisterous public feasts she sponsored in the north. She supported the planned women's community at Hitcham, for example, some of her letters explicitly linking her own financial success with the potential success of the Hitcham enterprise. She represents the true profits from exhausting labors as not personal but communal, the well-being of her family and friends. "I am very happy that you are to have Hitcham.... I have sent to Mr. Montagu the account of how ye present state of ye Colliery stands & you will rejoice to see the sum total," she wrote Scott in 1767, implying an intimate connection between the success of the collieries and her ability to help finance Hitcham (MO 5857, 12 September 1767). Shortly after, she wrote Scott about the specific financial arrangements for the Hitcham inhabitants: "I had great joy in yr account of Hitcham & when I am weary my mind finds recreation & repose there. If Mrs Friends income is so small as to make it at all a difficulty to her, could not you take a double share of ye House for me, & then I might beg her to live in it…? You need not have any scruples on this head for I am sure Mr Montagu will raise my wages" (MO 5859, 27 September 1767).

The question of wages was a vexing one. Despite her many responsibilities, until her husband's death Elizabeth remained dependent on an allowance. However, her own expertise in business provided a vantage point from which to critique, and often subvert, her husband's authority. Patriarchal family politics necessitated subterfuge on her part, she told Scott in one letter, in the interests of better management and thus a higher good:

> I have long seen that Mr Montagu's estate was capable of considerable improvement, & urged it to him; he being averse to trouble was always angry.… With the profoundest mystery I shall proceed in all these matters, & when the money comes into my pockets so one shall hear it chink, for they will be apt to say it is counters which I mistook for guineas. I have got Mr Montagu a handsome round sum already by his Colliery, tho ye coal trade labours under strange difficulties at present (MO 5859, 27 September 1767)

Despite the success of her subterfuges, however, her resentment over her financially dependent status, and indeed over all the dependencies ensuing from patriarchal power relations in her marriage, becomes increasingly explicit in her letters. By 1772, Elizabeth is writing Scott that Edward "has got to meddling among his papers which shifting from one box to another he calls doing business, & talks as gravely of this occupation as if it was very important" (MO 5927, 4 June 1772). Her rhetoric emasculates Edward as a paper-shuffling dotard. Nonetheless, despite her very real abilities, Montagu ultimately had to play a waiting game, hoping her husband would honor the unwritten contract she had worked so hard to fulfill—as in fact he did.

The entrepreneurial persona that Elizabeth Montagu creates in her letters, and in her life, offers a compelling counterpoint to eighteenth-century fictions about the economic lives of women. In *Women Writing about Money*, Edward Copeland notes that by the late eighteenth century, "Women found themselves vulnerable as economic beings, as authors now regularly noted in their novels that featured heroines with specifically economic lives: heroines barred from the possession of land (the period's single most important source of capital), or heroines with fixed incomes, usually in trusts, annuities, and stocks."[25] The eighteenth-century novel offers only a limited field of wealthy female protagonists, and of those few, most are victimized rather than empowered by their wealth. Frances Burney's *Cecilia* (1782) offers just one case in point; Burney's heroine staggers under the burden of her fortune, virtually forced to relinquish the reins of power to one unscrupulous and/or incompetent man after another.

Elizabeth Montagu, on the other hand, chose to reject the courtship plot and its attendant notions of female worth, embracing instead the sturdier Bluestocking ethos of female ability, imagination, and usefulness. The letters of the Montagu Collection demonstrate convincingly that Montagu seized the reins of family wealth with gusto. In this one case at least, real capital seems to have underwritten female autonomy, and money to have served not as nemesis but as muse.

*Trinity College, Washington, D.C.*

---

25. Edward Copeland, *Women Writing about Money* (Cambridge, 1995), 17.

# The Politics of Sociability: Public Dimensions of the Bluestocking Millennium

— Emma Major

On 15 October 1772, John Macpherson, later governor-general of India, wrote to Elizabeth Montagu:

> I sincerely hope the dark gloom of politicks which deaden'd inge-
> nious and Elegant life in London in the years 69 & 70 has van-
> ished before now. George the third does not know how much he
> is indebted to the chearful and Classic Assemblies of your Chinese
> Room. You gave that sweetness and refinement to the thoughts of
> our Statesmen which could alone counteract the acid and gloom
> of their Dispositions. Even Lyt[telto]n would have been more
> violent, had he not been soothed in his visits with you. Lady
> Shelburne never left you without being more pleased with the
> World; —Her friend received the good humour she brought away
> … indeed, Madam, we are all indebted to you … you … have thus
> humanized our Manners. (MO 1506, 15 October 1772)

According to Macpherson, Montagu's "sweetness and refinement," her "human-ising" effects, benefit not only the irascible politicians who are soothed by her company and influence but also, by extension, everyone: "we are all indebted to you." The nature of George III's great and particular "debt" to Montagu is in-triguing: as we shall see, it may be seen partly to reside in the example of femi-ninity she provides but also in the model of society offered by her assemblies. In this essay I am interested in exploring George III's indebtedness to the patriotic and public sociability of Montagu and her circle and, specifically, the ways in which religion is central to these polite forays into the realms of the public.

If politeness can be seen, in a sense, as the social practice of Enlightenment, then the version of politeness with which this essay engages is that suggested by

I am indebted to the editors and to Susan Green for their generous help and incisive comments and to Ian Howie and Charlotte Bates for discussion and careful readings. I am also very grateful to the Huntington Library for the fellowship that enabled me to work with the Montagu Collection in 1999.

J. G. A. Pocock's observation that "there were forms of Enlightenment, mainly Protestant in origin and character, . . . in which England's peculiar national institutions led it to take a part."[1] Macpherson's description of Lyttelton's lion-like submission to Montagu's taming presence aptly echoes the paradisiacal lines of Isaiah's pacific millennium: "The wolf also shall dwell with the lamb, and the leopard shall lie down with the kid; and the calf and the young lion" (Isa. 11:6). This praise of Montagu's social powers is in keeping with a millennial strain in the correspondence of the Bluestocking circle, in which polite assemblies are elevated to the divine; and Elizabeth Vesey's drawing room, for example, is spoken of as the setting for a "polite paradise." The entwined "peculiar national institutions" of the Church of England and the monarchy shape these polite millennial visions into distinctly Anglican and patriotic forms.

Polite practices were often underlaid with contemporary Anglican beliefs and strictures. One of the key tropes of eighteenth-century writings on polite conversation, the "via media," a golden mean between two opposing forces, is rooted in the Church of England, for the middle way symbolized the Church's position between Roman Catholicism and Puritanism. The via media of the Church of England was often personified as a woman.[2] In 1633, for example, George Herbert described the Church of England as the perfect woman, neither shabbily nor gaudily dressed, claiming, "The mean thy praise and glory is."[3] Such personification placed Anglican women in special relation to their Church: not only were women generally held to be more religious than men, but the ideal Anglican woman could also on occasion embody the Church of England. Slippage between the emblematic and the exemplary is intriguingly evident in religious conduct literature for women, and led to suggestions that membership in the Church of England might create a public role for women. John Langhorne, an Anglican clergyman and an early friend and admirer of Hannah More, argued that Anglican women—specifically, Anglican women of the upper rank—had duties to fulfill in "the province of public virtue."[4] The Church of England is thus important to both parts of George III's debt to Montagu: it informs her role as a

---

1.  J. G. A. Pocock, *Barbarism and Religion*, vol. 1, *The Enlightenments of Edward Gibbon, 1737–1764* (Cambridge, 1999), 295 and 292–308. See also Pocock, "Clergy and Commerce: The Conservative Enlightenment in England," in *L'eta dei Lumi: Studi Storici sul Settecento Europeo in more di Franco Venturi* (Naples, 1985), 525–62.

2.  See Emma Major, "Rethinking the Private: Religious Femininity and Patriotism, 1750–1789" (Ph.D. diss., University of York, 2000), 112–20, 165–67, 222–55. This article is based on material from pt. 3 of my thesis.

3.  George Herbert, "The British Church," *The Temple: Sacred Poems and Private Ejaculations* (Cambridge, 1633), 103.

4.  John Langhorne, *Letters on Religious Retirement, Melancholy, and Enthusiasm* (London, 1762), 37.

model woman, and it is central to the formation and validation of the paradigmatic society offered by her assemblies.

In emphasizing the importance of the Church of England to the politeness of Montagu and her circle, I am not supporting J. C. D. Clark's argument that there was an absolute Anglican hegemony during the eighteenth century. Over the thirty years or so covered by this essay—roughly, the 1760s to the 1790s—Montagu and her friends increasingly defined themselves against both an allegedly treasonous, dissenting middling rank and the ubiquitous mob. Macpherson's hopes that Montagu's "chearful and Classic Assemblies" would flourish unimpeded by further shadows from "the dark gloom of politicks" were not to be fulfilled: political turmoil caused by John Wilkes and his supporters, the war with America, the Gordon Riots, and the French Revolution formed a hostile background to the polite sociability of Montagu's circle. Indeed, the communities of religion, rank, and nation defined by Montagu and her correspondents might be seen as constructed within and against a series of opposed terms: upper rank and mob, Anglican and dissenter, public and private.

The political and religious controversies of these decades produced forms of patriotic activity that competed with and threatened the upper-rank Anglican sociability of Montagu's assemblies. Claims that polite society exemplified true patriotism were challenged by other, more violent, definitions of the patriotic Protestant Briton. Writers such as the Baptist Maria de Fleury offered less elite and more explosive visions of patriotic Protestant society, in which a vengeful Second Coming preceded the millennium's thousand years of peace. The millennium referred to in the correspondence of Montagu and her friends, by contrast, was rooted in Scottish Enlightenment theories of civilization: these implied that the thousand years of peace could grow out of the progress of society.[5] However, as I suggest in my conclusion, later in the century the letters of Montagu and her sister Sarah Scott were rife with apocalyptic language and imagery depicting the atheistic menace of the French Revolution. The central section of my essay explores the ways in which Montagu and her circle represented themselves as participating in a patriotic public. I look at their claims to be the true children of Israel—God's new chosen people—which they defended by both criticizing and attempting to reform the unruly classes. I would like first to begin, though, in a less polemical setting by considering the millennial potential of Elizabeth Vesey's conversational powers.

---

5.    On eighteenth-century debates about history and the millennium, see David Spadafora, *The Idea of Progress in Eighteenth-Century Britain* (New Haven, Conn., 1990), 107–32.

〜 〜

In a brief preface to a nineteenth-century edition of her 1782 poem *The Bas Bleu; or, Conversation*, Hannah More writes in praise of the Bluestocking "society" that had inspired her poem:

> May the Author be permitted to bear her grateful testimony . . . to the many pleasant and instructive hours she had the honour to pass in this company; in which learning was as little disfigured by pedantry[,] good taste as little tinctured by affectation, and general conversation as little disgraced by calumnity, levity, and the other censurable errors with which it is too commonly tainted, as has perhaps been known in any society.[6]

The conversation of the "company" is the indicator of their morality: the lack of vices in their conversation leads to More's rather awkwardly phrased suggestion that their company was as good as the least sinful of "any society." The claim lifts the "company" into "society" through analogy and turns their "general conversation" into a reflection of morality. Montagu was more explicit in her claims for the millennial virtues of Bluestocking society, writing to Elizabeth Carter in 1783 that Elizabeth Vesey's "drawing room puts me sometimes in mind of Paradise, when ye Lion dandles the Kid," offering as apparently conclusive evidence the observation that "[e]ven Samuel Johnson was seldom brutally rude in her company." For "such an influence has ye good humour & benevolent nature of our Vesey, that Persons of the most contrary dispositions are harmonized if not brought into unison in her Concerto's of conversation" (MO 3565, 15 December 1783).

In exerting such mute qualities as "good humour & benevolent nature" to promote conversation, Vesey was a model of female politeness: More's *Essays* described the role of sociable femininity as a facilitating silence that engaged with vision rather than speech. In her essay "On Conversation" she notes:

> How easily and effectually may a well-bred woman promote the most useful and elegant conversation, almost without speaking a word! for the modes of speech are scarcely more variable than the modes of silence. . . . A woman, in a company where she has the least influence, may promote any subject by a profound and invariable attention, which shews she is pleased with it, and by an illuminated countenance, which proves she understands it.[7]

---

6.  Hannah More, *The Poetical Works of Hannah More, with a memoir of the author* (London, 1839), [382].
7.  More, "On Conversation," in *The Works of Hannah More*, 6 vols. (London, 1834), 6:278.

Attention, then, seems to be the female contribution to conversation, and More is typical of writers on female conduct in describing it so. In *Bas Bleu* she defines the "charm" and "witchcraft" of Vesey's conversation as derived from the "mute angel" of "attention."[8]

Representations of Vesey as an "enchantress" with a "magic spell" and mysterious charms linked to witchcraft might themselves be seen as linked to the claims the poem makes for national excellence in conversation.[9] Montagu confessed to "great complacency" for "the Witches in Macbeth" and often referred to herself, Carter, and Vesey as witches. Her identification of eighteenth-century women with English witches asserts an important line of shared nationality: both are linked to Shakespeare and to the "Brittish stories" that Montagu prized (MO 3084, 3 October 1762), and the association draws upon Gothic notions of "literary nation."[10] In Montagu's Shakespearean frame of reference, the charge of witchery is one that strengthens the patriotism of Vesey's hostessing and, paradoxically, enriches her depiction as a facilitating Anglican angel.

Thus, conversation was seen as an important means of uniting religion and politeness, and it is in a specifically religious dimension that More locates the renewed powers of conversation. She gives a mock-epic introduction to her subject by according it a history through the ages and countries, relating how in Britain "conversation's setting light / Lay half-obscured in Gothic night," occluded by fashionable card games. Its eventual resurrection is achieved by attention to morality, and "conversation / Emerges into *reformation*."[11] It is significant that an early title for *The Bas Bleu; or, Conversation* was *Bas Bleu: or, The Progress of Conversation*, for the grand historical narrative in which More dresses conversation engages with more than the conventions of the mock-epic. The influence of Scottish Enlightenment stadial models of history can be seen in the pattern of the decline and rise of conversation, from its fall after classical times to its re-emergence as "reformation" in the present.[12] Read in this context, the

8.   More, *The Bas Bleu, or, Conversation,* in *Poetical Works,* 393. The poem was written in 1782 and circulated among the circle; it was published in 1786.
9.   Ibid., 388.
10.  On the Gothic and the literary, see Harriet Guest, "The Wanton Muse: Politics and Gender in Gothic Theory after 1760," in Stephen Copley and John Whale, eds., *Beyond Romanticism: New Approaches to Texts and Contexts, 1780–1832* (London, 1992), 118–39.
11.  More, *Bas Bleu; Poetical Works,* 384.
12.  According to stadial models, mankind passed through stages of development, designated by Adam Smith in his *Lectures on Jurisprudence* (1762–64) as the time of barbaric hunters, the time of nomadic shepherds, the age of agriculture, and the age of commerce. Commerce inevitably led to decay, and thus, it was feared, to a cyclical repetition of the stages. See also Adam Ferguson, *Essay on Civil Society* (1767); and John Millar, *Origin of the Distinction of Ranks* (1771).

poem's pretended history of conversation makes a serious assertion of national superiority for "our isle," an assertion to which religion was central.[13]

"'Tis more than wit, 'tis moral beauty, / 'Tis pleasure rising out of duty," More urges in the closing lines of *Bas Bleu*.[14] Her description of conversation as a duty as well as a pleasure freights the conversational and the social with the religious. In fact, the language of Christian duty permeates discussions of female friendship and of conversation between men and women in both literary and religious texts of the period. Montagu tells Vesey that "when I think of Mrs Vesey I feel how unnecessary it is to make friendship a duty, & enforce it by command," adding that Christianity is ideally suited to social life, because "[t]he temper, the state of mind recommended by the Gospel, the brotherly love, the justice, the charity, put you in a condition to do right in every circumstance & situation" (MO 6478, 15 May 1776). As we shall see, in speaking of the social aspect of religion Montagu is engaging with very public notions of a reformed nation and its possible progress.

There is a surprising and significant conceptual shift in *Bas Bleu*, for in this poem femininity is portrayed as rooted in the social rather than the familial. The idealized conversation of More's poem is emphatically polite rather than classical, and it is the property of a select few: its move into the social belongs to conservative hostesses rather than republican mothers. In the next section I will consider the public ambitions of these polite hostesses and their "conversaziones," or conversation parties.

❧ ❧

Elizabeth Montagu herself saw in Elizabeth Vesey's circle, she claimed, something more than human: a polite millennium. On 4 September 1772, Montagu wrote to Carter of her pleasure at seeing Vesey, nicknamed "Sylph":

> I delight already in ye prospect of ye blue box (alias Drawing Room) in which our Sylph assembles all the heterogeneous natures in the World, & indeed in many respects resembles Paradise, for there ye Lion sits down by the Lamb, ye Tyger dandles the Kid; the shy scotchman & ye [illegible] Hibernian, the Hero & Maccaroni, the Vestal, . . . the Mungo of Ministry and the inflexible partizans of incorruptible Patriots, Beaux esprits & fine Gentlemen all gather together under the downy wing of the Sylph,

13. More, *Bas Bleu; Poetical Works*, 385.
14. Ibid., 394.

> & are soothed into good humour: were she to withdraw her influ-
> ence a moment, discord wd reassume her reign, & we shd hear
> ye clashing of swords, the angry flirting of fans, & St Andrew &
> St Patrick gabbling in dire confusion the different dialects of ye
> Erse language. Methinks I see our Sylph moving in her circle, & by
> some unknown attraction keeping the whole system in due order.
> (MO 3304, 4 September 1772)

The reference to Isaiah 11:6 signals that the "Paradise" Montagu sees in these gatherings is situated within a religious framework. Although assembling "all the heterogeneous natures in the World," the paradise Vesey unites is also distinctly British, with its harmonious mix of the Scottish, the Irish, and the Patriots. The Sylph's influence is not explained in this letter—further on, Montagu describes it as "this invisible je ne scai quoi," "the gift of the Fairies"—but it clearly expresses itself in the linguistic fluency and union of her guests. Without it, the Scots and the Irish would be stranded, "gabbling in dire confusion." Vesey's gift might then be described as that of promoting conversation: a quality, as I mentioned earlier, recommended by all who write on the matter in the eighteenth century as not only peculiarly suited to polite, virtuous femininity but also as central to the union of religion and civilization in polite patriotism. Here it results in nothing less than a united kingdom, with the different nations harmonizing in a patriotic conversational concerto in Vesey's drawing room.

As in Macpherson's letter to Montagu, politicians are divested of "the dark gloom of politicks" in Vesey's circle, and so are able to countenance one another without anger. However, this does not mean that the political is extraneous to politeness; for the political is essential to the definition of polite society in two important ways. Firstly, as in the above quotation and Macpherson's letter, it is used to define by contrast: the harmony of polite circles is compared to the turmoil of politics, and as I shall show, polite society is defined against an unruly political mob. Secondly, the realm of the political is central to an important shift in the meaning of the public and private in the correspondence of this circle.

The correspondence of Montagu's circle is increasingly concerned with both public and private news from the 1760s onward. Yet the increased interest in these categories did not mark a greater desire to separate the two, as a 1779 letter in which Vesey is discussed shows:

> Our dear Sylph must have some Dragon to amuse her. . . . Our
> Sylphs apprehensions are a delicate essence, l'eau de mille fleurs.
> Mr Veseys fits, Mrs Hancocks palpitations, the loss of America, the

gutter that overflows in ye kitchen, & the Fleet superior to our
Navy, a Foreign army ready to land &c. (MO 3481, 28 July 1779)[15]

The heterogeneous mix of public, personal, and quotidian concerns that com-
prises the "mille fleurs" of Vesey's anxieties is suggestive of more than her tendency to worry about everything. The peculiarly public and private nature of the
"Dragon" that preoccupies her reflects a significant shift in the composition of the
private. For here we may see the inverse of Hannah Arendt's concept of society
as "that curiously hybrid realm where private interests assume national importance."[16] The public, in this letter, assumes the importance of the private to Vesey:
national concerns break in upon the private and become as pressing and real as
"the gutter that overflows in ye kitchen." This shift can be seen as marking a
move toward personal identification with the national, and it is central to the
formation of a notion of a national community: for a national realm needs to
be created before the private can assume national importance, as in Arendt's
formulation.

   An imagined "community of nation," to use Benedict Anderson's term,[17]
causes Vesey's worries about America, the Navy, and invasion. It also lies behind
Montagu's observation in 1782, on having some of her colliery property destroyed
by lightning, that "I did not grieve for them [the buildings] as I do for the de-
molition of ye Garrison at Gibraltar, a little oeconomy will repair a private disaster, but in publick all must inevitably, irrevocably fall" (letter to Vesey, MO 6575,
15 September 1782). Montagu and Vesey's private troubles are thus situated in
relation to a demanding public, one that permeates the private and whose fate
"inevitably, irrevocably" will involve "all." Public worries become a form of conversational currency, each exchange affirming both the friends' patriotism and
social position. A few years later, George III's illness prompted an anxious epistolary flurry in which they detailed their loyal responses, Montagu reporting that
"I have visited only my most intimate Friends, & our conversation has been on
the calamity of our Country, & the sad afflictions of their Majesties" (letter to
Elizabeth Carter, MO 3652, 18 December [1788]).

15.  Fears of invasion had started the summer of 1778. The references to the fleet and Navy allude to the
     controversy over Admiral Augustus Keppel, who had refused to fight against the Americans; he stood trial
     earlier that year but was acquitted. See Kathleen Wilson, *The Sense of the People: Politics, Culture, and
     Imperialism in England, 1715–1785* (Cambridge, 1995), 252–61; and John Brewer, *The Sinews of Power: War,
     Money, and the English State, 1688–1783* (1989; reprint ed., London, 1994), 176.
16.  Hannah Arendt, *The Human Condition* (Chicago, 1958), 35.
17.  Benedict Anderson, *Imagined Communities: Reflections on the Origins and Spread of Nationalism* (London,
     1983).

Montagu's claim that national events supersede her private worries can be read, then, as a sign that she felt a strong private involvement in the fate of the national public. Yet the mapping of the public onto the private can be read as doubly significant, a fundamental shift in language that not only signals a sense of community but also constructs that community in such a way as to protect it—in the very terms of the Scottish Enlightenment narratives that predict its fall (see n. 13). Montagu writes in July of 1779, a year of continuing failure and trouble in America and Ireland, and a summer in which, according to Paul Langford, Prime Minister Lord North's "fragile morale came close to collapse":[18]

> [T]he only Comfort I find amidst the dangers which surround, & the alarms which disturb this Country is, that every Nation which has enjoy'd uninterrupted peace & prosperity, for any long time, has degenerated into baseness, & the lowest Vices. Perhaps publick danger may awaken publick spirit, & selfishness be lost in the universal interest. My pride & selfsufficiency, as an Englishwoman, is mightily humbled as often as I reflect on the possibility of a Foreign foe insulting us on our Island. (Letter to Carter, MO 3481, 28 July 1779)

Again, Montagu's personal identification with the nation, to the point of participating in some of its errors, is evident: she, too, "as an Englishwoman," has become complacent in the civilization of her country and has fallen into "pride & selfsufficiency," qualities identified by Adam Ferguson as contributing to the fall of great nations.[19] Montagu's consolation, in the midst of political troubles, is explicitly related to the Scottish Enlightenment histories: she refers to the degeneration of civilized nations in times of peace in language very close to that of Ferguson. Her hope that danger may prompt a resurgence of public spirit that will reunite a country grown fragmented and complacent in peace also echoes Ferguson's links between military and public spirit. The sense of the public Montagu avows so strongly in her letters is an assertion of a polite patriotism that can also be read as a response to Ferguson's charge that "we . . . are accustomed to think of the individual with compassion, seldom of the public with zeal."[20]

The national public with which Montagu and her circle identified was not only threatened by troubles abroad. From the late 1760s onward, Montagu refers to civil war as a serious possibility: in October 1769, following months of repeated riots by the supporters of Wilkes, she writes that

18. Paul Langford, *A Polite and Commercial People: England, 1727–1783* (Oxford, 1989), 547.
19. See, for example, Adam Ferguson, *An Essay on the History of Civil Society* (1767; reprint ed., Cambridge, 1995): "They have entertained admiration of themselves"; and "The members of a community may . . . lose the sense of every connection, but that of kindred" (see pp. 196–220; quotations at 196, 208).
20. Ferguson, *Essay*, 214–20, and passim; quotation at 190.

> I hate war, but a foreign is preferable to civil War, of which we seem
> to be in great danger. Knaves & fools make a continual fermentation
> in a free Government. Bad Ministers, seditious Leaders of ye people,
> a wicked mob, & a foolish sort of folks who follow any popular
> cry, seem now to be brewing a terrible storm. A civil war is replete
> with every evil. (Letter to Carter, MO 3259, 17 [October 1769])

The "seditious" and "wicked" nature of the "Knaves & fools" involved in the
threats to civil peace is compounded, Montagu argues, by the "fraud & treachery" of their practice; she claims that "in former times" civil war "was accompanied with much violence but little fraud & treachery." Their cause, she
complains, is not worthy of war: "Israel resorted to his Tent because he thought
his House was not safe, now men will resort to the Tent if their Houses are not
large or splendid enough" (MO 3259). Her reference to Israel is telling: she is invoking God's chosen nation to draw an eighteenth-century parallel, and while the
revolutionaries' cause is dismissed as a war-mongering greed unworthy of Israel,
Montagu and her property-owning peers are shown to be the modern inheritors
of Israel's valid fears.

The image of treacherous underclasses recurs often in her correspondence
after the late 1760s. In September 1779 she tells Carter, "It is now I understand as
usual with ye middling sort of folks to talk treason, as to hum a tune, or whistle"
(Montagu to Carter, MO 3484, 17 September 1779). Montagu's identification of
the middling ranks as the source of radicalism was not especially perspicacious;
prominent radicals claimed the same, William Beckford asserting that "it was
not the mob, nor 200 great lords that made us so firm: the middling rank of men
it was in which our strength consisted."[21] In October 1779, Montagu describes
the coalminers' rebellion and the strike at her colliery to Carter, observing, "It is
generally inculcated, that it shews fine spirit to oppose restraint, & insult superiors" (MO 3487, 28 October [1779]). The only truly reliable and loyal successors
of Israel, her correspondence implies, are to be found among those who already
possess "large or splendid" houses. The middling ranks' radicalism and the poor
colliers' insubordination license representations of the upper ranks as the bas-
tions of loyalty and patriotism, and validate, as we shall see, the increasingly confident belief, in the arguments of some, that "all are not Israel that are of
Israel"[22]—that true patriotism belonged only to the loyal elite.

---

21.  Quoted in Nicholas Rogers, "Crowd and People in the Gordon Riots," in Eckhart Hellmuth, ed., *The
     Transformation of Political Culture: England and Germany in the Late Eighteenth Century* (Oxford, 1990),
     39–56 at 41.
22.  [William Jones], *An Essay on the Church* (Gloucester, 1787), 128.

The effects of the treachery she ascribed to the radicals were not confined to domestic affairs, but extended, Montagu claimed, to the loss of America. In 1784 she responds to Carter:

> I agree with you, that the great losses the Empire of great Brittain has sufferd have been owing to our pretended Patriots. Ministers oftcn do piddling mischief but as they are liable to be calld to account for their actions, their wickedness is under restraint. (MO 3572, 25 July [1784])

The blame is laid clearly on the unelected "pretended Patriots" whose untimely political activism undermined the interests of the Empire. According to Montagu, true patriotism lies in respect for the law, faith, and constitution of Britain, "& if there were not too many who wish there was neither God nor Judge in Israel, I shd not be afraid [of] such Wild Republican principles" (letter to Carter, MO 3342, 14 September 1774). Here the laws of Britain become the laws of Israel and God, and religious and civic law become one, in a rhetorical move that I shall examine in greater depth in the next section in the context of the possibilities Montagu found both frightening and exciting about Protestant societies in the 1780s.

I have suggested that from the late 1760s, the political becomes central to the self-definition of Montagu and her circle: in complex ways their polite society both appropriates the political and differentiates itself from it. Montagu and her friends repeatedly contrasted the alleged treachery of the poor and middling ranks with their own true loyalty and patriotism. "True patriotism," Montagu wrote in 1774, "is first pure, then peaceable" (MO 3342); and as we have seen, she described the society in Vesey's drawing-room as the polite version of Isaiah's pacific millennium. The appropriation of "true patriotism" for the polite is, I have argued, defended by their claims to have assumed the mantle of public responsibility. The representation of public worries as more personally important to Montagu than private anxieties maps the public onto the private in a way that not only validates her claims to patriotism but also engages with narratives of civilization in an attempt to combat corruption through public feeling.

ೞ ೞ

"I cannot help attributing the wild uproar and disorders in publick & private life to arise from the doctrines of a set of people who call themselves freethinkers," writes Montagu in 1779; their lack of religion, she claims, has "untied all the bonds of Society."[23] The 1780s saw various attempts to retie the bonds of society and restore order to "publick & private life" through the reformation of national manners: the 1781 Sunday Observance Act, George III's Proclamation of 1787 urging national reform, the Proclamation Society established by William Wilberforce to promote the Proclamation, and the sudden growth of Sunday Schools.[24] The most lasting of these campaigns was the Sunday School movement, of which Montagu was a keen supporter; she was friendly with some of the leading figures in the moves for reform during the 1780s, such as William Wilberforce and Beilby Porteus, bishop of Chester and later of London. Montagu writes with satisfaction in 1787 that Sunday Schools had resulted in a "great improvement in decency, & sobriety" (Montagu to Pepys, MO 4081, 9 July [1787]). In the 1780s such schools were often described as the means to establish a Protestant version of popular nationhood that affirmed public worship in the Church of England and by extension public laws. Porteus, supporter of the Proclamation England was the best means of promoting a sense of citizenship, and that "true Christianity will produce TRUE PATRIOTISM AND PUBLIC SPRIT."[25]

Joanna Innes has shown that the Proclamation Society drew its membership predominantly from the upper ranks, rendering it a "very elite society" with Pittite leanings.[26] The king's proclamation, the upper-rank, Pittite composition of the Proclamation Society and the involvement of women such as Montagu in the Sunday School movement are suggestive of a rise in the 1780s in specifically upper-rank, Tory attempts to reform society. Sabbath-breaking was criticized in all ranks, but reports of tradesmen making journeys on Sundays because "[t]ravelling on the Genteel Day will give [them] an Air of Consequence" suggest that some at least regarded it as incumbent upon the upper ranks to reform themselves and set a better example to others.[27] Queen Charlotte, who reputedly gave up her Sunday hairdresser in response to Hannah More's *Thoughts on the Importance of the Manners of the Great* (1788), also invited Robert Raikes and the author Sarah

---

23.  Montagu to Leonard Smelt, MO 5020, 10 June 1779.
24.  See Joanna Innes, "Politics and Morals: The Reformation of Manners Movement in Later Eighteenth-Century England," in Hellmuth, *Transformation of Political Culture*, 57–118 at 57–58.
25.  This was typical of lecturers representing the Society for the Promotion of Christian Knowledge; see Beilby Porteus, "Sermon XI: The Necessity of National Reformation. Preached before the Lords Spiritual and Temporal, on the General Fast, Feb. 10, 1779," *Works*, 6 vols. (London, 1811), 1:261.
26.  Innes, "Politics and Morals," 86–87 and 103.
27.  Minister of the Established Church, *The Observation of the Christian Sabbath Recommended, (in a Sermon) as Particularly Necessary to the Well-Being of Civil Society. Addressed to all Lovers of their Country, and especially to the Higher Degrees* (Northampton, 1789), vi.

Trimmer to discuss Sunday Schools in personal, well-publicized meetings. The *Gentleman's Magazine* reported in 1788 that

> her Majesty graciously said, that she envied those who had the power of doing good, by thus personally promoting the welfare of society, in giving instruction and morality to the general mass of common people. . . . What a glorious sentiment is this for a Queen!—Were this known amongst the ladies of the British nation, it would serve to animate them with zeal.[28]

These moves toward a fashionable reformation in which women played a key role can be seen as attempts to realize what Newton Ogle, dean of Winchester, termed "a moral taste." Ogle's phrasing is significant, suggestive of the union of religion and politeness praised in Montagu and Vesey's "conversaziones."[29]

Increased upper-rank interest in the reformation of manners was not, however, simply a passing attempt to map religion onto fashion to produce a purer, more civilized form of fashionable consumption; it was also a response to the civil unrest of the previous fifteen or so years, and so should also be read in the context of the virulently Protestant and patriotic Gordon Riots.[30] It was in these riots that Montagu feared she had finally seen let slip "ye Dogs of civil discord" (letter to Carter, MO 6541, [June 1780]),[31] and she wrote to Vesey that "religious zeal is very small, but the disposition of the people is very combustible. Indeed a long train of Gunpowder has been laid to blow up this explosion" (MO 6540, [June 1780]). The republican resonances of the gunpowder in Montagu's letter are accompanied by references to the nonconformist fervor that she claims lit the taper. Complaining that "[t]he thirty nine articles of our Church were discussed in all ye alehouses appeals made by their opponents in every three half penny newspaper," she then immediately goes on to write of Theophilus Lindsey's departure from the Church as if it were one of the events that formed the "long trail of Gunpowder," even though this had happened in 1773, seven years before the riots (MO 6540).

---

28. The *Gentleman's Magazine* (1788), 2, p. 654.
29. The term appears in his sermon for the Society for the Promotion of Christian Knowledge in 1775; Newton Ogle, *A Sermon Preached in the Parish-Church of Christ-Church, London, on May 4th, 1775; Being the Time of the Yearly Meeting of the Children Educated in the Charity-Schools, in and about the Cities of London and Westminster* (London, 1775), 13.
30. Described by Nicholas Rogers as "the most tumultuous of the century"; "Crowd and People," 41.
31. As so often, Montagu is reworking Shakespeare: "Cry, 'Havoc!' and let slip the dogs of war"; *Julius Caesar*, 3.1.273. On the role of the army in controlling the riots, see Brewer, *Sinews of Power*, 52–53.

For Montagu, then, Protestantism alone does not bring civil peace: her idea of an orderly society is tied firmly to the Church of England, and the attempts to shape the rising generation of Britons into orderly Anglicans can be seen in part as a response to the unruly citizen-patriots of the Protestant Association, whose more ecumenical vision of Britain as a religious nation was decidedly more apocalyptic.[32] The Protestant Association organized the petition and protests that prompted the Gordon Riots, and its advertisements calling for action against the Catholic Relief Bill of 1778 simply identified Protestantism with patriotism. "TRUE PROTESTANTS NO TURNCOATS, Or six plain reasons given why Protestants of all denominations should oppose the Growth and Establishment of *Popery*, with the greatest Vigour and without Delay" ran the heading of one of their advertisements, which after denouncing transubstantiation and the religious persecution of Protestants under Mary, appended a warning that Roman Catholics were targeting the children of the poor.[33] Such calls, with their representation of poor children as particularly vulnerable and references to the gory imagery of Foxe's *Book of Martyrs*, were powerfully emotive. Their appeals to a shared history, shared enemy, and shared Protestant identity formed a version of patriotism celebrated by the Baptist writer Maria de Fleury, whose "Address to the Protestant Association" (1781) opened with these lines:

> HAIL! Britons! Hail! associate band!
> Who, bold for Truth, united stand,
> Resolv'd to oppose the scarlet whore,
> Though men may frown, and devils roar.
> 'Tis well resolv'd, O! noble zeal!
> May ev'ry breast in Britain feel
> Its sacred influence, and glow
> With holy, gen'rous ardour too:
> 'Tis GOD whose cause you undertake,
> 'Tis for your king and country's sake,
> To guard your dearest rights, and prove
> Heav'n's sacred gifts ye prize and love.

32. The Protestant Association has not received much attention recently; see, however, Wilson's brief but fascinating accounts in *Sense of the People*, 366–72, 266–67; Colin Haydon, *Anti-Catholicism in Eighteenth-Century England, c. 1714–80* (Manchester, 1993), 262–64; Christopher Hibbert, *King Mob: The Story of Lord George Gordon and the Riots of 1780* (London, 1958); Eugene Charlton Black, *The Association: British Extra-Parliamentary Political Organisation, 1769–1793* (Cambridge, Mass., 1963), 131–37, 142–67; and Frank O'Gorman, *The Rise of Party in England: The Rockingham Whigs, 1760–1782* (London, 1975), 421–22.

33. Advertisement appended to Maria de Fleury's *Unrighteous Abuse Detected and Chastised, or a Vindication of Innocence and Integrity, Being an Answer to a Virulent Poem, Intituled, The Protestant Association*, 2d ed. (London, 1781).

The Britons de Fleury rallies are united against "the scarlet whore of Rome"; their "noble ardour" is both holy and patriotic, and their protests ventured for "king and country's sake." She urges: "Go then, ye champions for your GOD, / Follow the track your father's trod; / Be zealous! it will glory bring / To GOD, your country, and your king." The Protestant Association is here eulogized as a patriotic band of fearless citizens with a holy mission, united in faith, history, and nation against the Roman Catholics—who, de Fleury claims, were the real source of the violence in the Gordon Riots.[34]

De Fleury's poem personifies the Church of Rome as the "scarlet whore" of Babylon, and this figure represents a sinister twin to the polite female emblem of the Church of England. De Fleury's Protestant millennium comes not from the messianic verses of Isaiah but from the chaos of Revelation.[35] Yet although Isaiah was repeatedly invoked in descriptions of the gatherings hosted by Montagu and Vesey, the language of the two visions cannot so easily be separated out in the friends' correspondence later in the century. Glimpses of apocalypse haunt their discussions of politics and threaten to take over entirely in the 1790s, when everything, even the weather, assumed a portentous quality, and Montagu had to draw on her faith to reassure herself that the blighted seasons were not omens of divine wrath (letter to Carter, MO 3770 [1 October 1797]).

As the letters on Wilkes and the Gordon Riots suggest, there is much excited political debate in the correspondence of the Montagu Collection, but the increasing violence in the French Revolution marks a new degree of compelled engagement with the news. Britain's war with France was a righteous war for Montagu and many of her friends: the language of divine justice permeates their correspondence, with British victories ascribed to Providence—one typical claim that "[t]he impiety of the French makes me believe they will be afflicted with the most severe and terrible calamities" (Montagu to Carter, MO 3691, 2 September [1791]). There were worries that revolutionary fire might spread from the Continent, and Sarah Scott wrote of "a flame [that] has been blown up among the lowest rank of people by diabolical Incendiaries"; she particularly feared for the manufacturing towns, considering their large numbers of dissenters "well inclind to dissentions" of a civil as well as religious kind (letter to Montagu, MO 5511, 19 October [c. 1794]). Montagu countered such threats of domestic unrest by circulating Hannah More's tracts, which exhorted readers to preserve social order by being loyal to the Church of England and the king, promoting them among those "disposed to Rioting," and urging Carter to do the same (MO 3751, 9 September 1795).

---

34.  De Fleury, "An Address to the Protestant Association," *Unrighteous Abuse*, 21, 22, 9-11.
35.  See esp. Rev. 17:3–5, 2:20–23.

The tumultuousness of events and the fear and speculation they generated were such that in September 1792 Scott confessed to Montagu:

> I begin to think I am like Dr Young, & love a horror, for tho' the accounts from France chill my blood, & make it boil alternately, yet I never before felt as much impatience for news papers. The horrible events they relate keep my mind in a ferment, & almost entirely possess it. They so far exceed any thing one ever read of that were they transacted in a more distant part of the Globe one shou'd not believe them true; but we are almost on the spot, only happily just removed from being eye witnesses of them. (MO 5489, 23 September [1792])

The exhilaration of her rather Burkean response to the Terror is also evident in subsequent letters, in which Scott's "ferment" of mind is expressed as a religious fervor:

> The amazing talents & noble views of Mr Pitt fill my mind with wonder & veneration. It lessens my fears of the ill consequences threatn'd by the diabolical spirit that has gone forth among so many Nations, & I am almost ready to believe that the G[ates?] of Hell can not prevail against him. But the smallest chance of the destruction of a Kingdom arrived at such a pinnacle of prosperity & happiness as ours, is terrible. (Letter to Montagu, MO 5490, 4 October [1792])

Here, it seems, Pitt's "amazing talents & noble views" have elevated him to the level of Christ harrowing the French Hell; indeed, she goes on to write that Paris "must be rather a worse place than Les Enfers." Not all the circle would perhaps have concurred in Scott's identification of Pitt as Christ—a few months earlier, Pitt's successes had been met with more modest "joy" from Montagu and Carter[36]—but such descriptions of Pitt were not unprecedented. In 1789 More had observed that "[a]s to Pitt, if I were a Pagan, I would raise altars and temples to him"; and images of Pitt as Christ were evidently of some cultural currency, as they recur in graphic satire of the period.[37]

---

36. See, for example, Montagu to Carter, MO 3705, 26 August [1792].
37. More to Martha (Patty) More, 6 January 1789, in William Roberts, ed., *Memoirs of the Life and Correspondence of Mrs Hannah More*, 4 vols. (London, 1834), 2:140. On Pitt and millennial imagery, see Diana Donald, *The Age of Caricature: Satirical Prints in the Reign of George III* (New Haven, Conn., 1996), 163–65. See also Morris Eaves, *The Counter-Arts Conspiracy: Art and Industry in the Age of Blake* (Ithaca, N.Y., 1992), 86–87, on Blake's painting *The Spiritual Form of Pitt Guiding Behemoth* (1805–9).

Pitt's representation as Christ also makes claims for the "Kingdom" that he defends, which becomes, by implication, the kingdom of God. It is as if Britain's progress to "prosperity & happiness" has defied stadial history by continuing its progress into heaven instead of following the cycle that leads civilization down into decay. Yet though Scott's letter echoes the bloodshed and purification of Revelation, it nevertheless retains at its core the confident assumption of the earlier polite millennium: that its members represent God's chosen nation.

Scott's metaphor identifies public concerns with religion in a manner that equates piety with patriotism without intended blasphemy. It is evident from her choice of Christ-figure that the kingdom she hopes is saved is a conservative, Anglican one that excludes dissenters and "Incendiaries" with "diabolical" French tendencies. Leading a life of retirement, she did not mix with political public figures as Montagu did; but she nevertheless described herself as having "public Spirit," and in a letter to Montagu she explained that

> I rejoice in the continuance of your health & powers of enjoying it, no one can deserve it better, for you let others share in the blessing; you do not sink into solitary & retired enjoyment of ease, but communicate the blessing to numbers, & enliven their spirits by contact with your own. May you long be able to proceed in the same track! a wish formd not only from love of you but from benevolence & public Spirit. (MO 5463, 20 March [1790])

In this letter, there is slippage between Scott's benevolence, her feeling for the "public," and her love for Montagu: the three are elided intriguingly in the last sentence, while the whole passage is lent a religious aspect by the repeated mention of the undefined "blessing." Her description of the effects of the blessing her sister brings to the public is reminiscent of Macpherson's language when he wrote that Montagu "gave ... sweetness and refinement," "soothed" and "humanized." There is a hint that the manner in which "the blessing" is communicated is specifically Anglican: eschewing Methodist or nun-like "solitary & retired enjoyment of ease," Montagu benefits the public by letting "others share in the blessing."

As with George III's "debt" to Montagu, the "blessing" is conveyed by Montagu's sociability. The social, as we have seen, is the crucible in which private feeling may be transformed into public spirit, where an epistolary exchange can transform Vesey's "mille fleurs" of national and quotidian fears into an assertion of her membership in a national community. It is the union of religion and politeness in the social that produces the public dimension of the "Paradise" experienced in the Bluestocking drawing rooms, and allows us to comprehend the extent of George III's debt to Montagu. For the moments of social epiphany provided by these assemblies could be interpreted as premonitions of a glorious future, one in which Montagu and her circle turned George III's Britain into an earthly paradise of divinely blessed progress. The Bluestocking millennium, indeed, represents nothing less than an idealized version of that self-proclaimed most civilized and most patriotic public, the Anglican elite of God's chosen nation.

*Centre for Eighteenth-Century Studies*
*University of York*

# Two Versions of Community:
# Montagu and Scott

— BETTY RIZZO

Truly distinguished letter savers—in the eighteenth century, Lady Spencer of Althorpe, Horace Walpole, Emily, duchess of Leinster, the Burney family members, Elizabeth Montagu—must carry on an extensive and interesting correspondence. They also must have interesting lives; space and time for writing, preserving, and organizing; and, I think, a strong sense of the significance of their own existence. Elizabeth Robinson Montagu is a splendid example of such a letter saver. Those with a more acute sense of privacy burn their personal papers. Like Montagu's sister, Sarah Robinson Scott, they may make a greater distinction between what they choose to issue publicly and their private writings. Their lives—even an edited version of them—unlike the lives of letter savers, are not for general consumption.

Accordingly, those caches of letters that do survive, survive selectively. They are the correspondence of persons who are comfortable living public lives because they consider themselves successful. The letters saved, furthermore, are from certain loved or respected correspondents; they memorialize interesting events; they convey a flattering image of the recipient's character and concerns. Perhaps the act of collection manifests a passion for control, for managing and editing the lives of both recipient and correspondent. Discrimination in selecting letters for retention is indeed a method of editing one's life—even, we should be aware, a way of presenting and maintaining fictions. Paradoxically, however, we are dependent upon these efforts for our record not only of those who save the letters they receive but also of those who would destroy their own—which may be preserved by the savers but selectively, some having been discarded, some mutilated. It becomes interesting, then, beyond the accidents of longevity,[1] to know who compiled the collections, who preserved them, and what still lies in them, as well as to guess what has been discarded. A great deal can be extrapolated from the absences as well as the presences. Letter savers may discard

---

1. According to law, one's letters remained one's own property, though in the hands of recipients, and were properly returnable on the death of the recipient. Elizabeth Montagu outlived the greater number of her correspondents and so retained their letters.

correspondence from unfavored acquaintances as well as items too trivial, too unflattering, too unpleasantly revealing, or too confrontational. In all of these collections there are vital pieces that have gone missing, relics of critical periods that went into the fire.

The splendid Montagu Collection at the Huntington, about 6,900 pieces in all, contains many of Montagu's own letters and the letters of many of her correspondents, including a large number from her sister—whose correspondence with most others is wanting.[2] That Montagu saved her letters for posterity while Scott did not emblematically expresses their difference, a very great one between girls who began life as alike, it was alleged, as peas in a pod. Nonetheless, Montagu's sense of that difference as well as Scott's must be inferred from their differently preserved correspondence; a great deal of what we now know of them is to be gleaned only from their letters.[3] And their differing attitudes toward their lives correspond with their differing views of community.

Elizabeth Montagu kept many, perhaps most, of the letters from her younger sister Sarah. Montagu was the archivist, the family historian, and the would-be controller. Her control is exhibited by the fact that these letters, like others in the collection, are often mutilated and incomplete, with many of the final pages, presumably containing references to private or unpleasant matters, now missing. Sarah Scott, on the other hand, enjoined her executor—perhaps significantly *not* her sister—to burn her papers, manuscripts included, though evidently her sister's letters, and probably those of others, were properly returned to the surviving sender. Scott's death therefore ensured that her letters of many years remained in the hands of the sister who survived her. Had Scott been the longer lived, it is probable that the correspondence between the two sisters would have disappeared entirely.

The difference between the two women's attitudes toward the record of their lives is a critical one. Both women were irrepressible builders of community, but of very different sorts. Montagu presided over a Bluestocking assembly in London to which any person of any importance came. Her aim was to provide the preeminent salon and to blaze in it. The community she built, and of which her salon was the focus, was of the elite. The salon was undoubtedly of use as an inspiriting gathering place for individuals with talent and genius. But though she could be beneficent to the members of her court, her purpose was egotistical, to

2.  Scott's letters to her brother William do survive; they were apparently given to Montagu after William's death in 1803.

3.  Letters from the Huntington's Montagu Collection are identified hereafter in the text by manuscript number. For a fuller discussion of the lives of these two sisters, see Betty Rizzo, *Companions without Vows: Relationships among Eighteenth-Century British Women* (Athens, Ga., 1994), chaps. 6 and 13; for Scott, see the introduction to Sarah Scott, *The History of Sir George Ellison*, ed. Betty Rizzo (Lexington, Ky., 1996).

show off her wisdom and her wit, of which she had inordinate amounts. (Her letters are full of them, as they are full of the names of her eminent friends.)

Scott too, it may be said, presided, with her friend Lady Barbara Montagu, over a community. But it developed in opposition to her sister's, which she heartily disliked, and can perhaps most fruitfully be viewed as an anti-salon. A number of Bath residents, most of them women, gathered to discuss social reform. They gathered formally and informally, and their deliberations were focused not principally on the politics and publications of the day (though Scott took an intense interest in both) but on their charitable cases, their plans to make their own lives useful and the lives of others more comfortable, and, most notably, their development of a plan for a British utopia where the social evils they were attempting to alleviate would be obviated. Their gathering was no end in itself. A community of their own, they constructed a model for another ideal community and tried to live their own lives as citizens of that community. In the end they actually implemented an experimental community.

The letters show that the sisters, though from their twenties on widely differing in their lifestyles, never ceased to love one another—and that each had the other in view as she labored to vindicate her own vision of community. In negotiating these differences, Scott often obliquely critiqued the social eminence that Montagu vaunted while Montagu, always mindful of her sister's moral superiority, sometimes professed the same objectives and schemes and subtly advertised her superior capacity for implementing them. Scott undertook a modest school; then Montagu undertook to educate all the children of her Yorkshire miners. Scott designed a utopian community; then Montagu joined with enthusiasm and provided the money and "good things," as the sisters called them, that made it practicable. Scott may have dedicated her life to proving her sister's values wrong; Montagu, who loved her sister and also feared the scandal of a public breach, often labored mightily to prove herself right.

Possibly—even probably—the ambitions of the two diverged at the time when, aged twenty, Sarah fell ill with a disfiguring smallpox and Elizabeth fled the house, stayed entirely away, and managed her first reunion with her sister outdoors and at a distance, without embrace. Scott was throughout their later years to replicate that distance herself. In Scott's fictions there are incidents where girls smitten with smallpox thank God that it has restrained their vanity and turned their minds to more serious matters, one of which was systematized study.[4] A second heartbreaking rejection for Scott immediately followed when Montagu left home to be a companion to the young duchess of Portland. When

---

4.  See Scott, *A Description of Millenium Hall*, ed. Gary Kelly (Peterborough, Ont., 1995), 41–42; and *History of Sir George Ellison*, 199.

her cousin's husband, William Freind, reproached her on behalf of Sarah, she responded, "Her Grace has a friendship for me I can never find in any one else; nor indeed would it give the same pleasure from any other person; because then I must be ungrateful, as it would be impossible for me to love any one as I do her."[5] Montagu, who had her eye on the main chance and who, from her new milieu, made a lucky marriage, was to revise this opinion, but her sister never forgot it; in 1754 she translated the French novel *La Laideur aimable*, in which the elder pretty sister, vain and selfish, goes into the world as companion to an aristocratic lady, is disgraced, and is then replaced by her plain but virtuous younger sister. In succeeding years Montagu was, in fact, indicted by everyone for her vanity, if not her selfishness, while Scott applied herself to serious, selfless matters. Both used their letters to inscribe their differences, their successes, and their strained devotion.

∿ ∾

Ideology controlled the sisters' difference but, secondarily, finance and geography supported it. The notion of the salon as a form of community was natural to both, for their father—unable with his nine children to afford a London season—had created a salon of their own in the family drawing room in Kent. His children were to be heard as well as seen, and he required the wit to fly. Most of them—a member of Parliament, lawyers, a divine—kept it up in adult life, and most, like Elizabeth and Sarah, wrote. Montagu, who married for money and eventually had three establishments to maintain (including houses in fashionable London, respectably in Hill Street and then magnificently in Portman Square), could easily gather about her the authors of the moment, the great ladies, and the statesmen eminent in the public eye. The silent and the bashful were not made welcome and *mauvaise honte* was a cardinal sin (as was the failure to pay particular obeisance to the hostess). In her drawing room one sat in an inflexible semicircle, signifying the hostess's control. Whether contributing to general or more particular conversation, however, one went there to contest.

One might meet there any and every luminary—Hester Thrale, Frances Burney, and the other Bluestockings Frances Boscawen, Elizabeth Carter, Elizabeth Vesey, Mary Monckton, and Mrs. Orde; also Lyttelton, Johnson, Burke, Wilkes, Garrick, Lord Bath, Walpole, and William Mason. The salon welcomed successful people who might be and often were kind and generous in

5. *The Letters of Mrs. Elizabeth Montagu, with Some of the Letters of Her Correspondents, 1720–1761*, 4 vols. (London, 1809–13), 2:8n; references to this work are given subsequently in the text.

their fashion but whose principal business there was personal display and the advancement of reputation.

Montagu's community, then, confined to the genteel, the affluent, and the successful, consisted of her rich and complaisant husband, her invited guests, and the large staff that made her parties possible. Democratic gestures were represented by her taking up such celebrities as the shoemaker poet James Woodhouse, but she soon returned him to his more natural place by appointing him her steward. Respectable distinction was the ticket of entry to her house and wit was the currency that bought applause. The spirit was entirely competitive. As Lady Louisa Stuart wrote, Montagu lacked the "art of kneading the mass well together. As her company came in, a heterogeneous medley, so they went out, each individual feeling himself single, isolated, and (to borrow a French phrase) embarrassed with his own person. . . . Everything in that house, as if under a spell, was sure to form itself into a circle or semicircle."[6]

Scott with considerable transparency describes her sister as Lady Brumpton in *A Description of Millenium Hall* (1762):

> The adulation which she received with too much visible complacency, inspired her with such an opinion of herself, as led her to despise those of less shining qualities, and not to treat any with proper civility, whom she had not some particular desire to please, which often gave severe pains to bashful merit, and called her real superiority in question; for those who observed so great a weakness, were tempted to believe her understanding rather glittering than solid. (Pp. 192–93)

The beginning of the portrait was perhaps even more pointed; Montagu showed considerable forbearance when she overlooked it:

> She sought to be admired for various merits. To recommend her person she studied dress, and went to a considerable expence in ornaments. To shew her taste, she distinguished herself by the elegance of her house, furniture, and equipage. To prove her fondness for literature, she collected a considerable library, and to shew that all her esteem was not engrossed by the learned dead, she caressed all living genius's from the ragged philosopher to the rhiming peer. . . . She aimed at making her house a little academy. (P. 190)

In Montagu's house, as in Lady Brumpton's, the prevailing mode was "the extreme endeavour to shine," which "took off from that ease in conversation

6. *Lady Louisa Stuart: Selections from her Manuscripts*, ed. Hon. James Home (New York, 1899), 158–59.

which is its greatest charm. Every person was like a bent bow, ready to shoot forth an arrow; which had no sooner darted to the other side of the room, than it fell to the ground, and the next person picked it up, and made a new shot with it" (p. 193). She confidently attempted to incorporate her younger sister into this life (while maintaining superiority over her) and, as the two girls had been equal and vociferous wits in their girlhood home, probably never doubted of success, but perhaps too much anticipated from her sister awe and admiration for herself. In fact, the experience of the youthful Lady Mary in the salon of Lady Brumpton may have been Scott's. Begging for guidance in reading to keep up with the brilliant throng, Lady Mary is directed to read all the most recent publications: moral essays, a new play, a new history, a volume of sermons— a melange producing confusion (p. 192).

Scott's own community, then, was certainly a critique of her sister's. It focused on the disadvantaged rather than the advantaged, on giving rather than receiving, on selflessness rather than egocentrism. But it may arguably be seen to have evolved gradually and, at least in part, exactly as her sister's did, as the result of geography and resources. And that "bashful merit" Montagu despised was precisely what Scott had sought out, even in marriage. Montagu had married an older man of wealth; Scott, against her sister's interdiction, married an older man with no means of support until in 1751 he was appointed sub-preceptor to the future George III. While she was married to him (briefly) her community probably consisted of one friend only, who lived with the pair— Lady Barbara Montagu, the only unmarried daughter of the earl of Halifax.

Lady Barbara, with whom Scott had bonded at Bath, had an ailing heart. When Scott's marriage ended in a separation enforced by her own father and brothers, who came to carry her away—that was probably the style in which wives were separated from men adjudged homosexual,[7] and certainly Montagu identified her sister thereafter as a virgin (Montagu to Scott, MO 5880, 26 [March, 1768])—the two friends repaired to Bath. They lived there together until the death of Lady Barbara—another person of great but bashful merit—in 1765. Scott was poor after her separation from her husband in 1752, living on his quarterly payments of £25 and donations from her father. Lady Barbara had an annual income, probably, of about £200.[8] They had not, even with combined

---

7.    See, for instance, Randolph Trumbach, *The Rise of the Egalitarian Family: Aristocratic Kinship and Domestic Relations in Eighteenth-Century England* (New York, 1978), 284. Scott wrote that "the name of old Maid never had any terrors for me, & the thing I like best in my situation is that I am one in effect" (MO 5346, 5 September 1767). Letters from the Montagu Collection cited henceforward in the text by MO number; conjectural completions to dates for the letters are enclosed in brackets.

8.    For more details about the Bath lives of Scott and Lady Barbara, see *Companions without Vows*, chap. 13.

resources, income sufficient to entertain in the style of their families, a social course into which otherwise they might naturally have settled, for both were sociable. Bath constantly entertained people of rank and talent known to them both, and with adequate funds they might easily have fallen into the course of maintaining a private place of resort for the chosen.

Both sisters put great creativity into adorning their homes, but the difference is illuminating. Montagu created the great and famous feather drawing room in Portman Square; Scott and Lady Barbara painted toilet articles, festooned shell ornaments above their mantels, and collected nuts and grains to arrange decoratively.

Perhaps the lack of means to entertain properly also helped to impel them to project quite a different community in Bath, a community of permanent and quiet residents of a serious and altruistic disposition. Having little social power, they were nevertheless able to exert considerable power in implementing a genuine Christian charity, very noticeable both in its difference from the charitable giving of their more affluent connections and in the moral superiority thereby accruing to them.

Montagu's guests are often familiar to us still. The friends of Scott and Lady Barbara are largely unknown, but form a group of women who accomplished much in their organized good works, their theorizing about an alternative plan of life in which women could be publicly effective, and their support of women writers. The core of the group consisted of women who, like Scott and Lady Barbara, though well born and well educated, had become irrelevant to society from the perspective of those to whom the major purposes of women were the procreation of children and the transmission of possessions.[9] There were many such women relegated to the sidelines in places such as Bath or Tunbridge, women whose slender provisions were often grudgingly seen as detracting from the family fortunes. Their fathers and brothers were usually content, though, to countenance and even enable their separate lives with funds just sufficient to prevent their disgracing their connections. They clustered together here and there. In London they could not live as they had been brought up to live; one needed an income of £1,000 there to keep a carriage and a footman and everything else in proportion, whereas many of these women subsisted on as small an income as Lady Barbara's £200. In Bath one could lodge with respectability more cheaply,

9.  I have identified and considered this group rather cursorily in *Companions without Vows*, chap. 13; they have subsequently been further noted by Linda Bree, "Sisterhood and Sarah Fielding," in Rebecca d'Monte and Nicole Pohl, eds., *Female Communities, 1600–1800: Literary Visions and Cultural Realities* (Basingstoke, England, 2000), 184–98.

one could walk or hire a chair and thus keep no carriage, one could also nurse one's health, and—an additional advantage—with no expense to oneself one would be visited at various times by all one's family and friends.

Sarah Robinson, still unmarried at twenty-seven, visited Bath with her sister and her sister's husband in 1747, met Lady Barbara Montagu, and stayed on with her instead of returning home with her sister—perhaps the first desertion, then, was Scott's. Lady Barbara was young—younger than Scott—but frail, and she was the only one of the earl's six daughters not to marry. Her delicate health was probably her excuse for living alone at Bath rather than with one of her sisters, in dependent grandeur; like Scott she seems to have disdained both dependence and grandeur. To live alone, however, was inconvenient for a young woman, even unseemly. Scott, who suffered mightily from headache, who could not live with her father (who was by this time in lodgings in London and whose housekeeper was his mistress), and whose services were not required in the homes of any of her brothers, readily adopted Lady Barbara's plan of life. When she deviated from it briefly in 1751 to marry George Scott, Lady Barbara went with her. When ten months later she separated from her husband, she returned to Bath, then settled in with her companion and devised with her a new scheme of life, one adjusted to their circumstances. A serious view of life resulted in a desire to mitigate the sufferings, particularly but not exclusively, of women of their own class and condition. Theirs was the state, in both its conditions and its inequities, that they knew best. They longed for increased power and agency for women like themselves, and, disadvantaged themselves, recognized the disadvantages of others.

Scott, and Lady Barbara no doubt as well, took a view of marriage not uncommon in their time, that courtship should culminate not merely in coupling but in integration into a community where a man and woman might disseminate their influence for good to the fullest of their capacities. This view—emblematized in the pattern dances of the time in which a couple remained together but performed, in their turn, intricate and harmonious designs among a group of dancers—is explicit in Scott's published works. In *The History of Cornelia* (1750), written as she prepared for marriage, the action concludes not when her hero and heroine at last marry but when they have succeeding in regulating the entire neighborhood in which they live. In *The History of Sir George Ellison* (1766) Scott unites Sir George at last with his beloved, but the pair must consciously avoid the self-indulgence of being too absorbed in one another, must discipline themselves by meeting only after they have seen to their heavy social responsibilities.

Scott and Lady Barbara took a similar view of the purpose of the lives of the unmarried. As a pair, the two devoted the rest of their life together—from 1752 to Lady Barbara's death in 1765—to this model. Their vision demanded first that they gather a like-minded group about them and next that they act as far as their circumstances would allow for the benefit of their neighbors. Their closest associates in their endeavors were Elizabeth Cutts and Miss M. (Mary?) Arnold. They were inspired by the companionship and utopian proposals of Sarah Fielding. All were exemplars of the intelligent, well-educated, and high-minded but deracinated single women who settled in Bath. Indeed, as Scott noted in *Millenium Hall*, only such women could have entered into such a circle's activities: if Miss Mancel had married, "her sincere affection for [her husband] would have led her to conform implicitly to all his inclinations, her views would have been confined to this earth, and too strongly attached to human objects, to have properly obeyed the giver of the blessings she so much valued" (p. 161). Only single women could dedicate themselves to objectives beyond the well being of their families, and among its other remarkable achievements the Bath circle constructed and provided a model for the deployment of such single women superior to that of useful aunts—a model actually suggesting that women with a sense of mission might make a *choice* of the unmarried state rather than fall into it.

❧ ❧

Mrs. Cutts, probably born, like her brother Mordecai, about 1700, apparently had no close surviving family save him and, though he was said to take good care of her,[10] lived alone on an adequate but unprincely income in Bath. She did have some income of her own, being possessed of lands in Thorn and in Braffit in Yorkshire.[11] Mordecai Cutts functioned throughout his life as a man of business to the successive Viscounts Irwin of Yorkshire.[12] His connection to the Bath community

---

10. *Letters from Mrs. Elizabeth Carter to Mrs. Montagu, between the years 1755 and 1800*, ed. Montagu Pennington, 3 vols. (London, 1817), 2:201, 19 June 1773; cited henceforward in the text.

11. Will of Mordecai Cutts, P.C.C. Prob 11/1161/9. I am grateful to Cynthia Comyn for very kindly locating and abstracting this will for me.

12. As always, it is far easier to garner information about the brother than about his sister; Cutts's social position can be extrapolated from that of her brother as among the respectable middling professional class. Mordecai Cutts, who died in Hatfield, Yorkshire, took a B.A. degree from University College, Oxford, in 1724, and in 1745 was a man of business for Henry Ingram, seventh Viscount Irwin (or Irvine) in the Scotch peerage, Lord Lieutenant of East Riding, 1736–61. In December 1745 Cutts was reporting from the north on the movements of the rebel army to Irwin; in May 1751 he was relaying political and social gossip from London. As late as 1774 Scott noted that he passed by on his way to Sussex with Lord Irwin, who was visiting his constituency (Historical Manuscripts Commission. *Reports on Manuscripts in Various Collections, Vol. VIII. The Manuscripts of the Hon. Frederick Lindley Wood; M.L.S. Clements, Esq.: S. Philip Unwin, Esq.* [London, 1913], 141, 148, 157–58, 174–75; letter of Scott to Mary Robinson, Huntington Library, HM 17454, 10 October [1774]).

is witnessed by his willingness to subscribe to their publishing enterprises: he acquired two copies of Sarah Fielding's *Lives of Cleopatra and Octavia* (1752) and a
copy of his sister's poem *Almeria* (1775).[13] Cutts was enabled by her income to live
on her own among her congenial Bath friends instead of living on sufferance in
her brother's house, but as was typical of the Bath group, she was careful to extend the community outward, to include her brother and other friends as well.
One's influence could extend significantly through one's pool of acquaintance. All
the members of the group cultivated their connections, who were frequently
helpful, as in the important cases of book subscriptions and charitable donations.
The group's influence, in fact, percolated into most of the upper and professional
reaches of English society.

Cutts was a faithful friend to Scott and Lady Barbara, at various times living
with them, tending their health, deliberating on their projects, and, in the terrible period for Scott after Lady Barbara's death in 1765, remaining with and con-
soling her. Indeed, Lady Barbara bequeathed the remainder of her house lease in
Beaufort Square to Cutts,[14] and Scott for some time lived there with her. By the
late 1770s, Cutts lived elsewhere but spent the summers with Scott.[15]

Cutts was one of the trio that designed the community at Hitcham (discussed in detail below). She was, in the manner of many of the Bath group, an
occasional author but a consistent benefactor. When she published her long poem
*Almeria* in 1775, with her usual modesty anonymously, it was published by subscription—not at all, as Cutts with wry humor pointed out, at "the earnest be-
hest of friends," the hackneyed excuse of many women writers, but to benefit
through its healthy subscription "two needy people."

Apart from Cutts, Scott's closest companion was the much younger Miss
Arnold, who remained with Scott for the rest of her life and was probably the literary executor who destroyed her papers.[16] There was good reason for their close
association: Miss M. Arnold was apparently a natural daughter of Scott's favorite

13.   Not all subscription lists are included in the Chadwyck-Healey Biography Database, 1660–1830, but it
      provides a fine sampling. Information from disks 1 and 2 will be cited below.
14.   Will of Lady Barbara Montagu, P.C.C. Prob. 11/913/15, administered 1765.
15.   Because Cutts was still alive in 1777 but dead in 1780, it is tempting to speculate that she was the Mrs.
      Cutts of Arundel Street in London who died on 4 January 1780, "much regretted by all her acquaintance"
      (*Daily Advertiser*, 8 January 1780).
16.   Miss Arnold signed a letter of 1800 to Mrs. Morris Robinson "M. Arnold" (MO 147, 28 August 1800). She
      writes from Boston, Lincolnshire, to Mrs. William Robinson about the death of Jane Greenland
      Robinson, refers to her mother's recent death (apparently in Boston), and gives her address as of next week
      as at Mrs. Wright's, Dean Square, Norwich. I thank Mary L. Robertson, curator of manuscripts at the
      Huntington, for providing me with a copy of the letter. In it Arnold announced her imminent return to
      Norfolk, where she still apparently resided five years after Scott's death there.

brother, Morris,[17] who in 1757 had married Jane Greenland, a vulgar woman of low birth and small mind given to meannesses and fits of passion—and despised by his sisters.[18] Miss Arnold (though letters referring to her membership in the family are frequently among those missing)[19] was an accepted member of the Robinson family and visited both Morris and "Mrs. Morris," as she called her stepmother. Probably five years older than her stepmother, Arnold regarded her visits to Mrs. Morris as a necessary penance—"in ye vinegar bottle" as Montagu expresses it (MO 5917, 23 [January 1769])—and was expected to visit her in Charlton, east of Greenwich, when Morris himself, a lawyer, was in chambers in Chancery Lane. In the letter of 1800 written to the wife of Matthew Montagu (Mrs. Morris's son, adopted by the Montagus) on Mrs. Morris's death, Arnold noted that her father's wife "never proved herself much attach'd to me; but having known her so long, and at times, much in the habit of seeing her, I often felt kindly towards her, though it could not be call'd affection" (MO 147, 28 August 1800). Mrs. Morris, known to have described Morris's family to him as "your crew" (Scott to Montagu, MO 5346, 5 September [1767]), seems in an odd relationship to his daughter, often demanding visits from her in a manner suggesting that she may have found her stepdaughter useful about the house. That Arnold was the Robinsons' niece but could not openly be acknowledged by her father explains her closeness to Scott, who was in a position to claim her without scandal; but Montagu habitually mentioned her specifically in her letters—"love to Miss Arnold and compliments to Mrs. Cutts." On occasion Arnold visited not only Morris but also both Montagu and her uncle the Rev. William Robinson.

Arnold, like the others, was straitened in means and among them seems to have had the least money of her own. Lady Barbara, on her death in 1765, bequeathed to her all her choicest clothing, her watches, rings, and garnet earrings. She subscribed to fewer books than other members of the group, none listed before 1775. Most of the women of the Bath group were deracinated, but Scott, a woman separated from her husband but not divorced, and Arnold, a woman

17. Miss M. Arnold may be the Mary Arnold born without notation of a father to Rosamond Arnold and christened at Sandal Magna, Yorkshire, on 22 April 1733 (International Genealogical Index [IGI] of the Church of the Latter Day Saints). In 1732 the Robinson family still lived in or near York; Morris Robinson was seventeen. Miss Arnold's relationship to the Robinson family was first noted by Linda Bree; see "Sisterhood and Miss Fielding," 193.

18. One reason for their detestation (though apparently her character provided ample justification) is that, as revealed by the IGI, they married on 13 February 1757 and their son Morris was christened on the following 9 August.

19. In 1768 Montagu requested Arnold to buy her a pretty black-eyed cherry-cheeked doll as much like her "mother-in-law" (stepmother) as possible, to be dressed for that lady's daughter, Arnold's half-sister (MO 5900 [30 September 1768]).

who could not openly lay claim to her own family, were doubly so, and clung to each other. Arnold lived with Scott for at least forty years and, the youngest of Scott's group, was also the longest lived and the most faithful, moving with her and Cutts into the Hitcham experiment, and later to Norwich as her aunt's only companion.

Sarah Fielding was the third member, after Scott and Cutts, of the central group. She contributed the goodwill of her own connections, most importantly the prominent Bath resident Ralph Allen. Always impoverished and subsisting on donations and contributions, Fielding lived in or nearby Bath from 1754 until her death in 1768. *The Adventures of David Simple* (1744) and its bleak sequel *Volume the Last* (1753), in which a utopian community is destroyed by outside forces, were an essential influence on the group's theories about the equality of women, control over the tyranny of men, and the construction of community. Though ill, Fielding probably continued to contribute to the plans for Hitcham, realized just after her death. Certainly she had been considered an important member of the utopian group. Scott's *A Description of Millenium Hall* and *The History of Sir George Ellison* are direct attempts to contend with the forces that destroyed the community in Fielding's *Volume the Last* by constructing stronger, more invulnerable communities. The books were in their conception collaborative but in writing and organization Scott's.

Scott, Lady Barbara, Cutts, Fielding, and Arnold were the loyal nucleus of the Bath community—the nucleus of a radical salon—in the 1760s, its productive years. They supported one another, sharing their resources including housing and labor, but most importantly refusing to accept their consignment, as women unproductive of any man's heirs, to contingency and societal periphery. No longer desired in their parental homes (to which their brothers had succeeded), they created an important new center for the idea of an alternative society in which women like themselves could be active and creative, and serve as benefactors to society with central societal roles. They sought to affirm the significance of women like themselves. Had they been men they would doubtless have been parliamentarians, college dons, clergymen, and legal scholars, like their brothers. Confined as they were by their sex,[20] piqued no doubt by their unjust confinement to their prescribed roles, they would imagine a liberating utopia, to be described in Scott's books, and then they would attempt a real utopia of their own.

The associates and satellites of the central group were many—more, no doubt, than will ever be identified. Among their important friends were the

20. Perhaps it should be noted, however, that among the Bluestockings Montagu became a coal magnate and author, Scott (like Sarah Fielding) a celebrated author; and that both, like all their brothers save one, found mention in the *Dictionary of National Biography*.

affluent Margaret Pigott Riggs (ca. 1714–88).[21] A spirited widow, Margaret Riggs built a beautiful villa in Batheaston[22] where she lived with her great friend Mary Margaret Ravaud, the daughter of Marc Antony Ravaud (died ca. 1727), a Huguenot burgess of Geneva who had settled in Hammersmith.[23] The Ravaud family was genteel and the daughter at least adequately provided for. Far more elegant and subdued than Riggs, Ravaud was counted among the Bluestockings at Bath and numbered among her own connections Mary Delany, the duchess of Portland, and the Countess Cowper. Riggs and Ravaud, whose Batheaston villa was one of the obligatory places of resort for polite visitors to Bath, were a particularly important resource to the group in terms of networking.

There was one atypically married, although childless, member of the group, Mary Hoare Adams, who involved her unusually complaisant husband, William, as well. Adams (1714–67) was the daughter of Richard Hoare, elder brother of Henry of Stourhead, Wiltshire; she was therefore the cousin german of the rich Henry the Magnificent (1705–85). Her connection to Stourhead, conveniently near Bath, was close; in 1762 "little Miss Hoare," probably the daughter of her cousin Richard, Henry the Magnificent's younger brother, was living with her, and following Adams's death in 1767, Miss Hoare, very ill in December 1768, was Cutts's charge.[24] Cutts and Adams were close friends, sometimes living together, visiting together at Stourhead, and drawing the wealthy Hoares in among the community's most useful friends. The dire fate of David Simple's community at the hands of destructive outsiders could be fended off, the community probably believed, by the acquisition of powerful friends its members could call on.

Mary Adams, who predeceased her husband, had achieved the unusual right to dispose of her money by her own will (a right provided in her marriage settlement). Of the £5,000 she brought to her marriage, William Adams was paid

21. She was the widow of Edward Riggs of the Middle Temple, a commissioner of the excise (d. 1743), and daughter-in-law of Edward Riggs, Irish M.P., commissioner of the Irish revenue, and member of the Privy Council.

22. Scott explains in a letter to Montagu (MO 5208, 19 September 1748) that Dr. Oliver, the Bath physician, had sold them a cottage at Batheaston and then "deliver'd them to Wood to torment them" in enlarging it. John Wood was one of the foremost architects and designers of Bath; he transformed the city.

23. See "Refugee Families of La Meloniére, Langlois, and Ravaud," *Miscellanea Genealogice et Heraldica*, n.s. 4 (1884): 322–23; the will of her brother Stephen David Ravaud, P.C.C. Prob 11/1023/400 was kindly provided me by Cynthia Comyn. The will, proved in 1776, designated Mary Margaret Ravaud as her brother's executor and residual heir.

24. Little Miss Hoare was probably Jane or Elizabeth, one of the two daughters of Richard (1709–54), the younger brother of Henry the Magnificent, and his second wife, Elizabeth Rust, who died in 1752. Her children included Henry (1744–85) and two daughters otherwise unmemorialized. Her children were orphans in 1754, and Mrs. Adams was the cousin of their father. She was dead in 1767 but Cutts had shared in the charge in 1762, and perhaps she had remained in charge.

£2,000 and given all the silver, plate, and so on; £3,000 went to buy a quarterly annuity for Cutts, payable on her death to her husband.[25] From his home in Walcot, after his wife's death in early 1767, William apparently continued to nurture the group; he owned the Bath property in Miles Court where Scott, in later 1767 and 1768, nursed Fielding until she died.[26] He was also a moderate subscriber to their projects, in 1757 to Fielding's *Lives of Cleopatra and Octavia* and in 1775 to Cutts's *Almeria* (and, incidentally, in 1764 to Sterne's *Sermons of Yorick*).

Grace Robinson Freind (1718–76), the cousin german of Scott and Montagu and wife of the Rev. William Freind (1715–66), dean of Canterbury, was an intimate friend of her cousins, as, indeed, was her husband. She is not known to have become involved in Scott's communal plans until the death of her husband—whose sons inherited most of his possessions—left her free, with some limited resources. Her attraction to Hitcham, like Montagu's, would be deep, compensatory, even a kind of expiation. Her involvement in the community would facilitate it (the place had been her husband's and was now the property of a son) and eventually, precisely because she was not childless and had divided loyalties, wreck it; indeed, though not recognized as an outsider, she was to become the dreaded destroyer.

❧ ❧

The various activities of this group of women—a group always in flux but always flowing together, gathering in others, and in communication with their own circles of friends—are revealed in their surviving letters. Scott and Lady Barbara dominated and led with their first objective, to be instruments of social good. Everything they did was calculated to lead toward this end. Scott is found in Bath shortly after her separation with an experimental menage of two servants, one disadvantaged mentally, the other deaf; as neither could do the shopping, Miss Arnold, probably by then living with her, did it (Scott to Montagu, MO 5223 [December 1752]). Scott and Lady Barbara set the neighborhood women to knitting mittens and marketed their product to their friends. They instituted a school in which they taught twenty-four poor children, twelve girls and twelve boys, and then added a Sunday school (*Letters of Elizabeth Montagu,* 3:335–37,

---

25. P.C.C. Prob 11/928/161. A yield of 4 percent would have returned Cutts £120 a year. William Adams's will, on the other hand, proved in 1777 (P.C.C. Prob 11/1305/406), secures Cutts's annuity but among many bequests of annuities, buildings, choice books, and paintings distinguishes no other member of the Bath group. Cutts's annuity he disposed of, at her death, to other legatees. By that time Lady Barbara had died and Scott had left Bath.

26. In his will he devises the property to Elizabeth Barton.

16 October 1755). Lady Barbara's will is an indication both of their activities and of their careful struggle to stretch their limited incomes for charitable purposes. It names beneficiaries of their labors not otherwise known to us: Mrs. Anne Aust, living with Sarah Morse in Lady Barbara's house in Beaufort Square; Scott's servant Mary Aust; the cook who had a boarded-out child to apprentice; a young protégée to be apprenticed and set up in a shop; Mary Groom of Teddington. Sarah Fielding got £10 a year for life and Miss Arnold, as noted above, got the best clothes and jewelry.

The group, probably again inspired by Fielding—who habitually published not only for the proceeds but also and most importantly to propagandize for her views—devised a number of publications and underwrote others as a charitable endeavor. Miss Arnold was writing a history, perhaps anonymously published, that has never been attributed; Montagu's *Essay on the Writings and Genius of Shakespear* (1769), first published anonymously, was acknowledged at last on the title page of the fourth edition (1777).[27] Lady Barbara supported the anonymously published *Histories of Some of the Penitents in the Magdalen House* (1760), thought by some to be by Fielding.[28] She also negotiated to have a set of instructive cards for school children printed. Cutts, as mentioned earlier, published her poem *Almeria* for the benefit of two needy people.

They supported worthwhile publications through subscription, especially the works of other women. The nonalphabetical subscription list of Mary Leapor's *Poems upon Several Occasions* (1751) reveals something about the ways in which networks of friends subscribed. A Bath group, listed together, names Mrs. Cutts, Bab Montague [sic], Mrs. Montegue [sic], Miss Roberts (a friend of Adams and Cutts), Miss Robinson (that is, Scott), George Scott (her fiancé), Mrs. Riggs, Mrs. Ravaud, Lady [Frances] Williams (a cousin of Lady Barbara's), and Mrs. Scott (perhaps George Scott's mother). Quite naturally the Bath circle supported the publications of Sarah Fielding. Subscribers to her *Lives of Cleopatra and Octavia* included Adams and her husband, Cutts and her brother, Henry and Mrs. Hoare, Lady Barbara Mountagu and Mrs. Mountagu [sic], Mr. and Mrs. Morris Robinson, Mr. [sic] Riggs and Mrs. Ravaud, George Scott, and Lady Frances Williams. One can detect Mrs. Ravaud's hand in the subscription of the duke and duchess of Beaufort and the Rev. Dr. Delany, Montagu's in the subscription of her friends Lords Bath and Lyttelton. Five years later William and

27. Until recently, the catalogue of the New York Public Library suggested that Scott's most famous work, *A Description of Millenium Hall*, was by Christopher Smart or Oliver Goldsmith.
28. "There is a novel published which I believe to be chiefly written by your friend Mrs. Fielding"—a statement that suggests she may have known of some collaborative effort; *Letters of Mrs. Elizabeth Montagu*, 4:216, n.d.

Mrs. Adams, Miss Arnold, Mordecai and Elizabeth Cutts, Henry and Mrs. Hoare, Miss Hoare,  Richard Hoare, Lady Barbara Montagu and her many sisters, Mrs. Montagu and her husband, Mrs. Riggs and Mrs. Ravaud, a number of Robinsons and Robertses, and Mrs. Scott subscribed to Fielding's translation *Xenophon's Memoirs of Socrates* (1762), as did many of their acquaintance, including Montagu's intimates Lord Lyttelton, Dr. Moysey, Lady Frances Williams (three books), and Mrs. Boscawen. A similar assortment of friends subscribed to Cutts's *Almeria;* the networking is clearly evident: patrons included not only such familiar names as Adams, Arnold, the duchess of Beaufort, Freind, Hoare, Ravaud, five Robinson brothers, and two of Lady Barbara's sisters, but also Samuel Johnson and Mr. (John?) Hawkesworth.

~ꙮ ꙮ~

The Hitcham experiment was Scott's great effort to prove the utopian scheme of *Millenium Hall* practicable, though it was much reduced in scope. Millenium Hall is run by women with varying amounts of income, some large, who contribute what they have. What they have is sufficient to run a village of various benevolent enterprises: a home for the single women who administer the whole, a refuge for the physically disadvantaged, an industry to employ workers and crafts to employ the old, an ecological system established in the ample and beautiful grounds. Scott, Cutts, and Arnold envisioned, more modestly, a country home with a garden, a community of themselves, each contributing not her whole income but a fixed annual amount of £50 that would support the project, and then almost certainly (though they never got to that aspect) an outreach into the neighborhood to set up schools and useful employment.

Finding the right home took a lot of effort, and when Grace Freind, newly widowed and lonely with her daughter having just married, suggested Hitcham in Buckinghamshire, an estate bequeathed to her son by his father, they were delighted.[29] Hitcham was only about twenty-eight miles from London, and the women had no mind to isolate themselves from their friends. It had a tenant who would sublet the place for £13 a year. Scott, Cutts, Arnold, Montagu, and Freind would each make their yearly contributions, and Montagu offered secretly to add to Fielding's meager store the rest of the required sum so that she could join them.

29. On Hitcham House, see Royal Commission on Historical Monuments, *An Inventory of the Historical Monuments in Buckinghamshire*, 2 vols. (London, 1912), 1:205. For more on the Hitcham project, see Rizzo, introduction to *Sir George Ellison*, xxv–xxix.

Hitcham was slowly put into order as Scott remained in Bath nursing Fielding, whose recovery sometimes seemed possible; she might then join the community. But Scott would not desert her in any case, for she had been and was a vital member of the group. Meanwhile Montagu found herself trying to juggle her wealth and luxurious lifestyle, her sister's ideal of hard work and austerity, and the demands of female benevolence and charity. She contributed to the project with a vehemence that suggested both her loneliness for her sister—so long alienated by their differing views—and her deep desire to be counted (publicly) among the millennialists. The importance of the Hitcham project—the interest it aroused, its fame in polite circles—can be reckoned from Montagu's keen desire to take a dominant part. As long as the only standards of excellence had been those of the London *ton* and intelligentsia, Montagu had confidently reigned, but the new standard of benevolent and active Christianity made more and more prominent by her sister presented a challenge she could not ignore, for to ignore it would be to allow herself to be judged by it and found woefully wanting and frivolous. She did at least publicly ignore the problem that one could scarcely romp through the eye of the needle.

Hitcham was near the Bath road, halfway between London and Montagu's country estate, Sandleford, and she was delighted by the promised convenience of using it as a stopping place between her properties—her other life. Moreover, her aging and ailing husband had been diagnosed as unable to withstand another winter in England; she was told more than once that he would die unless taken abroad, but somehow no plan to travel there ever materialized. Instead, it would seem, Montagu happily envisioned herself as free to join the community at her will. She had, in the summer of 1767, actually (at last) replaced her husband at his coal fields in the north by herself visiting and making decisions, thereby adding a great deal of money to his revenues; and she had money at her own disposal that she spent lavishly at Hitcham while she took on the principal trouble of arranging the lease.

She now almost humorously underscores in her letters to Scott her own millennial activities and the difference between herself and her insensible husband that aligns her more closely to Scott. From his coal fields in the north she is at pains to detail her worries about the colliery workers—a little boy who went into the pit every day, a wife who miscarried in the harvest fields to whom she sent a midwife and other good things, the schools she has instituted to teach the children to read and write despite her fears that the other colliery owners will resent the precedent (Montagu to Scott, MO 5859, 27 September [1767]; MO 5861, 7 October [1767]; MO 5864, 28 October [1767]). In regard to this schooling project her bewildered husband looks in vain for his advantage, and she reports his meditation on the subject and her own conclusion: "Perhaps it may be some use in her being beloved in that Country. So I got well out of ye scrape. Poor man he has killed his benevolence out of a principle of prudence." Moreover, at Sandleford she has taken in "blind John" and has found him tasks to do. Her husband hates even to see the old man, but she advises him, "when you meet blind john say to yrself there is a fellow creature whom I redeem from misery & if you have not very pleasant feelings I am mistaken. Oh says he that is Christianity. I am glad says I to hear you own that, Christianity can never from its most zealous disciples receive greater honour than by ascribing to it the love of mankind" (Montagu to Scott, MO 5863, 8 November [1767]). And she has been forgiving to her husband's errant and undeserving man of business, removing him from his place but promising him compensation, and "I shd be base if I did not keep my word" (Montagu to Scott, MO 5867 [12 November 1767]). In keeping with her rendition for her sister of this unfashionable and uncustomary role, she continues eagerly occupied in dissociating herself from her husband's attitude to the less fortunate. In the cold weather of January 1768 she rejoices that her husband's tender feelings of woe have been roused by the plight of the poor whom he has been assisting, for "no temper is so unfit for a share of the general bliss as the unfeeling and unsympathizing" (Montagu to Scott, MO 5874, 12 [January 1768]).

Scott certainly recognized the chasm between her own and her sister's views of benevolence, charity, and class responsibility. She herself, as closely as possible for a person wishing to retain the power to alleviate and regulate, lived and labored at the level of the unfortunate. Montagu never considered giving up her exalted life style. When she was confronted with the misery of the pitiful small sweeps that removed her coal dust from the nation's chimneys, her solution was to offer them a splendid banquet once a year, thus for a few tantalizing hours providing them a glimpse of how she herself lived.

It was Montagu who declared the greater desire to live once more with her sister, to whom she now wrote in more loving terms. She was "extremely happy in the sweet hope of passing many of my days in your company," and could not express to Scott "how happy I am that we shall now be rejoyned, reunited. God grant us comfortable years together" (Montagu to Scott, MO 5871, 26 December [1767]; MO 5879, 16 [March 1768]). She was now declaring herself of the millennial community, as she must have been declaring herself, with, one can imagine, a far-away (and superior) look, even in the midst of her London salon—where, she announces, she has been entertaining her acquaintance forty at a time (Montagu to Scott, MO 5880, 26 [March 1768]). Montagu is of two minds. In the cold January of 1768 she deliberates over her court dress for the queen's birthday, has some scruples at wearing anything fine in so calamitous a time, "for it seems insulting ye wretched"; but then describes at length her dress and its splendid effect (Montagu to Scott, MO 5874, 12 [January 1768]; MO 5875, 25 [January 1768]). She is also planning to equip her own retreat at Hitcham. She must have the ice house furnished, "for I much love eatable Ice" (Montagu to Scott, MO 5871, 26 December [1767]). She needs little but a bed, a chair, a table, and her sister, for "I wd not belong as many people do to the things about them for ye World." But she sends a good bed, pillows, and a servant, for she is a poor sleeper, and she positively refuses to monopolize the study, having no objections whatever to anyone else's being in there as she works. She refuses the best bedchamber, demanding instead the worst, but it is unlikely Scott took her at her word. She assures Scott that she can do without a dressing room, but at Sandleford, she notes, she is enlarging her dressing room to be thirty-six-feet long with a view over the garden (MO 5875, 8 [March 1768]; MO 5876, 16 [February 1768]; MO 5880, 26 [March 1768]; MO 5883, 3 May [1768]; MO 5884, 5 May [1768]). And in the same spartan spirit, in July she writes that she can do with four rather than six coach horses, particularly as she uses the chaise so often (MO 5889, 9 [July 1768]).

Scott may well have been embarrassed by her sister's enthusiastic largess, but she could not afford to refuse it. As Fielding lay dying in Miles Court, Montagu sent her butler, Joseph Woodhouse (brother to her steward, the poet), to Hitcham to arrange the garden and engage a manly gardener who would double as protector to "so many Virgin Ladies." She will send furniture and has deputed Woodhouse to look over the cows before they are purchased. She will supply hogs, pigs, and garden produce until their own garden is productive. Woodhouse will go down to Hitcham a day or so before Scott arrives to attend to the fires and airings (MO 5880, 26 [March 1768]; MO 5882, 4 April [1768]).

❧ ❧

Fielding died on 9 April 1768, and at once the group made their long-deferred move to Hitcham. (One may consider the contrast between Scott's deferral of her favorite scheme while her friend was dying and Montagu's ignoring the advice that she must take her husband abroad.) Edward Montagu was now too ill to be left for very long, but his wife made visits to Hitcham. Meanwhile, at Sandleford she took in the poet Woodhouse's wife, Daphne, as her housekeeper and had the children on the premises too (à la Sir George Ellison) which at first even Mr. Montagu found delightful, though later a screaming infant had to be removed some distance. She is now, in May, eating her own poultry and killing most of her own meat, and she knows at what houses pigs are to be serviced. She must rival her sister even in country expertise: "As you are also a Farmer we may communicate our experience" (MO 5883, 3 May [1768]). In July she reports that the rain has ruined the barley (MO 5890, 18 [July 1768]). She sends poultry, carp, eels, pigeons, mushrooms, cucumbers, a salmon, tuberoses, chickens, artichokes, a melon. But still at Sandleford in September and itching to return to London, she cannot forbear boasting that as she and Lady Hervey were "the only Women who have circles of beaux esprits, there might be supposed to be some envy," and again, in her solitude, declares her "love of Beaux esprits": "I shd love to have some person to whom to say que la solitude est belle" (MO 5898, 4 September [1768]).

The Hitcham experiment was short-lived. It was destroyed, as David Simple's community had been destroyed, by turbulence from the outside that could not be shut out as effectively as at Millenium Hall. Grace Freind's daughter had foolishly married a lieutenant of marines who had no way to keep her and was demanding payment of the £4,000 due her only on her mother's death. Freind, torn, insisted on taking her daughter in at Hitcham, where she was to lie in. The place was her son's and he too thought it an ideal repository for his sister. The resultant imbalance, distraction, and division of loyalty produced a total disruption of the community just as it was establishing itself. In August, Scott, always plagued by headaches but now incapacitated by them, had to flee to Chelsea, to the medicinal baths of Dr. Dominiceti. Cutts and Arnold went with her, leaving the Freinds in possession of Hitcham. Scott would return there once again, but only to determine that in the Freinds' family residence the community could no longer function. The lease was up early in the year 1769, and soon enough Montagu was working hard to find another country retreat suitable for renewing the experiment. But such a retreat was never to be discovered.

The group's utopia, well publicized through Montagu's efforts, had been of great interest, especially to women, and its failure was an embarrassment shared by many; Montagu apparently could not bring herself to apprise her most intimate friends. Elizabeth Carter wrote to her in December, "You have never told me, that the society at Hitcham was dissolved. My informant makes grievous lamentation for the scandal which she supposes this event will reflect on female friendship" (*Letters of Carter to Montagu*, 2:16–17, 4 December 1768). Scott felt the failure more acutely, of course, than did Montagu. She never again mounted such a practical effort, confining herself in future to writing—novels and histories, but not utopias. In fact her next and last novel, *A Test of Filial Duty* (1772), emphasizes the disasters that ensue when a daughter marries against her father's (family's) wishes, and thus appears to represent the shrinking of Scott's vision to the domestic—her ruminations on the consequences of the foolish marriage of Grace Freind's daughter.

But Fielding's and Scott's utopian writings were not entirely ineffectual in contemporary society. The Bath circle may have looked to the work of the philanthropist John Howard, who from 1756 had been building model cottages for villages, encouraging their industry, and establishing schools for children at Cardington, Bedfordshire. He in turn may have been inspired by Fielding's *David Simple*. Montagu's friends the Nathaniel Chomleys had built by the 1780s a village near their house, fitting up residences for old and married servants and supervising a school for the children.[30] And Matthew Lewis's reformations on his Jamaican plantation were probably modeled on those of Sir George Ellison.[31] Moreover, authors of utopias subsequent to Scott's in the eighteenth century kept her work in view.[32]

Scott, however, had run out of heroic energy, and Montagu returned to her wonted ways. She also continued to yearn after her sister, but not to much avail; Scott persisted in her not-so-gentle rejection and sealed it through her geographical distance: after the death of Cutts, instead of settling with or at least near Montagu, Scott and Arnold chose to live in Norfolk. With their straitened means, aunt and niece did not have to sacrifice more hedonistic alternatives when they chose there a sober, spartan, and Christian life among the clerics of a cathedral city. Montagu would seem to have acceded to their choices and even approved them when, after her husband's death (which without benefit of winters abroad occurred at last in 1775), she bestowed a nicely calculated annuity of £200 on her sister—an income neat but certainly not gaudy.

Montagu herself unleashed her exhibitionistic nature when, following her accession without hindrance to her husband's wealth, she built her great mansion in Portman Square and gave her splendid parties. Thus, after the strain of the sisters' attempt at reconciliation during the Hitcham experiment—Scott's accepting Montagu into the project, Montagu's attempt to remake half of herself after her sister's likeness—they diverged again, as they had at the outset of adulthood. Scott had never shared her sister's attraction to *beaux esprits*. Montagu must have felt some relief as she slipped back into her Hill Street mode, no longer having to sustain two utterly disparate lifestyles. The sisters continued to love one another and to maintain their distinctions, Montagu demonstrating her supremacy in the areas of taste, wit, and the best society; Scott demonstrating that the best

---

30. *DNB;* and Historical Manuscripts Commission, *Calendar of the Manuscripts of the Marquis of Bath,* vol. 1 (London, 1904), 349.

31. See Matthew Lewis, *Journal of a West Indian Proprietor* (London, 1833).

32. See, for instance, Ruth Perry, "Bluestockings in Utopia," in Beth Tobin, ed., *History, Gender, and Eighteenth-Century Literature* (Athens, Ga., 1994), 159–78.

society was really in some other place, among the provincial clerical sort at Nor-wich, for example, and that she, not her sister, was on the high road.

We must take into account, however, that the narrative of the lives of the two sisters has been cautiously committed to writing by the one and carefully edited by the other. We have almost certainly been deceived by emphases on the positive and eliminations of the negative. We must work with what remains but remember that what remains is certainly skewed and that what is omitted we cannot really guess. All of what we know, we know because Montagu was a let-ter saver and because she must have concluded that the letters she saved displayed her to advantage and recited the narrative she herself was writing. Nor would she have intended disadvantage to her sister. The coal magnate and *salonnière* had her own éclat; the utopian reformer had hers. For a brief period they collaborated in the Hitcham utopia, Scott participating full-time, Montagu in part. The tensions between them, almost resolved, in the end drove them apart again, Montagu remaining thenceforward the pursuer, Scott, in tacit reproach, the eternal eloper.

*City College of New York and the CUNY Graduate Center*

# Subjectivity Unbound: Elizabeth Vesey as the Sylph in Bluestocking Correspondence

DEBORAH HELLER

## RECOVERING ELIZABETH VESEY

To the London society of her day, Elizabeth Vesey's name was virtually synonymous with the term "Bluestocking." Readers of the morning newspaper could be expected to relish the rumor that "there are now 2 parties of the blue stockings," with Mrs. Vesey and Mrs. Montagu at their rival heads. As Elizabeth Montagu wrote to her friend Elizabeth Carter:

> I hope you have met with an absurd paragraph in ye morning
> Herald, which says, that at Mrs V: ys ye other night, there happend
> such a dispute between ye blue stockings, that had it not been for
> ye timely interference of ye unletterd part of ye company might
> have ended very fatally; that there are now 2 parties of ye blue
> stockings, Mrs M$^u$ at ye head of ye seceders.[1]

In fact, "[Vesey] probably invented the term [Bluestocking], and had a proprietary interest in keeping it alive," according to Sylvia Myers.[2] And in 1783, when the term had enjoyed at least twenty years of currency, and Hannah More wrote her popular poem celebrating the Bluestockings—*The Bas Bleu; or, Conversation*—it was to Vesey that the piece was dedicated. The poem was published in 1786, thus further circulating in public the name and program of the original Bluestockings as well as reinforcing the Bluestocking fame of Elizabeth Vesey.

If, then, Vesey was such a famous Bluestocking in her own day, why has she received so little attention in recent work devoted to the Bluestockings? One reason

I wish to thank the Western New Mexico University Foundation for its generous support, which helped me to complete this project.

1.   MO 3565, 15 November 1783[?]. The Huntington's Montagu Collection is cited henceforward in the text; all transcriptions from the manuscripts are my own.
2.   Sylvia Harcstark Myers, *The Bluestocking Circle: Women, Friendship, and the Life of the Mind in Eighteenth-Century England* (Oxford, 1990), 251.

for neglect is that Vesey's life remains largely unknown, except through verbal caricature passed down uncritically via nineteenth-century accounts through to our own day. Reginald Blunt, for instance, wrote an essay on Vesey in 1925 for the *Edinburgh Review* that made her out to be childish, comical, even a bit imbecilic.[3] Blunt himself is not entirely responsible for this sort of representation; the picture he provided relies on memoirists such as Frances Burney who, knowing Vesey only at the end of the latter's life, transmitted a very limited and distorted portrait.[4]

Fortunately, there are primary sources that can help us learn more about this important Irishwoman and first-generation Bluestocking. Some of these have been published, such as the letters Elizabeth Carter wrote to Vesey and to Montagu about Vesey. Of course, as is well known, the reliability of Carter's letters is diminished by her nephew's "gate-keeping editorship" of the now missing originals.[5] But the most valuable sources on Vesey have remained largely untapped. I refer to the ninety-six letters in Vesey's own hand that have been preserved in the Huntington Library Montagu Collection, ninety of which are addressed to Montagu (the other six are to George, Lord Lyttelton). In addition, the collection contains two hundred and fifty-four letters from Montagu to Vesey, most of which have never been published. The correspondence between the two women spans nearly twenty-five years (1761–86), tracing the development of an intimate friendship and showing from the inside, as it were, the work and ideas of these Bluestocking pioneers.

The self-understanding of the Bluestockings—the way they saw their own role—has not previously been much discussed; the scholarly emphasis has understandably been on the incursions these women made into the public sphere. This public exposure, after all, was the reason for isolating the Bluestockings as an identifiable historical phenomenon in the first place, and it remains the focus and organizing principle even of more recent treatments. Gary Kelly's collection, *Bluestocking Feminism*: *Writings of the Bluestocking Circle, 1738–1785*, for instance, is organized around women who published works of literary or scholarly import. Vesey, who never published anything, is absent from the collection. And yet no one deserves to be called "Bluestocking" more than Vesey, especially if one takes the term, in its historical specificity, as designating the interlocking social circles and literary assemblies organized around Vesey, Montagu, and a few others, some

3.  Reginald Blunt, "The Sylph," *Edinburgh Review* 242 (October 1925): 364–79; 364–66.
4.  See, for instance, Burney's depictions of Vesey in *Memoirs of Dr. Burney, Arranged from his own Manuscripts . . . by his Daughter, Madame D'Arblay*, 3 vols. (London, 1832), 2:264, 266.
5.  *Bluestocking Feminism: Writings of the Bluestocking Circle, 1738–1785*, 6 vols., gen. ed. Gary Kelly (London, 1999), vol. 2, ed. Judith Hawley, xi.

of them like Vesey not copiously documented. But even Myers's groundbreaking book *The Bluestocking Circle*, which focuses on the first generation of Blue-stockings, devotes only a few pages to Vesey. More recently, Betty Rizzo has provided a more extensive treatment, analyzing Vesey's triangular relationship with companion Mrs. Handcock and husband Mr. Vesey in terms of a model of patriarchal family dynamics. Her chapter on Vesey brings valuable information to light, especially around the issue of her problematic second marriage, and she includes several of Vesey's hitherto unpublished letters; but in the end Rizzo seems to me to come dangerously close to the old stereotype of Vesey as childlike and inconsequent. In Rizzo's account, Vesey remained throughout her life "in her role as charming, impulsive child," impractical and helpless.[6] In my view, this portrayal fails to take account of the very positive appraisal of Vesey by her friends in their character of her as the "Sylph."

In this essay I take up a specific discourse surrounding Vesey—her figuration as the "Sylph," an unpredictable, mysterious, and indeterminate being who enjoyed almost magical powers of invention, energy, and freedom. The Sylphic figure, I argue, was the embodiment of a discourse of the subject available to the Bluestockings—the modern notion of the autonomous subject, which, looking to its own interiority as constituting its identity, possesses the potential for resisting the identities assigned to it by public discourse or culture on the basis of rank or sex. By claiming its own particularity and uniqueness—indeed its very inaccessibility to the common measure, or *ratio,* of identitarian reason and language—the Sylphic self claims a space free from constraining definitions and norms. My argument—that the notion of an ungendered, autonomous self actually provided a resource for women's practices of freedom in the second half of the eighteenth century—is contrary to received opinion. The widely accepted view is that the discourse of the subject had become bound up with the discourses of femininity, domesticity, and the civilizing arts to produce a stabilizing ideological complex centered on women and tending to reproduce middle-class culture and society. Women of the middle classes, so the view goes, were given an important role in the perpetuation of society, but at the price of their own activism and change: the policers of the margins became themselves the policed.

This received account of subjectivity and women has seemed to cover a range of phenomena fairly well, but it has also *covered over* phenomena worthy of our attention. Binding subjectivity inextricably with femininity, domesticity, discipline, virtue, reason, and so on, the received account has occulted the continuing influence of the discourse of the subject as an ungendered, autonomous, and

6. Betty Rizzo, *Companions without Vows: Relationships among Eighteenth-Century British Women* (Athens, Ga, 1994), 219.

authentic point of origin. This "unbound" subject continued to offer—as it did in the Sylph discourse, for example—strategic possibilities for resisting the dominant ethos for women, especially through the notion of interiority or indecipherable depth in the self.

The theory of a bound, feminized subjectivity is formulated most clearly by Nancy Armstrong. As she tells the story in *Desire and Domestic Fiction*, representations of women before 1740 tended to construct them, not so much as subjects ("selves" marked by psychological depth), but as objects whose value was assessed by their physicality and surface appearance. But shortly before midcentury, owing to the proliferation of novels and conduct literature, there was a rapid transformation, and a powerful new identification of women with subjectivity. The invention of "depth in the self," Armstrong writes, "provided the rationale for an educational program designed specifically for women, for these programs strove to subordinate the body to a set of mental processes that guaranteed domesticity." These disciplinary programs created an "essential self" for women that was marked by domesticity, supported by discourses of reason and virtue, and managed through practices of self-regulation. Becoming a subject for women meant subjecting oneself to roles and practices of domesticity and discipline. The allegedly gender-neutral self of Locke and other philosophers, says Armstrong, had no effect whatever on the formation of the female subject: "If the Lockean subject began as a white sheet of paper on which objects could be understood in sets of spatial relations, then pedagogical literature for women mapped out a field of knowledge that would produce a specifically female form of subjectivity."[7]

More recently, Gary Kelly has extended Armstrong's gendered model of subjectivity to the case of the Bluestockings. Kelly's version of subjectivity, while less essentializing than Armstrong's, nevertheless binds it strongly with domesticity and the feminine. Emphasizing that he is speaking of a rhetorical and cultural "figure" and not of actual individual women, Kelly states that "'woman' linked the major themes of cultural revolution," which included subjectivity, domesticity, civil society, and the nation. He then adds: "Actual women, especially in the professional and other middle classes, and including the Bluestocking women, could see themselves in this figure, participate in it, or help construct it in writing. . . . Because of the historic association of women with emotionalism and the feelings, 'woman' could represent the new eighteenth-century culture of subjectivity."[8] The ideological complex Kelly describes thus strongly feminizes subjectivity

7.  Nancy Armstrong, *Desire and Domestic Fiction: A Political History of the Novel* (Oxford, 1987), 75–81; quotations at 76, 14.
8.  Gary Kelly, "General Introduction" in *Bluestocking Feminism*, vol. 1, ed. Elizabeth Eger, xxiv–xxv.

and attaches to it traditionally feminine qualities. To do so seems to me to blur the focus on the salient aspect of modern subjectivity: namely, an interiority that can elude the identities constructed for it by discourse or culture. I argue here that the Sylph—as constructed by Montagu, Carter, and Vesey herself—was based on, and expressed, a notion of the self that viewed it as an indeterminate, undefinable and, hence, unbounded origin of action. Because of its hermeneutic inaccessibility—its ability to elude the categories that quickly sorted into male and female—this indeterminate self allowed women an extra dimension of freedom within the discursive constraints of masculinist hegemony. In the second part of this essay, I try to show that the Sylphic self was at the same time obliged to seek its freedom within the context of, or over against, a series of identities constructed for women through "discursive clusters" such as those described by Armstrong and Kelly. My disagreement with those two scholars is that they (especially Armstrong) emphasize almost exclusively the degree to which female subjectivity was a discursive construct imposed upon women, and they neglect the self-reflexive or self-constituting structure of the modern subject, with its opening for resistance. For this reason, I propose to reserve the notion of autonomous subjectivity or interiority as a way of speaking of the "active" component of the modern subject, one that could resist the passive, discursively constituted subject.

My disagreement with Armstrong and Kelly parallels the shift in Michel Foucault's thinking about the subject that occurred between his middle and final periods, sometime between the first volume of *The History of Sexuality* and the two works that succeeded it (*The Use of Pleasure* and *The Care of the Self*). Foucault came to realize that the modern subject is historically structured as self-reflexive and, therefore, self-constituting. This way of looking at the subject as self-relation allows us to describe the modern subject as a kind of tension between fixed or given identities (handed down through discourses and technologies of the self) and an autonomous self that takes up various relations to those discourses and technologies.[9] This notion of the subject as a multiple set of relationships between autonomous self, on one hand, and games of truth and technologies of self, on the other, offers needed flexibility to our descriptions of eighteenth-century women's identities, and it allows us to formulate actual women's resistances (if any) to such identities. My treatment of the Sylph discourse proceeds from the

---

9. In Foucault's words, "[The subject] is not a substance. It is a form, and this form is not primarily or always identical to itself"; see "The Ethics of the Concern of the Self as a Practice of Freedom," in *The Essential Works of Michel Foucault, 1954–1984*, ed. Paul Rabinow, trans. Robert Hurley et al., 3 vols. (New York, 1997), 1:281–301; 290.

belief that the late eighteenth century witnessed a certain intensification of the notion of subjective interiority, and that that interiority provided a basis of resistance that found expression, among other places, in the Bluestockings' construction of Elizabeth Vesey as the Sylph.

## "Be yourself, be the Sylph"

Elizabeth Vesey's identity as the Sylph seems to have been current among her friends as early as 1750, when Mary Delany refers to her by this name: "We heard from the Veseys yesterday. I was really afraid the storms had blown the remains of their castle about their ears, *but Mrs Vesey is a sylph,* and the spirits of the air protect her, or something better!"[10] How much Delany and others among Vesey's early acquaintances intended to import from Pope's *Rape of the Lock* in so nicknaming Vesey, I cannot say. It is clear, at least, that Pope's borrowed (Rosicrucian) notion of elemental spirits must have lent an association of airy mobility and protean changeableness. Pope's sylphs, "freed from mortal Laws, with ease / Assume what Sexes and what Shapes they please."[11] Whoever first adopted the epithet and whatever their intentions might have been, we can say with certainty that Vesey's two closest English friends, Montagu and Carter, developed what might otherwise have remained a mere nickname into an elaborate discourse of peculiar richness. Their Sylph was a character not to be pinned down. Her airy insubstantiality allowed her to disappear and reappear unexpectedly, to travel great distances without hindrance, and generally to perform feats of the the improbable, the impossible, and even the miraculous.

Not everyone, of course, saw Vesey under this magical rubric. To some of her non-Bluestocking acquaintances, Vesey was simply eccentric, merely odd in her personality and actions. Caroline Fox, for instance, found her a "queer little woman."[12] To her Bluestocking friends, however, she was a figure of magical potency and unbounded energy: she was the Sylph. They configured the Sylph in their correspondence by continuously weaving together description and theorization of her unique characteristics and amazing exploits. Even casual browsing of the Carter or Montagu letters will repeatedly turn up this or that Sylphic feat—whether raising an "American hut" on the banks of the Liffey, or graveling an

---

10. *The Autobiography and Correspondence of Mary Granville, Mrs. Delany*, ed. Lady Llanover, 6 vols. (London, 1861–62), 1st ser., 3:21, 28 February 1750–51; cited hereafter in the text.

11. Canto 1, lines 69–70; *The Poems of Alexander Pope*, ed. John Butt (New Haven, Conn., 1963), 220.

12. *Correspondence of Emily, Duchess of Leinster, 1731–1814*, ed. Brian Fitzgerald, 3 vols. (Dublin, 1949–57), 1:211.

upstairs drawing room to aid a friend on crutches, or breaking the circle of formal conversation in her magic "blue" drawing room.[13] But the discourse of Sylphic innovation is best understood not as an ad hoc celebration of one woman's eccentricities. I believe it expresses a larger element in the Bluestockings' self-understanding. The ability to be different, to do something new, to transcend the bounds of convention—these were desiderata for women who were going to establish a place for themselves in society as female intellectuals. The role of female intellectual was not a preestablished one, waiting to be adopted. Considerable struggle and courage were needed, even for these privileged women. The Sylph, I suggest, emblematized for them the possibility of a female self soaring beyond the limitations of conventional female identity and conduct.

Montagu and Carter often imagine the aerial mobility of the Sylph as their own and connect it with their sense of doing something new as Bluestockings, as in the following letter from Montagu to Carter:

> My imagination without wing or broomstick oft mounts aloft, rises into ye Regions of pure space, & without lett or impedement bears me to your fireside, where you set me in your easy chair, & we talk & reason, as Angel Host & guest Aetherial should do, of high & important matters. We will not deign to say a word of Mobs or Ministers; of fashions or the fashionable; of the Great who are without Greatness, or the little who are less than their littleness. Pray say you dont let us talk nonsence! no my dear friend, nor will we talk sense, for that is worse. We will say what has not been said before, or if the substance be old, the mode & figure shall be new. (MO 3258, 10 October 1769)

Elizabeth Eger picks out this passage as exemplary and correctly notes the link between its "sense of space and freedom" and its "utopian impulse": "Here, and throughout the correspondence between Carter and Montagu, the reader can sense their self-conscious attitude to writing, and to conversation, their effort to carve out a space in which 'the mode & figure shall be new'" (*Bluestocking Feminism*, 1:lxii). Furthermore, as Eger points out, their sense of being Bluestockings, their sense of doing something new, of enlarging their "sphere of action" (MO 3034, 1 May 1760), existed within a self-conscious sense of Bluestocking

---

13. On the "American hut," see *Letters from Mrs. Elizabeth Carter to Mrs. Montagu, between the years 1755 and 1800*, ed. Montagu Pennington, 3 vols. (London, 1817), 1:311, 12 July 1766. On the graveling of a drawing room see ibid., 2:180, 28 November 1772; edition cited hereafter in the text. Stories of Vesey's experiments in her "blue room" are legion: Montagu writes of "that blue room where all people are enchanted tho ye magic figure of ye circle is banished, thence" (MO 6525, 13 November 1778).

community. Their feeling for the expansive possibilities of self was inseparable from their sense of belonging to a group providing mutual support, identity, and friendship. It was within this group that the discourse of the Sylph was invented.

Let me introduce the Sylph as unencumbered, free, and mobile self by quoting a letter from Montagu dated, simply, "Sunday morn." Montagu has invited Vesey to a dinner party, but Vesey has declined because of another engagement. Montagu urges her to resist her "over exquisite discretion" and to come anyway: "Dine with me therefore, & let some body call you out at 7 o clock, then glide into your chair & Sylph like—vanish. No one will know where you are gone, I will say you melted into air, into thin air, but will embody again when ye atmosphere is more dense. Be yourself, be the Sylph" (MO 6441, n.d.). The Sylph as self: this is perhaps more than homophony with a difference. It is the Sylph's unique self—as insubstantial as aether or air, but still peculiarly the Sylph's—that gives her her astonishing mobility and that grants her permission to elude the constraints of social decorum and "over exquisite discretion." This Sylphic self, emanating from a mysterious and ineffable interiority, is what makes Vesey incomparable, absolutely unique. "Indeed," writes Carter to Montagu, "it would be in vain for you to seek for a likeness of our Sylph, in the environs of Tunbridge, or in any other region below the moon; you can never find it except among the visitors of your own imagination" (2:101, 2 July 1771). Again, remarking on the Sylph's "heterogeneous assemblies" in her "blue room," Carter comments to Montagu: "The singular art, by which she produces the effects which you so well describe, certainly depends upon the singularity of her character, which I apprehend to be a matter of deep investigation, and made up of a great variety of particulars" (2:184, 20 December 1772). The true origin of the "effects" of her actions is undescribable, as it is hidden in the depths of subjectivity.

Any attempt to describe the Sylph's singularity inevitably falls back on metaphor. In one letter Montagu compares the Sylph's "je ne scai quoi" to a unique blend of scents and flavors:

> . . . eau de mille fleurs, made from a bouquet collected by the Graces, and infused in a peculiar fountain in Parnassus, all shaken together by les jeux & les ris: sometimes Minerva throws into it a spice of wisdom; the Laughter loving dame a little gayety; & Apollo a little (& but a little) sheer witt. There is a dolce piquante in this essence which is composed without rules, & made without labour, & renderd perfect without study, that triumphs over all the endeavours of art. Le je ne scai quoi is not to be found in the art of cookery. you, yourself, cannot give a receit for it. (MO 6571, 12 January 1782)

The Sylph's qualities ultimately escape capture by language. Remembering the Sylph and "all those qualities which made me so happy [last year at Tunbridge Wells]," Montagu concludes, "I have no names for many of them": like the "nameless stars" of the Milky Way, the Sylph's qualities diffuse a "gentle brightness" but cannot be separately identified (MO 6423, 26 June 1772).

The Bluestockings' fascination with the magical indeterminacy of the Sylph crystallizes around the issue of illegibility and decipherment of handwriting. The obscurity of Vesey's writing, in fact, is a constant theme in the letters of Montagu and Carter, attracting much comment and theorization. Sometimes a word or line in a Vesey letter defies all interpretive efforts. Montagu writes to Vesey on one occasion: "One line in your last letter seem'd to defy the bold presumption of a Bentley, the sagacious conjecture of a Warburton.... Long the matter lay in its safe & secure illegibility, but at length, as every thing that relates to you is deeply imprinted in my memory, there I read, last night, what I could not read in your letter" (MO 6490, 31 October 1776). Elizabeth Carter comments similarly in a letter to Vesey:

> [T]here is not a decypherer in the world who could have made out your last Letter except myself, not that I am vain enough to ascribe this special power to the particular sagacity of my head, which would never have got me out of such a scrape. Oh what perplexity and confusion of all the twenty-four letters of the alphabet! if it had not been aided and abetted and comforted by my heart.[14]

Vesey's friends not only lovingly indulged Vesey's notoriously illegible handwriting: through their Sylphic discourse they virtually transmuted it into something above mere writing. Throughout the correspondence, Vesey's chirographic vagaries are refigured as the magic embodiments of her particular genius and spirit. In the place of Vesey's "scratch" or "scrawl," her Bluestocking friends found "magick characters" and "hieroglyphicks."

In sanctioning their friend's uniquely slovenly hand, Carter and Montagu were once again giving Vesey leave to circumvent the rules of propriety. It is clear from midcentury discussions of handwriting that literate women were expected to write legibly. To Hester Chapone this point was so obvious as to need no justification: "To write a free and legible hand" was simply an "indispensable requisite."[15] Mary Delany's instructions to her niece provide more clues as to what

14.  Elizabeth Carter, *A Series of Letters between Mrs. Elizabeth Carter and Miss Catherine Talbot, from the year 1741 to 1770. To which Are Added, Letters from Mrs. Elizabeth Carter to Mrs. Vesey, between the years 1763 and 1787*, ed. Montagu Pennington, 4 vols. (London, 1809), 4:65, 12 June 1772. Cited hereafter in the text.

15.  Rhoda Zuk, vol. 3, ed. *Bluestocking Feminism*, p. 331.

was ordinarily expected of well brought-up ladies: "Your letters, my dear Mary, always are most welcome to me, I think your last was tolerably written considering you have not practiced much without lines; *your f's do not stick out their elbows quite so much*, & in time you will have a *free & easy air*!" (Delany, 1st ser., 3:600, 1 September 1760). Straight lines, unobtrusive conformity, standard correctness—these were exacted in handwriting just as certainly as in other bodily and verbal gestures.

There is more at stake here than simply releasing Vesey from some of the strictures of proper behavior, however. Carter's and Montagu's refashioning of Vesey's writing as hieroglyphics illustrates how their Sylphic discourse depends upon a notion of self as interiority and depth. Their hermeneutics of decipherment parallels their hermeneutics of self: in both cases, the outward signs or manifestations cover over a mysterious depth that cannot be fully interpreted or cannot be interpreted at all. In a response to a particularly brilliant letter from Vesey, one describing a costume ball at Lady Moira's in Dublin, we witness Montagu transmuting Vesey's difficult handwriting into a sublime and mysterious script. Vesey, as so often, had apologized for her handwriting: "I think I might set a state decypherer at defiance—but don't I conjure you expose the uninteresting pot hooks of yr friend for I wou'd not venture to plague any but such a friend who can find some affection tho no entertainment in my wretched blots which I am too careles to mend & which has almost discourag'd me from writing" (MO 6284, 28 April [1768]). To this Montagu responds:

> [E]very thing is embellish'd by your pen. Your cabalistical characters do not only differ in form, but in power, from common letters. With the help of a, b, c, & c, many can contrive to convey to a distant friend some imperfect idea of what they have seen or heard, but to give such glowing colours, & lively touches belongs only to my Dear friends scatter'd characters. They certainly contain the virtues of hieroglyphicks & letters, paint images, & convey spirit with ye united power of both. For sensible objects they have the hieroglyphical art, for witt the brevity of alphabetick marks, in one respect they savour of ye Chinese characters, which is, that one must bestow a good deal of time to learn them perfectly. I have long attain'd to an entire knowledge of them, & never was any of Lettré so well paid for their trouble by reading the works of Confucius, as I was by [your letter]. (MO 6394, 8 June [1768])

We can place Montagu's discussion of different kinds of writing (hieroglyphs, Chinese characters, alphabet) in the framework of the eighteenth-century debate on the history of writing, or grammatology. In seizing upon the notion of hiero-glyphs here, Montagu may be recalling the work of Bishop Warburton, whose 1741 treatise on hieroglyphs she clearly knew at least by reputation (she mentions him by name in MO 6490). However, unlike Warburton, who maintained that hieroglyphs were in principle decipherable—that is, could be assimilated to the words and ideas of another language—Montagu sees Vesey's hieroglyphs as not commensurable with any other language or script. Indeed, Montagu might be said to incline to what Jacques Derrida has dubbed the "hieroglyphist prejudice" of Athanasius Kircher, whose more mystical approach Warburton was attempt-ing to answer scientifically.[16] Kircher did not believe that hieroglyphs were trans-parently reducible to the words or concepts of another language or renderable into another script; they had to be grasped at once (*uno intuitu*) and corresponded to an ineffable reality. In the same way, both Vesey's script and the spirit of the writing behind the script can be grasped intuitively but not analyzed or merely translated. In one letter, Montagu speaks to Vesey of "the [Sylph's] dear magic characters which always convey something better than ever was express'd by sym-bol, Hieroglyphic picture, character, or alphabet. I believe your letters are written with ye true sympathetick Ink for I catch your sentiments sometimes before I can lay hold of the Words" (MO 6478, 15 May 1776).

The Sylph's scribble is not open to Warburton's modern science of interpre-tation. It more resembles what Derrida playfully calls "scrypt"; it conceals its meaning except to those already in the know, those possessing a special gnosis or initiation.[17] Similarly, the Sylph herself is not reducible to transparent and uni-versally understood terms. Her mysterious interiority is uninterpretable by the identitarian logic that seeks to reduce singularity to common measure, to uni-versal laws. As she escapes definition, so she escapes control. Her behavior and her personality are unaccountable in every sense of the word.

The Sylph's indeterminacy allowed her to operate freely in the middle spaces between the public and private domains, where women's proper role and terms of participation had not yet been rigidly defined. One of these middle spaces was personal letter writing, and there Vesey was not only allowed but indeed en-couraged to follow her particular genius. Vesey's letters, Montagu writes, "act with a living agency on the heart of her friends, & are as superior in their energy to studied formal letters, as Mr Garrick on ye stage is to the Puppet that by meer Mechanism assumes the gestures of the Hero or the Lover" (MO 6437, 9 February 1774). Ordinary rules of writing or grammar were no obstacle: "your letters give

16. Jacques Derrida, *Of Grammatology*, trans. Gayatri Chakravorty Spivak (Baltimore, 1976), 80.
17. Jacques Derrida, "Scribble (Writing-Power)," *Yale French Studies*, no. 58 (1979): 117–47; 124.

me the highest pleasure, they are not laboured compositions like ye letters of Mr Pope but your pen in its flight knows how to snatch a grace beyond ye rules of art & if by accident you break Priscians head you hang such a garland on it as makes a great ornament" (MO 6584, 29 July 1784). In comparing Vesey's letters to those of Pope, Montagu is implying a literary, or paraliterary, status for Vesey's letters. This is perhaps nothing new in the eighteenth century. As Cynthia Lowenthal points out with respect to the correspondence of Mary Wortley Montagu, the letter was a "sanctioned, legitimate vehicle" for women's literary ambitions: "The letter, because it occupies an indeterminate status between public and private, … [allows] a woman writer to cultivate and capitalize on her literary skills without transgressing the boundaries of her class and gender."[18]

The Bluestockings were well aware of the opportunities that the indeterminate status of the letter offered. Because the letter was not an officially public and, therefore, manly province, women's role and identity in letter writing had not been codified as somehow in a minor key, as subordinate. The Bluestockings used the personal letter not only to fashion their cerulean identity, which they cultivated among themselves and turned outward toward the public world, but also as women who wrote in a certain way, with flair and excellence. One sees a more ambitiously "literary" epistolary style among Bluestockings than among non-Bluestockings such as the women who composed the networks of correspondence around Hester Pitt or Emily Lennox.[19]

Sometimes the literariness of the Bluestocking correspondence borrows from the toolbox of established literary genres and inventories of language craft: for example, parts of letters resemble moral essays, loco-descriptive set-pieces, literary criticism, and dialogue; rhetorical flourishes include figures such as tricolon, parallelism, personification, and antithesis. Carter and Montagu, with their classically-oriented educations, tended toward established literary genres and their rhetorics. Vesey, on the other hand, is not so easy to classify. She was able to exploit her singularity as Sylph to underwrite her experiments in letter writing, straying from traditional male styles, creating something uniquely her own. In the following excerpt, describing Lady Moira's Dublin "habit Ball," Vesey transfigures the matter-of-factness of costumes into a "fairy Vision" of language:

18. Cynthia Lowenthal, *Lady Mary Wortley Montagu and the Eighteenth-Century Familiar Letter* (Athens, Ga., 1994), 3.
19. The letters of Emily Lennox, Duchess of Leinster (see n. 12 above) present an informed, well-read, but entirely unintellectual writer. There is more discussion of wallpaper than of reading material. Similarly, while Hester Pitt was a well-educated, fully literate woman, letters to and from her contain little in the way of literary talk or politics; see *So Dearly Loved, So Much Admired: Letters to Hester Pitt, Lady Chatham from her Relations and Friends, 1744–1801*, ed. Vere Birdwood (London, 1994).

Stiff Bodice & farthingale with silver gauze beads & Ermin made of black & white persian & cou'd not have been better dress'd from the Wardrobe—Ossians Harp was hung in the Musick Gallery—the Irish Stuffs have the greatest variety of rich & beautiful Colours in the World since the days of Solomon & with the addition of jewels & tinsel it was the gayist glittering fantastical Assembly you can form an idea of— . . . the river Liffy crown'd with Sedge her robe embroider'd with water plants an Urn upon her Head—a Bachanal wreath'd with ivy a Tygers skin acros her Shoulders & a Thirses in her hand danced a Cottilon with Comus & a Witch—the Witch was dress'd in a high crown'd hat a nightrail & apron a broom & a pair of Spectacles fasten'd in her girdle & as she was naturaly very deform'd one cou'd not help believing she had come down the Chimny the Demons rewarded her good humour for as her shape seem'd to be only part of her Character she never pleas'd or look'd so well in her life two beautiful Children of Lady Moiras were Cupid & Psiché their Wings contrived to look as transparent as the spotted net work of a flys— (MO 6284, 28 April [1768])

It was to this letter that Montagu responded with raptures, praising its unusual "power," which she ascribed to Vesey's "cabalistical characters." Such extravagant praise can only have encouraged Vesey to take further chances in a medium in which she was clearly gifted.

There is a mode of writing in Vesey's letters that one might call epistolary epiphany, in which the line between writing and life becomes blurred, almost nonexistent. Often the epiphanic moment is signaled by the sudden arrival of an avian visitor to the writing Vesey—almost a signature event of Vesey's letters. One of the burdens of Vesey's life, as she saw it, was her isolation in Ireland, far from the brilliant, candle-lit drawing rooms of London society. She was forever trying to get her friends to undertake the dangerous and fatiguing passage across the channel. In one letter, the writing Vesey appears to be brooding on this "seperation from friends"; then, suddenly, an avian visitant appears: "here is a young Hawk has just now perch'd upon the top of my book case how he stole in or who he is I can't tell he seems quite tame & is staring at me with his fine Eyes—I believe you have sent him I will take the Omen." Her imagination at this point itself takes flight and she leads the reader on a fantastical journey. The reverie dissolves with the sound of Mrs. Handcock calling Vesey to supper, but the letter's work has been done: Vesey and her friends united in reverie; separation overcome: "this enchanting reverie has just got possession of me dont contradict it let me at least live in the Castle for *this* year" (MO 6292, [July 1773]).

A similar epiphany arises in a letter to Montagu of September 1768, again transcending their separation.[20] Vesey discusses her hope of visiting England this winter: "I begin now to be certain I shall have that pleasure this winter—the month uncertain & I very impatient to secure it—Mr Vesey proposes I shou'd go first but I don't like his offer—here is a flight of Rooks just risen from the ivy'd Towers of a Convent within a few yards of my window as if it were to reproach me with this undomestick desire of rambling." The flight of rooks triggers a lengthy reflection on the "undomestick desire for rambling," for which Vesey feels reproached. Her accusers—the rooks and, by extension, the nuns—she then addresses in an extended apostrophe in which she contrasts her desire for colorful London society with the gloomy monastery and its inhabitants. On the side of the rooks and nuns are "yr black letter'd history of the Martyrs," the "sable demure Prioresse" with her "superstitious Etiquette" and "Cloister'd ignorance," and the chatter of "jack daws & Nuns." On the side of Vesey and her desire are an "Elegant composition," a table "surrounded with Orators Bards & Philosophers," a *salonnière* "animat[ing] her company with the fire of her own imagination," "the modest wisdom of an Athenian maid." Just as telling are the verbs lodged in the passage, as she addresses the nuns: "you never pray'd . . . much les did you ever dream . . . you never desired . . . or expected." Desire denied, a somber routine of stasis and discipline, a life devoid of imagination and art: this is the opposite of Vesey's "undomestick desire for rambling." Vesey concludes her reverie (and her letter): "I believe I may as well leave the jack daws & Nuns to chatter for themselves—I am afraid I shall never practice any of the Lessons they might give me" (MO 6291).

I have argued that beneath the construction of the Sylph lies the notion of a free, unencumbered self: an interiority or subjectivity beyond the reach of definition and, therefore, control. The Bluestockings associated the Sylphic idea with Vesey, no doubt because of her actual characteristics—her energy, her unusual creativity, and her personal charm. Yet the Sylph was never identical with the person of Elizabeth Vesey; rather, the Sylphic notion served the Bluestockings as a

20.   This letter (MO 6291) has been dated in the Montagu Collection as from 1772. However, this must be incorrect. A letter from Montagu to Carter, dated 29 September 1768 (MO 3227), clearly refers to this letter: "I had a charming letter from the Sylph last post, & the most charming of many charming things it contain'd, was an assurance of her coming to us this Winter. . . .The Rooks that fly over her head seem to her to be Orators Poets & beaux esprits, & thro the grate of a ruin'd Nunnery she fancies she hears the whispers of Athenian maids." Dating Vesey's letters is particularly difficult, as her autograph letters often omit the year, even the month, and frequently bear no date at all. I have been able to date many of Vesey's letters securely through cross-reference with letters of Montagu (and of Carter, though the autographs, of course, are missing). The letter cited above about the "young Hawk," for example, can be dated as shortly after a letter from Montagu to which it responds (MO 6429), dated in Montagu's hand "July ye 19th, 1773."

metaphor for their impulse to free themselves from some of the constraints of convention—to find for themselves a space of activity where the mode and figure could indeed be new. When Carter and Montagu consider Vesey outside of the metaphoric horizon of Sylpherie, when they enter into relation with her as a person with a specific body and a discernable set of behaviors, then her inscrutable interiority ceases to be celebrated. She becomes instead a difficult patient whose dangerous symptoms demand analysis (her own self-decipherment) and intervention (self-management through the imposition of technologies of the self).

## "More than a spoonful, poison": Rational Self-Control and Ethical Self-Formation

Montagu and Carter often commiserated about the state of Vesey's mind and health. In July 1771, after much coaxing, Montagu had at last persuaded Vesey to join her at Tunbridge Wells for a therapeutic session. Vesey came, but alas, she left after only a few days. "[You are like a] bird of paradise," Montagu tells Vesey. "[Y]ou are never to be met or seen but upon the wing.... I have reflected much on the state of your health since you left me, & I realy think you hurt it, & also your spirits, by being too much in action" (MO 6413, 18 July [1771]). There was much epistolary back-and-forth between Montagu and Carter about the precarious state of Vesey's health and about her early departure from the Tunbridge waters. Carter had written Montagu on 14 July:

> But, alas, it grieves me to find that mixed up with the aerial qualities of the Sylph, there is so alarming a proportion of the more mortal woman. Indeed her present state of health is terrifying, for it appears to me more eccentric than ever I knew it; and one feels the more uncomfortable about it, from the knowledge that she will never keep long enough to any one remedy, to allow it to be as beneficial to her as it *can*, merely because she does not find it as beneficial to her as she *expects*.... But, indeed, it is our poor, dear Sylph's misfortune, in every pursuit, to raise her expectations too high, for the condition of mortality; and this gives her that perpetual restlessness of body and mind, which harasses and wears out both. (2:108–9)

Carter speaks here of Vesey's health as *eccentric*, like a planet on an erratic flight; and, like Montagu, she comments on Vesey's lack of stability of body *and* mind. Likewise on 20 September 1773, Carter worries to Montagu about Vesey's well-being. She feels that "the hurry of the world too much withdraws her thoughts [from meditation on salutary subjects]." She urges Montagu to counsel her: "It would, I am sure, be a great comfort to her to hear from you. . . . But do not let me propose any task which will be too painful for you; only keep this general hint in your mind, and improve it to her good, when you have an opportunity, and can do it with ease" (2:220–21). As we learn in Carter's letter of 19 October to Montagu, Montagu had already made her recommendations to Vesey: "It gives me pleasure to find you had anticipated my intimation with regard to our dear and amiable friend. Indeed she is formed for enjoyments much superior to that *foolish* world, which too much engages her mind, and leads it on by the dancing phantom of an *ignus fatuus* of pleasure, which she wearies her spirits in pursuing, and which she never is able to overtake" (2:225).

Montagu's and Carter's concern for their friend's welfare—what Foucault has called "soul service"[21]—takes the form of advising a certain kind of care of self: rational self-control. They recommend to their patient not only measures to manage bodily health but also meditations of a sort appropriate to settle mind and spirit. If Carter's advice often took a philosophical cast, Montagu's prescriptions are more apt to recommend practical therapies of self-regulation and method. She proposed that Vesey adopt a "system of life" to manage health of body and mind (MO 6413, 18 July [1771]); for the very nature of human beings requires, she believed, order and method: "there is something in human nature that requires a pursuit, health is an object, the drinking waters is a business" (MO 6444, 11 June 1775).

The importance of cultivating rational self-management is cleverly formulated in a letter Carter writes to Vesey in 1766. Through a seemingly casual anecdote, she gently insinuates to Vesey a parable of self-control through reason and measure. Speaking of the use of antimony as a medicine, she writes: "It is so undistinguishable from Madeira, that to prevent any body tasting it in any hurtful quantity, I had labelled the bottle 'more than a spoonful, poison.' My maid happened to see it on a shelf, and came to me lately with a look of the utmost consternation and terror." After pacifying her maid's fears, Carter writes, she began to reflect on the "great difference of intellectual character" that separates two sorts of people: "They whose understandings are exercised by thought and observation, trace things through their successive stages to probable and remote consequences. Uncultivated minds [like the maid's] on the contrary perceive no intermediate degree either in nature or in action, but pass on directly to extremities; and thus discover nothing in poison, but the idea of irremediable and instant death." The lesson intended for Vesey is twofold. On the most elementary level is the maxim that the difference between limit and excess may mark the difference between health and disaster: more than a spoonful, poison. But the

---

21.  Foucault, *The Care of the Self*, trans. R. Hurley (New York, 1986), 54.

profounder lesson concerns the distinction between cultivated and uncultivated minds. The cultivated mind, trained through constant exercise of thought and observation, will remain calm in circumstances of hope and fear; but the uncultivated mind will be helplessly swept on to extremities of thought or action. Such mental training, Carter insinuates, would be very helpful for Vesey, whose body and mind were thought to be particularly susceptible to the disturbances of pathos and passion, respectively. An Rx of rational self-control was just what the wily doctor ordered, and she concluded her letter to the hypersensitive Vesey thus: "Pray, my dear Mrs. Vesey, keep your imagination employed in decorating the banks of the Liffy [Vesey had a rustic cottage there], and it will be less at leisure to disturb the tranquillity of your heart" (2:293–97, 15 July 1766).

The unmanageable Vesey never did practice any of the lessons her friends (or the rooks) gave her. Her intellectual curiosity, her powerful affections, her irrepressible imagination continued uncorrected. As late as 1782, an exasperated Carter warns her against reading "dangerous" books like those of the French *philosophes*: "[W]hy . . . will you idly spend your time in reading what ought never to have been written? But you do it, you say, merely for amusement: 'tis dangerous amusement to a mind like your's, indeed to any mind" (4:300–301, 9 January 1782). Or she scolds Vesey for her religious doubts: "You say you are as well satisfied as 'a mind formed for doubt can be.' Pardon me, my dear Mrs. Vesey, our doubts are our own making, and perhaps there never was a mind naturally formed for doubting. The regulation of our understanding is a moral quality, and as much under the power of the will, as the regulation of one's outward actions" (3:252–53, 2 January 1765). And, like our understanding, so also must our affections be regulated, Carter thinks. They are required as engines for our actions, but they "require the strictest guard, and the most careful direction" (*Carter to Vesey*, 4:83, 16 July 1773).

Imagination, like the affections and the understanding, is a wonderful faculty, but it too requires limits. Carter puts it on the reservation, sequestered like the noble but potentially unruly savage, as it were. The imagining faculty may be given free rein only in certain spheres, where it provides the "sublimed and noble amusements of delicate and refined imagination" (*Carter to Vesey*, 4:15, 28 April 1770). One such safe sphere of imagination was appreciation of wild nature. Carter, allowing that she, like Vesey, is "pastoral-mad," writes: "Indeed I am so far from thinking it necessary to check my imagination in this respect, that I give it free scope, and gladly pursue every innocent extravagance to which it directs me" (*Carter to Vesey*, 3:263, 6 December 1765). But if Carter can occasionally pursue an "innocent extravagance" on the wings of her imagination, she is careful to partition imagination off from the real world of common sense: "I have always endeavoured, my dear friend, to keep my imagination and my common sense in separate apartments" (*Carter to Montagu*, 2:218, 20 September 1773). Indeed, to the letter already quoted from Montagu, which begins, "My imagination without wing or broomstick oft mounts aloft" (MO 3258), Carter replied:

> Fly as far as you will, my dear friend, into the regions of imagination, and I will engage to meet you half way. I perfectly subscribe to your scheme, and will very readily leave all common topics, and all common sense, to the dull mortals who are plodding below, as mere useless incumbrances in our etherial excursions; there is no manner of danger but we shall easily recover them, when we drop again into this thick atmosphere, and return, as return we must, to the ordinary transactions of vulgar terrestrial life. . . . To mere reason, indeed, it is very necessary that, after all our flights, we should descend, not only as it is a good useful drudge in the business of common life, but as a remedy against our pride. (2:48–49, 12 October 1769)

Montagu's report of her soaring imagination notwithstanding, she would not have disagreed with Carter's strictures on the imagination, the affections, or the intellect; nor would she have disagreed about the need to impose such disciplinary strictures on Vesey.

What, then, are we to make of the obvious disparity between Carter's and Montagu's attempts to impose self-government on Vesey and the Bluestockings' construction of the Sylph as unimpeded, autonomous self? They were torn, I believe, between two conflicting models of subjectivity. On the one hand, the Sylph is constituted as a self relating only to itself, according to a notion of interiority available since Descartes; and such a notion would have had obvious attractions for the Bluestockings, as I have argued. On the other hand, the Bluestockings, like the rest of their society, were also working from a more traditional, ethical model of self-formation, genealogically related to the ancient theme Foucault has called "care of self." In this case, the subject constitutes itself as self-relation, but only through practices that are, in effect, self-other relations. In "care of self," the self constitutes itself as an ethical subject by means of two major kinds of operations: subjectivation of truths, and technologies of the self. The "mode of subjectivation," in Foucault's words, means "the way in which people are invited or incited to recognize their moral obligations [in the name of certain truths or discourses]."²² "Technologies of the self" Foucault defines as "the procedures . . .

---

22. Foucault, "On the Genealogy of Ethics: An Overview of Work in Progress," in *Essential Works*, 1:253–80; 264.

suggested or prescribed to individuals in order to determine their identity, maintain it, or transform it . . . through relations of self-mastery or self-knowledge."[23] Foucault's concepts are useful in showing how ethical subjectivity (produced through care of self) is bound up with the "truths" of one's society: in other words, who one is and how one is situated among others is inseparable from established truths and techniques that are handed down.

The Bluestockings' schemes of rational self-control were instances of care of self, and as such they were subject to the paradox of "governmentality": that is, when the individual regulates herself through relations to existing truths and techniques, how autonomous is she, really? When Montagu and Carter try to get Vesey to take active charge of herself—to free herself from passive thraldom to mental passions and bodily pathos—they are not enjoining a specific code of behavior on her, or a specific identity; rather, they are urging her to apply general principles based on reason. And yet, the "approved" patterns of ethos and conduct somehow get smuggled in, so that self-power becomes other-power: autonomy becomes heteronomy. The problem with so general a principle as rational self-control is that it tends to form the subject in accord with the already existing assumptions about one's proper ethos.

In the practice of rational self-regulation for women, "reason" tended to amount merely to the injunction to be reasonable—that is, to obey conventional standards of conduct and morality. Notice, in the following quotation, how Carter holds up a mirror/portrait to Vesey with stereotypical female features already painted in, and how Carter "presupposes" virtuous self-control:

> I could not help pleasing myself with the persuasion, that a mind so delicate as yours, when left to its own sensibilities, would naturally attend to the lessons which solitude is so fitted to inspire; at least when the current of the thoughts is not ruffled by any outrageous passion, nor the heart by any dark principles rendered impenetrable to the whispers of instruction. If *you* have either outrageous passions or dark principles, I will allow myself to be as much mistaken in your character as you seem to apprehend me to be. (3:251–52, 2 January 1765)

The "lessons" appropriate to the female mind meditating in solitude are, as it were, whispered to Vesey *sotto voce*. What Carter *presupposes* about Vesey's character she *prescribes* for Vesey's character. No "outrageous passions" for the heart, no "dark principles" for the intellect really means: I assume you are abiding by the

---

23. Foucault, "Subjectivity and Truth," ibid., 1:87–92; 87.

accepted standards for female behavior. When Carter invites Vesey to enter the circle of truths and practices and thereby to form her own ethos, she invites her to enter the cycle of accepted truths about women and about acceptable behavior.

To show Carter's and Montagu's urgings of self-government upon Vesey is not to tell a simple story of their capitulation to convention; nor is it to unmask them as traitors to their own emancipatory impulses. What we see in their letters to and about Vesey is evidence of a profound contradiction in their assumptions about freedom. On the one hand, Montagu and Carter were drawn to the Sylphic elements of Elizabeth Vesey—and they made metaphoric capital of those elements—because of the promise of freedom that they contained. Sylphic subjectivity, after all, consisted of pure self-relation and, as such, offered a resource for resistance against certain constraints of convention: Vesey need only be the Sylph to be herself, and under that spell she could soar above the barriers of decorum and custom. On the other hand, Carter and Montagu also believed that their regimens of rational self-regulation could help secure liberation on other fronts—liberation from mental perturbation and unfreedom. Carter prescribed limits for Vesey's affections, imagination, and thinking (more than a spoonful, poison) under the assumption that this regime of measure would secure freedom for her friend from the physical and mental turbulence that threatened her. The revolving door that such assumptions tended to share with conservative standards of female conduct did not seem to worry Carter or Montagu.

But before we submit to disappointment about the Bluestockings' subscription to some of the compelling orthodoxies of their day, we ought to recall Foucault's late thinking about subjectivity, which reminds us of the myriad relationships the subject can take up with respect to available games of truth and technologies of self. The Bluestockings took up, and made use of, two contradictory discourses of the self in their attempt to negotiate a partial autonomy for themselves as intellectual women. Whether they might profitably have adopted different gambits or strategies within the various truth-games in which they found themselves is perhaps not our most fruitful question. It is enough, I believe, to see them as active players in a game of freedom, truth, and power, and to try to understand their historical situatedness within that game. The existence of the Sylph and what she stood for—and the existence of Elizabeth Vesey—must surely be reckoned with in any such appraisal of the Bluestocking achievement.

*Western New Mexico University*

# "Rags of Mortality": Negotiating the Body in the Bluestocking Letters

Elizabeth Carter's poem "A Dialogue" (1741) records a spirited discussion between Body and Mind. Each has complaints: Body complains that Mind is so preoccupied that she pursues her mental pleasures with little regard for the needs of Body; Mind counters that her pursuits are often curtailed by the inconsiderate demands of Body. Although the poem gives voice to both sides of this difficult relationship, Carter's sympathies lie with Mind, whose crimes seem to be, if not necessarily less grievous in consequence, at least less vindictive and intentional. Body suffers from neglect, Mind from forcible control. And Mind will win, in the end, when Body will be condemned to decay, allowing Mind to "snap ... off [her] chains and fly freely away."[1] Within this poem, the body is represented as a kind of "other": distinguishable from, yet tied to, a self that is closely identified with the mind. Body is a demanding presence, concerned with material necessities such as food and sleep. Mind, a more ethereal presence, abandons Body to converse with "good friends in the stars" and finds herself "cramped and confined like a slave in a chain" by the corporeal mass that imprisons her.[2]

"A Dialogue" is firmly situated in a post-Cartesian world with a long tradition of philosophical thought that separates body from mind and pits the two entities against each other. Conventionally, mind has been the privileged term of this dualism, and body has been constructed as what must be transcended, disavowed, rejected. Carter's poem participates in this lengthy tradition by invoking the fantasy of transcendence. However, the poem offers a daring and radical challenge. Conventionally, this mind-body dualism is gendered: mind is masculine and body is feminine. "Woman" was typically relegated to the body and represented in opposition to the purely masculine province of mind; or bound to a

1. Elizabeth Carter, "A Dialogue," in Roger Lonsdale, ed., *Eighteenth-Century Women Poets* (Oxford, 1990), 168.
2. On the gender implications of Carter's poem, see Lisa A. Freeman, "'A Dialogue': Elizabeth Carter's Passion for the Female Mind," in Isobel Armstrong and Virginia Blain. eds., *Women's Poetry in the Enlightenment: The Making of a Canon, 1730–1820* (London, 1999), 50–63.

body that is less perfect because more frail, more unreliable than that of man.[3] One of the effects of this gendered dualism is that a life of the mind has been conventionally denied to women. For example, although the eighteenth century witnessed a growing interest in and debate about the education of women, assumptions of women's "natural" mental inferiority and "natural" maternal function persisted in contemporary discourses. Thus learned women were usually regarded with suspicion and often represented as cultural oddities.[4] In "A Dialogue," though, Carter reverses the familiar pattern of gender. In the domestic dispute in the poem, Mind is female while Body is likened to a petulant husband. Her poem explicitly challenges convention, asserting that women, too, can develop their intellectual capacities, can participate in the fantasy of corporeal transcendence.

The legacy of first generation Bluestockings Elizabeth Carter and Elizabeth Montagu demonstrates the practical application of Carter's poetic assertion. These women challenged contemporary attitudes and strictures to pursue scholarship.[5] The voluminous epistolary correspondence between Carter and Catherine Talbot, and Carter and Montagu, includes not only gossip and discussions of travel and politics but also numerous "conversations" about the scholarly work that absorbed them. Carter's translation of *Epictetus* (1758) began in response to

3.  There are several texts that provide particularly useful and succinct summaries of the history—from Plato, through Augustine, to Descartes—of this well-known Western dualism and its implications. See, for example: Genevieve Lloyd, *The Man of Reason: "Male" and "Female" in Western Philosophy* (London, 1984); Erica Harth, *Cartesian Women: Versions and Subversions of Rational Discourse in the Old Regime* (Ithaca, N.Y., 1992); and Susan Bordo, *Unbearable Weight: Feminism, Western Culture, and the Body* (Berkeley, Calif, 1993). See Elizabeth Grosz, *Volatile Bodies: Toward a Corporeal Feminism* (Bloomington, Ind., 1994), esp. for the implications of Western dualism for women. See also Theodore M. Brown, "Descartes, Dualism, and Psychosomatic Medicine," in W. F. Bynum, Roy Porter, and Michael Shepherd, eds., *The Anatomy of Madness: Essays in the History of Psychiatry*, 2 vols. (London, 1985), 1:40–62, for a discussion of the influence of Descartes on medicine.

4.  Eighteenth-century debates about women's education faced assumptions that women had "shallow minds incapable of 'intense and continued application' or of a 'close and comprehensive reasoning'"; Bridget Hill, *Eighteenth-Century Women: An Anthology* (London, 1984), 44. Bluestockings Hester Chapone (*Letters on the Improvement of the Mind, addressed to a Young Lady* [1773]) and Catharine Macaulay Graham (*Letters on Education* [1790]) engaged explicitly with these debates in extensive treatises on education. Chapone's took a conservative, conduct book–like approach, urging that education should prepare girls for their roles as wives and mothers. Macaulay's treatise, however, is an anomalous, radical piece advocating a redefinition of gender expectations.

5.  Kathryn Sutherland remarks on events that perhaps contributed to the intellectual passion of Elizabeth Montagu: Elizabeth Drake (Montagu's mother) may have been educated by the famous Bathsua Makin, author of *An Essay to Revive the Antient Education of Gentlewomen* (1673); and Elizabeth Elstob, an Anglo-Saxon scholar, was employed as a governess in the home of the duchess of Portland, a friend of Montagu's from her adolescence; Sutherland, "Writings on Education and Conduct: Arguments for Female Improvement," in Vivien Jones, ed., *Women and Literature in Britain, 1700–1800* (Cambridge, 2000), 25–45 at 30.

a request from Talbot, who then encouraged her and discussed the project with her at length by post. Similarly, while writing her *Essay On The Writings and Genius of Shakespear* (1769), Montagu argued and conferred with Carter by letter. The letters between these women create both friendship and intellectual community, recording the process of claiming the conventionally masculine province of mind; and thus, like Carter's poem, challenge the conventional gendering of the mind-body dualism. The correspondence, though, is more radical and more nuanced than the poem. Even as they claim a life of the mind for women, these letters explore and often validate the role of the body, undermining the very premise of the dualism and suggesting a more complex, even mysterious, partnership. "You bid me tell you," Carter writes to Elizabeth Vesey, "what neither I, nor any other mortal can tell. The manner in which soul and body is affected by each other is one of those impenetrable secrets with which, because it is impenetrable, we have no concern."[6] And, later, she explains to Montagu, "the effect of the union between body and spirit, must ever be unaccountable to all human researches. Perhaps they are different in every individual."[7] These excerpts stress the close relationship of body and mind, as does the correspondence as a whole, recording a struggle not so much to overcome the body as to balance embodiment with intellectual life.

Because both women suffered from chronic physical ailments (Montagu from digestive disorders and Carter migraine-like headaches), their bodies could not easily be ignored in daily life. Neither are they transcended in the epistolary representations of the life of the mind. Carter, for example, responds to Montagu, "You kindly bid me mention my health, which is, thank God, very well, except head-achs, rheumatisms, and sometimes little fevers, all which I consider as so many non-naturals, which there is no living without" (1:91, 5 September 1760). And the letters themselves illustrate not only the difficulties but also the rewards of *living with*. Carter's poem may suggest corporeal transcendence, but these epistolary selves are not represented as disembodied. Rather, they are complexly and intricately "embodied." My essay engages with this complexity to explore the rich mind-body dynamic in the correspondence. I begin by demonstrating that these bodies are, not surprisingly, often represented as is Body in Carter's poem— as irritating and constraining obstacles to intellectual pursuits. However, I suggest that the correspondence undermines this conventional dualism by evoking

6. *A Series of Letters between Mrs. Elizabeth Carter and Miss Catherine Talbot, from the year 1741 to 1770, To Which Are Added, Letters from Mrs. Elizabeth Carter to Mrs. Vesey, between the years 1763 and 1787*, ed. Montagu Pennington, 4 vols. (London, 1809), 4:101, 25 January 1774; cited henceforward in the text.
7. *Letters from Elizabeth Carter to Mrs. Montagu, between the years 1755 and 1800*, ed. Montagu Pennington, 3 vols. (1817; New York, 1973), 3:87–88, 19 September 1778.

a more fluid and nuanced relationship, both literal and metaphoric, between body and mind. At times, the presence of the body becomes a cooperative grounding force—a form of conscience—working with, not against, the mind. This cooperation becomes more intense during discussions about what were, for these women, morally problematic experiences of depression, where the suffering body becomes the guarantor of moral absolution. While it grounds and absolves, the body sometimes functions as a kind of co-conspirator, a willing scapegoat, that provides a certain degree of agency. The interconnection of body and mind is also vividly articulated when the body appears in these letters as a powerful metaphoric presence. Throughout the Bluestocking correspondence, I suggest, the body is represented literally as essential to the development of the mind/self and metaphorically as the medium that connects these women to one another.

## THE BODY AS ANTAGONIST

The letters exchanged between Carter and Montagu and with their other friends demonstrate particular interest in corporeal matters, especially physical health. Most of the letters between Carter and Montagu contain a report of the health of the sender and a query about that of the recipient. Often, they also include a plea not to sacrifice health to the indulgence of writing a letter. In 1765, for example, Carter begs Montagu, "Pray never write to me when there is the least danger of its hurting your health" (1:282, 14 October 1765). In making this request, Carter has apparently forgotten her vexation of five years earlier when she admonished Montagu:

> Surely, my dear Mrs. Montagu, it is quite an age since I heard from you, and my patience will hold out no longer. I find there is no end to wearying myself with conjectures whether this silence is occasioned by your not having recovered the sight of your eyes, or by your having lost the feeling of your heart. . . . You may urge, in excuse of giving me this solicitude, that I desired you not to write till you could do it with perfect ease. Very true: but then you might, at least, have sent me your kind love and service by the carrier, or the waggon, or any such other conveyance, as folks who cannot write written hand, make use of, to tell their friends that they are in good health, hoping they are the same. . . . I am sometimes in a fright about you, and sometimes in a tiff, but in either disposition, Your most affectionate, &c. (1:74–75, 2 February 1760)

Although it seems here that Carter would rather envision her friend ill than cooling in her affections, delayed correspondence often did signal illness and thus caused great concern to the waiting party. Carter writes to Talbot, "You cannot tell, dear Miss Talbot, how rejoiced I am to hear the good news of your recovery, unless you know how very sure I was you had been sick; for your long silence had made me certain of it" (1:273, 13 July 1748).[8]

The focus on health marks these correspondents as typical eighteenth-century letter writers. Dorothy and Roy Porter state that in this "golden age of diaries and letter-writing . . . health is prominent in both."[9] And this epistolary convention attests to the nature of the material experience of the body in the eighteenth century, which was, so often, the experience of illness. In his historical survey of illness and death over the last four hundred years, James Riley reports that much of the European population suffered a wide variety of diseases over the course of their lives, and many suffered repeated bouts of the same illness: "To live in Europe between 1600 and 1870 was to face a series of vivid and recurrent disease risks."[10] Childhood mortality was particularly high, as was maternal mortality—sometimes from difficult delivery but more often from post-delivery infection. Dorothy and Roy Porter claim that "being a fertile married woman in a pre-contraceptive age, when most married couples did not practise what Malthus called 'moral restraint,' was perhaps the highest-risk occupation of all."[11] If a woman survived both childhood and childbearing, her life expectancy

8. In relationships where circumstances and geographical distance typically meant that visits were limited and far between, and friendships were maintained, to a great extent, through the post, the letter was often the only guarantee of the health, even the continued existence, of the other party. When Catherine Talbot was dying, for example, she was unable to write to Carter herself. Although others kept Carter informed of Talbot's situation, it was the absence of letters in Talbot's hand that signaled the seriousness of her condition; see *Letters between Carter and Talbot,* 24 October 1769, 26 October 1769, 28 October 1769; 3:196–200. Talbot died in January 1770. And a few years earlier, Carter had written to Montagu about the silence of another friend: "I have for some time feared, from Madame de Blum's very long silence, that there was some melancholy alteration in her health. I had only waited till my return to Deal for a convenient opportunity of making some enquiry after her, but all enquiry is now unnecessary, for I yesterday received an account of her death from Monsieur de Blum, *le fils*" (1:299, 31 May 1766).

9. Dorothy Porter and Roy Porter, *In Sickness and in Health: The British Experience, 1650–1850* (New York, 1989), 12.

10. James Riley, *Sickness, Recovery, and Death: A History and Forecast of Ill Health* (London, 1989): "Although the feature most remarked upon of this panorama of risks has been its intensity—the probability of dying in an epidemic—the most remarkable feature of it appears, in the formulation offered here, to be the probability of being ill repeatedly. . . . the ordinary individual appears to have experienced both a continuing series of infectious diseases and the risk of concurrent infections." What surprises Riley is how many people survived these diseases over and over again; see pp. 112–14.

11. Dorothy Porter and Roy Porter, *Patient's Progress: Doctors and Doctoring in Eighteenth-Century England* (Oxford, 1989), 174; and Elizabeth Burton, *The Pageant of Georgian England* (New York, 1967).

was fairly long, but these longer lives were apparently punctuated by a series, often repetitive, of illnesses.[12]

The letters of Carter and Montagu record their sufferings with fleeting illness as well as their struggles with chronic conditions throughout their long lives. In a letter to Elizabeth Vesey, Carter comments on the pervasiveness of her headaches: "As every external remedy has failed, my mind has long been accustomed to submit quietly and cheerfully to that condition of health which seems to be inseparably connected with the principles of my constitution" (3:231, 6 December 1763). And a few years later, she cautions her friend, "do not be in any manner of concern about me. The head-ache you know belongs to me, as much as any thing external can" (3:309, 13 October 1766). Her letters repeatedly record the physical discomforts with which she is familiar. Similarly, in a letter to her husband, Montagu refers to her perpetual ill health by informing him, "I am so well in health, that I do not know myself, and I think I am a little like the humorous Lieutenant, that would run no hazards while he was well, though he was prodigal of life, when he had a pain in his side."[13] Throughout the correspondence, both women stress the prominence of ill health in their lives.

In many of their epistolary representations of illness, their bodies become the Body of "A Dialogue." Self is separated from body, which is distracting, irritating, or incapacitating; but the demands of the body claim the attention of mind/self: "I do not know what to say for my idleness last post," writes Montagu to her sister from Whitehall, "but indeed I was so oppressed by a cold, I could not disengage my mind from its attention to a disordered body, long enough to write a line" (1:121, 1740). In Montagu's apology, the similarities to the terms of Carter's poem are striking: the mind is responsible for writing—a kind of intellectual pursuit—but is prevented from this pleasant task by the need to attend to the body. Significantly, where Montagu blames the body for hampering the mind, Carter's chronic physical distemper was often blamed, by others, on a kind

12. See Riley, *Sickness, Recovery, and Death,* passim. Significantly, neither Elizabeth Carter nor Catherine Talbot married; Elizabeth Montagu married, but she bore only one child (John, "Punch"), who died while teething. Although Talbot died of cancer when she was just short of forty-nine, Montagu lived eighty years and Carter eighty-eight. Neither Carter nor Montagu suffered anything as serious as the cancer that killed Talbot; Montagu even managed to avoid the smallpox that marked her sister. She was unsuccessfully inoculated several times over her life and lived in perpetual fear of exposure; Carter was convinced that her friend must have contracted a minor form of smallpox (probably from inoculation) that provided her with immunity: "I should be more alarmed at your being in such infected air, if I had not long ago comforted myself with the persuasion that you have had this vile disorder, though I think you are perfectly right to keep out of the contagion" (*Letters from Carter to Montagu,* 3:108, 22 September 1783).

13. *The Letters of Mrs. Elizabeth Montagu, with Some of the Letters of Her Correspondents, 1720–1761,* 4 vols. (1809–13; New York, 1974), 3:169–70, 30 September 1751.

of neglect as she catered to her mind.[14] Montagu Pennington, Carter's nephew and rather sententious editor, attributes his aunt's ailments to study habits when young. He reports that she was a slow but determined scholar, "and her unwearied application injured her health, and probably laid the foundation of those frequent and severe head-achs, from which she was never afterwards wholly free." Pennington reports that her disciplined study schedule meant that she customarily rose very early (between four and five o'clock) and also retired very late, keeping herself awake to study with a combination of green tea, snuff, a wet towel around her head, and another wet cloth on her stomach. Pennington suggests that forcing herself to remain awake was "to the great injury of her health, for she was always very much inclined to sleep, slept soon, and very soundly, even in her chair."[15] In her biographical work on Montagu, Emily Climenson mentions Carter's "excruciating headaches," and recounts that "Lord Bath said that if she would drink less green tea, take less snuff, and not study so much, they would disappear."[16] Sylvia Myers has traced the first mention of her headaches to a letter from Carter's father when she was in London, "in which he says he has heard that she has been having headaches, and advises her not to study so hard."[17] Carter herself seems to have rejected this explanation for her persistent headaches, variously blaming overexertion in social settings, the weather, and a lack of exercise—ultimately, like Montagu, representing her mind as the victim of her head.

This representation of the body echoes the Body of Carter's poem. In "A Dialogue," poor Mind complains:

> I did but step out, on some weighty affairs,
> To visit, last night, my good friends in the stars,
> When, before I had got half as high as the moon,

14. In this, Carter is not alone. Lady Mary Wortley Montagu, for example, reports a discussion in which acquaintances of hers "fell into good-natured discourse of the ill consequences of too much application, and remembered how many apoplexies, gouts, and dropsies had happened amongst the hard students of their acquaintance"; *The Complete Letters of Lady Mary Wortley Montagu*, 3 vols., ed. Robert Halsband (Oxford, 1965–67), 3:217, 19 July 1759. In her midcentury poem "The Headache. To Aurelia," Mary Leapor represents her own headaches as sinister punishment for her poetry: "For camps and headaches are our due: / We suffer justly for our crimes, / For scandal you, and I for rhymes"; Lonsdale, *Eighteenth-Century Women Poets*, 195–97.
15. Montagu Pennington, *Memoirs of the Life of Mrs. Elizabeth Carter, with a New Edition of Her Poems; To Which are Added, Some Miscellaneous Essays in Prose, Together with Her Notes on the Bible, and Answers to Objections Concerning the Christian Religion*, 4th ed, 2 vols. (London, 1825), 9, 22.
16. Emily J. Climenson, *Elizabeth Montagu: The Queen of the Blue-Stockings: Her Correspondence from 1720 to 1761*, 2 vols. (London, 1906), 1:207.
17. Sylvia Harcstark Myers, *The Bluestocking Circle: Women, Friendship, and the Life of the Mind in Eighteenth-Century England* (Oxford, 1990), 58.

You despatched Pain and Languor to hurry me down;
*Vi & Armis* they seized me, in midst of my flight,
And shut me in caverns as dark as the night.

(Lines 23–28)

Similarly, throughout the correspondence, the body is often represented as a confining, petulant force, weighing down Carter's mental self and hindering Montagu's pleasures, both intellectual and social. Many of Carter's letters begin with an apology similar to this one, offered to Montagu: "I should before this, my dear friend, have answered your kind letter, had I not been absolutely disqualified by a bad fit of the headache. I find a much greater obstacle to writing from want of health, than from want of leisure" (3:82, 7 August 1778). Early in their friendship, Carter explains to Montagu that her aching head confines her to bed an average of two days per week (1:47, 20 June 1759), and although she finds this an inconvenience, she reports that she cannot control the influence her body has on her intellectual life: "I am too sensible of the mischievous consequence of being obliged so often to keep to my bed: but I cannot avoid it. I sometimes struggle out a day's head ach in great pain and inability of doing any thing: but the usual effect of this effort is being obliged to take to my bed the next, and having two bad days instead of one" (1:286–87, 3 November 1765). Repeatedly, Carter represents herself as the victim of an unpredictable, demanding body that frustrates her best intentions.

For Montagu, it is not so much her writing as her social converse that suffers because of the constraints imposed by her body. As a vivacious, energetic woman, known for the intellectual exchanges at her London parties and her extensive social life, Montagu found the indolence forced upon her by her body to be inconvenient and frustrating. During one period of ill health, Carter praises her for "submitting to the prescription of indolence. Indeed one can scarcely imagine how such an active spirit as yours can comply with such a regimen, unless Dr. Mousey [*sic*] has put you into a bottle hermetically sealed" (1:21, 13 January 1759). Later, Carter, who refused to blame her headaches on her own mental pursuits, cautions Montagu about the possible effects of mental exertion:

> If you were a sober economical gentlewoman . . . I should be much more inclined to lament the weakness of your eyes, than I am at present; as I believe it will prove a salutary restraint on those intellectual riots in which you would too naturally be hurried, and which might lavish away all the health which you have been acquiring during the course of your penance at Tunbridge. (2:150–51, 22 July 1772)

Sometimes, for Montagu, it is not ill health but merely the danger of ill health that necessitates the curbing of certain activities; Carter cautions her about over-activity and praises her for practicing restraint.[18] Montagu's body, not unlike her unpredictable and often irritating husband, is something to be soothed and humored. It is a kind of petulant companion to the self that compels compromise in the interests of domestic harmony and peace.

## A Mind-Body Partnership

That the body is often represented as a hindrance in the correspondence of Montagu and Carter is hardly surprising. What is surprising is that the body is sometimes represented quite otherwise. At times the relationship between body and mind does not appear as the antagonistic marriage of Carter's poem but rather as a cooperative companionship in which the body supports, enables, and even absolves the self, which is identified with the mind. Sometimes this body is a grounding force, acting as a kind of conscience that provides a welcome reasonableness and stability to the intemperate mind. From Bristol, for example, Carter writes, "An aching head is an excellent antidote against the extravagances of a giddy one; and by this security, in spite of all the infection of the Pump-room, and my very little care to prevent catching it, I remain as wise, and as sober, and as dull, as if I dwelt opposite to it, in some hermitage on the side of the rock" (*Letters from Carter to Montagu*, 1:46, 20 June 1759). Here, the physical head grounds the metaphorical head. Although Carter's letter registers, not without wit, a degree of disappointment regarding her sober state, it also implies that her wisdom results, to a certain degree, from the check her health provides on an inclination toward frivolousness and extravagance. In a similar vein, Carter suggests that illness might work as an antidote to outrageous behavior in the British Parliament. She asks:

> Do not you think it might tend very much to the quiet and good
> order of these nations, if many of the speakers in both Houses, had

---

18. See, for example, a letter of 14 November 1771: "I most highly applaud your resisting the evening society, which would have succeeded a fatiguing morning. I hope, *de tems en tems*, to be informed that you persevere in this laudable opposition to seduction, and then I shall flatter myself with the happiness of finding you in full possession of all that treasure of health, which you collected from the air and water of Tunbridge" (2:127); and another of 22 November 1775: "you have already begun to exhaust yourself with company. That society, to a certain degree, is good for your health and spirits, I believe, but it should be under strict regulations. If you would make it a part of your invitation to dinner, that all people are to go away at seven o'clock, or that if they stay longer, you would retire, all would be well; but if you exhaust your strength and spirits on them, you had better have travelled your thousand miles, and been out of their reach" (2:344).

such health as you and I have? I do not by this in any degree propose to make an exchange, as it is by no means clear whether it
would do any good to ourselves or the world, if we had such health
and strength as they have. (2:345, 22 November 1775)

Although Carter seems to insinuate that dubious health would provide a desir-
able grounding or sobering effect on members of Parliament, she does not embrace the idea of an exchange of roles, even in her fantasy. This reluctance possibly
registers modesty—good health would be wasted on her—however, it also implies that health and strength would not provide the necessary condition for the
good she already does do, intellectually, in the world. Her bodily infirmity con-
tributes to her mental nature, and not in the obvious negative ways.

The body grounds and it also, more seriously, absolves. Both Carter and
Talbot seem to have suffered from bouts of what today we would call depression, which they referred to as a "splenetick disposition" or as a particular condition of spirits—"languor of spirits," for example—"spirits" represented in
opposition to the body.[19] For Carter and Talbot, this state appears to have been
accompanied by a sense of shame and by the desire to hide it from others. Early
in their relationship Carter confesses to Montagu:

> [T]hough I am really much inclined to be pleased and amused, I
> have such a strange languor of spirits, and such a painful lassitude
> in endeavouring to exert them, as is not easy to be imagined by
> any one who has never experienced it. This is a disposition to which
> I have always been, in some degree, by fits, subject; and the events of
> last year have, I believe, greatly contributed to increase it. I write this
> account of myself to you, because I write only to you, for it is a secret
> with which very few people are to be entrusted, unless one would
> chuse to be thought whimsical or discontented. (1:39, 23 April 1759)

Carter's letter demonstrates the considerable trust placed in her relatively new
friendship with Montagu, and it is particularly poignant in its vulnerability.
Fifteen years earlier, she had to be coaxed to reveal her depressive tendency by
Talbot's assurance that she understood Carter's problem from her own experience: "it would be a great consolation to me, to know what had occasioned the
whimsical fit of spleen you complained of; . . . pray be charitable enough to gratify
my curiosity. I promise you I will receive it with true sisterly candour, as I am so

19. See *Letters between Talbot and Carter,* 1:52–53, 19 May 1744; *Letters from Carter to Montagu,* 1:38–40,
23 April 1759; see also *Carter to Montagu,* 1:21, 21 January 1759, where the distinction and connection is
made between spirits and corporeal health: "Indeed my health and spirits have been much more affected
than I have ever discovered."

great a sufferer in that way myself" (1:52–53, 10 May 1744). Talbot may empathize, but there is no guarantee that she will sympathize with Carter. Talbot's letter continues by explaining that she suffers her own depression "against [her] conscience," and she asserts, "I have no notion that any body can be seriously in the spleen; I think a very little serious reflection enough to set life and all its concerns in a very different light from that in which fancy places it upon every little vexation" (1:53, 10 May 1744).

The depressions that the two suffered were experienced and represented within the context of medical discourses that prevailed during the eighteenth century and that were particularly complex and contradictory, as the relationship between body and mind was increasingly represented by a model of nervous physiology rather than the circulation of the four humors. According to the humoral theories of the body, psyche and soma affected each other in a kind of fluid relationship. This interaction between mind and body was also a cornerstone of an evolving medical discourse influenced by Thomas Willis, who gave us "nerves," and George Cheyne, whose *English Malady* (1733) "identified the spleen, vapours, lowness of spirits, hypochondriacal and hysterical distempers as constituting the cluster of nervous diseases to which he believed the English were especially prone."[20] The nervous system was a new way of mapping the mind-body integration central to the older, holistic humoral theories, but it registered several decided changes. The most significant was that the mind gained a new primacy as the seat of physical well-being, a portal through which everything was channeled, often privileged as the causal factor in all illness. Because the mind could produce and cure various ills, "state of mind" became an essential component in maintaining good health.[21]

The Bluestocking correspondence both embraces and resists this evolving medical philosophy and physiology. The numerous discussions between the women about nerves and nervous constitutions demonstrate their awareness of and participation in this emerging medical discourse. Carter often discusses the effect of the weather on her "elasticity" and the adverse effect of the "damp" or "relaxing" weather on her "weak nerves." But the mind is just as likely to act on

20. W. F. Bynum, "The Nervous Patient in Eighteenth- and Nineteenth-Century Britain: The Psychiatric Origins of British Neurology," in *Anatomy of Madness*, 1:89–102 at 91. See also Robert Martensen, "The Transformation of Eve: Women's Bodies, Medicine and Culture in Early Modern Europe," in Roy Porter and Mikuláš Teich, eds., *Sexual Knowledge, Sexual Science* (Cambridge, 1994), 107–33.

21. G. S. Rousseau, "Nerves, Spirits, and Fibres: Towards Defining the Origins of Sensibility," *Studies in the Eighteenth Century*, no. 3, ed. R. F. Brissenden and J. C. Eade (Toronto, 1976), 137–57 at 155. Rousseau affirms that, "all diseases, not merely those considered hysterical and hypochondriacal, were eventually classified as 'nervous' and . . . internalised by persons of fashion as visible emblems of refinement and delicacy."

the body, in terms of the new role of nerves. When Carter's nephew was gravely
ill, for example, she reported to Montagu that "the danger of this poor little boy;
and the distress of his parents, you will easily imagine have hurt my nerves"
(1:209, 24 December 1763).

Carter in particular refuses to embrace the newer medical paradigm completely, although her letters are littered with the language of nervous physiology.
She often reconfigures popular medical discourse in order to avoid its moral implications. One of the possible consequences of the popular eighteenth-century
theory that the mind affected and even effected illness was that, as Dorothy and
Roy Porter remark, "every disease, every pain, had its meaning, and meanings typically had their moral."[22] Within the Bluestocking correspondence, the moral
implications of illness are particularly acute in the discussions between Carter
and Talbot regarding depression. In her exchanges with Talbot, Carter resists
popular nervous discourse, adamantly arguing for depression's somatic rather
than psychic origin. Talbot, on the other hand, seems to regard her depression as
a mental state that has undesirable consequences for the body. She laments to
Carter, "spirits that have any thing of delicacy are easily and strongly affected, and
influence the body so as to make it a very troublesome companion, and I know
nothing one would not do to avoid being nervous" (1:152, 21 June 1746).
Throughout their correspondence, Carter attempts to comfort her friend by arguing against the representation of depression as morally problematic. At one
point she admonishes, "but the low spiritedness, my dear Miss Talbot, of which
you complain, assures me you cannot be well, nor ever will be, while you have
the strange imagination, that a weak system of nerves is a moral defect, and to
be cured by reason and argument" (2:156, 14 February 1754).

Talbot remained unconvinced, and, almost a decade later, she wrote to
Carter, "I am convinced now that *bad nerves* (as one is pleased to call the indulgence of humour) are little short of a mortal sin. They disgrace one's best
principles, grieve one's best friends, and make one's whole being ungrateful" (3:2,
14 May 1762). Significantly, in her response to this letter, Carter refuses to engage
directly with the issue of whether melancholy is sinful. Rather, she insists that
Talbot's mental distress has a physical cause. Carter writes:

> My real intention was to make you judge more equitably of your-
> self, to remove the painful imagination that there was any thing
> voluntary in an inactivity, the mere effect of constitutional disor-
> der.... Your mind, my dear friend, has the dispositions of angelic
> natures: but your constitution has alas too much of the weakness

22.  Dorothy and Roy Porter, *In Sickness and in Health*, 72.

of frail mortality.... In this state of imperfection, the kind and extent of our duties must be regulated by the extent of our animal powers. To these, beyond a certain degree, no effort of resolution can make the least addition: and you might just as reasonably accuse yourself for not being able to fly. (3:6–7, 17 May 1762)

Carter repeatedly insists that Talbot's melancholy is physical at its root—resisting popular medical discourse by arguing that "nerves" are primarily of the body rather than the mind. This insistence suggests not that she disagrees with Talbot but rather that she agrees. They both view a primarily mental or spiritual depression as a moral lapse—perhaps a reflection of their Christian beliefs. Regardless of how fashionable affective nervous complaints may have become over the century, depression—the first step on the rocky road to despair and the turning away from God—has always been morally complex for the pious. And the letters between Carter and Talbot suggest that depression escapes censure only if it can be represented as somatic in origin.

On one level, this representation of the body does not seem very different from "Body" in Carter's poem, or the body that restricts Carter and Montagu by enveloping them in illness. In both cases, the body appears to control and constrain the mind/self. I suggest, however, that context and tone create the difference, nuanced though it may be. When it comes to depression, the body is not being blamed for hindering the self; rather, the self (Talbot) is being liberated, freed because the burden can be laid on the body. In 1773, for example, Carter writes to Montagu that the final years of Swift's life, "which in any other view, form so deplorable a part of the history of such a genius, appear in a comfortable light, when they are considered as merely being proofs that his aberrations from decency, and his neglect of, or want of attention to religion, did not proceed from a corrupted heart, or from scepticism; but from physical infirmity" (2:198, 12 June 1773). And, in reference to Elizabeth Vesey, whose behavior was becoming more erratic and disturbing as she aged, Carter writes to Montagu that "much allowance is due where the mind is weakened by bodily disorders" (3:279, 30 August 1787). In these cases, moral judgment is suspended because of the somatic scapegoat, and the body provides a kind of moral absolution that cannot be granted to the mind alone.

## The Body as Conspirator

Often, in the correspondence, the body also appears in a more active or potentially active role than that of grounding or absolving. It functions as an ally, enabling the choice of pleasurable pursuits and providing a way around the socially prescribed duties and functions that must have structured a very great proportion of these women's lives. Once she married, Montagu's life was largely dominated by her husband, although she did become fairly adept at manipulating him for her own purposes. Similarly, Elizabeth Carter's first duty was to her father; both during his life and after his death she took all of her family responsibilities seriously, tutoring one nephew for Oxford and hosting the visits of various other relations. The correspondence reveals that the prescribed duties of these women often took considerable energy, and in one of her letters Carter cautions the weary Montagu, "do not harass your health by more business and engagements than your reason, not your imagination, pronounces to be necessary. Take notice, as a good woman at whom I ungraciously laughed, used to say to me, that you are flesh and blood, and not iron and steel" (1:375, 25 November 1767). Significantly, this flesh and blood is frequently represented as a morally and socially acceptable excuse for pursuing one's own pleasures. As a young married woman, Montagu yearned for the society and intellectual stimulation of Tunbridge Wells. Unfortunately, her husband was not fond of the place and preferred to stay at home. Montagu explains her difficulty to her cousin Mr. West:

> You cannot imagine I should not be glad to come to Tunbridge, where I have always improved my stock of health, and have acquired such valuable friends, . . . but Mr. Montagu is happier here. . . . My constitution is not so strong, that it would not receive benefit by the waters, but I cannot say I am ill, and must content myself with the advantages of air and exercise which this situation affords. (3:309, 13 July 1755?)

Montagu's letter almost laments the fact that she is not unwell enough to warrant a visit that was against her husband's desires. His wishes come first, but the passage makes it clear that if she were ill, her body would provide the necessary justification for satisfying her wishes.

At times this corporeal potential is realized, and, in fact, pursuit of health did on many occasions afford Montagu the intellectual society of Tunbridge Wells. Similarly, although Carter's headaches most often frustrated her attempt to write letters, sometimes, particularly in her younger years, they provided the excuse she needed to take the time to write.

> I write to you, dear Miss Talbot, to the sound of a fiddle: not that I am dancing, but within the sound of people who are. All the world is gone to the assembly, and I am at least as well amused at home in bed with the head-ache, regaling myself with balm and lavender, and regaling myself still more with the thoughts of how

much happier I am with the head-ache while my friends are at the assembly, than I should be if I were at the assembly, and they at home in bed. (2:339, 30 June 1760)

The headache that precludes submitting to the rigors of society does not necessarily interfere with intellectual pursuits; and it may facilitate the creation of an epistolary intellectual community. On one occasion she writes to Talbot, "A fit of the head-ache furnishes me for a plea to stay at home alone, and as talking is a mighty good remedy, I am going to chat with you the whole afternoon without interruption, a circumstance very rare in this racketing place" (1:245, 20 January 1748). Here, the headache that is often said to curtail correspondence actually enables her writing. It provides time and opportunity in an otherwise hectic life filled with social obligations.

The illness of the body also affords an acceptable excuse for leaving things undone. Although there is a fine line between the body as hindrance and the body as excuse, a distinction is made by the Bluestockings themselves in the representation of their bodies. Montagu, for example, bemoans the fact that she cannot plead a physical excuse for not having written to Mr. West. She laments, "I am so ashamed that I cannot plead a broken arm, or some terrible disease or unhappy disaster, as the reason of my not thanking you for the favour of your last kind and obliging letter, that I hardly rejoice in the perfect health I am in" (3:315, 27 July 1755). Later, however, in a particularly colorful passage, Montagu can and does claim moral clemency based on the illness of her body:

> I should make some apology for not having answered your letter, if I did not consider that an invalid is not a moral and accountable agent. It is a poor animal that has not ease enough to sleep, nor spirits enough to be awake, but with eyes half shut, half open, passes its time in a situation of mind between thought and delerium, to which the polite give the name of reverie. . . . In the order of beings it . . . ranks next to a creature you will find in my friend Mr. Stillingfleet's book, under the name of *Sloth*, which he represents to be without any quality that could make it loved, feared, or desired, but by certain piteous tones it moves compassion, and makes every one avoid hurting it: you may be assured that I am ready to claim all the privileges of my sister Sloth. (4:215–16, n.d.)

Montagu's representation echoes the discussion of depression between Carter and Talbot. The body provides an amnesty, functioning as a kind of essential scapegoat, guaranteeing forgiveness from others and ensuring moral absolution.

As in the discussion of depression, the body in these examples is not, in it-self, markedly different from Body in Carter's poem. It is ill, or might become ill; it is tired; it is in pain. What distinguishes it from the rather vengeful Body that sends "pain and languor" to bring Mind back to her rightful place, though, is the variety of meanings assigned by the writers in their epistolary representations. Assigning meaning to the body gives these women a degree of agency within their letters (and perhaps within their lives). Carter and Montagu are not only vic-tims of their bodies but also agents because of them. Carter resists the explana-tions others provide for her headaches, but she also resists consistency in the meanings she herself assigns. She determines whether the headache is caused by atmosphere or activity, and she determines whether the headache has prevented or enabled her. Similarly, Montagu regards her illnesses, variously, as inconve-nient, as liberating, or as an acceptable excuse. Agency for these women rests in their control over the representation of illness. The correspondence situates them as the autonomous arbiters of the significance of their bodies, providing the con-text and owning the meaning.

## THE BODY AS METAPHOR

The mind-body dualism is complicated not only through literal representations in this correspondence but also through metaphor, where intimate physical con-nection evokes the passion of intellectual communion, and body and mind are not separated but intertwined. In the Huntington Library's Montagu Collection, there is a letter from Montagu to Carter that is breathtaking in its intensity and vulnerability and in the power of the bodily metaphor so vividly described. Not surprisingly, this letter is not published in Matthew Montagu's collection of his aunt's letters, nor is it mentioned in Emily Climenson's edition. It is perhaps surprising that Matthew preserved this letter at all or that sections of it did not fall victim to his censoring pen—the brown ink that makes it impossible to read certain words and sentences in a number of the other letters. Perhaps, though, it is only in the wake of late-twentieth-century scholarship that we have a frame-work allowing us to be stunned by this letter, with its eroticism and its maternity, in which breast milk represents the complex relationship between Montagu and Carter.[23]

---

23. Elizabeth Mavor's *The Ladies of Llangollen* (London, 1971); Lillian Faderman's *Surpassing the Love of Men: Romantic Friendship and Love between Women from the Renaissance to the Present* (New York, 1981); and Emma Donoghue's *Passions between Women: British Lesbian Culture, 1668–1801* (New York, 1993), among other works, have drawn our attention to a number of intense and passionate relationships between women in the eighteenth century.

The letter is dated 17 February 1759, but a note supplied by Sylvia Myers in the manuscript folder suggests that the letter is misdated, in fact being a response to Carter's letter of 13 March 1759. Carter and Montagu met in late 1757 or early 1758—their friendship was fairly new—and from the letters it seems that they had recently spent a significant amount of time together in London, Carter's visit occasioned by the illness of Talbot. Carter left London at the beginning of March to journey to Bristol with Talbot and her mother. There they remained until the following September. On 13 March 1759, Carter wrote to Montagu from Newbury: "It seems an immense time, since I have heard any thing of you my dear Mrs. Montagu; after being accustomed to the expectation of seeing you every day. . . . there are some hours in which I feel strangely vacant, at finding I know no more about you, than if I was in another planet. If you are at all sensible, how much I have set my heart upon finding a letter from you when I get to Bristol, I am sure you have too much good nature to disappoint me" (1:26–27). According to Myers, Carter was not disappointed, but whereas Carter simply declares her longing for Montagu's company—"I longed for you extremely the other night at Reading, to ramble by moonlight amongst the ruins of an old abbey"—Montagu's letter represents longing with physical metaphor. It is worth quoting in its entirety:

> Dear Madam: I have ever had great compassion for infants at the period of their weaning, it is their first taste of regret and so perhaps may be more lively than after they are used and accustom'd to the breaking off agreable habits; but then poor things they can whimper, cry, be peevish, thrust away with indignation the spoonfulls of tasteless pap that are offered to them in lieu of the soft nectar they had fed on, but we older children who have stronger passions and more discerning palates must not indulge complaints but be placid in disappointment and when our nectar'd bowl is taken from us must bow and simper over any tasteless or nauseous draught that is given to us; so our external manner [is] fashion'd but the economy within is mightily discomposed by this same weaning. I have not yet been able to reconcile myself to your departure. Twenty people have occupied the chair you used to sit in, they have offered me very good bread and milk, some have put sugar into it but I had no stomach to it; I was in hopes time would reconcile me to vulgar fare but on the contrary I grew more discontented and more impatient; you think perhaps you have been superlatively generous in writing to me twice, but your liberality has not furnish'd more than a base subsistence. I felt such an impatience for a

letter yesterday that if it had not arrived I really believe I should have whimpered. I think I could have justified myself if I had, how can my grief be childish when it is all that is not childish in me that weeps for the absence of Miss Carter! (MO 3024)[24]

Here, Montagu represents herself as a child, confronted with the intense pain and frustration of being weaned from Carter, who does not merely have the breast; rather, she is the breast that is now lost to her friend.

This letter exhibits a tangible, almost unbearable physical desire. Its eroticism derives in part from the intensity of the detailed imagery and in part from the structure of the passage. After invoking the metaphor of weaning to describe Carter's departure, Montagu makes a distinction between a child, who can act out the pain and the anger and herself—with stronger passions that must be repressed. Her writing enacts this repression by moving away from the image, focusing on her adult self and providing a rational description—almost a report—of the number of people who have been to visit her. The "bread and milk" contains the echo of the earlier image, but the passage as a whole seems to be moving away from it. Suddenly, though, at the end of the passage, the two images are brought together again. The intensity of the weaning experience is refreshed with the repetition of the word "whimpered," and it merges with the "stronger passions" and the intensity of "all that is not childish in me." The result is that the powerful image of a hungering child fuses with the image of the bereft thirty-eight-year-old woman, whose yearning becomes both primal and erotic.

The power of this image captures the initial passion and excitement of the growing intimacy between Montagu and Carter, representing not only physical desire but also intellectual yearning. The first letter we have from Montagu to Carter notes the importance of intelligent converse to their relationship. Montagu writes:

I can perfectly understand why you were afraid of me last year, and I will tell you, for you won't tell me; perhaps, you have not told yourself; you had heard I set up for a wit, and people of real merit and sense hate to converse with witlings; as rich merchant-ships dread to engage with privateers: they may receive damage and can get nothing but dry blows. I am happy you have found out I am not to be feared; I am afraid I must improve myself much before you will find I am to be loved. If you will give affection for affection "tout simple," I shall get it from you, and even if you won't part with it without other good qualities, I hope to get them of

24. Letters from the Montagu Collection in the Huntington Library are cited in the text by manuscript number.

you, if you will continue to me the happiness and advantage of your conversation. (4:75–76, 6 June 1758)

It is conversation, and particularly the exchange of ideas, that draws Montagu to Carter, and their letters provide a space for discussions about history, literature, politics, and about Carter's recently published *Epictetus* and Montagu's upcoming publication of her *Essay on Shakespear*. In fact, Montagu's admiration for Carter's translation of *Epictetus* probably inspired her to establish a connection. Elizabeth Eger comments that "Montagu and Carter were proud of each other's works.... As authors of moral philosophy and Shakespeare criticism, Carter and Montagu shared the experience of making successful incursions into spheres still dominated by men, and they relied on each other's support and friendship in a world still hostile to learned women."[25] The intensity of their intimate relationship depended on the intellectual stimulation they provided for each other, and when they fantasized in their correspondence it was often about conversation. Early in their friendship, Carter admits to "pleasing [herself] in imaginary conversations with [Montagu]" (1:12, 1 November 1758). A few months later, she dreams, "instead of conversing at the distance of a hundred miles, you and I should have been sitting *tête-a-tête*, and we should have been the quietest, prettiest, properest company for each other imaginable.... What a number of subjects should we have discussed" (1:32–33, 31 March 1759). And ten years later, Montagu claims, "My imagination without wing or broom stick off mounts aloft, rises into ye Regions of pure space, and without lett or impediment bears me to your fireside, where you can set me in your easy chair, and we talk and reason, as angel Host and guest Aetherial should do, of high and important matters" (MO 3258, 10 October 1769). Here, Montagu's representation of ethereal conversation echoes Carter's "Mind," stepping out to converse with the stars, marking the importance of the intimacy created by mental exchange. Montagu's early letter to Carter recognizes and foreshadows this significance, and she emphasizes its importance by using the body as metaphor.

Thus, the early erotic passage signals intense physical longing, but that bodily desire also represents the intellectual conversation craved by Montagu. Carter's conversation is compared to a nectar, delicious and nourishing for Montagu— possibly the "good qualities" Montagu hoped to draw from Carter and her conversation. In this bleak vision of deprivation, however, the breast disappears, and Montagu is forced to try to sate herself with the unappetizing conversation of those who now occupy Carter's chair. Spoken conversation merges with written

---

25. *Bluestocking Feminism: Writings of the Bluestocking Circle, 1738–1790,* gen. ed. Gary Kelly, 6 vols. (London, 1999), vol. 1; *Elizabeth Montagu*, ed. Elizabeth Eger (London, 1999), lx.

when Montagu grudgingly admits to having received two letters from Carter; however, she protests that these letters provide barely enough nourishment for survival. In Montagu's letter, ideas become breast milk, and their absence becomes physical starvation. The complexity of this passage—the blurring of the maternal and the erotic, of the adult and the child—and its raw emotional intensity show the importance of the intellectual relationship between these two women, and the body becomes a powerful metaphor for conversation and correspondence—for connection of a noncorporeal nature.

## NEGOTIATING THE BODY

In 1761, after Carter had spent seven weeks of the summer with Montagu, Montagu wrote to her, responding to letters in which she wrote about the pain of separation:

> How much I felt your kind disposition to turn back when you were on the stairs, I cannot express to you in words; there started a tear on reading that paragraph which declared the sentiment better. Words serve well for common occasions, but there are so many on which they cannot explain the movements of the heart, and the delicate feelings of the soul, that in a state of natural religion only, it would have helped to have convinced me of our being to exist in another life, in which we should not use an inadequate interpreter of our thoughts, as language is. Thought is of the soul, language belongs to body; we shall leave it in the grave with our other rags of mortality. (4:362–63, 6 September 1761)

By linking pure thought with soul (true self) and envisioning their eventual escape from body and language—these "rags of mortality"—Montagu's passage invokes the fantasy of corporeal transcendence. It echoes Carter's poem, and like it alludes to a long-standing dualistic heritage. However, Montagu's two sides are not antagonistic. Words, Montagu suggests, are necessary—they interpret, if inadequately—making pure thought intelligible. This passage is particularly poignant because it recognizes both that language is limited and that there is no alternative to it. By analogy, then, soul/mind may transcend the body after death, but until that point the body is necessary—as essential to the existence of the soul during its mortal tenure as language is to sustain communication and connection between minds. While the fantasy of transcendence is evident in this letter, the relationship between body and mind is more like that between thought and language—imperfect, but cooperative.

Montagu's analogy between body and language can be extended and complicated to encompass the letters upon which the friendships between these women depended. A letter communicates the presence of the writer just as language communicates thought, and body does soul. It is in some ways doubly limited because it is both constructed of language and marked by the body of the sender. Letters are intimately physical documents, an observation perhaps most applicable to handwritten letters, where the blank paper becomes, when covered with words, etched by the particulars of its writer. It is not only the words themselves but also the physical process of writing that stamps each letter with corporeal traces. In the Huntington collection, for example, Montagu's strong, relatively clear handwriting changes during illness and becomes more cramped, more difficult to read, as she ages and as her eyesight fades.

In a number of Carter's letters, the physical impact on the epistolary document is linguistically recorded. When her missives are interrupted by illness, letters often foreground the interruption: "I had begun a letter to you, my dear friend, last week," she writes to Montagu, "but my head prevented me from going on" (1:293, 25 December 1765). On another occasion she reports, "I have for this last ten days been too ill to walk, or almost to do any thing, (and this must account for this letter having been begun these four days)" (2:86, 3 October 1770). In these examples, the process of the writing parallels the condition of Carter's body. The letter remains suspended, like the body of the writer, waiting for the return to health. "Three days has this letter laid in my drawer, unfinished, so ill have I been," Carter writes to Montagu in December 1768 (2:15), and her description equates the poor, insufficient letter, languishing in the drawer, with Carter languishing in bed. In another letter, Carter provides a graphic example of the "writing-to-the-moment" technique so popular in eighteenth-century novels. She apologizes to Montagu for the quality of her penmanship, asserting, "I believe you will find it difficult to make out this scrawl, as I have been let blood in the midst of it" (1:307, 29 June 1766). Here, Carter's letter becomes a kind of body double, affected, like Carter's body itself, by the experience of bloodletting. The letter does not merely describe the body; rather it becomes a kind of partial textual embodiment, eventually cradled in the hands of the reader. As Montagu's erotic "weaning" passage makes clear, the letter is an inadequate substitute for the presence of the writer. However, like language and body—which Montagu suggests are imperfect but essential to mortal existence—and marked by both, the letter was essential to the intellectual relationships between the Bluestocking women.

Montagu's description of the relationship between thought and language, soul and body encapsulates the complex and nuanced relationship between body and mind expressed throughout her correspondence with Carter and Carter's with Talbot. In Carter's poem, claiming a life of the mind for women involves inverting the conventional dualistic paradigm and devolving the burden of the body onto an "other" who functions like a confining, constraining, childish, and complaining husband; however, the epistolary relationship between these women suggests another kind of relationship between body and mind. Their letters suggest that claiming the life of the mind for women often means fighting against or succumbing to the heavy, confining chains of corporeal existence that hinder intellectual pursuits. But they also suggest that transcendence over the burdensome body is not the only way to claim a life of the mind. When the body is represented as conscience, moral absolution, excuse, and enabler, it liberates the mind not despite but because of the connection between them. When it is invoked as an erotic metaphor, it makes visible the intensity of the intellectual communion between Montagu and Carter; and when it becomes part of Montagu's analogy, the body interprets, translates, speaks. Body and language are united as essential to communication, to existence itself. The references in the correspondence to the physical letters themselves also mark the significance of the body. The letter is intimately connected to the body of the sender, and, because so much of the intellectual communication and friendship between these women was conducted through correspondence, the letter—and by metaphorical analogy the body—becomes the condition for the very existence of the intellectual relationships between them. While Carter's poem offers a radical challenge to the conventional gendering of this key Western dualism, the Bluestocking correspondence challenges the underlying premise of that dualism. According to Montagu, human communication, imperfect though it is, requires that thought be embodied in language. Similarly, claiming a life of the mind for women, these letters suggest, requires not freedom from or transcendence over, but a constant process of shifting negotiation with, the body.

*University of Prince Edward Island*

# Bluestocking Sapphism and the Economies of Desire

## Susan S. Lanser

**W**ere the Bluestockings queer?" So asks Celia Easton in a compelling essay on Elizabeth Carter's poems of "Uranian friendship" that is less provocative and more nuanced than its title might indicate.[1] While my title poses the question in tamer terms, there are good reasons for Easton's challenging rhetoric. For even as female friendships are celebrated as a sine qua non of Bluestocking society, Bluestocking propriety has continued to circumscribe scholarly interpretations of those friendships in terms not only of behavior but of desire. In the one scholarly book devoted exclusively to the Bluestocking circle, Sylvia Myers sets "blue" and "lesbian" explicitly at odds, arguing that Bluestocking friendships were never erotic and that to suggest otherwise "lead[s] to some serious distortions about friendships among women in general, and the Bluestockings in particular."[2]

It is no wonder that Celia Easton chose to "queer" this conversation: as concepts with very different investments, "Bluestocking" and "lesbian" figure in the scholarly imagination as a rather unnatural coupling. It will be my project here to scrutinize both terms, to ask why ink has been spilled to keep them separate, and to suggest ways of considering their possible intersections by exploring the economies—that is, the management, the restrained or careful usage, the production, arrangement, and distribution—of Bluestocking desire. I will take for my Bluestocking circle five closely connected women writers usually identified with the group—Elizabeth Robinson Montagu, Elizabeth Carter,

---

1. See Celia Easton, "Were the Bluestockings Queer? Elizabeth Carter's Uranian Friendships," *The Age of Johnson* 9 (1998): 257–94.
2. Sylvia Harcstark Myers, *The Bluestocking Circle: Women, Friendship, and the Life of the Mind in Eighteenth-Century England* (Oxford, 1990), 18. Myers is by no means alone in objecting to characterizations of Bluestocking women as homoerotic; several other scholars, including Betty Rizzo and Rhoda Zuk, have objected to such suggestions, especially as they are formulated in Lillian Faderman's *Surpassing the Love of Men: Romantic Friendship and Love between Women from the Renaissance to the Present* (New York, 1981). See Rizzo, *Companions without Vows: Relationships among Eighteenth-Century British Women* (Athens, Ga., 1994); and Rhoda Zuk, in the introduction to Catherine Talbot in vol. 3 of *Bluestocking Feminism: Writings of the Bluestocking Circle, 1738–1785*, gen. ed. Gary Kelly, 6 vols. (London, 1999).

Catherine Talbot, Hester Mulso Chapone, and Sarah Robinson Scott—but the question of who counts as a Bluestocking is also part of my concern.

For of course what we call the "Bluestocking Circle" has no definitive membership. In its narrowest usage, the term was already applied retrospectively if not defensively, signifying a coalition of femininity, philanthropy, Anglican piety, English propriety, and intellectual pursuit, all integrated into a public identity that could promote women's participation in literary culture as decorous, salutary, and safe. Hannah More put it well when she averred, in a passage explicitly mentioning Carter and Montagu, that "good matronic gentlewomen" give "no offence, / *When* female virtue joins with female sense."[3] Viewed in this light, Bluestocking feminism was also a project of constraint; one can guess that it wasn't easy being Blue.

It still may not be easy being Blue, for it is difficult to know where the Bluestockings' own self-fashioning ends and where the historical construction of them begins. I want to propose that scholarly decisions about who is true Blue have been somewhat arbitrary and somewhat circular: it may not be simply that the Blues behaved in a certain manner but that those who behaved (or were perceived to behave) in a certain manner got to be Blue. Indeed, if we look at the range and number of intellectual English women active between 1740 and 1780, we might well think the label rather narrowly applied. Is Charlotte Lennox omitted from the Blues because she wrote for money or because she was a protégée of Johnson rather than Montagu?[4] What distinctions of genre, class, or situation may have excluded Sarah Fielding? And when Myers says that "to be a Bluestocking meant to be an impeccable member of an intellectual community which included both men and women,"[5] is it only impeccability, or is it also heterosociability, that is at stake?

"Bluestocking," in short, may be as much a screen in the twentieth century as it was a shield in the eighteenth. For whether from scholarly identification with our objects of inquiry, reverence for their public images, or the need to resist the denigration of learned women that has continued through the years, scholarly discussions of Bluestockings have dwelled little on questions of desire. As if replicating the body-mind conflict of Elizabeth Carter's "A Dialogue," Blue

---

3.   Hannah More, "Epilogue" to *The Search after Happiness: A Pastoral Drama* (London, 1796), 57; emphasis added. Although the play itself was first published in 1773, the epilogue did not appear until the third (1796) edition.

4.   In Janet Todd's *Dictionary of British and American Women Writers, 1660–1800* (Totowa, N.J., and London, 1985), Katherine Shevelow notes that Lennox was "not part of female literary circles" (p. 197).

5.   Myers, *Bluestocking Circle,* 11.

scholarship has tended to let mind conquer body, inscribing desire mostly in the negative: as renunciation (for example, when Myers describes Catherine Talbot giving up young George Berkeley and coping with her loss, or as control (for example, when Betty Rizzo explores Elizabeth Montagu's attempts to maneuver a marriage between her nephew and Dorothea Gregory as a way of hanging on to Gregory).[6]

A scholarly investment in Bluestocking proprieties may help to explain the vehemence of scholars such as Myers toward any suggestion that Bluestockings might have experienced—or, worse, enacted—same-sex desire. In a language riddled with misprisions, Myers insists that Bluestocking friendships "were neither passionate nor exclusive," not "erotic attachments" but "stable, supportive relationships." Turning modern fictions into eighteenth-century facts, Myers implies that the Blues could not be lesbians because lesbians "exclude themselves from friendships with men."[7] With similarly skewed assumptions Elizabeth Mavor, faced with the intimate letters of Carter and Talbot, links lesbianism to possessiveness or at least to monogamy: since Carter was a flirt and Talbot had other friendships, says Mavor, their relationship is merely "*pseudo*-sexual coquetry."[8] And some scholars have argued that if language between women was overtly passionate in the eighteenth century, that language could not also have held an erotic charge. But as I have written elsewhere, class politics worked to purify passionate language, and the fact that not all friends used it underscores its distinctive potency.[9] In mid-eighteenth-century England, a time when sexualities that were coming to be recognizable as modern (*mutatis mutandis*) had begun to coalesce, a fine line of perception separated chaste female intimacies from suspicious liaisons, and proprieties of class and gender helped to keep female friendships on the safe side of the line. I submit that scholarship has sometimes also toed this line, accepting the period's public fictions for private truths.

The private truths are nonetheless elusive, and I am not suggesting that sexual scandals lurk beneath the Blue line. Rather, I want to ask that we broaden our sense of the erotic, and hence also of what I am calling the *sapphic*, beyond explicit sexual acts or even overtly enunciated sexual wishes to encompass desires and penchants that give primacy—even momentary primacy—to same-sex

---

6.   Ibid., 113–17; Rizzo, *Companions without Vows,* chap. 6, 112–41.
7    Myers, *Bluestocking Circle,* 76, 18.
8.   Elizabeth Mavor, *The Ladies of Llangollen* (Harmondsworth, England, 1971), 87.
9.   See Susan S. Lanser, "Befriending the Body: Female Intimacies as Class Acts," *Eighteenth-Century Studies* 32 (1998–99): 179–98.

bonds through words and practices amenable to an erotic rendering.[10] Gary Kelly sensibly reminds us that the intimate relationship between Sarah Scott and Barbara Montagu was "recognized as such by those who knew them well," that "there is no unequivocal evidence of a sexual dimension to the relationship," but that this "lack" of evidence "in itself proves nothing either way."[11] I'd like to take this important intervention one step further by suggesting that observers lack "unequivocal evidence of a sexual dimension" to most relationships and that in the absence of proof, we tend to surmise a sexual dimension in male-female intimacies and to assume the absence of one in same-sex bonds. Moreover, sexual behavior does not provide reliable evidence of sexual orientation or desire. Particularly where marriage is a compulsory institution, "unequivocal evidence" of sex proves neither a "relationship" nor the sexuality of either participant and says virtually nothing about female desire.

Yet because an inequitable burden of proof has rested on historians of the homoerotic, the study of lesbian and gay sexualities has been, as Martha Vicinus observes, "excessively concerned with knowing-for-sure," insisting on "evidence of sexual consummation, whereas heterosexuality is confirmed through a variety of diverse social formations."[12] Although we may safely guess that we "know for sure" in the single case of Anne Lister, we are unlikely to find many other women of the eighteenth and nineteenth centuries whose letters or diaries are equally frank; Lister herself wrote the most revealing of her diary entries in code.[13] Eleanor Butler and Sarah Ponsonby, the "Ladies of Llangollen" who eloped to Wales and openly proclaimed themselves a loving couple, would never have

---

10. I am using the term "sapphic" to designate female-female attractions, orientations, desires, and behaviors as these are represented or configured in relation to eighteenth-century gentlewomen. My research suggests that certain social formations of female same-sex affiliation become textually visible in the eighteenth century in ways that distinguish them from both the early modern "homoerotic" and late modern "lesbian" formations. While no single word can accommodate the inchoate representations of female homoeroticism in the eighteenth century, the fact that the words "sapphism" and "sapphic(k)" are deployed with some frequency in the middle and later eighteenth century, but very little before that time, gives some basis for my imperfect choice of terms. That I have seen no instances of its use to describe women below the gentry class underscores the class-specific nature of my inquiry.

11. Gary Kelly, introduction to vol. 5 of *Bluestocking Feminism*, xii.

12 Martha Vicinus, "Lesbian History: All Theory and No Facts or All Facts and No Theory," *Radical History Review* 60 (1994): 57–75 at 57, 59.

13. Halifax gentrywoman Anne Lister kept voluminous diaries recording a lifelong exclusive same-sex orientation enacted in sexual relationships with several women. Excerpts from the diaries can be found in *I Know My Own Heart: The Diaries of Anne Lister, 1791–1840*, ed. Helena Whitbread (London, 1988; New York, 1991); *No Priest But Love: The Journals of Anne Lister from 1824–1826*, ed. Helena Whitbread (New York, 1992); and Jill Liddington, *Female Fortune: Land, Gender, and Authority: The Anne Lister Diaries and Other Writings, 1833–36* (London, 1998). Of these three, only Liddington's volume distinguishes between the coded and uncoded sections of Lister's diaries.

declared themselves sexual partners and indeed may not have been, but their acknowledged lifetime of intimacy in a shared bed also reminds us that what counts as sex and what counts as sapphism are questions that scholars need to continue pondering. For by no stretch would it make sense to consider Butler and Ponsonby either heterosexual or undesiring given the fact that they brooked rejection and penury to live together and stay together as passionately united partners until death. Their life is clearly a (class-based) *social formation* built around same-sex desire, and the term "gentry sapphists" that I have elsewhere applied to them (in "Befriending the Body") honors the primacy not of bedroom behavior but of a life organized, against the grain of social and familial injunctions, around that governing same-sex interest.

If we stop seeking sex acts and examine the formations within which women's desires were expressed, restrained, and managed, we may open different dimensions of Bluestocking lives and works. Such an inquiry would begin, as Vicinus encourages, by assuming a range of sexualities in any woman rather than taking a heterosexual starting point. It is that heterosexual departure point, for example, that compels us to explain *away* Elizabeth Carter's refusal to marry as motivated by her desire to write and study rather than asking whether her desires ever seemed oriented toward men. The difference is more than trivial; it asks us whether (feminist) *ideas* have governed our biographical constructions of literary women where (sexual) *feelings* might be equally relevant.

❧ ❧

What, to adapt a phrase of Jacques Lacan, are the *addresses* of Bluestocking desires? How do the Blues constitute their lives and writings in relation to such desires? How do they approach, restrain, deploy, displace—in short, manage— erotic longings and interests? For even if Myers is right that "as respectable women . . . committed to virtue and chastity, the Bluestockings resisted the intrusion of eroticism into both their male and female friendships,"[14] we might want to know which "intrusions" they felt compelled to resist or perhaps to accommodate. Ironically, given the social proprieties governing male-female relations for gentlewomen of the period, we may be able to learn more about Bluestocking sapphism than about Bluestocking desires for men. This difference, within an already uneven and censored written record, must temper any claims about Bluestocking desires, including those I am about to suggest.

---

14. Myers, *Bluestocking Circle*, 17.

But if we begin as Vicinus proposes by considering a range of erotic possibilities in the five women of my Bluestocking circle, then I might agree with Celia Easton's implication that the Blues were rather a queer lot, all the more if we set them against the "ordinary" women of their class featured, say, in Amanda Vickery's *The Gentlemen's Daughter*.[15] Among the five, Hester Mulso Chapone seems to me the only one *not* invested in women in some primary way. She alone of these women seems to have married more from desire than from social imperatives, and there is no sense in any of her writings that same-sex bonds are an erotic or even affectional preference.

Certainly Chapone promoted female friendship, and that fact too helps us distinguish routine friendship from erotic pull. About to marry in 1760, Chapone wrote reassuringly to Elizabeth Carter of her

> most perfect dissent from an opinion of . . . Johnson, "that a married woman can have no friendship but with her husband." I flatter myself my heart will be improved in every virtuous affection by an union with a worthy man, and that my dear Miss Carter, and all my friends, will find it more worthy of their attachment, and better qualified for the best uses of friendship, than it ever was before. At least I think it will not be less kindly disposed towards them, nor less desirous to cherish and cultivate all my valuable connexions.[16]

But this surely heartfelt avowal does not seem to me an erotic one. There is a limit, too, to the importance Chapone grants female friendship. The "Matrimonial Creed" she addressed to Samuel Richardson claims that in the best marriages a man would rank his wife "his *first* and *dearest friend*,"[17] and her *Letters on the Improvement of the Mind* (1773) conceives female friendship as above all a project of mentorship.

Chapone's husband died but a year after their marriage; and even though Chapone's small income required her thereafter to reside frequently with friends, I have found no suggestion of a permanent attachment with a woman in all the forty years between her husband's death and hers. Moreover, Chapone distinguished her own desires—or at least their fulfillment—from those of Carter and Montagu: writing about *Evelina*, she tells Carter that Frances Burney's novel gives "a just and natural picture of the purest and most elegant love," but that

15. See Amanda Vickery, *The Gentleman's Daughter: Women's Lives in Georgian England* (New Haven, Conn., 1998).

16. Hester Mulso Chapone, *The Posthumous Works of Mrs. Chapone*, 2 vols. (London, 1807), 1:118.

17. Chapone, "Matrimonial Creed," *Bluestocking Feminism*, 3:253.

"Mrs. Montagu, *entre nous*, is an ignoramus on this subject, as I have observed on many occasions, nor are you quite an adept."[18] None of Chapone's personal or public writings suggest passion for women; her admiring "Irregular Ode to Mrs. Eliz. Carter," for example, strikes a dramatically different tone from Carter's own passionate poems to Miss Lynch. Chapone's is thus a valuable test case: because her model for friendship is not manifestly erotic, her writings illuminate the important distinction I want to posit between Bluestocking feminism— a matter of conviction—and Bluestocking sapphism—a matter of desire.

In the lives of the other four women who are my focus here, some form of sapphic affiliation is arguably legible. In making this claim, I am not alleging homoerotic exclusivity or even homoerotic activity. Two of these women were married—Scott briefly and apparently unhappily, Montagu with seeming equanimity for over thirty years—though, as I have suggested, the external evidence of these relationships tells us little about the women's desires. More revealing is the textual evidence of Catherine Talbot's desire for George Berkeley, whose proposal of marriage she refused, probably because of a disparity of age and the likely disapproval of both families. Loss and longing are writ large in some of the posthumously published poems that scholars have connected to Talbot's relationship with Berkeley. Whatever their provenance (and it seems plausible that they are addressed to Berkeley), these are certainly poems of desire, and of desire thwarted. Talbot's "Song—," for example, writes its refrain so that absence becomes the very signifier of the self: "Oh think of Absence—think of Me," the poet pleads.[19] While this poem may well have been addressed to Berkeley as scholars speculate, the dynamics and poetics of Talbot's longings, whether for Berkeley or for her friend Elizabeth Carter (or for an imbrication of the two), would be well worth scholarly inquiry. It would also be useful to set the textual fabric of these relationships against the letters Talbot wrote to Jemima Campbell, the closest friend of her youth, from whom she was grieved to separate when Campbell married. Indeed textual desire—or, more accurately, textual evidence of desire—seems to me more reliable than speculations about sexual behavior and thus more capable of our pursuit.

I have already argued that in most instances when we are dealing primarily with textual materials, we will find little evidence of erotic acts, especially in the writings of women; in the case of the Blues, it is quite impossible on the basis of available evidence to know whether and in what ways they may have been actively sexual or even how they understood the sexual: what would have counted to them as sexual behavior, or how their bodies were implicated in the enactment

---

18.   Cited in Zuk, *Bluestocking Feminism*, 3:185.
19.   Catherine Talbot, "Song—," *Bluestocking Feminism*, 3:156–57.

of feelings for anyone. Yet signs of same-sex desire can be read, variously and sometimes differently, in the lives and works of Scott, Montagu, Talbot, and Carter: in Sarah Scott's long cohabitation with Lady Barbara Montagu, in Montagu's particular friendship for Carter, and in the thirty-year intimacy between Carter and Talbot as well as in both women's apparent attractions to other women, and in Carter's many attractions especially. Each of these "sapphic formations" is biographically and textually distinct, but there also seem to be some shared textual practices through which I believe these Bluestocking women were able to entertain, restrain, and sustain same-sex desire.

~ ~

Sarah Scott may or may not have been "indifferent to the other sex,"[20] as one of her fictional characters proclaims herself, but without question her closest and longest attachment was with another woman, Lady Barbara Montagu. Scott and Montagu lived together for some seventeen years before, after, and during Sarah's brief and abruptly ended marriage to George Scott, until Lady Barbara's death in 1765. Scott told her sister that she and "Lady Bab" maintained "as little distinction of property as any married couple," and her life speaks an attachment for Barbara Montagu for which the financial benefit of cohabitation clearly does not suffice to account (Huntington Library, Montagu Collection; MO 5302, 26 May 1763). That Scott's relationship with Lady Barbara might have caused concern is suggested by Elizabeth Montagu's early response to it. In 1748, the year in which Sarah Robinson moved into Lady Barbara's house in Bath, Montagu wrote to Lady Barbara, "My sister tells me you have been very good to her, the Girl is good enough, I allow you to Coquet a little with her but do not fall in love" (MO 1646, May 1748; quoted in *Bluestocking Feminism,* 5:xii). Two years later—perhaps, as Gary Kelly suggests, by way of warning—Montagu complains about two other women who had decided to cohabit:

> I must confess I am sorry for [it], as it will add to the jests the men made on that friendship, & I own I think those sort of reports hurt us all. And fall in their degree on the whole Sex: and really if this nonsense gains ground one must shut oneself up alone; for one can not have Men Intimates, & at this rate the Women are more scandalous. So we must become Savages & have no friendships or connexions: I cannot think what Mrs L[yttelton] and Miss R [or K?] can mean by making such a parade of their affection, they might

20. Sarah Scott, *The Test of Filial Duty* [1772], Letter IV, in *Bluestocking Feminism,* 6:20.

know it wd give occasion to Lies. (MO 1646, May 1748; quoted in
*Bluestocking Feminism,* 5:xii).

It is worth noting that Montagu worries less about private behavior than about
public performance; Mrs. L and Miss R have crossed the protective fine line between female friendship and suspect sexuality and are giving all female friends a
bad name. If Montagu's comments are representative, then permanent cohabitation between unrelated gentlewomen in midcentury England may have been
less common, less innocent, and more significant than some modern scholars
have imagined it. This may explain too why Elizabeth and Sarah Robinson's father apparently refused in such vehement terms Elizabeth's request that he contribute financially so that Sarah and Lady Barbara could maintain both their
town house in Bath and their summer house in Batheaston, which Mr. Robinson
allegedly found to be "a monstrous proposal and unreasonable," and it was perhaps not only in monetary terms that "he could not afford to comply with it."[21]
If Montagu's and perhaps her father's fears and suspicions are representative of
wider concern about female couples, then the cohabiting Sarah Scott and Barbara
Montagu would likely have been aware of a need to manage the public face of
their relationship.

It may be no accident, therefore, that it is almost solely the public relationship between Sarah Scott and Barbara Montagu that has been left to us. Unlike
Eleanor Butler and Sarah Ponsonby, who preserved letters and diaries testifying
to a bond that they made no attempt to minimize, Scott apparently intended
her private papers to be destroyed. I want to speculate that this quest for privacy
may have been one of Scott's and Montagu's management strategies, and that
Scott may have wanted to shelter the relationship even (or especially) from her
sister. Elizabeth Child has described to me in the extant correspondence a "perhaps telling sequence of letters in the early 1750s," in which Scott, traveling to
London with Lady Bab, "explains at great length to Elizabeth Montagu why they
prefer to lodge together and not at Montagu's house," seeming "a bit defensive
but very definite about these arrangements.[22] There may already have been other,
unrelated strains between the Robinson sisters but, given Elizabeth Montagu's
earlier concerns, Scott may also have wanted to evade her elder sister's prying eye.

It does not take a reading of *Millenium Hall,* which legitimates female cohabitation on the basis of Christian philanthropy, to speculate that Scott and
Montagu also managed their relationship within a philanthropic economy,
engaging in a spectrum of publicly visible charities that would have underscored

21. Cited in Myers, *Bluestocking Circle,* 138.
22. Private correspondence with the author, April 2001.

their virtue and justified their ménage à deux. It is important to note, however, that the intimacy between Scott and Lady Barbara, like that between Mrs. Morgan and Miss Mancel in Scott's novel, predates the philanthropy rather than forming as a result of it. In *Millenium Hall* we can also see the workings of other strategies through which Scott may have been managing not only fictional but also personal relationship. For strikingly, the novel that Elizabeth Mavor calls the "*vade mecum* of romantic friendship,"[23] written at a time when female friendships were supposed to have been physically demonstrative and verbally effusive as a commonplace, carries hardly a single instance of touch, and very few inscriptions of passionate feeling, between women friends. Even Miss Mancel and Mrs. Morgan, whose hearts were "strictly united" and without distinctions of "Meum and Tuum," are represented as caressing only when Louisa Mancel is still a child.[24] It is worth asking whether, among its range of purposes, *Millenium Hall* is also responding to Elizabeth Montagu's cautionary tales about the proper limits of female attachment. *Millenium Hall*'s "cover story" is perhaps what leads Betty Rizzo to argue that Sarah Scott and Barbara Montagu "were not even discernibly romantic friends" and "not, apparently, in love with each other," but rather engaged in "low-keyed bonding." Yet Rizzo also speculates that the marriage between Sarah and George Scott may have ended "because her husband discovered the two women in a compromising state," and she argues, perhaps more plausibly, that some tension of triangulation could explain why, when Scott left her husband, she lived alone for a time rather than returning to Lady Barbara, even though the two had lived together before and during Scott's marriage.[25] Ultimately, Scott and Lady Barbara do seem to have succeeded in organizing their relationship within the economy of virtue and intellect for which the first Bluestockings became renowned; despite the brief scandal surrounding Scott's divorce, the two women do not seem to have been subjected even to the occasional sexual suspicions that were cast a few decades later upon the more publicly coupled "Ladies of Llangollen."

Elizabeth Montagu's relationship with Elizabeth Carter, enacted through letters and visits, does not seem to have been under such public scrutiny. The relationship may have been somewhat lopsided, with Montagu the emotionally more demanding of the pair as well as the materially wealthier. Elizabeth Eger believes Montagu's "correspondence with Elizabeth Carter stands out as the defining relationship of her life." It is a "friendship of profound spiritual and intellectual

---

23.   Mavor, *Ladies of Llangollen,* 83.
24.   Sarah Scott, *Millenium Hall* [1762], ed. Gary Kelly (Peterborough, Ont., 1995), 93.
25.   Rizzo, *Companions without Vows,* 295, 304, 308.

importance," "an emotional relationship of rare intensity." I myself would depart from Eger when she terms it a "sort of rational or platonic love ... grounded in their shared Christian principles," for I don't think "rational or platonic love" quite accounts for either the intensity or the particularity of the desires Montagu's letters to Carter manifest.[26] If Carter's letters to Montagu suggest that this intensity may not have been fully reciprocal, Carter nonetheless clearly reveals a deep attachment to, and emotional reliance on, the woman she addresses in letter after letter as "my dear friend."

Elizabeth Carter's "passion"—her word—for Catherine Talbot, if more effusive than Talbot's at the start, seems to have become a deep, reciprocal, and complex bond that lasted from 1741 until Talbot's death in 1770. Dwelling in their family homes, sometimes visiting there or in London, the two women were separated more than they were together, so that their letters had to carry the relationship for most of its twenty-nine years. With a rich admixture of melancholy, spirit, vulnerability, and wit, Carter and Talbot coped with the material as well as spiritual constraints on their desire. It is therefore perhaps all the more significant that the letters, even after Pennington's censorship, reveal so much.

Looking primarily at letters exchanged between Carter and Talbot and incorporating some correspondence between Montagu and Carter as well as telling moments in *Millenium Hall*, I want to suggest some of the ways in which these Bluestockings seem to have economized their desires. Their economies cluster around three elements: the imaginative management of time and space; the husbanding of signs and tokens; and a sparing and displacing use of bodily figurations. I will also take up the question of gender play in Catherine Talbot's letters to Elizabeth Carter in order to suggest that in Carter's case what is being managed may be not only her relationships with specific women but also a more diffuse same-sex desire and perhaps modest transgressions of gender as well.

❧ ❧

Talbot wrote to Carter early in their relationship, "what a pity it is now we are so much better acquainted, that we can never meet."[27] Coping with the constraints of time and place becomes a dialogic project within Carter and Talbot's correspondence. At first it is Carter who seems most to chafe at separation from

---

26. Elizabeth Eger, introduction to vol. 1, *Bluestocking Feminism*, lix–lxi. Elizabeth Child has told me that after reading "about a year's worth of letters from Elizabeth Montagu to Elizabeth Carter ... I can't help noticing that Montagu is really writing love letters to Carter"; personal correspondence with the author.

27. *A Series of Letters between Mrs. Elizabeth Carter and Miss Catherine Talbot, from the year 1741 to 1770*, ed. Montagu Pennington, 4 vols. (London, 1809), 1:110, 4 September 1745; cited henceforward in the text.

Talbot and her other women friends, while Talbot's is the voice of what we might consider Bluestocking restraint: "We must e'en lower our ideas of friendship to the pitch of common life, and be content with loving and esteeming people constantly and affectionately amid a variety of thwarting, awkward circumstances, that forbid all possibility of spending our lives together. Let people in such a situation be glad that they have known enough of one another to make affection mutual, and then let them resign the complete enjoyment of it, as inconsistent with such a world as this" (1:59, 27 June 1744). "I have a great notion," she writes elsewhere, "that half one's business in this world is to make the best of every thing" (1:111, 4 September 1745), and "as for seeing the people one likes—why one must learn to like the people one sees I think" (1:176, 14 November 1746). Clearly desire here is a challenge of management. But if Pennington's editing is to be trusted, after 1760 especially, Talbot seems to be the one who most resents constraints and writes out her longings: she laments that "I can have no longer patience, dear Miss Carter, 'tis ages since I heard from you; 'tis near three weeks since I sent away my last" and that "*to be sure you are so taken up with all the fine places and fine folks at France, that you have no time to write*" (3:45, 21 July 1763). Or: "I wish I could have an hour's conversation with you … I verily believe the degree of feeling for others which I certainly want, you have most undoubtedly stolen from me" (2:356, 3 November 1760). Or again: "I dare say we remember one another daily, (I am sure I do *you*;)" (3:357, 30 December 1760). And perhaps the most characteristic Talbot comment: "I denied myself the telling you how very sorry and grieved I was to part with you," a denial that of course enacts the telling it has denied (3:316, 17 April 1760).

But if Talbot keeps trying to accommodate "such a world as this," Montagu and Carter seem to me more openly to push against that world. I am struck by the frequency of fantasies in which each of them creates a scene of imaginary visitation, or invents a utopic space for a same-sex relationship. In *The Apparitional Lesbian*, Terry Castle has argued that "the literary history of lesbianism" is "a history of derealization" enacted through "spectral metaphors."[28] In these Bluestocking letters, spectral metaphors become a strategy for *realizing* the desire for intimacy by projecting it into imaginary space or time. A letter from Montagu to Carter in 1759, for example, places Carter on an island and then leads her back to London and to Montagu: "I want a little Island for you which would be suitable to you, you should read upon violets be fanned by zephyrs & shaded by woodbine & roses in a moral sense, … our moral atmosphere our material World is not worthy of you but if you must lead ye usual life come to Clarges street. My

28. Terry Castle, *The Apparitional Lesbian: Female Homosexuality and Modern Culture* (New York, 1993), 34.

heart rejoices at ye thought & echo's come to Clarges streets" (MO 3033, December 1759; cited in *Bluestocking Feminism,* 1:155). Or in 1769: "My imagination without wing or broom stick oft mounts aloft, rises into ye Regions of pure space, & without lett or impediment bears me to your fireside, where you can set me in your easy chair, & we talk & reason, as angel Host & guest Aetherial should do, of high & important matters. . . . We will say what has not been said before, or if the substance be old, the mode & figure shall be new" (MO 3258, 10 October 1769; cited in *Bluestocking Feminism,* 1:190). Carter brings both Montagu and Talbot to herself in fantasy: "I longed for you extremely the other night at Reading," she writes to Montagu in 1759, "to ramble by moonlight amongst the ruins of an old abbey." Much earlier, she fantasized "seven-league boots" that would allow her to leap across England to visit Talbot.[29] Such fantasies lessen the magnitude of separation evident, for example, in a letter to Montagu of 13 March 1759 in which Carter, daunted by the vastness of time and space that separates the friends, writes: "It seems an immense time, since I have heard any thing of you my dear Mrs. Montagu . . . there are some hours in which I feel strangely vacant, at finding I know no more about you, than if I was in zet" (1:26–27).[30]

It is no wonder, then, that Carter's poems often resolve themselves through heavenly solutions that imagine another and better world. In the letters Carter also uses otherworldly though more secular, indeed ghostly, language to imagine herself with Talbot. Two of her very first letters to Talbot speak of "haunting" her, and a third elaborates a suggestively nocturnal fantasy: "I have a strong inclination, dear Miss Talbot, to visit you like an apparition at this unseasonable hour, which I may safely indulge as it will do you no harm, for I may talk to you as long as I please, without any danger of disturbing your slumbers, or depriving you of an agreeable dream" (1:56, 24 May 1744). But the apparitional in Carter can also turn dark: she writes on one occasion in 1745, "'Tis surely a fatal error to give one's self up to certain enchantments that lead the mind into fairy regions of dreams and shadows, where it is amused and fixed on imaginary forms of happiness and perfection, which vanish with the fickle cause that gave them being, and one is left in the midst of a wild perplexed solitude, astonished, and utterly at a loss what road to take" (1:114, 20 September 1745). This anxiety may explain why another of Carter's strategies is to try to inhabit only the moment:

29. Elizabeth Carter, *Letters from Mrs. Elizabeth Carter to Mrs. Montagu, between the years 1755 and 1800,* ed. Montagu Pennington, 3 vols. (London, 1817), 1:27 (13 March 1759); and 1:62, 27 June 1744 (cited henceforward in the text).
30. Cited by Jane Magrath in her essay in this volume, p. 251.

"With regard to our happiness in this world, the more closely our thoughts are confined to the present day, the better; whenever they are sent out to wander too far beyond it, the mind is soon lost and confused in the darkness and variety of human events, and distracted by the tumult of hopes and fears" (1:360–61, 26 October 1750). If such a focus on the present seems philosophically opposed to Carter's heavenward solutions, it is striking that both the heavenly *telos* of the poems[31] and the epistolary restriction to the present erase precisely the space that desire would occupy: a future that is foreseeable but not yet achieved and for which one could therefore long. There is a similar tendency in Talbot's anticipation of a long visit: "To see you now and then . . . is very enlivening; but to have you for a while first, evenings and all, is comfortable to think of; and God be thanked that we have the prospect once again as cheerfully as ever—when one parts for the summer one dares not look so far forward" (3:128, 20 November 1765).

Within this tight economy of time and space, signs and tokens gain special significance. The letters themselves are figured as visits, as when Carter writes in 1748 that she is alone at home and that Talbot is "the only person to whom I could think of making any" visit by post (1:245, 20 January 1748); or when Montagu proposes that she and Carter read the same book and write about it every day. The letters are also stored up as tokens, to be revisited in ways that sustain the intensity of the ties. Reading over a parcel of Carter's early letters around 1752, Talbot brims with renewed pleasure and gratitude "that such a mind and heart as your's should be desirous of a near acquaintance with mine" (2:85, n.d.). At another point, Talbot studies a single letter "over and over" with increased "affectionate gratitude" (3:9, 21 May 1762). Carter is especially invested in signs and markers of her relationship with Talbot. She makes much of the first anniversary of their meeting, citing Petrarch to bless the day, month, year, hour, and minute when they met. She is delighted when Talbot sends a rose—and triumphant when she finally sends a lock of hair. She apparently also kept Talbot's letters carefully arranged.

In Montagu's letters to Carter, a rather more literal economy prevails as financial favors turn into tokens of what Montagu calls "not friendship" but a "Covenant." Even helping Talbot becomes for Montagu a sign of her love for Carter: "I look upon her life as a publick concern," she says, but adds: "Then as your friend I am most terribly interested for her welfare." A discourse of value permeates Montagu's desires: when she learns that Carter plans to come to London, she cautions: "If you do not come to Town now you have flatterd me with hopes of it you have done an ill thing, you cannot imagine how many things

---

31. See Easton, "Carter's Uranian Friendships."

before this news pleased me very well have now lost their value, agreeable people sell at no price, many even wise & good are fallen below par" (MO 3031, 24 November 1759; cited in *Bluestocking Feminism,* 1:155). And in a rather startling image of domestic improvement, Montagu tells Carter that "you let me buy more pleasure with ye money than it could possibly purchase me any other way. My domestick expenses will be so much below my Income that I am as much obliged to those I love if they will accept some of it as I should be to any one who wd turn a stream of waste water out of my grounds into a little brook that wd beautify my prospect. I reckon my love & affection is certainly not worth less to me" (MO 3365, 7 July 1775; cited in *Bluestocking Feminism,* 1:193). I want to read these moments not simply as evidence of Montagu's economic heavy hand but as effusive displacements of desire.

One may rightly wonder at the virtual absence of the Bluestocking *body* within these managed discourses and tokenizations of desire. Jane Magrath describes a letter from Montagu to Carter written in 1759 as "stun[ning]" with need, in which Montagu figures her grief at separation as a weaning from the "nectar'd bowl" of Carter's breast, a deprivation worse than a child's loss by virtue of the "stronger passions and more discerning palates" of adults: "how can my grief be childish when it is all that is not childish in me that weeps for the absence of Miss Carter!"[32] Montagu fashions another image of deprivation when she compares Carter's conversation to a "luxurious feast" and then admonishes, "You have made me nice and dainty so look that you do not leave me to starve." And Montagu defines her closeness to Carter much as *Millenium Hall* describes that between Mrs. Morgan and Miss Mancel: Montagu and Carter are "so joined" that Montagu "would defy the splitters of a hair and the dividers of a polypes to disunite them" (MO 3091, 31 December 1762; cited in *Bluestocking Feminism,* 1:lix). Carter writes in 1749 that she "was delighted with the description of [Talbot's] dress, and heartily wish I had seen you in it; but mistake me not, 'tis you and not the dress I would have seen" (1:313, 20 June 1749).

But these are very modest hints of bodies, and while censors such as Montagu Pennington may bear some responsibility for the corporeal silence, it is also worth noting that the body represented in these writings is not the body in pleasure but the body in pain or distress. "Whenever you suffer I am in pain," writes Montagu to Carter in December 1759 (MO 3033; 1:154–55). Talbot worries often about Carter's headaches and wishes she could relieve them; Carter frets over Talbot's lassitude. And there is a cryptic exchange in 1762 in which Talbot is "haunted with the thought of having grieved" Carter, and says "I believe you

32. MO 3024; also discussed by Jane Magrath in this volume.

would have come into my room again that night, as I wished you then; and as I am *now* glad you did not; —had you been aware into what a solemn train of thought I was led by the shutting of the door" (3:1–3, 14 May 1762). Carter replies with self-reproach for not returning to the room, and admits that "I have had many a secret painful feeling that with such superior goodness you are less happy than I" (3:5–7, 17 May 1762). Nighttime intimacy here is less pleasure than solace from misery. I am not the first to wonder whether Talbot's melancholia and Carter's headaches become sites, and perhaps also effects, of physical longings otherwise denied. It is certainly worth asking—and Mary Wollstonecraft's *Mary, a Fiction* (1788) would be another case in point—whether pain here legitimates attention to bodies and becomes in queer ways a displacement for erotic desire. It is also worth recalling that the most intense affirmation of Mrs. Morgan and Miss Mancel's love in *Millenium Hall* also appears as pain; when they must undergo their "cruel separation," the "severest affliction they had ever experienced," "the connection of soul and body did not seem more indissoluble, nor were ever divided with greater pain." Pleasure, by contrast, is displaced in *Millenium Hall* into pastoral, and hence into more public outdoor space, where it takes on a hyperbolic language of desire: the ladies are "epicures in rural pleasures, and enjoy them in the utmost excess to which they can be carried."[33]

Thus managing its resources carefully through imagination, displacement, and restraint, the Bluestocking sapphism that emerges from these writings is indeed an *economy* of desire, a husbanding of small rewards. It is also an economy of *desire*—of longing and missing more than of getting and having—and is thus importantly different from the more satisfied if still vexed sapphism of Anne Lister or of Butler and Ponsonby. Yet Carter in particular seems to me to push again and again beyond these modest Blue satisfactions by enacting a rather capacious desire that attaches itself widely as well as deeply and that becomes, as Easton argues, one important template for reading Carter's work. Like one of Scott's characters and perhaps Scott herself (*Bluestocking Feminism*, 6:20), Carter seems to have been "indifferent to the other sex." If we can trust Carter's own letters to Talbot, relationships with men were out of the question for Carter long before a decision not to marry could have been simply intellectual: at the age of ten, she tells Talbot, "I looked upon having a *sweetheart* with as much horror as if it had been one of the seven deadly sins." On other occasions she tells Talbot

33.  Scott, *Millenium Hall,* 131, 223.

that "I never was tempted by any voluntary connexion to engage myself," claims her heart is "square-cornered," and says she "ran away from matrimonial schemes as far as dry land goes" (2:315, 14 February 1760; 2:29, 21 May 1751). These vows are far too adamant to be read as motivated either by Carter's intellectual pursuits or by pure practicality. Myers believes that Carter avoided marriage "at least partially in order to be free to continue her studies," laments that the plan backfired because "she was not very productive," and speculates that "marriage to another scholar might have helped her to pursue work in a more systematic way."[34] But in light of Carter's own avowals, one must surely question the assumption that marriage was for her a matter of practicality rather than desire.

Furthermore, the number of women to whom Carter seems to have been intensely attached throughout her long life is in itself significant. Rather than seeing this fact as evidence that these were ordinary (since not necessarily exclusive) friendships, as Myers or Mavor might, I read in Carter a kind of free-floating homoerotic desire that attaches itself, much as Lister's does, if less openly, to women-in-general as well as to particular women. Myers herself describes the close relationship between Carter and a Miss Sharpe that began around 1777, entailed a great deal of travel together, and altered in 1782 when the younger Sharpe became engaged to a much older man. Myers finds evidence that Sharpe's decision to marry "hurt" Carter deeply, creating a "temporary estrangement" between the two, even though Carter considered Sharpe's choice, if she had to marry, "respectable."[35] It seems entirely logical to read Carter's behavior here as the wounding of someone deeply attached in ways that simply do not make sense if we begin from the assumption that Carter had either a hetero-erotic orientation or no erotic orientation at all.

Carter also seems to have relished some modest transgressions of femininity. Hester Thrale, that litmus test for hetero-propriety, once drew up a ranking of "her male and female acquaintances according to gender-specific criteria." Of a possible 120 points, Montagu earned 101 but Carter garnered only 60.[36] One might also wonder whether Chapone has only intellect in mind when she writes to Carter that "you carry your partiality to your own sex farther than I do";[37] such a comment suggests that Carter's sense of identification with women is more than a matter of intellectual egalitarianism. Talbot at one point calls Carter a "Belle Sauvage" (2:322, 25 December 1749), and Montagu identifies with her

---

34. Myers, *Bluestocking Circle,* 120.
35. Ibid., 307.
36. Hester Lynch Thrale Piozzi, *Thraliana: The Diary of Mrs. Hester Lynch Thrale* (*Later Mrs. Piozzi*) *1776–1809,* ed. Katherine C. Balderson, 2 vols. (Oxford, 1942), 1:330–31.
37. Chapone, *Posthumous Works,* 1:64.

"wild and intractable love of liberty" (MO 3031, 24 November 1759; 1:150). Carter rambunctiously charges along on her walks, leaving everyone behind, and chafes against the propriety of the chaperone, "a little disconcerted . . . with the reflection, that in a world, with which I was much inclined to be pleased, it should have been found improper for me to return alone, and that when the sun was set I must not travel without a guard; and I could not help considering the poor man who was obliged to trudge after me, in the same uncomfortable light, as I always look upon a lock, or a bolt, as a most severe satire upon mankind" (2:135–36, 30 August 1753).

Carter is frequently forthright about her attachments to women. She acknowledges a "strange delicacy of friendship" as a "weakness," and is perhaps only half joking when she begs Talbot's "advice how to conquer it" (1:57, 24 May 1744). She is especially depressed when she loses women friends to marriage; at one point Talbot counters that Carter must learn to accept these losses or else "you must turn Roman catholic, and go into a convent, where you may have a whole sisterhood of friends secluded from the rest of the world" (1:59, 27 June 1744). And Talbot's letters to her when she goes to Europe in 1763 are startlingly obvious, if teasing, about Carter's attractions to other women: of a German baroness who seems to have captivated Carter, Talbot writes, "The description you give of her has had such effects as would make Mrs. Montagu, amid all her flaunting with Altesses, pale with envy. . . . I do not know whether I shall be quite satisfied with your taste, if you do not espouse some German Baron, in order to pass the remainder of your days in her neighbourhood." And then: "I have just received your's of the 31st, in which you talk to me of a belle Hollandoise and a Chanoinesse angelique, for neither of whom do I care, and so no more of la Baronne than if no such amiable being existed. I begin to suspect this is really the case, and that she is only un être d'imagination, whom you dreamt of on the inspiring brink of the Geronstere spring. The Archbishop says, No, you are only fallen in love with another woman, and the first is forgot. A pretty gentleman you will come home indeed." "Go to Deal," pleads Talbot, "and grow domestic again, and return in spring just such as you used to be" (3:50–51, 11 August 1763). In this light, the masculinization of the body into a demanding husbandly figure, which Lisa Freeman so astutely identifies in Carter's "A Dialogue," might have yet another significance: Carter may have been enacting not only "a passion for the female mind" and a "less-than-positive" attitude toward marriage but also some recognition of her own irrational and thwarted bodily desires.[38] At the very least,

38.   See Lisa A. Freeman, "'A Dialogue': Elizabeth Carter's Passion for the Female Mind," in Isobel Armstrong and Virginia Blain, eds., *Women's Poetry in the Enlightenment: The Making of a Canon, 1730–1820* (Basingstoke, England, and New York, 1999), 50–63.

it makes almost as little sense to construct Carter from a heterosexual presumption as to construct Butler, Ponsonby, or Lister in that way. We might then speculate that the effort to feminize and domesticate Carter as a maker of puddings is a doubly defensive task.[39]

Indeed, for one final and speculative moment, I want to push the envelope on Bluestocking propriety by revisiting the split I initially posited between "Bluestocking" and "lesbian." I have been suggesting that insofar as "sapphic" stands for a location of desire in other women, some Bluestockings could be called "sapphic" even though they were proper and virtuous. I now want to turn the question: is it possible that they were also proper and virtuous—or reinvented as proper and virtuous—in part *because of* their sapphic desires? That is, were Blue proprieties what I have called (in "Befriending the Body") a "compensatory conservatism" for managing not only intellectual interests but erotic and affectional interests as well? If so, then the two terms with which I opened are closer together than we might have imagined, true Blue might itself be a little bit queer, and Elizabeth Carter might be the queerest of the Blues. It may be time, then, to explore more fully the economies not only of the Bluestockings but of our own scholarly investments and desires.

*Brandeis University*

---

39.  I refer here to Samuel Johnson's famous remark that Carter "could make a pudding, as well as translate Epictetus from the Greek, and work a handkerchief as well as compose a poem."

# Index

*Page numbers in italics indicate illustrations.*